AMERICAN RAJ

AMERICAN RAJ

★★★★★★★★★★

LIBERATION OR DOMINATION?

ERIC S. MARGOLIS

KEY PORTER BOOKS

Library and Archives Canada Cataloguing in Publication

Margolis, Eric S.
    American Raj : liberation or domination? / Eric S. Margolis.

ISBN 978-1-55470-087-5

1. East and West. 2. Islamic countries—Relations—Western countries. 3. Islamic countries—Relations—United States. 4. Western countries— Relations—Islamic countries. 5. United States—Relations—Islamic countries. I. Title.

DS35.74.U6M37 2008   303.48'2176701821   C2008-901754-4

ONTARIO ARTS COUNCIL
CONSEIL DES ARTS DE L'ONTARIO

The publisher gratefully acknowledges the support of the Canada Council for the Arts and the Ontario Arts Council for its publishing program. We acknowledge the support of the Government of Ontario through the Ontario Media Development Corporation's Ontario Book Initiative.

We acknowledge the financial support of the Government of Canada through the Book Publishing Industry Development Program (BPIDP) for our publishing activities.

Key Porter Books Limited
Six Adelaide Street East, Tenth Floor
Toronto, Ontario
Canada M5C 1H6

www.keyporter.com

Text design: Marijke Friesen
Electronic formatting: Alison Carr

Printed and bound in Canada

08 09 10 11 12 5 4 3 2 1

DEDICATION

To Dana B Baines for all her help, advice, encouragement and patience

To my Muse, LC

ACKNOWLEDGEMENTS

To Grainne Jones and Stephanie Blok
for their unceasing support, patience and help

TABLE OF CONTENTS

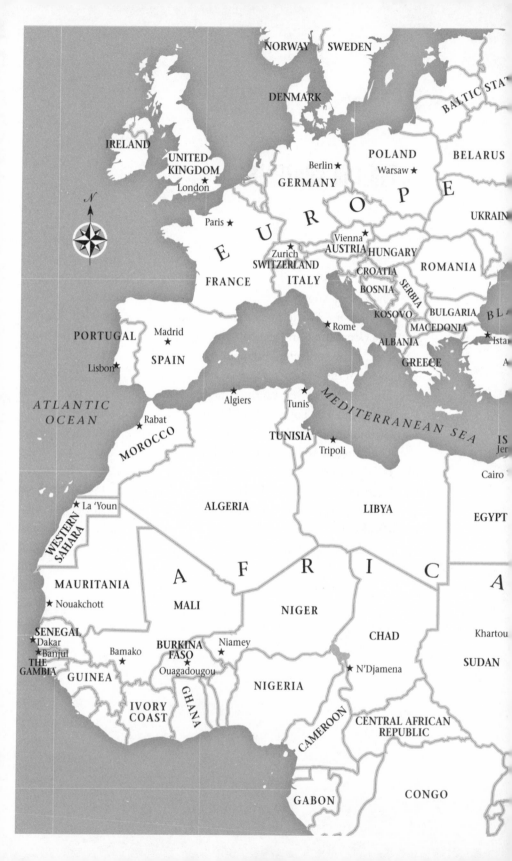

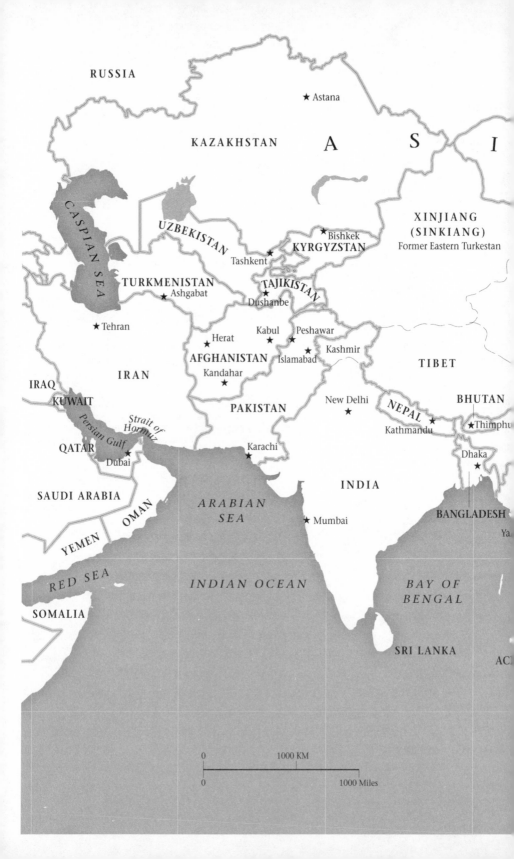

Israel's repression of the Palestinian "intifada" is being telecast around the globe, producing rage against Israel and its patron, the United States, and a worldwide surge of anti-Semitism. America's strategic and economic interests in the Mideast and Muslim world are being threatened by the agony in Palestine, which inevitably invites terrorist attacks against US citizens and property.

—Eric S. Margolis, *Sun Media*, September 2, 2001 (nine days before the September 11 attacks against New York and Washington, D.C.)

THE JOURNEY BEGINS . . .

This book is going to take you on a far-flung, sometimes disturbing, and often controversial journey across the political and emotional geography of the Muslim world, a voyage through a landscape fraught with violence, anger, and hatred that is seething with irrationality, delusions, and the still-raw wounds of past defeats and human tragedies.

Like all explorations, *American Raj* will be challenging. But, in the end, this work will, hopefully, offer the reader a better understanding of the Muslim world's anger against the West and what we westerners can do to lower its intensity, and eventually transform antipathy and confrontation into fruitful cooperation.

I have been covering the Muslim world for just over 50 years, first as a student, then businessman, military analyst, and finally as a journalist and author. My travels and residencies, and the conflicts I covered as a war correspondent, have taken me repeatedly to every Mideast nation and most of the Muslim states of Asia and Africa.

A half century in the souks and battlefields of the Mideast, or in the mountains of Central Asia, Afghanistan, Pakistan, and India have left me bearing a score of scars, both physical and mental, but they also provided me unusual insight into a fascinating, turbulent part of the planet that too few westerners have seen. My years with the Afghan mujahidin (holy warriors), and, later, Taliban, provided remarkable insights and understanding of radical political Islam, and a measure of acceptance, even trust, by leaders of these movements that allowed me to sit with the them, cross-legged, in remote mountain caves or in ill-lit back alleys, from Cairo to

Peshawar, or join them on battlefields, from Africa to the Himalayas.

I wrote my first book, *War at the Top of the World—the Struggle for Afghanistan and Asia*, because I was deeply concerned that the western world, and particularly the United States, was unaware of the dangers that would shortly emanate from Afghanistan, Pakistan, and India (collectively known as South Asia).

I warned in the book that "the first major world crisis of the new century would come in this turbulent region."

At the time, few westerners were interested in what for them was a remote, confusing part of the world. Two years after the first edition of *War at the Top of the World* came out, New York City and Washington were attacked by aircraft hijacked by members of al-Qaida, and the United States declared its so-called War on Terror that continues to this day.

The instructive intent of *War at the Top of the World* was amply fulfilled by its updating and reprinting in new editions, and its use by the United States Air Force and US government agencies as a primary text and guidebook for understanding South and Central Asia's complex problems.

Having very nearly gone on to do a PhD at Cambridge University and then become a history professor, I was deeply satisfied that my knowledge was being put to productive use.

Many Americans and Canadians asked me, "How did you know that an explosion was about to occur in South Asia?" The answer was simple. I had long been fascinated by this exotic region and had taken the time over decades to travel its badlands and pay attention to what was going on there. Accordingly, this new book, *American Raj*, is written with the same goal: to cast light into parts of the world that are causing the West enormous pain and anxiety, yet are either poorly understood or misrepresented.

I cannot but write with profound sympathy for many of these places. I have sometimes been accused by critics of trying to be a "Lawrence with a laptop," intoxicated by the mystery and romance of the places about which I report. Lawrence I am not, but, as one brought up on Rudyard Kipling and stirring tales of the great British Indian Raj, I do plead guilty to the later charge. South Asia—wild Afghanistan and Pakistan, and Central Asia—long ago captured and held my heart and imagination.

Where else can one go on earth and suddenly be transported back into the Middle Ages. After flying for 25 or 30 hours, when I arrive, I want to see turbaned, gun-wielding tribesmen, not the kind of dreadful cookie-cutter shopping malls one encounters in Singapore or Seoul after punishing trips. Go to South Asia and you are on a different planet. A trip there is the closet most of us will ever come to space travel. Small wonder so many of the names and costumes used in science fiction productions like *Star Trek, Next Generation* are copied from there.

But promoting Asian exotica is not my objective. I have always written for three reasons: the admittedly quixotic and presumptuous mission of trying to educate my fellow North Americans to the complexities of the Mideast and South Asia; my lifelong, unrelenting battle against all types of propaganda, disinformation, and lies; and my attempts to speak for those who have no voice. That is my creed as a journalist—and one that has kept me in hot water all my professional life.

As tensions and violence between the western and Muslim worlds continue to grow and take new, ever more dangerous directions, *American Raj* is my determined attempt to speak for those in the Muslim world who have so utterly failed to explain their motivations and passions to westerners, or whose voices have been drowned out by the high-amp thunder of western governments, media, and special interest groups of all sorts.

Let me start at the beginning, as Mideastern tellers of tales are wont to say when they begin a narrative.

My first taste of the Muslim world came from my mother, Nexhmie Zaimi. During the 1930s, at the age of 16, she fled from her family in little Albania, and somehow managed to come to America and become the first woman in her country to attend university, prestigious Wellesley College. In 1937, she wrote a national bestseller, *Daughter of the Eagle*, a gripping, poignant autobiography about growing up in impoverished, backwards Albania, which was then just emerging from 500 years of Turkish Ottoman rule. She went on to Columbia Graduate School of Journalism. There she met an up-and-coming New York City lawyer, Henry Margolis. They were married just before the war, soon divorced though they loved one another, and proceeded to fight like cats and dogs for the next half century.

My mother, a brilliant, fearless woman of volcanic temper and fierce determination, set out in the early 1950s to cover the Mideast for New York–area newspapers. At that time, there were few American journalists in this little-known and even less understood part of the world, and certainly hardly any women traveling on their own.

But my mother scoffed at caution and over the next five years investigated and extensively wrote and lectured on the region, interviewing in the process Egypt's new leaders, Gamal Abdel Nasser and his deputy, Anwar Sadat, as well as Jordan's King Hussein and the leaders of Syria and Iraq.

She managed to obtain this unusual access because of her beauty, nervy refusal to take no for an answer, and, equally, because of her understanding of Arab culture and custom. Growing up in Albania, which was 70 percent easygoing Muslim and 30 percent Christian, had given her a natural key to the Muslim world and a keen, natural understanding of its often convoluted mentality that escaped confused, frustrated, or annoyed westerners.

At home in New York City, I grew up on Albanian-Turkish food, listened to Turkish love songs, went to sleep with Balkan fairy tales, and awoke to reports from my mother of her latest adventures and discoveries in the Mideast.

My eyes began to open to this fascinating part of the world, about which I began to read voraciously.

Our home was always filled with diplomats and writers from Europe, the Mideast or South Asia. When my mother went on her frequent foreign trips, I was parked with her best friend, a majestic but fearsome Irish aristocrat who, I learned years afterward, also happened to be the chief fund-raiser in New York for the Irish Republican Army. I soon became a revolutionary and have remained so to this day.

My mother came back from Jordan with harrowing reports of hundreds upon hundreds of thousands of hungry, sick, terrified refugees from Palestine—now the new state of Israel—who were near starving in unheated tents and shacks made from tin cans. She had "discovered" the Palestinian refugees—the first harbingers of a whirlwind that was to smite the United States and the western world.

She began writing and lecturing about the plight of these refugees, calling on the US government to feed and clothe them. Even though the concerns she expressed were entirely humanitarian, her reports and lectures quickly produced a firestorm. Newspapers that carried her reports were forced to drop her when major retailers threatened to pull all of their advertising. Speaking engagements were suddenly canceled.

My mother remained defiant and kept trying to circulate reports on the refugee problem. At that time, memories of the Jewish Holocaust were still horrifyingly fresh and passions ran high. We began to get threats, obscene callers, and people banging on our apartment door in the middle of the night. These threats grew ever more frightening.

One day, my mother was told acid would be thrown into my face if she kept talking about the Palestinians.

She finally had to give in. Her voice was silenced. One woman with a vulnerable child could not stand against a storm of fury and threats. But she had one last Parthian shaft to loose. In 1953, she wrote a study of the Mideast for the US State Department, "Gauge of Arab Anger."

In this remarkable paper, she predicted that unless the Palestinian refugee problem—for which she laid ultimate blame on the United States—was resolved in a fair, humanitarian way, it would come to poison the then warm relations between the Muslims and America. In 50 years, she predicted with remarkable foresight, the entire Arab and much of the Muslim world would turn violently against the United States.

Her uncannily accurate prediction was, of course, ignored by the US government. Few Americans even thought about the Palestinian problem until the ninth day of November 2001.

At the tender but boisterous age of 14 my mother sent me to Cairo to live with the family of the president of Esso in the Mideast. Thus began my travels in the Mideast which continue, half a century later. In ensuing years, I ran businesses across the Muslim world, covered wars and revolutions, followed the endless travails of the Arab-Israeli conflict, saw kings and dictators come and go in a dreary tableau of backstabbing, murder, treachery, and greed. My father remarried a heroine of the Israeli independence struggle. I was jailed in Lebanon, nearly killed in Yemen, branded a CIA agent in Libya, held hands with Muammar Khadaffi, whipped in Saudi Arabia, drank tea with Yasser Arafat and airplane bomber George Habash, was threatened by both Syrians and Iraqis with hanging as an Israeli spy, and managed to arrive in Beirut for the first day of the Lebanese civil war.

In the early 1980s, as I recount in *War at the Top of the World*, I became deeply interested in the then almost unknown struggle being waged in Afghanistan against Soviet occupation, and began raising medical supplies and funds for the mujahidin resistance. In 1985, President Zia ul Haq of Pakistan read my columns on the growing Afghan war and invited me to come interview him. So began my new adventures in the region I like to call, "the Mideast, East."

Doing business across the region from Morocco to India also gave me unusual access to the real thinking of wealthy merchants in this area. Businessmen are often much better sources of political, economic and strategic information than government officials or academics. I thus had a rich second source of information that was usually given with remarkably frankness.

Extensive intelligence contacts from my military and post-military days, my access to both Islamic radicals and Muslim governments, my extensive experience in the Muslim world, and my business contacts provided a steady flow of inside information. Because my information was often so reliable and unusual, many people became convinced I was actually in the intelligence business. A cbc announcer once accused me of being a senior cia officer. In fact, I was running a one-man intelligence agency and my information on the Muslim world was often more reliable and timely than that obtained by the cia.

There was nothing mysterious about my operations. I often got things right because I had long experience in the region, kept up to date, and knew what to look for—the very opposite of blundering US intelligence in the Muslim world, which so often ended up barking up the wrong tree, was just plain wrong, or was being misled by "allies" with hidden agendas.

What I have seen in recent years troubles me deeply: Muslims, from Morocco to India and Indonesia, who believed the United States was out to destroy Islam and impose dictatorship across their lands; Muslims who were convinced the age of European imperialism had simply been replaced with that of American imperialism, only more efficiently, with Britain and France tagging along to gobble up the crumbs.

Arabs and Israelis—and their foreign supporters—so blinded by endless cycles of violence and retaliation, by a 50-year legacy of fear and disinformation, that they had become incapable of resolving their sterile confrontation in a rational manner. I saw these warm, generous peoples of ancient civilization, high intellect, and honor at one another's throats, fighting like cavemen over a bone.

One day I would have tea with Holocaust survivors who believed, with good reason, that only a Jewish state armed to the teeth would save them and their offspring from another attempted extermination in a hostile Christian world. The next, with Palestinians who had lost their homes three or four times and lived like beggars on handouts from international charity organizations, and felt betrayed by the entire world.

I met with Chechens fighting for their lives against the Russians who had inflicted a Holocaust upon their parents. I sat with Bosnians and Albanian Kosovars, many shaking, their eyes filled with horror, who had seen their homes and mosques burned, and their mothers, sisters, and daughters raped. And with Kashmiri Muslims who had experienced the same horrors six thousand kilometers away to the east in the Himalayas.

I met in Pakistan with high-ranking politicians and generals, many of them public allies of the United States, and equally with ordinary citizens, who called Osama bin Laden a saint and hero, and believed America richly deserved all the suffering it endured in the 9/11 attacks. As I traveled over the decades, I encountered a growing tide of bitterness and anger directed against the western world, and one that was equally mirrored in North America, where Islamophobia became the modern version of 1930s anti-Semitism and a basic tenet of right-wing parties from Washington to Ottawa to Canberra.

The growing irrationality on both sides of the conflict was equaled by the mutual ignorance between westerners and Muslims about their respective cultures, faiths, and ways of life. I watched the fear and hatred of Islam, that had been embedded like a toxic bulb deep in western culture since the early Middle Ages, spring again to life. I saw Muslims accuse the West of all sorts of nefarious intent, including a new crusade to destroy their faith. I heard Israeli commentators claiming Islam was determined to destroy Judaism and Christianity, loudmouthed Muslim mullahs urging their illiterate followers to lay fire and sword on the impious West, and Christian televangelists calling for the destruction by heavenly fire of Islam and all its believers.

How, I wondered, could such stupid, brutish medievalism come to afflict us at the dawn of the twenty-first century? Have we learned nothing from the last century about racism, religious hatred, and the folly of rampant nationalism? Evidently not.

This book is an attempt to say, "sit down, take a deep breath, and let me try to explain what is going on behind the current storm of invective and threats." Let us pause for a moment from all the Sturm und Drang and try to dissect, analyze, and understand the component parts of the Muslim world's anger and hostility.

Let us also try to comprehend, the largely invisible, yet immensely powerful control mechanisms, the American Raj, by which the United States and its allies still dominate and shape the affairs of the Muslim world a half century after the age of colonialism was supposed to have ended. For it is these mechanisms, and the increasingly violent reaction to them, that are largely responsible for what we in the West call terrorism.

I invite those who will be surprised or angered by these assertions to be patient and turn to Chapter One.

Eric S. Margolis
April 2008

CHAPTER ONE

★ ★ ★

THE ARC OF ANGER

Mblida, Morocco

Three hard-looking men in their mid-30s, skins aged and darkened by the harsh sun and incessant winds that lash Morocco's wild Rif Mountains, squatted on the dirt floor of a small, stone-walled house set in a tiny village whose forty families were achingly poor even by the meager standards of the arid, treeless region.

The men sat on their haunches around a sputtering, foul-smelling kerosene lantern, chain-smoking cheap cigarettes, coughing to clear their throats from the swirling dust that always shrouded the village. They spoke in low, muted tones, keeping an eye on the rough-hewn door of wooden planks that let in thin rays of light and drafts of air.

One took out a folded paper from inside his brown woolen burnoose, opened it up, and smoothed it out on the floor. The others crouched lower to get a look at the thin sepia lines on the dirty rectangle of worn paper.

The man with the plan—his name was Ahmed—explained:

"This, *al-hamdilah* (Allah be praised), is from Syed the Tunisian. It is a plan of the American consulate in Barcelona, Spain. He was able to get it from the company that did electrical work on the building. He works for them as a floor cleaner."

The other two men grunted approval, clearly impressed.

Ahmed continued. "In studying this plan, I have found an old, unused tunnel that runs from the sewer system into the basement of the building. It was bricked up thirty years ago. That's why the Americans do not know about it."

The glow of their cigarettes and the flaring lantern cast a yellowish-red luminescence over their faces and the plan.

"I will go to Barcelona and pass this on to Brother Mehdi and his jihadis there. They have been waiting for over a year to find a way to attack the nest of the American crusaders. Now we have the way, praise Allah!"

"You must raise enough money from your families and friends to pay for my trip and obtain more money so we can buy the explosives in Spain."

"Brother Ahmed," said the second man, "your punishment will be felt all the way back in the American capitol. It will remind the Spaniards that they must live in peace with us, not the Americans."

The third man, a noted tribal elder, lit another cigarette, put his arm over Ahmed's broad shoulders, and said to him, "My brother, may God's blessings shower on you and your family, and their offspring. You have done very well. We will raise the money for you even if we must go hungry. Give me one week. This is my word."

The men stood, embraced, kissed one another on the cheeks in the style of the mountain Berbers, and left the dismal, smoky room one by one. Ahmed got into an ancient pickup van, battered by sand, rocks, and time, and began the long, arduous, two-day drive back to Casablanca. From Morocco's seaport, he would take a ferry to Spain, where he had a resident labor visa, and then go to Barcelona to meet Brother Mehdi's cell of jihadists.

As Ahmed maneuvered his van around deep potholes, he pictured in his mind's eye the American consulate in Barcelona, with its high walls, cement barriers, and electronic systems, suddenly torn apart by a volcanic eruption from deep within its fundament. "Allah be praised," he said aloud to himself once again, deeply impressed by the scene of destruction he had imagined.

"We will strike them a terrible blow. We will make them pay, and pay again for their crimes against the Muslims." Hate and adrenaline coursed through his veins. The setting sun burned into his eyes as he kept driving down from the mountains, planning his vengeance against Americans, a people he had never met, who had never done him any personal injury, and who would not have the slightest understanding of why a group of Berber tribesmen in the remote mountains of Morocco would want to harm them.

DHEISHEN REFUGEE CAMP—PALESTINE TERRITORIES

Adel Jabarra was a very bright, 23-year-old honors graduate in mechanical engineering from the prestigious Beir Zeit University, a handsome young man much admired by the ladies and who, it was widely said, possessed that much-desired positive life-force and innate good luck known in Arabic as "baraka."

On this day, Adel the Fortunate, as his friends sometimes called him, was standing in a cold, dank auto garage in the center of the refugee camp, naked to the waist, his arms spread wide.

Two men, one short, scruffy, and bearded, the other clean-shaven and professorial looking, who went by the nom de guerre Asim the Teacher, were busy taping a fine mesh belt covered with pockets filled with rectangles of the military explosive RDX that had been smuggled to the Palestinian Territories through a tunnel that began in Egyptian-controlled Sinai near el-Arish—RDX, highly prized for its explosive power, stability, lack of telltale odor, and light weight.

The two men finished taping the explosive belt around Adel's narrow waist, carefully inserted detonator cords into each explosive packet, then put the young Palestinian man's white shirt back on, and handed him a black dress jacket, Jewish yarmulke head cover, and an armload of books and notebooks that was to transform his appearance from young Arab student into young Jewish student.

Adel's mission was straightforward. A busload of American Midwestern religious tourists was coming to Bethlehem.

Once the Israeli Egged bus disgorged its passengers in front of the Church of the Nativity, Adel was to work his way among the tourists then push the button on a cell phone in his right pocket. The evangelicals, he mused sardonically, would attain their long-desired paradise rather sooner than they had expected.

Adel's mother had done everything in her power to dissuade her son from committing mass murder.

"Adel, Adel, my eagle," she'd pleaded with him on her knees. "My darling, you must not throw your life away like this. You are young, you have an entire good life in front of you. I beg you, I beg you ..."

She had pled like this for a month, ever since her son had confided that he was determined to become "shaheed," a martyr, for the cause of Palestine.

His older cousin, Kassem, had told him, "Listen, Adel, to hell with Palestine, to hell with the Israelis, to hell with the Americans, to hell with them all. Palestine will always be a mess. It's our nature. We can't help it. Don't throw away your life for a lost cause ... for nothing ... go find yourself a girlfriend and get married."

The logic of age is impotent faced by the passion of youth. Like almost all young Palestinians, Adel was buffeted by inner emotional storms that combined fury, fear, shame, and youth's quixotic hopes that one's personal actions could lessen the world's evil and alleviate its suffering.

"Kassem," Adel had patiently explained, over and over, "I cannot go on living under this occupation. It makes my life worthless, meaningless. Every day I wake up humiliated. I don't want to keep bowing my knees to the Americans and the Israelis.

"If I don't fight back, and if all my friends take the same attitude, we will remain slaves forever, and the Israelis will push us back to starve in the desert. I'd rather die resisting than go on living like a convict in our miserable prison of a Palestine.

"I want to kill as many of those Americans as I can. Perhaps that will send a message back to their country that they can't go on persecuting us. I don't know if there really is a paradise, but if there is, I will look down upon their defeat."

"Adel, how is killing a bunch of old tourists going to change America's policies?"

"Fear, Kassem, fear. They are cowards. Fear is the only way we will drive them from our homeland. I am going to shoot an arrow of fear into their black hearts."

Adel the Fortunate put on his black jacket and yarmulke, kissed the other two men on their cheeks, hugged them, and walked out into the sharp sunlight. He got into a rickety old Mercedes sedan and was driven from the refugee camp, where 11,000 Palestinians had lived since 1949 in squalor and simmering hatred against the world, into Bethlehem, where Christ the Prophet of Peace had been born.

He alit three blocks from the Church of the Nativity and walked towards its door. Nearby, a large bus filled with sunburned American tourists in loud shirts and blue baseball caps, furiously snapping photographs, was just pulling up.

Kunar, Afghanistan

"Ma'shallah," exclaimed Mullah Mahmud, "by God, we will strike the Franks just at dawn tomorrow and send them straight to hell."

The Afghans, an ancient people, still referred to westerners, and particularly the American and British troops occupying their nation, by the same name by which the medieval Europeans and, later, the crusaders had become known to the Muslim world, "Franks." The Frankish kingdom of Charlemagne and Charles the Fat had vanished over 1,200 years earlier, but the Islamic folk memory of the fierce Frankish knights whom the early Arab invaders of Europe had battled remained vivid and respectful.

Mullah Mahmud—a local village prayer leader who had gained renown during the 1980s as a mujahid, or holy warrior, in the "Great Jihad" against the Soviets and the hated Afghan Communists, studied the British army's temporary encampment in the flat valley floor below the mountainside on which they lay concealed among dun-colored boulders and scrub.

The mullah had lost an eye fighting the Soviets, and had suffered three additional, near-fatal wounds. Like all the other Afghan mujahidin wounded in the eleven-year struggle against Soviet occupation, he was given only the most rudimentary field medical treatment. Wounded warriors either died in silence or, thanks to the grace of Allah, recovered to fight another day.

Mullah Mahmud had been fighting foreign invaders for twenty-nine years. He had given up farming to become a permanent warrior for Allah. In doing so, his reputation as a fearless and skilled commander who showed no mercy to the foe became known and admired across southern Afghanistan.

A member of the notoriously warlike Pashtun tribe, the mullah was fond of saying that he had thought he hated godless Communists more than anything else on earth—until he met the American and British invaders.

"The American Franks and their dogs the British are even more godless than the Russian Communists. They believe only in money and making the world their slaves. They are bigger enemies of Islam than the Communists, much stronger, much more clever.

"We are poor, but we are not stupid. We know they invaded our country to build oil pipelines across our land. They think they can keep a puppet government in power in Kabul. They want to force us to become Christians and buy their products and kiss their feet."

The black-turbaned mullah spat on the ground twice and cradled his beloved AK-47 Kalashnikov automatic rifle in his arms.

Another Afghan warrior, a thick white scar transecting his hawk-like face, spoke. "My brother, I have just heard that the men of Hadji Asif are ready to attack the Franks from the other side of the valley just as soon as morning prayers are done tomorrow. He has ammunition for his two mortars. The hadji sends you the message to kill all the invaders without mercy and give glory to God the Deliverer."

Winter snow still lay thick in many parts of the mountains and uplands. But two of Hadji Asif's mujahidin, men too poor to afford boots, had left at dusk, pulled their thick shawls about their shoulders, and trudged over snowy mountains in their sandals for seven hours to the camp of another mujahidin commander who had a supply of 81mm mortar shells. Each filled their backpacks with 110-pound loads of shells, then trekked back to their camp across the mountains for another seven hours through the freezing cold and deep snow.

"The American Franks have every sort of advanced weapon that Shaitan (Satan) can devise," Mullah Mahmud was fond of repeating. "They can bounce messages off the moon and send out little mechanical birds to spy on us. They shower storms of fire from the sky, and blizzards of sharp metal darts. They like to fight from far away, where there is no risk."

"We have nothing . . . except for our Din, our faith. The Franks do not understand that they cannot defeat a people who have nothing, nothing except faith and honor.

"Faith is stronger than any of their hellish Frankish devices. We defeated the British and the merciless Russians. We will defeat the Americans and the British, and the Russians when they come back one day. And when that is done, we will go down to Pakistan and cut off the heads of all the apostate unbelievers who have befouled that nation."

The mujahidin could not light a fire lest the American drones with infrared devices that always hovered overhead located their position. It began to snow lightly. The Pashtun warriors huddled together for warmth, rubbing their hands, shivering as the cold bit into their bones. They ate some stale bread and pieces of dried fruit, said their last prayer of the day, the Isha, and tried, without much success, to doze off.

Before the first rays of the sun appeared, the seventeen mujahidin performed their ritual washing with snow, then gave their predawn morning prayer, or Fajr, which, by tradition, is often ended by the line "Prayer is better than sleep."

Mullah Mahmud's fighters moved down the mountain, bent low, working their way around boulders in the darkness. Half a kilometer away was the British temporary camp, a group of vehicles formed into a laager, or defensive circle, a form of circular encampment the British learned during the Boer War. The mujahidin worked their way into a nullah, or dry streambed, thereby escaping detection by British sentries who always had night-vision devices and, sometimes, movement detectors.

Just as the first carmine rays of the sun were breaking over the mountain ridge to their east, Hadji Asif's mortars opened up, delivered a shower of the 81mm shells that his men had so laboriously backpacked over the snowy mountains. His experienced crews quickly found the range. The British base was enveloped in a series of explosions whose thunder echoed off the surrounding mountains.

Mahmud's men broke cover, crying out the ancient Muslim war cry "Allah Akbar," and began firing into the base. Sheets of return fire, at first erratic, then steady, came back. Five of the mullah's mujahidin managed to get close enough to the British laager to fire RPG rockets into the vehicles, which burst into flames, killing the crews of two of them who had been firing back at the attackers with heavy machine guns.

Two more of Mullah Mahmud's men penetrated the circle of vehicles and shot down three groggy British soldiers who were emerging from their dugout. The two mujahidin were quickly shot down in turn.

Minutes later, US aircraft appeared overhead and began bombing and rocketing the scattered mujahidin. Only their proximity to the British camp saved them from immediate destruction. Once the US warplanes had spent their munitions, they departed.

But the mujahidin knew a giant American B-1 bomber would soon reach the scene and shower them with deadly precision munitions. They ran for the cover of the nullah, and then back into the safety of the mountain, The holy warriors sheltered in a small cave that they fortuitously discovered, safe from the furious American bombing that they knew would shortly resume.

Of the original seventeen mujahidin, only ten had returned alive from the attack. The survivors gave prayers for the souls of their martyred comrades, then embraced.

Mullah Mahmud's fierce, black-bearded face split into a smile of rapturous joy. "We have shown the Franks today what we can do. Let them take this lesson. We have many more to teach these kaffirs (unbelievers). Honor and feel envy for our brothers martyred in jihad. For they are truly in paradise. Allah Akbar! God is great."

Cairo, Egypt

Gamal, a heavyset man in his fifties, carefully pinned a large color picture of a cruise ship on the wall of a small, second-floor room above the modest shop of Murad, the sweet-seller, deep in the heart of Cairo's old bazaar that was known as the Mouski.

"Brother Selim in Naples reports that the cruise ship *Queen of the Seas* will be calling on Alexandria on July 28."

Five other men in the room, the executive council of the banned and hunted underground organization Islamic Jihad, listened intently. "Brother" Gamal was their chief of military operations. He had once worked closely with the legendary Dr. Ayman al-Zawahiri, the deputy emir of al-Qaida, who had cofounded their revolutionary movement. It was said that Gamal had taken part in the attack on European tourists in 1997 at Luxor that left sixty-eight dead and ruined Egypt's vital tourist industry for three years.

If tourists stopped coming to Egypt, its economy would collapse, and with it the American-supported military regime in Cairo that they called a brutal puppet of the Americans. How many times had Dr. Zawahiri repeated that once the flow of foreign currency to Egypt's oligarchy was cut off, it would collapse like a rotten house and take with it Egypt's American masters who had openly and arrogantly ruled their nation since the days of that modern pharaoh and loathsome traitor Anwar Sadat?

"*The Queen of the Seas*," declaimed Brother Gamal, who had been named after Gamal Abdel Nasser, Egypt's only true patriotic national leader in the past 2,000 years, "will leave Naples on the night of the twenty-sixth of July and dock at Alexandria three days later, early in the morning, around 6 a.m. According to our information from Naples, it will have at least 260 members of a tour group aboard, as well as other American and European passengers.

"Twelve of the dockworkers are members of our groups. My plan is simple. We will create a diversion at the dock's front gate by exploding some grenades at the guard post. When most of the dock guards run to see what is happening, our brothers at the dock will cut a hole in the wire fence and allow our special strike group to enter. It will immediately storm the ship, killing the few guards and customs agents left at the gangway.

"If our timing is correct, the American tour group will just have assembled ahead of the other debarking passengers in front of the gangway exit. We will kill them all with grenades and gunfire. Our mujahidin will then seize the lists of passengers from the purser's desk and go from cabin to cabin killing any more Americans, British, Australians, and Canadians that we can find."

"How will the mujahidin escape, Brother Gamal?" asked one of the men.

"They will not. This is a martyrdom mission. All have accepted."

Another of the men in the small room, teacher of English by profession who wore a shabby western-style suit, interjected, "Your plan is brilliant. The attack will drive a dagger into the heart of our tourist industry, and it will also horrify America, and make Americans too frightened to leave their homes."

"Strike the Americans where they will feel the most pain," another man quoted a favorite maxim of Dr. Zawahiri. "Strike them in their wallets by hitting their industry and their finance, for only there is America truly vulnerable." Zawahiri had spent enough time in the United States to know of what he was speaking.

Zawahiri was merely echoing the words of his leader, Sheik Osama bin Laden, who kept advising his followers around the globe to strike at America's Achilles' heel, its economy. "The religion of America is money," bin Laden kept repeating.

Had not the 9/11 attacks and George W. Bush's predictable response by launching a war on terror and invading Afghanistan and Iraq already cost the Americans nearly one trillion dollars? Even impossibly rich America could not long bear this titanic expense. The 9/11 attacks on New York had alone cost America $100 billion, which, Sheik Osama gleefully pointed out.

Another man, named Nawar, cleared his throat. "Brother Gamal, yours is an excellent plan and I am sure it will put the fear of Allah into the Americans. But what about our cause?

"The Luxor attack brought worldwide condemnation on our group and made us give up such attacks, as you well recall. Won't massacring large numbers of tourists blacken our name, hurt our cause, and injure the good name of Islam? How do we explain killing so many innocent civilians?"

"My brother Nawar," Gamal replied patiently, as if lecturing an errant child, "what has world opinion done for us until now? Did it rescue the Palestinians and restore their stolen land? Did it save the Chechens or Kashmiris? Did it stop the butchery in Iraq and Afghanistan?

"I say, spit on world opinion. Let them fear our wrath. That's what they will understand. The Americans have real compassion only for their pet dogs.

"Besides, foreign tourists are a legitimate target. Their money supports the tyrants who enslave us. Attacking them is no different from attacking other economic targets like factories, bridges, and railroads. Ask the British and Americans about this . . . and about the millions of Germans and Japanese civilians they killed in World War II. Or ask them about Vietnam where they killed two million civilians and called it 'collateral damage.'"

There were no more objections or questions. It was decided.

"I will leave for Alexandria tomorrow," said Gamal, "to begin planning for our operation. May Allah guide your footsteps and mine."

We have now reached one of those dangerous confluences in history where powerful political and economic forces have combined with surging currents of violent nationalism, demagoguery, racism, and religious bigotry to produce an explosive mixture that seems at times to threaten a worldwide conflict between the Muslim world and the West.

On one extreme, we heard President George W. Bush calling for a global crusade against "Islamic terrorists" as US military forces battled Muslim guerrillas in Iraq, Afghanistan, Somalia, Pakistan's Waziristan, in both East and West Africa, and in the Philippines. American televangelists damn Islam as "the work of the devil." Millions of American Protestants believe claims that Biblical Israel of 1000 BC is about to be re-created, bringing the return of the Christian Messiah and the fiery destruction of all mankind—except for the true believers—in Armageddon and the End of Days.

Some American congresspeople urge nuclear strikes on Mecca. Pope Benedict XVI calls Islam a "violent" faith, somehow forgetting the Crusades, the Inquisition, slavery, Europe's religious wars, and nineteenth-century colonialism, and two prominent leaders born into the Christian faith, Josef Stalin and Adolf Hitler. Benedict's influential personal secretary warned of the danger of the "Islamisation of Europe." American neoconservatives demand "World War III" against Islam, and stoke Islamophobia—the evil twin of anti-Semitism. In the meantime, the US–led war in Iraq grinds on and western powers plunge ever deeper into Afghanistan as neighboring Pakistan seethes with violence and anti-Americanism.

At the other extreme, Osama bin Laden calls on his many followers for a worldwide holy war against "Crusaders and Jews," and urges nuclear attacks against the United States. New, particularly violent anti-western jihadi groups keep emerging in Asia, Europe, and Africa. Anti-Semitism and hostility towards the West grows apace across the Muslim world. Islamic schools known as "madrassas" teach children to hate and despise the "evil" western world. More recruits rush to become suicide bombers, deluded into believing they do the work of Islam by killing innocent people.

In 2006, a deeply disturbing World Public Opinion survey found that a large majority in four leading Muslim nations—Egypt, Morocco, Pakistan, and Indonesia, which comprise a third of the Muslim world's people—believe the US is determined to destroy or undermine Islam, and overwhelmingly support attacks on US forces based in their nations. These same sentiments are unfortunately common across the Muslim world.

The West and the Muslim world have indeed fallen into a confrontation. Not yet the notion of a "clash of civilizations" advocated by neoconservative scaremongers, but certainly a bloody, prolonged, and unpredictable conflict that threatens to be as dangerous as it is utterly unnecessary. Since this conflict is developing at a slow, erratic tempo, we are fortunate in still having time to halt it before events run out of control and assume a life and direction of their own. Most wars begin by miscalculation, mistaken information, misjudgment of one's foes, and overblown estimates of one's own strength. America's debacle in Iraq offers the latest example.

The current clash between the West and the Muslim world is not a new phenomenon: its current phase has been slowly building up since the nineteenth century, though its historic origins date back to the time after Islam's birth in the seventh century when the newly united Muslim Arabs assailed the Byzantine Empire, conquered Spain, and harassed Italy and the kingdom of the Franks.

Two events caused the current explosion of violence. First, the criminal 9/11 attacks mounted by al-Qaida, a tiny radical organization that never numbered more than three hundred adherents. Second, the Bush administration's decision to use 9/11 as a pretext to launch a campaign to dominate two of the world's major energy sources—Mesopotamia and the Caspian Basin—and bring the Muslim world ever more firmly under the arc of US influence I call the American Raj.

The suicide attacks on America of September 11, 2001, ignited fury against Muslims in much the same manner the surprise raid on Pearl Harbor on December 7, 1941, aroused hatred of Japanese. In both cases, the attacks appeared unprovoked and to come out of the blue. Very few people had any understanding of the geopolitical context underlying these attacks, or the other side's motivations in launching them. Few Americans knew their nation had been engaged in sporadic, low-intensity warfare in the Muslim world for the previous three decades, any more than their parents had seen or understood the relentless growth of tensions between the United States and Japan over Manchuria and China from the 1920s until Pearl Harbor.

Not since the medieval Crusades has the western world been so deluged with alarms over the "menace" of Islam, or appeals for what the British writer G.K. Chesterton, in "Lepanto," his magisterial poem about the clash of Europe and the Ottoman Empire, called "swords about the cross." President George W. Bush, a born-again Christian, repeatedly warned that the United States was at war with "evil," a code word the Muslim world took to mean Islam. In September 2006, Bush boldly asserted his so-called war on terror would prove the "decisive struggle" of the twenty-first century, a claim reminiscent of the fatuous slogan that World War I was "the war to end all wars."

In the same month, President Bush, Vice President Dick Cheney, and Defense Secretary Donald Rumsfeld unleashed a new ideological offensive, branding Muslims who opposed US influence "Islamofascists." The president sought to link his war on terror to the heroic era of World War II, and his own leadership to that of Winston Churchill. Muslims who resisted the New World order were cast as neo-Nazis in turbans.

Ascribing surging anti-Americanism across the Muslim world to the revivified ghost of Adolf Hitler showed just how far the Bush administration had drifted from the shores of reality. Disturbingly, a majority of

Americans at that time agreed with the president. By contrast, polls in Pakistan found that some 90 percent of Pakistanis called Osama bin Laden a hero, while an equal number saw George W. Bush as a threat to all mankind.

Former senior Bush administration officials have confirmed that the White House had decided to attack Iraq and likely Afghanistan well before 9/11. In July 2007, the normally soft-spoken former Soviet chairman, Mikhail Gorbachev, went public with stinging criticism of the Bush administration that summed up the world's prevalent view of US foreign policy. Nobel Peace Prize winner Gorbachev accused the Bush White House of being committed to a policy of "aggressive imperialism" that created "turmoil" around the globe. His view was widely shared in Europe, even among staunch American allies.

Washington threw away the historic opportunity offered by the collapse of the USSR to forge an era of international law and mature cooperation, charged Gorbachev, who himself refused to use military force to save the disintegrating Soviet Union and its East German satellite in spite of demands by Soviet marshals and the KGB to use troops and tanks to crush the growing uprising. Instead, Gorbachev, one of the most humane, principled statesmen of our time, specifically accused Republican neoconservatives in Washington of adopting an aggressive, "empire-building policy" that led the US to commit a series of major strategic mistakes.

"The idea of a new empire, of sole leadership, was born," Gorbachev charged. "Unilateral actions and wars followed," adding, the US "ignored the Security Council, international law and the will of its own people." Gorbachev's accusations may sound naive and utopian to some, but in refusing to use force to keep the unraveling Soviet Union intact, he followed exactly what he preached. His predecessors, by contrast, crushed unrest with usual Soviet ruthlessness. So did his successors.

America's failure of grand strategy began during the Clinton administration. Instead of seizing the unprecedented opportunity offered by the end of the Cold War to build an international great power understanding— a sort of modern version of the Treaty of Vienna that ended the Napoleonic era and brought peace to Europe for nearly a century—the Clinton White House sought to nurture a client government in Moscow by means of massive payments to the corrupt, bankrupt Yeltsin oligarchy.

Scornful of seemingly moribund Russia, and infused with hubris, the new Bush administration decided to seize this opportunity to pursue a policy of world military, political, and economic domination. But like many past leaders whose ambitions outran their resources, President George W. Bush and Vice President Dick Cheney seriously overestimated their nation's military and economic power, and underestimated the resistance their imperial strategy would inevitably encounter.

Being top dog in the world was indeed one splendid way of assuring America's security, but only if you are big and powerful enough. However mighty and incredibly rich, America lacked the military and economic power to forcefully impose its will on the globe. In fact, when George Bush invaded Afghanistan in 2001, US conventional military forces were weaker than they had been since the end of the Vietnam war and no longer had the capability to fight 2.5 or even 1.5 major wars at the same time that had long been America's strategic baseline for minimum military power.

The vainglorious, overreaching neoconservative grand strategy—one that often recalls Mussolini's arrogant plans to re-create the Roman Empire by conquests—was certain to eventually provoke violent resistance and cause other world powers to coalesce against a hegemonistic United States, just as Europe had united to defeat Napoleon's aggressive France, and Britain had assembled alliances to thwart the march of German power. Nor was it likely the rest of the world would accept Bush's announced strategy of preemptive attacks against all perceived threats.

History may look back on the Bush administration's foreign policies as one of the most counterproductive of any presidency in US history, and its domestic-security measures as the most serious violations of America's core democratic values since the 1950s McCarthy-era Red Scare.

Instead of advancing America's interests abroad, the Bush administration's bull-in-the-china-shop policies fostered virulent anti-Americanism around the globe. As we shall shortly see, the Muslim world turned violently against the United States and its allies. President Bush and Vice President Cheney's scornful unilateralism alienated many of America's stoutest traditional allies, notably France and Germany, where polls showed that the Bush administration was widely regarded as the leading threat to world peace and good order. Similar views were common in Asia.

The rupture with Europe over Iraq in turn provoked widespread anti-European sentiments across the United States, particularly among less educated Republicans who reveled in baiting the French. In spite of having helped create the United States, France was scourged as a deceitful, unsanitary, cowardly nation in constant need of American succor while the ever-accommodating British, who also had to be rescued by American power in two world wars, were rapturously praised. It did not take long for the Bush administration's aggressive, crusading tone to make Russia and China regard Washington's intentions as increasingly hostile.

The surge of anti-Americanism around the globe proved an unexpected but most welcome boon and rallying point to leftist and Marxist parties everywhere who had been aimless and without a popular cause since the collapse of Communism.

A June 2003 bbc international survey of 11,000 people in eleven nations found that 57 percent of those sampled had a very negative view of America's leadership. The figure rose to 60 percent when American respondents were eliminated. When asked who was more dangerous to world peace, the United States rated higher than al-Qaida in some Muslim nations.

Another bbc poll of 26,000 people in twenty-five nations taken in 2007 found 49 percent believed the US was playing a mainly negative role in the world, and 68 percent felt the ongoing US military presence in the Mideast provoked more conflict than it prevented. Over two-thirds of all respondents disapproved of the way Washington had dealt with Iraq, the Guantanamo detainees, the Israel-Hezbollah war, Iran's nuclear program, and Washington's handling of global warming and North Korea.

Not only had the world turned sharply against the United States by tragically failing to resolve the festering Arab-Israeli conflict, a primary generator of what we call terrorism, the Bush administration ensured such violence would persist. But it was the administration's clumsy, ultimately catastrophic efforts to dominate global energy resources by invading Afghanistan and Iraq that led to a head-on confrontation with the Muslim world. A confrontation, one must assume, in which the Rasputin-like figure of Vice President Dick Cheney and his neoconservative Praetorian Guard took full advantage of the president's simplistic, biblical view of the Mideast, and his limited knowledge of history and foreign affairs, to advance their aggressive imperial agenda.

From the Atlantic shores of Morocco and Mauritania to the jungles of the southern Philippines, the Muslim world—23 percent of the world's population—has become an arc of anger seething with hostility at the United States and its allies. This anger is generated by specific causes, but it is also diffused into a miasma of hatred, fear, and distrust of the United States and the West that has come to permeate the entire Muslim world and all classes of its societies, even those that depend on America for their protection and wealth.

These emotions and the violent actions flowing from them have become one of the engines of what is known in the West as "terrorism," a largely meaningless term that serves as a propaganda weapon used by both sides. Terrorism is a tactic: the UN defines it as "attacking civilians for political purpose." One cannot wage global war on a tactic.

By contrast, in many parts of the Muslim world, acts of violence and defiance against the West are hailed as "resistance" against oppression and injustice, two terms that are rarely used in the West these days. Distant as they may be from our own experience, these terms still resonate across the Muslim world, where, according to Islamic thought and tradition, injustice and oppression are not only primary evils, but are also urgent calls to action for pious Muslims.

Seven years after the 9/11 attacks, we are inundated by innumerable books about terrorism, and works claiming Islam is a sick, violent faith, all written by "experts," many of whom have little on-the-ground experience in the Muslim nations about which they so readily pontificate. Many confirm current anti-Muslim prejudices and mistaken views of the Muslim. North Americans have yet to understand what really motivated the 9/11 attacks, and why increasing numbers of people in the Muslim world are literally up in arms against the United States and principal allies Britain, Canada, Australia, the Netherlands, and Denmark.

While the US invasion of Iraq in 2003 was seen in many parts of the world, and certainly the Muslim world, as an old-fashioned imperial grab for oil, a majority of Americans believe Saddam Hussein was behind the 9/11 attacks and strongly backed the invasion of Iraq, which President Bush called, "the central front in the war on terrorism."

We need to drop the emotionalism associated with the term "terrorism" and begin taking a hard look at the sources of anti-western violence and animosity. Trying to understand the motivations of those who attack the West in no way seeks to justify such acts, or suggests we allow our policies to be dictated by suicide bombers or religious fanatics.

A basic intelligence map is essential to understanding our opponents' order of battle and strategy. We have to stop flying blind. Most important, before we advance any further towards the notion of an unlimited series of wars in the Muslim world, we need first to understand what has turned so many Muslims against the West, and what can be done to lessen, or even end, this growing hostility. Muslims, for their part, need to examine why their too-often violent responses to western actions are goading their opponents to further violent action and are profoundly counterproductive to Muslim causes.

In the first decade of the twenty-first century, much of the Muslim world is gripped by a profound sense of being exploited or wronged by the West, and, increasingly, the desire to inflict retribution on the supposed western authors of these wrongs. Meanwhile, in the West, there is a growing sense that the Muslim world is a hotbed of violence and a growing danger to the United States, Britain, Canada, and the rest of the NATO alliance. For some, the "Green Peril" of Islam has become a replacement for the former "Red Peril" of Communism.

While wide-scale antipathy for the West in the Islamic world is obvious, it still remains almost unthinkable that 1.5 billion Muslims, who until a few decades ago regarded the United States as a friend, potential liberator, and role model, could become so deeply embittered against America. It is even more astounding that America, the world's sole superpower, lives in daily fear of becoming the target of nuclear, biological or chemical attacks by fanatical Muslim suicide squads.

Only a brief decade after America had emerged victorious from the fifty-five-year Cold War against the Soviet Union, a redoubtable, extremely dangerous foe, the US found itself locked in a bizarre, shapeless conflict with little-known, poorly understood opponents armed only with improvised bombs and small arms who are waging what the Pentagon calls "asymmetric warfare" against the United States and its allies. During the Cold War, the rules of conflict between the US–led West and the Soviet

Bloc were clear and carefully observed, thus limiting the danger of an outbreak of all-out war. But in the new, post–Cold War era of conflict, there were no rules, and no constraints on the actions of the parties engaged.

America has been facing a shadow war, a murky struggle against a faceless, almost invisible foe bent on both giving Americans a national nervous breakdown and blasting or scaring US influence out of the Muslim world. America's military had been armed and trained to fight the conventional armed forces of hostile nations, and not a bunch of ragtag transnational guerrillas. This totally unexpected development produced widespread consternation, bureaucratic tumult, and political confusion in Washington, eliciting quaintly Victorian calls by the Pentagon for America's elusive Muslim opponents to stand up, be cricket, "Stop hiding behind civilians. Fight fair in the open, like real men."

But the unsporting Muslim wagers of what we mistakenly call "holy war," and they call jihad, refused to comply with western rules by making themselves targets for the US Air Force's cluster bombs. The jihadis became a swarm of angry Lilliputians stinging the legs and ankles of the giant American Gulliver. No sooner would he stomp on a few and squash them than another swarm would issue from cracks in the wall to continue harassing the infuriated giant.

The Bush/Cheney administration incessantly warned there was a global terrorist threat against the United States from a vast, multi-armed conspiracy centrally directed from al-Qaida's hidden headquarters. The facts were otherwise.

First, and most important, the rising wave of violence westerners call "Islamic terrorism" is primarily directed against the western-supported dictatorial regimes ruling the Muslim world. Attacks on the West, however spectacular, are of secondary importance. This point cannot be overemphasized. "Terrorism" literally begins at home.

Second, the United States and its allies are fighting a collection of like-minded but completely unconnected and uncoordinated anti-American groups. Nothing at all, save their hatred of the United States and its allies, unites the disparate jihadi groups that have emerged from nowhere to challenge and bedevil the West. What, one might rightly ask, does a Moroccan jihadi have in common with a Yemeni revolutionary, a Pashtun tribesman from Pakistan's Waziristan, a Muslim university student in France, or an Indonesian Islamist from Sumatra?

All observe the same faith, in varying ways and intensity, and according to different styles and sects, but besides religion, they hold no evident beliefs or causes in common. Historic religious schisms, such as Shi'ism and Sufism, had long ago shattered the early monolithic nature of Islam. Modern Muslims share no more common bonds than do Spanish Catholics with Protestant Finns in Lapland, or Orthodox-Christian Greek fishermen in Salonika. In short, the dots do not appear to connect.

But a deeper look into Islamic thought and tradition reveals there is indeed a common thread that links many of the world's Muslims. That is the sacred duty of jihad. Thanks to Hollywood, most westerners think of jihad as a sort of primitive mass religious hysteria that produces eruptions of Islamic violence.

Many Christians—and most lately evangelical Christians and even, unfortunately, Pope Benedict xvi—have long spread the canard that jihad means a holy war designed to spread Islam by the sword. While Islam was certainly born in battle, and owed its early success to the defeat of pagan Arab, Byzantine, and Persian armies, it is an historic fact that Islam's near-lightning expansion from Morocco to the Great Wall of China and deep into Africa was the result of its ready, often eager acceptance by non-Muslim populations as a dynamic new faith that liberated them from Christian religious infighting, serfdom, rapacious, exploitive rule by Byzantines and Persians, or from India's pernicious Hindu caste system that amounted to a form of serfdom.

The primary propagators of Islam were merchants, traders, and sailors. Today, ten African animists are becoming Muslims for every one that converts to Christianity, a fact that has fired the deepest animosity against Muslims among American Protestant evangelical groups and contributed to the surging wave of Islamophobia in the United States.

The proper translation for jihad is "struggle." There are two primary forms of jihad: inner and outer. For Muslims, jihad is a mandatory religious duty.

Inner jihad means struggling with one's own demons and desires, and such common human failings as greed, gluttony, sloth, envy, lust, and ill will. It means fighting corruption, poverty, dishonesty, and hypocrisy. For all observant Muslims, inner jihad is a daily physical and mental struggle. The Holy Koran commands all Muslims to live modestly and austerely, eschewing the trappings of wealth and power, and to share a fixed measure of one's income with the needy, a duty that is widely ignored in many of the rich Muslim oil kingdoms.

Outer jihad means fighting against political, social, religious, and economic oppression and injustice. The Holy Koran commands all good Muslims to defend Islam and go to the rescue of fellow Muslims who are in danger or being oppressed, either by non-Muslims or by apostate Muslims. "Defend thy neighbor" is a cardinal tenet of Islam. So, too, is the duty to go to the aid of Muslims who are not being allowed to practice their faith.

The Koran clearly defines the conduct of jihad:

Fight in the path of God those who fight you, but do not aggress. Surely God does not love the aggressors. And fight them where you come upon them, and send them out from where they have sent you out, for persecution is a worse thing than fighting. And do not fight them at the Sacred Mosque (in Mecca) unless they fight you there, but if they fight you, then fight them back. That is the reward of the rejectors. Then if they cease, so God is All-Forgiving, Gentle. And fight them until there is no more persecution and the religion is for God. But if they cease, so let there be no hostility except against wrongdoers.

—Surah al-Baqarah, verses 190–193

The Holy Koran, written in a time of constant warfare, has many references to fighting unbelievers. These are routinely cited by some Christian and Jewish conservative critics as evidence of the inherent aggressiveness and bellicosity of Islam. As the old Hungarian saying goes, "The Devil uses the Holy Scriptures to preach his case." One could just as readily find blood and thunder calls to war and aggression in the Old and New Testaments.

The point to remember is that Islam is first and foremost a faith of compassion, brotherhood, and submission that rejects all divisions of wealth, class, race, and geography. Muslims are no more violent than any other humans. They certainly played no part in the past century's horrors, like Stalin's and Hitler's death camps, Hiroshima, and Mao's Great Leap Forward. The mass industrialized violence of modern warfare has been a phenomenon of the non-Muslim world.

The concept of defending fellow Muslims in danger is of paramount importance to our understanding of the Islamic world and what we term terrorism. When a Muslim is being oppressed in Iraq, or the southern Philippines, or Bosnia, it is the duty of Muslims to go to their rescue and fight those who oppress them.

For Muslims, jihad is an intimate, personal action. While covering the Great Jihad in Afghanistan in the 1980s, I repeatedly heard mujahidin say, "I am waging my jihad," rather than "I have joined the jihad." In other words, each jihadi is performing an imperative religious and moral duty.

If the jihadi falls in battle, the Koran says his soul will go immediately to heaven. The oft-quoted notion about scores of virgins awaiting the fallen warrior is a minor comment in the Koran that has been blown out of proportion by those trying to portray Muslim jihadis as demented or misled fanatics seeking lust through death. This writer has met many jihadis but never one who really believed bevies of virgins awaited him, though some did joke about the concept. Most were as uncertain as the rest of us about what awaited them after death.

The Holy Koran imposes strict rules for external jihad. It must only be waged in the cause of Islam, not for material or personal gain. Jihad must end once its goal is achieved. Civilians, particularly women and children, are to be protected. So are their means of livelihood, like farms, orchards, wells, and animals. Only the oppressors, the malefactors must be targets. The essence of Koranic external jihad is selectivity: only the wrongdoers deserve punishment.

By contrast, in the view of many Muslims, the West does precisely the opposite by waging indiscriminate, mass war against civilians and razing entire towns and cities—or even nations—that resist, Iraq and Afghanistan being cited as prime examples. The 9/11 attacks against New York were a stark violation of the Islamic laws of jihad and were widely condemned across the Muslim world, while the attack on the Pentagon was viewed as legitimate. However, Muslim nations and clergy failed to condemn Saddam Hussein's genocide against rebellious Kurds.

Naturally, these strict tenets of jihad are far more observed by lip service across the Muslim world than by deed, particularly when it comes to Muslim governments. While Muslim women were being raped and mosques blown up by Serb neofascists in Bosnia, the governments of the Muslim world—Iran and Afghanistan excepted—averted their eyes or simply issued polite protests. Osama bin Laden's constant exhortations to his followers to attack innocent civilians egregiously violated the basic tenets of Islam.

There are many in the Muslim world who are prepared to follow the Holy Koran's commands to perform jihad. During the anti-Soviet Great Jihad in Afghanistan during the 1980s, over 100,000 Muslim volunteers came to fight from as far afield as North Africa and Sumatra. Afghanistan marked the first time in the modern era that jihad went beyond being local or national and became a transnational cause for Muslims from different nations. The anti-Soviet struggle in Afghanistan became the first major event in our era to internationalize the call to jihad.

In the thinking of many radical young Muslims, and the imams, or prayer leaders, the closest things Sunni Islam has to a clergy, who electrified their minds by fiery blood-and-thunder sermons, jihad was as great, if not greater, duty than praying, fasting, and helping the needy. The concept of outer jihad naturally had enormous appeal to idealistic young men and women. It channeled their potent youthful emotions into religiously sanctioned pursuits that not only aided suffering fellow Muslims, but brought religious benefits and a sense of spiritual fulfillment that so many in the West lack. In the hands of fanatical local prayer leaders, or mullahs, and other religious teachers, warped, hate-filled versions of jihad became a lethal weapon that inflamed the minds and passions of credulous youth and gave them a wholly undeserved sense of self-worth and importance.

Colonialism and centuries of decline had left much of the Muslim world broken into inward-looking political fragments whose inhabitants' insular interests rarely extend beyond family, clan or tribe, and whose geographical horizons were rarely farther than a nearby village or modest provincial city.

To many Muslims, jihad has became synonymous with a renewal of long-lost Islamic virtues. Jihad offered a path of morality and rectitude through the swamp of corruption and immorality that had contaminated so much of the Muslim world. It was a rebellion against the corrupt dictatorships sustained by the West that violated every tenet of Koranic good government and public morality. Jihad promised new links to the rest of the Muslim world.

The second, and equally powerful, force in internationalizing the thinking of Muslims was television and, later, the Internet.

I journeyed through Yemen in 1976. At the time, this magical, antique land of the Queen of Sheba was just creeping into the eighth century AD. At dusk, a ram's horn was blown, and the city's great wooden gates closed for the night.

When asked what Yemenis did in the evening to entertain themselves, a local resident of the capital, Sanaa, replied, "We get together with the neighbors and our relatives to eat dinner. We do traditional dances, we tell our children fairy tales and stories from Yemeni history. We play games, the women sew and do weaving, we hold poetry contests ... since we all love poetry so much."

He paused for a moment. "That, of course, was until two weeks ago."

"What happened two weeks ago?" I asked.

"We got television. Now everyone stays at home and watches TV."

Two thousand years of rich Yemeni culture had been eradicated in one night by television. It was appalling, but, of course, inevitable. Poetry and history had been permanently replaced by reruns of "Mork and Mindy" dubbed into Arabic, and endless harangues by Yemen's prolix president. It was horrifying.

Television in the Muslim world quickly became a tool of government, broadcasting nonstop propaganda, political instruction, and religious programming. So it remained until the founding in Qatar of the al-Jazeera network in 1996 dropped a bombshell into the laps of every Muslim regime.

Al-Jazeera's uncensored broadcasts were carried by the new technology of satellite and cable to every corner of the Muslim world. Until then, the repressive regimes that ran much of this vast region, where illiteracy runs high, had minimized or completely ignored reports or even references in their heavily censored media to the suffering of Muslims in other parts of the "ummah" (Muslim world) except, of course, when it suited them. Not surprisingly, many Muslims had little knowledge and even less understanding of events outside their own nations. In fact, many westerners knew more about events in the Muslim world than did Muslims themselves, shut away as they were in their hermetically sealed nations where all news was the property of the state.

The founding of al-Jazeera by the forward-thinking Emir of Qatar, Sheik Hamid bin Khalifa al Thani, proved to be one of the most profoundly revolutionary and positive acts in modern Mideast history. Ironically, it was done by a traditional royal ruler who, at least at first glance, hardly seemed to fit the role of Mideast revolutionary. But a true revolutionary he certainly was. Sheik Hamid did more to bring the Mideast into the modern world than any number of previous Arab revolutionaries by liberating the minds of Muslim viewers from their usual steady diet of boring state propaganda. Like his fellow enlightened emirs in the United Arab Emirates, Sheik Hamid also showed how their little nations could live, and thrive, when oil eventually runs out, by developing new high-tech industries and tourism.

Al-Jazeera became the free voice of the Muslim world and quickly earned the fury of the Bush administration for reporting news Washington desired to suppress. The US even bombed al-Jazeera's office in Kabul and blasted its Baghdad office with tank fire, killing one of the network's correspondents. In mid-2007, intense pressure from Washington forced Qatar's royal family to purge its staff and adopted reporting "more friendly" to US policies. So much for Washington promoting free speech.

But before being partially muzzled, al-Jazeera's satellite-TV broadcasts suddenly brought into living rooms across the Muslim world the suffering of Muslims in Palestine, Chechnya, Kashmir, Iraq, Bosnia, Afghanistan, and Central Asia. Complacency was replaced by anguish, horror, and outrage as Muslims nightly saw reports on al-Jazeera, and other TV stations, including CNN and BBC, of the many human and political disasters afflicting the Islamic world.

Young Muslims, in particular, who gained access to the liberation technology of the Internet were deluged by a ceaseless flood of tragic, angry, and shameful news about the sufferings of their fellow Muslims. Most upsetting of all, for Muslims, night after night on TV they witnessed infuriating examples of what they believed was western hypocrisy and double standards over Palestine, Iraq, and Chechnya. They witnessed harrowing scenes of Muslim suffering in those nations that were only rarely shown on North American television.

This drumbeat of ugly revelations not only inflamed passions across the Muslim world, it also brought cries for jihad to rescue fellow Muslims in peril. If Muslim jihadis could defeat the mighty Soviet Union in

Afghanistan, many young people asked, why could they not go and battle for their fellows in Iraq, Afghanistan, Kashmir, or Palestine?

The Muslim world's long-simmering collective anguish and growing sense of injustice, now intensified by more open television and the Internet, inevitably became directed at their own governments, which did nothing to stop the suffering and exploitation of the Muslim world. This growing anger then turned on the distant imperial power in America that, many believed, defended, manipulated, and used these repressive regimes for its own strategic and economic interests.

This process had begun in the 1960s, when the suffering of Palestinians and the shameful double-dealing and backstabbing by Arab governments over Palestine began to become known. Israel's military triumph in 1967 and 1973 left the Arabs humiliated and increasingly disgusted by their own governments that had been so martial in word, yet so feeble in battle.

The frightful persecution of Muslims in Bosnia and, later, the Albanian Kosovars, heaped more shame on the Muslim nations. The Muslim world watched the tiny flickering flame of Chechen independence flare bravely, and then slowly sputter out as its defenders were massacred or assassinated one after the other.

As the first and second Palestinian "intifadas," or national uprisings, erupted, and Israel used tanks, heavy artillery, and warplanes to crush the insurgency, the Muslim world once again made only peeps of protest, and did nothing. Egypt, arguably the most important nation of the Arab world, piously advised Palestinians to seek "fruitful compromise" with Israel.

Muslim youth, like youth everywhere, found it difficult to stomach the hypocrisy, cowardice, and unprincipled accommodations that characterizes politics and international affairs. Disgust and contempt at the rampant corruption, incompetence, brutality, and kowtowing of their nation's weak governments to western interests formed a river of fury that coursed from one end of the Muslim world to the other.

While the rest of the world, black Africa excepted, was racing forward into the twenty-first century, the Muslim world was left behind in the dust. Government propaganda could no longer conceal the fact that most Muslim nations were almost bereft of political rights taken for granted in the West, and disgracefully backwards in science, education, cultural expression, and free thought.

In 2000, aside from Pakistan's nuclear program, and Turkey's modest industrial base, the Muslim world, a millennium earlier the global vanguard of science, medicine, astronomy, navigation, mathematics, and literature, was stagnating, or even slipping backwards. Half the food consumed by the Muslim world had to be imported, thus making Muslim nations as strategically vulnerable to a food embargo as were western and Asian nations to the threat of a Mideast oil cutoff. As one cynic quipped, "The most advanced piece of technology to come out of the Muslim world since the fifteenth century was the car bomb."

Though most westerners thought of the Mideast as a region of fabulous wealth, in reality, the region's combined total economic output was less than half of France's gross domestic product (GDP).

Every political route the Muslim world tried to follow since World War II had turned into a dead end. Monarchy clearly failed and was an anachronism. Communism was violently rejected by nearly all Muslims, save a handful in Iraq, Syria, and Lebanon. The East European–style socialism adopted by Iraq and Syria produced grim police states notorious for corruption and economic stagnation. The fiery nationalism and pan-Arab unity advocated by Egypt's hugely popular Gamal Abdel Nasser was thwarted by tribalism and jealousy, or by western opposition. So-called free markets proved a bonanza only for corrupt elites connected to government, particularly in Egypt.

Pakistan, founded in 1947 as a beacon of moral rectitude and good government for the Muslim world, has never been able to run a successful democratic state and too long remained an icon of dictatorship, instability, cronyism, and corruption. Turkey, a special case, long had a military-industrial oligarchy that dominated its weak parliamentary democracy. Only with the advent of the moderate Islamist AK Justice and Development Party did Turkish parliamentary democracy come alive. Indonesia, the world's largest Muslim nation, is only now emerging from half a century of dictatorship. Malaysia suffered under one-party rule until March 2008, when the opposition won important electoral victories.

Algeria's revolution, which once electrified the Muslim world by its seeming nobility, purity of purpose, and hope, turned into a Maghrebian nightmare of slaughter, beheading, and torture. Algeria's military junta, which proudly calls itself "the eradicators," is one of the world's most repressive, abusive regimes.

Iran claims to be a popular democracy, though it remains, in reality, a quasi-democratic state grafted on to a repressive theocracy in which supreme power remains with the mullahs. Perhaps the only two genuine democracies in which Muslims today live are, ironically, India and Israel, though in the former they are mostly at the bottom of society and in the latter they remain second-class citizens. Nigeria, whose Muslim population comprises 75 percent of its 127 million people, is so consumed by voracious corruption and malfeasance that its claim to be a democracy challenges credulity.

It is against this backdrop of social and economic ferment that increasing numbers of young Muslims have turned against their governments and embraced assertive versions of Islam. They are clamoring for an end to autocracy and military rule, for democracy, free speech, and social renewal.

Today's Muslim world in many ways resembles the moribund Soviet Union of the 1980s. Beneath the hard crust of totalitarian rule, powerful ferment is under way. A youth revolution is welling up that will one day sweep the old order away.

The uprisings of the early 1990s that overturned East Europe's hidebound Communist order was more a generational revolution than a political one. Young people from East Germany to Moscow craved western consumerism and junk culture; they demanded free speech and freedom from state controls. They were fed up with being told what to do by elderly Marxist "dinosaurs," and wanted a chance to make money and have the kind of fun not available in socialist Komsomol youth camps.

East Germany's politburo, Russia's chairmen Leonid Brezhnev and Yuri Andropov, had fretted endlessly about the dangers of television bringing the infection of western culture into their closed societies. So did South Africa's ultraconservative apartheid regime that had long banned TV. These Marxist dinosaurs, unlike those of the Cretaceous era, foresaw their impending doom. But they were helpless to halt the explosion. Today, over half the population of the Muslim world is under twenty-five. The repressive governments of the Muslim world will soon be similarly powerless to stop the oncoming demographic and political earthquake that will alter the region's landscape.

Most of the Muslim world's governments have a single priority and sole focus: keeping themselves in power, and their enemies out of power.

The hereditary monarchs, military men, and assorted despots who rule so much of the Muslim world are not interested in the plight of Palestinians or Chechens, and they are certainly not likely to risk arousing dangerous Islamic passions among their own nations for the sake of distant causes in which they have absolutely no interest.

The three cardinal rules of government in the Muslim world are: holding on to power at any cost by crushing all actual and potential dissent; enriching yourself and your family as fast as possible; and keeping in the good books of the United States, which has become the ultimate guarantor of most of the region's regimes.

These rules have worked well for the Muslim world's feudal and oligarchic elites. The men with the guns make the rules. Raising the cry of terrorism is usually successful in getting Washington to send its cavalry to the rescue and shower the supposedly threatened regime with tens of millions in secret payments and overt aid. It also is a most useful pretext for locking up political opponents and critics.

Little wonder then so many Muslims, both young and old, have become thoroughly disgusted by the corruption, impotence, and servility to the western powers of the regimes that rule them. Over the past twenty years, small but growing numbers of Muslims said to the devil with their do-nothing governments and decided to literally take matters into their own hands.

The Great Jihad in Afghanistan showed what organized groups of freelance mujahidin could achieve. If they could defeat the world's greatest land power, the Soviet Union, which at the time had 100 active Red Army divisions, could they not purge their own nations of the "hypocrites," apostates, and "evildoers" who had made the term "Muslim" synonymous with backwardness, incompetence, and grotesque ostentation. However, many Muslims simply forgot that the Soviets would never have been defeated in Afghanistan without the decisive military, intelligence, and financial intervention of Pakistan, the US, and Saudi Arabia.

Academics refer to this eruption of freelance fighters as "non-state actors." A better term is "private enterprise resistance." Hitherto, in our era, states held a monopoly on international violence and warfare. Communist states held a monopoly on both military action and domestic crime, which they more or less supervised.

The dawn of the twenty-first century saw an explosion of free enterprise violence wherein individuals and like-minded groups decided to take the forceful action that their own useless governments could or would not. "If Egypt will not liberate Palestine," went the call from Cairo's streets that echoed across the Muslim world, "we will."

The call to resistance resonated loudly through every corner of the Islamic world. Muslims who normally could agree on almost nothing beyond the fact that Allah was great suddenly found themselves agreeing that they had to fight back against perceived exploitation and oppression by the West and its Muslim satraps. This explosion of popular sentiment came at the very same time that the Muslim world's youth was discovering new forms of reenergized Islam to replace the failed creeds of nationalism and Arab socialism—and the liberating influence of the Internet.

This tidal wave of Islamic fervor infused Muslim societies everywhere. Muslims quickly adopted the term "resistance" as their new battle cry. Even harsh Arab dictatorships, like Syria and Iraq, and theocratic Iran, were ennobled, in the eyes of Muslim youth, by their resistance to Washington's diktat. So, too, Palestine's intifada and its rejectionist Hamas movement, and Lebanon's Hezbollah, the only force to ever defeat Israel. So did Iraq's Sunni resistance groups fighting US occupation until they were bought off with large bribes and gifts of arms. Resistance to perceived oppression became a nationalist and spiritual duty among many young Muslims. Those who "resisted" became the new heroes and role models for the youth of the Muslim world.

The attacks against the US on September 11, 2001, initially generated enormous sympathy and compassion for America in all Muslim nations. But President Bush, in one of the most politically revealing verbal slips of our era, called for a "crusade" against what he called "Islamic terrorism." The term "crusade" echoed throughout the Muslim world. President Bush's ensuing war on terror both poured gasoline on the rising flames Muslim anger, and inflamed anti-Muslim sentiment in the West.

The US invasion of Afghanistan in 2001 seemed at the time an appropriate counterterrorism response. A few old Afghan hands, this writer included, warned the US to uproot al-Qaida, then get its troops out of that fierce nation as quickly as possible or else risk getting drawn into a disastrous occupation that would end in another Afghan jihad against foreign occupation.

The invasion of Afghanistan and the so-called war on terror were, for many Muslims, proof the US had indeed embarked on a multi-front crusade against Islam. The Muslims world's post–9/11 sympathy for America quickly evaporated. The ruthless efficiency of the US invasion of Afghanistan, threats of war against Pakistan if it did not immediately comply with Washington's demands, and a rising volume of anti-Islamic rhetoric by the US and its media convinced many Muslims that the crime of 9/11 had been eagerly used by the Bush administration to launch a long-planned war for oil and worldwide domination. Washington's use of B-52 heavy bombers to carpet bomb primitive Taliban tribesmen reinforced the image of imperial punishment. So, too, the massacres of thousands of Taliban captives under the eyes of US Special Forces and CIA teams.

A very important, in-depth February 2007 World Public Opinion/ University of Maryland survey of four leading Muslim nations, Egypt, Morocco, Pakistan, and Indonesia—all close US allies—found large majorities in these nations believed that undermining Islam was a key goal of US foreign policy. Most respondents wanted US troops out of the Mideast and approved of attacks against them. Large majorities supported the political goals of al-Qaida but rejected attacks on civilians. Majorities also supported the idea of an enhanced role for Islam in their nation's affairs. Most backed globalization and favored freedom of religion and democracy.

This highly revealing study put US relations with the Muslim world in sharp and deeply disturbing perspective. After seven years of the war on terror, President Bush's crusade to supposedly promote democracy, two foreign wars, the expenditure of a trillion dollars and countless lives, all the Bush administration had accomplished was to turn the entire Muslim world against the United States and make Osama bin Laden its new hero. But this dramatic survey also showed that beneath the mantle of western-supported dictatorships, Muslims were yearning for the same values common to western democracies.

The Muslim world's opinion makers also seemed much better informed than most Americans about the decisive role played by Washington's neoconservatives in the vice president's office, Pentagon, the Project for the New American Century, the American Enterprise Institute, the Heritage Foundation, the Institute for Near East Policy, and the American Israel Public Affairs Committee. The neoconservatives' purported plans to overthrow the governments of Iraq, Syria, and Iran, and, eventually, Saudi

Arabia, were well known in the Muslim world, but little appreciated in North America.

To Muslims, as well as Europeans and Asians, President Bush unfortunately appeared to personify many of the negative stereotypes foreigners held of Americans: a jarring lack of education and culture, hyperaggressive nationalism, and an overriding arrogance.

These unfortunate traits were not just confined to President Bush or Vice President Dick Cheney, they characterized much of the administration's decision-makers and other senior officials. When Bush ordered the invasion of Iraq, not one high-level official resigned in protest. By contrast, Britain's principled foreign secretary, the late Robin Cook, and influential Labour MP Clare Short, both resigned from cabinet after Prime Minister Tony Blair joined the rush to war against Iraq. The Bush cabinet and senior echelons of the Pentagon and CIA went along with the invasion of Iraq with the same careerist acquiescence and synthetic institutional optimism as did the Soviet politburo and KGB with Brezhnev's disastrous 1979 invasion of Afghanistan.

The scene vividly recalled across the Muslim world was the deeply disturbing image of then Secretary of State Colin Powell presenting an audiovisual farrago of lies and disinformation at the UN about Iraq's nonexistent weapons programs while CIA chief George Tenet and UN ambassador John Negroponte sat behind him, hooded eyes cast down on their laps like Benedictine monks at vespers, listening to Powell's stream of falsehoods that rivaled the preposterous accusations produced by prosecutor Andrei Vishinsky at Stalin's infamous 1936–37 show trials. Powell's little phial of fake anthrax quickly became an icon of deceit and propaganda. How this decent man and fine public servant could have become a party to such dishonesty remains a mystery.

The almost universal view among Muslims—however mistaken—that the US had embarked on a full-scale war against Islam was reinforced by bloodcurdling calls by prominent Washington neocons for America to launch World War III against Muslims and nuke Mecca, as well as fulminations against Islam by demagogic Christian televangelists. Muslims, who rarely understand the diversity of America, heard these hate-filled messages and assumed they were government-sanctioned acts designed to whip up more hatred against Islam.

America's unqualified support of Israel in its repression of the Palestinian intifada, and Washington's defense of Israel's highly destructive 2006 mini-war in Lebanon, as well as the ongoing US campaign against Islamic charities and groups that Muslims considered legitimate resistance organizations, convinced lingering Muslim doubters the US had launched a multi-front campaign against any and all expressions by Muslims of opposition to what they deemed injustice and occupation.

The rise of youth-oriented Islam, intense feelings of injustice and victimization, and America's war on terror radicalized many Muslims and provided extremists of every type, from medievalist religious firebrands to western-hating nihilists, fertile ground for cultivating violent opposition to the West and its allies. Equally important, the Muslim world's continuing agonies in places like Algeria, Palestine, Iraq, Afghanistan, Kashmir, and Somalia were salt rubbed nightly by TV into Muslims' open emotional wounds. So long as these tragic situations festered, they continued to pump hate into the Islamic world's bloodstream, unfortunately making too many Muslims believe the mistaken idea that the source of these sorrows is a hostile, wicked, and rapacious United States and its allies.

My father, who fought his way up to Park Avenue from poverty on New York's Lower East Side, never forgot his roots and supported many social causes. "You will never know what it is like to be black in the United States until you are black," he said to me one day when I asked why he was sending money to civil rights groups. Similarly, most Americans will have trouble comprehending what it is like to be a Muslim in the western world in a time when Muslims are reviled, denied boarding on aircraft, depicted in TV and films as maniacal villains, called terrorists, and generally regarded as third-class citizens. Only Jews will understand the creeping, gut-wrenching fear experienced by North America's Muslims as they saw thousands of innocent Muslims arrested after 9/11, felt increasingly threatened by their own government, and experienced the current wave of Islamophobia that begins to recall the early stages of 1930s anti-Semitism.

Americans will have even more trouble comprehending the passions that have seized Muslims and propelled them to violent resistance against the West. To understand this much-debated question, which is now the most important security issue of our era, we have to take some steps back into recent history and see where this wave of what we call "terrorism" and Muslims term "resistance" really came from.

Why are Muslims causing so much trouble? What has provoked such hatred against us? What forces drive ordinary Muslims from such diverse places as Sudan or Uzbekistan to acts of extreme and, in our view, mindless violence? Is Islam a religion of violence? Are we in the West innocent victims of Islamic malevolence, or part of the problem? What can or should America and its allies do to take themselves off the target list?

The story begins in the heady fall days of 1945, when Germany and Japan lay defeated, and the world celebrated what just about everyone believed would be a new era of peace and prosperity.

CHAPTER TWO
★ ★ ★

THE MUSLIM WORLD IN CHAINS

In 1945, at the end of World War II, a conflict described as the Great War for Democracy, almost the entire Muslim world lay under European, Russian, or Chinese colonial rule. Such had been the status quo since the 1920s, when the victorious Allies of World War I finished dividing up the spoils of the defeated Ottoman, Austro-Hungarian, and German Empires. Many of the current travails of the Muslim world, and of black Africa, date to the post–World War I period, which saw the last, and ultimately pernicious, flowering of European colonialism.

At the end of World War II, there were only five Muslim nations that could truly be called independent: Turkey, though it was officially a non-Muslim, secular state; Saudi Arabia, by then already a de facto American protectorate; North Yemen, too poor, remote, and obscure to rouse the appetites of the Great Powers; and even more remote and worthless, Afghanistan. There was also the obscure Muslim Republic of Eastern Turkestan, which was fated to be erased by China four years later.

The rest of the world's Muslims, then nearly one billion people, lived as colonial subjects. To comprehend the magnitude of this fact, and its profound effects upon current history and international relations, we must first understand why Muslim nations had become so weak and vulnerable to foreign colonial rule and exploitation.

Two devastating historical events struck the Muslim world in the past thousand years: the great Mongol invasions and European colonialism. Compared to these catastrophes, the medieval Crusades were a minor coastal skirmish.

When in the thirteenth century Genghis Khan's Mongol horse armies burst forth upon the Muslim world from the Central Asian Steppe, they found before them one of mankind's two most advanced civilizations.

The glittering cities of the Khwarzimian Empire in what is today Kazakhstan and Uzbekistan, and the great cities of Persia and Mesopotamia, were the beating heart of the resplendent cosmopolitan Muslim civilization.

Baghdad, the largest city on earth outside those of the other great civilization, China, had over a million people, sewers, public lighting, hundreds of bookstores, hospitals, and universities. Western Europe did not reach this level of civilization until the early nineteenth century. In the 1300s, London was a collection of hovels with only a few thousand malodorous inhabitants.

The Mongol armies destroyed everything in their path. Their terrifying strategic objective was to raze all cities, massacre all populations, and destroy agriculture on their march westward, thus eliminating the need to control hostile subjects and, even more important, providing open pastureland for their ponies.

These ferocious, pitiless, militarily invincible nomads razed to the ground many of Islam's greatest cities: Bukhara, Samarkand, Khiva, Kars, Kabul, Meshed, Tabriz, Isfahan, Basra, Baghdad, and Damascus. At Baghdad in 1258, Hulagu Khan was said to have raised a pyramid of 100,000 heads. Drunken Mongol soldiers spent days torturing prisoners from the captured cities before beheading them. Women and girls were gang-raped and either killed or sold into slavery. Eight hundred thousand of Baghdad's people were thus slaughtered, the remainder enslaved.

The Mongol was finally stopped near Gaza in 1260 at the decisive battle of Ain Jalut by Baibars, the redoubtable Mameluke Sultan of Egypt. The Mongol hordes, which had reached as far as Gaza, Germany, and Poland, quickly withdrew into Asia. After the death of Genghis Khan, his empire, briefly the largest in history, simply vanished into dust.

But however ephemeral, the Mongols left total destruction in their wake: ruined ghost cities, barren lands denuded of people, shattered irrigation systems, slaughtered herds, poisoned wells. The Mongols were the thirteenth century's equivalent of a nuclear war. In fact, the Mongols killed far more people than all the bombs, including atomic weapons, dropped in World War II. So immense and complete was the Mongol devastation that Iran's population did not reach thirteenth-century levels until the

1970s—700 years later. Baghdad only reached the same population it had had in 1258 during the rule of Saddam Hussein.

Islamic civilization never recovered from the Mongol onslaught, and fell into 600 years of relentless decline. Behind the Mongols came more afflictions. Christian crusaders seeking plunder and religious glory, more waves of Turkic-steppe nomads under the merciless Timur the Lame, their cousins the Seljuk Turks, and then the last great wave of invaders from Central Asia, the Ottoman Turks, who would soon go on to subjugate the Mideast. The Ottomans were mighty conquerors, but consistently inept when it came to the proper administration and financial management of their sprawling, multiethnic empire, and near hopeless at fostering industry and commerce. Under Ottoman rule, the Mideast degenerated into an intellectual, economic, and political backwater.

The stunning cultural, artistic, and technological achievements of Islamic civilization were lost, replaced by obscurantism and rank superstition. Much of the Muslim world fragmented, becoming misruled by petty warlords and tyrants, and suffering endemic poverty and social disorder, all overseen by pitiless Ottoman tax collectors who cared for naught but how many coppers they could squeeze out of the sultan's unhappy subjects.

It was upon the moribund body of Islamic civilization that fell the second great scourge to afflict the Muslim peoples: the era of European colonial adventures that began soon after the most advanced and resplendent remaining Muslim state, al-Andalus (today, southern Spain), was conquered by the Catholic forces of Ferdinand and Isabella.

The fall of Granada in AD 1492 marked the beginning of the explosion of European discovery and ensuing conquests that changed the world's history for the next 450 years. Europe's rapacious powers used their maritime technology and military superiority to seize much of the known world's wealth and subjugate many of its peoples.

After a ferocious struggle with bitter colonial rivals France, Spain, Holland, and Portugal, Great Britain emerged by the late 1700s as the world's dominant imperial power. Britain went on to defeat its European colonial rivals in a series of sharp wars that spanned two centuries. By 1900, the British Empire controlled a quarter of the earth's land, and all its seas. The oft-termed "jewel in its crown" was the British Indian Empire, better known by its Hindi name, the British Raj.

British colonial expansion followed a set pattern: provoke an incident with an intended victim nation or tribe, attack them with disciplined western troops armed with quick-firing guns and artillery, smash the enemy's forces, install a compliant ruler, set local tribes at one another's throats, rule through favored minorities while plundering treasures and natural resources, and use the captive markets of these new colonies as dumping grounds for cheap manufactured goods.

Great Britain justified this highly successful system of organized piracy by claiming it was all being done in a noble effort of self-sacrifice to bring the benefits of Christianity and the light of civilization to benighted Asians and Africans. The darker sides of British colonialism, such as the forced addiction of millions of Chinese to British-grown opium, the mass slaughter of independence-seekers in India, and, of course, slavery and indentured servitude, were not discussed in polite company.

A century and a half later, the successor to the British Empire would justify its occupation of Iraq and Afghanistan as part of another selfless campaign to bring the blessings of "democracy" to benighted Muslim peoples.

Let us return to 1945 and take a brief *tour d'horizon* of the Muslim world.

Morocco was ruled by a monarchy "guided" by Paris and garrisoned by French troops.

Algeria was an integral part of the French state, or the "metropole," as France called it. Two million French and other Europeans had settled in Algeria since France invaded it in 1830 after its local ruler, the Dey, committed an alleged act of war by striking the French ambassador with a horsehair fly whisk.

Tunisia was run by a French-appointed pasha, who was replaced in 1957 by Francophile dictator Habib Bourguiba. Tunisia has had only one other ruler since 1945, the US–backed general Zine ben Ali, who seized power in 1987. Responding to President Bush's calls for democracy in the Mideast, the general reduced his tally in the latest rigged election to only 94.5 percent from the customary 99 percent and arrested even more political opponents.

Libya was ruled by decrepit old King Ibn Idris, who spent most of his time in European spas and casinos, and left the running of his country to British political advisers.

Egypt, home of a third of all Arabs, was nominally independent but under British tutelage, a colony in all but name. British troops garrisoned the Suez Canal, the jugular of Britain's imperial lifeline, and ensured that Egypt's government followed orders from Whitehall. Egyptians were not allowed in Cairo's exclusive Gezira Sporting Club.

Egypt's figurehead ruler, King Farouk, was directly descended from the famed Albanian soldier of fortune Mehmet Ali, who, four years after Napoleon abandoned his army and returned to France, conquered Egypt in 1805 with only 600 Albanian soldiers of fortune.

Farouk, an obese, unfortunate creature who boasted the world's largest collection of elephant pornography, had not always been a subject of derision. Before the war, he was handsome and dashing, and the great hope of Egyptian nationalists. But in 1941, Farouk refused to declare war on Germany, insisting his nation was sovereign and neutral. The British ambassador had Farouk's palace surrounded by tanks and artillery and gave the king an hour to declare war, or face death. This experience broke Farouk. When I met him in 1958, he had become a drug-taking debauché and fawning servant of the British.

Sudan, Africa's largest nation, had long been administered as an "Anglo-Egyptian condominium," meaning that British officials in Cairo and their local flunkies administered the vastness of Sudan under orders from London. During the nineteenth century, Britain's imperialists had grabbed huge swathes of African territory to the east and west of the Nile, in part to prevent their French rivals from getting their hands on the great river's headwaters.

British imperial nation-makers drew a border around this huge conglomeration of disparate tribes, peoples, languages and religions that stretched from the steamy jungles of central Africa to the Saharan wastes of Darfur, creating a geopolitical monstrosity that was inevitably predestined to endless secessionist movements, tribal and religious strife, and enormous headaches for all concerned. They repeated this error once again by creating the West Africa state of Nigeria, Africa's most populous nation.

With the exception of British Nigeria, Ghana, and a few colonial flyspecks on Africa's West Coast, British East Africa, and the Cape Colony, the balance of Africa's Muslims lived under French colonial rule in the vast state of French West Africa. Their kings and rulers spoke French at home, lived on the Côte d'Azur, and looked to Paris for financial support, military protection, and guidance. So deep were the Franco-African links that many leaders of the region considered themselves Frenchmen first, and Africans second. Like the Francophile rulers and elite of North Africa, they were widely known as "brown Frenchmen."

During the funeral of President Charles de Gaulle, the distraught, weeping "Emperor" Bokassa I, of the grandly styled Central African Empire, threw himself on the French leader's grave, piteously wailing, "Papa! Papa! Papa." This pathetic scene said more about France's pervasive influence over West Africa and its peoples than a library full of scholarly studies.

In the Mideast, formerly known as the Near East (in the nineteenth and early twentieth century the Balkans were called the Near East), Imperial Britain created after World War I the little desert state of Transjordan (today Jordan) for its Arab ally, Emir Abdullah of the Beni Hashim tribe, as a reward for fighting the Ottoman Empire. Abdullah had expected the more important crown of Iraq or Saudi Arabia, but he was left only with a consolation kingdom of sand and rock.

Transjordan settled down into a picturesque little country ruled by Britain through the puppet king's Bedouin army, commanded by one of the most colorful figures of that era, the dashing British general Sir John Bagot Glubb, better known as Glubb Pasha.

In a wonderful comment that seems to conjure up all the glories of Britain's imperial days, after he retired, Glubb was asked which of his multitude of decorations meant the most to him. He immediately replied, "My medal 'Defender of the Shepherds of Iraq.'"

Glubb had been protecting Iraqi herders from raids by the Ikhwan, Saudi religious extremists who regarded other Muslims as infidels. Interestingly, these same followers of the Wahabi Ikhwan movement would resurface seventy years later in our own time to bedevil the Mideast, South Asia, and the United States.

Syria and the future Lebanon were apportioned to France as spoils of World War I under the infamous and stunningly cynical Sykes-Picot Agreement, a conspiracy no less tawdry or criminal than the 1939 Nazi-Soviet Pact.

While France was laying the groundwork for future mayhem in Lebanon, Britain was doing the same thing in a new state it created in Mesopotamia. The Royal Navy's switch from bulky, inefficient coal to the superior propulsive fuel oil demanded that Britain secure the Fertile Crescent's recently discovered sources of petroleum.

Awkwardly, oil was located in the south of Mesopotamia, near the Shia port city of Basra, and far to the north, in the Kurdish highlands, around Mosul and Kirkuk. To tie these distant regions together, Great Britain created the Frankenstein state of Iraq.

The nexus between Iraq's oil-rich extremities was an impoverished intermediate region without oil populated by Sunni tribes. In the middle of this artificial state was its new capital, Baghdad, then, in the 1920s, a small, scruffy little city of around 25,000 among whose largest ethnic groups were Jews and Armenians.

Another important British ally in the revolt against the Turks, the Hashemite emir, Faisal, was due to have been rewarded by Britain with the throne of Syria. But in the postwar rape of the Ottoman Empire, Syria went to the French. They wanted no part of Britain's would-be puppet king or his dashing mentor, Lawrence of Arabia. As a consolation prize, Faisal was subsequently given the throne of newly created Iraq.

RAF bombers and fighters were based at Iraq's giant Habbaniyah air base, the bastion of British imperial control over Iraq. Villages of tribal malefactors who disturbed the Pax Britannica were routinely bombed into quiescence by the RAF.

France detached the most economically productive part of Syria, Mount Lebanon and its wealthy Mediterranean ports of Beirut, Tyre, Sidon, and Tripoli, and created a new protectorate, Lebanon. Great Britain did the same thing in Mesopotamia by detaching a chunk of barren territory on the Gulf next to Basra that contained both oil and a good deepwater port, calling it Kuwait. London put a penurious local chieftain, whose principal income came from fishing, onto its new throne. Thus was born the al-Sabah dynasty, today one of the world's wealthiest families that is lucky enough to own their very own oil-rich country, thanks to the grace of Allah and the British Colonial Office.

In a similar manner, Imperial Britain's warships sailed into anchorages along the length of the Gulf and, after solemn ceremonies and the promise of more gold than the dirt-poor pearl fishers and camel herders who lived along these bleak, wretched coasts had ever dreamed of, signed treaties making the Gulf emirates tributaries of Her Majesty.

Thus came into existence what were known until recent times the

Trucial States. When oil was discovered along the Gulf coast, these local emirs waxed immensely rich under Britain's favor, ceding to London management of their foreign, military, and economic affairs. Their millions were deposited directly into British banks, their children went to British public schools, then Sandhurst Military Academy, and their palaces were guarded by mercenary troops provided by Great Britain.

In 1871, Oman, once a major regional trading power with possessions in Zanzibar, East Africa, and Pakistan, became another British protectorate. In the next century, Oman would become a virtual colony of Britain's foreign intelligence service, MI6, and Her Majesty's renowned assassins, the Special Air Service. This was the first time a western intelligence service had its very own country.

North Yemen was wild, mountainous, offering nothing but rock and hostile tribesmen addicted to the narcotic shrub qat. As a result, it was left alone by the imperial powers.

By contrast, South Yemen, with its great port of Aden, became a major British naval, land, and air base and principal link in the "Imperial Lifeline" that extended from Liverpool through the Suez Canal and on to India and Singapore.

Europe's fifteen to eighteen million Muslims were all but forgotten. Muslim minorities in Yugoslavia, Greece, and Bulgaria, the human detritus of the shattered Ottoman Empire, subsisted in fear of their Orthodox Christian neighbors, who blamed them for past depredations of the Turks. Tiny Albania, about 75 percent Muslim, was independent, but later suffered horribly under a Stalinist dictator, Enver Hoxha, who turned his nation into a giant prison camp and crushed all religions, reserving particular hatred for Islam.

Turkey was an independent state in 1945. But it is difficult to characterize it as a Muslim state, even though most of its citizens were ardent followers of Islam. Turkey's dictator, Mustafa Kemal, a brilliant general and iron-fisted dictator much influenced by both contemporary European fascism and Bolshevism, declared war on Islam in much the same manner as did the Soviets in the USSR. Both saw Islam as a threat to their power and a scourge that kept their nations backwards and ridden by superstition.

Ataturk, as he came to be known, sought to tear out Turkey's eastern, Islamic roots and transform the nation and its people into modern Europeans. Islam was severely constrained; mosques and the religious establishment were put under state control, just as were churches and mosques in the USSR. What clergy remained in both nations became agents of the secret police.

The Arabic alphabet, the fez, women's headscarves, all other Islamic symbols—even traditional Muslim expressions—were banned under pain of prison. Ataturk compelled Turkey to become a secular state that, at the time of his death in 1938, was neither European nor Islamic but a confused hybrid of the two. Turkey's minority of secularists and majority of Islamists continue to argue about their nation's basic nature to this day.

Iran's Shia Muslims had managed to escape both European colonialism and frequent attempts by Imperial Russia to conquer their northern provinces. Most of Iran's energies had gone into battling its bitter historic rival, the Ottoman Empire. Remoteness and poverty helped spare Iran foreign occupation until the strategic importance of oil was understood in the early twentieth century.

Of all Muslim nations, Afghanistan was, in 1945, probably the most free of western political influence and economic domination. There was nothing of value in Afghanistan. It became a buffer state between the southern Soviet Union and western-dominated Pakistan and Iran. The strategic value of the land corridor it provided between the future oil-rich hinterland of Central Asia and the ports of the Arabian Sea remained in the future.

About 15 percent of British India's huge population were Muslims, concentrated most heavily in the western regions of Punjab, Sind, and Kashmir, or in the eastern region of Bengal. All lived under the rule of the Imperial British Raj. Queen Victoria—and her successor monarchs—had more Muslim subjects than British ones and could rightfully claim to be the most important "Muslim" monarch on earth.

The world's single-largest number of Muslims was found in the 1,200-mile long chain of islands that formed the oil-rich Netherlands East Indies, today called Indonesia. In 1945, Muslims of Java and Sumatra revolted against three centuries of harsh, rapacious Dutch colonial rule and fought for independence. Britain, and later Holland, rushed in troops to put down the uprising.

Holland, which made much of its suffering under German wartime occupation, furiously resisted Indonesia's freedom struggle, killing large numbers of Indonesians, bombing Indonesian cities, and conducting massacres in a series of brutal counterinsurgency campaigns. After four years of fighting, the United States forced Holland to grant Indonesia full independence by threatening to suspend Marshall Plan aid to the Hague. Indonesians have never forgotten America's role in their liberation and independence.

Malaysia, a largely Muslim nation, had long been a rich British colony. The Muslims of the southern Philippines were ruled by the United States through its Christian Filipino colonial government in Manila.

The Muslim Turkic tribes of Central Asia that dwelt from the Caspian Sea to the Great Wall of China, modern descendants of the Mongols who had terrorized Europe and the Mideast, had fallen under the rule of Russia or China.

At the same time America was expanding west into its vast continent, Imperial Russia was sending its explorers, Cossacks, and settlers into the uncharted wilds of Siberia, and to the Pacific Coast, thousands of kilometers distant from Moscow and Saint Petersburg. Russian armies were dispatched to conquer the independent Muslim khanates or emirates spread across the vastness of Western Turkistan.

In a long, fiercely resisted colonial campaign, the czar's armies relentlessly occupied what is today Kazakhstan, Uzbekistan, Turkmenistan, Kyrgyzstan, and Tajikistan. These artificial states were all creations of Moscow's divide-and-rule strategy. Russia's advance was only halted when it encountered Britain's Indian Raj. Afghanistan was agreed upon as a buffer state between the realms of the Queen Empress and Czar of All the Russias. Thereafter, the British and Russian Empires would wage "the Great Game," a long, romantic struggle for influence in the most exotic reaches of Central Asia, Tibet, and Persia, a contest that continues to our day, only with different players.

Imperial Russian armies began invading the Caucasus during the reign of Peter the Great. For the next 300 years they would fight with utmost ferocity and cruelty to impose imperial rule on the fiercely independent Muslim peoples of the region, notably the Chechens, Ingush, Cherkass, Dagestanis, and Abkhaz.

Another Asian Muslim people, the little-known Uighurs of Eastern Turkistan—today known as China's province of Xinjiang (or Sinkiang)—had battled China for centuries. In 1944, Sinkiang's Muslims established an independent republic but it was crushed five years later after an invasion by the Chinese People's Liberation Army.

China's occupation of independent Tibet a year later provoked a worldwide outcry that continues to this day. By contrast, China's occupation of the Muslim Republic of East Turkistan went virtually unnoticed and, of course, unchallenged. China's other non-Uighur Muslims in the regions of Gansu and Shaanxi, known as Hui, remained under Beijing's control.

The greatest war in world history had liberated Western Europe from German occupation, but threw Eastern Europe into the hands of Stalin's Soviet Union. In late 1945, large parts of the rest of the globe still remained under British, French, American, Portuguese, Dutch, Russian, or Chinese colonial rule. Freedom, liberty, and democracy, it seemed, were to be reserved only for western peoples.

CHAPTER THREE
★ ★ ★

THE GREAT MUSLIM REVOLTS

There is a commonly held perception in the West, and particularly in North America, that the spasms of violence emanating from the Muslim world are new phenomena. This belief is mistaken, though hardly surprising, given the steady decline of the teaching of history and geography in North America.

To understand and put into proper context the passions and violence coursing through the Muslim world today, we must understand the series of anticolonial uprisings—or jihads—that exploded in the Muslim world during the nineteenth and twentieth centuries, and their lingering influence upon current Muslim political and religious thinking.

The historical record of these uprisings, usually described as "native revolts," comes down to us through the eyes of the very colonial powers involved in repressing them, thus leaving us with highly colored, distorted, and invariably self-serving pictures that are further tainted by prejudice, colonial arrogance, war propaganda, and misunderstanding.

These revolts were not simple uprisings by run-amok natives, or explosions of religious fanaticism, but regional or national rebellions against foreign rule. They represent the first major anticolonial struggles in Asia and Africa, and are crucial to ensuing historical events on these continents.

Each one of the following conflicts continues to resonate in our day, however unaware of them we in the western world may be, and to shape the Muslim world's hostile attitudes and often violent reactions to the West.

They merit a brief examination because these seemingly long-distant, faraway events and conflicts serve as the intellectual and emotional underpinning and inspiration of many of today's jihadist movements. It is impossible to adequately understand what is going on in North Africa, Sudan, Somalia, Kashmir, and the Caucasus without a look back into their recent past. History is the essential frame for our understanding of current events.

THE GREAT MUTINY

By 1857, the British East India Company, based in Calcutta, had managed to conquer, annex, or otherwise bring under its control large parts of India.

At that time, India was a dizzying collection of hundreds of principalities, some small, others large and powerful, all ruled by feudal monarchs who had no concept of a greater India and were entirely focused on their own selfish affairs and the aggrandizement of their little kingdoms at the expense of their hostile neighbors. In short, a perfect geopolitical condition for a powerful, ruthless, and clever interloper to expand its influence.

At that time, India was effectively ruled by only 40,000 British colonial troops of the East India Company, a rapacious private merchant enterprise, backed up by 200,000 "sepoys," as native mercenary troops were called. Britain's bitter colonial rivals, France and the Netherlands, also used chartered trading companies, the eighteenth century's equivalents of today's powerful multinational corporations, and native levies to advance their political and economic interests.

The British were able to dominate the vast continent through skillful diplomacy, playing off petty rulers, bribery, intimidation, and that always useful colonial device dividing and turning groups and religions against one another. When necessary, the East India Company launched small but very brutal wars against recalcitrant rulers who refused to accept British hegemony.

Widespread unrest and hostility to British rule had been simmering among many Indians. Attempts by the British to convert Indians to Christianity provoked outrage. So did Britain's massive looting of gold, silver, jewelry, art, and natural resources from India, which were sent to Britain where they helped finance the Industrial Revolution and found some of Britain's greatest family fortunes. Other great British fortunes came from the opium trade.

Many of India's industries were forcibly shut down to make way for shoddy British imports made in Midlands factories financed by loot stolen from India. Indian farmers were compelled to grow specialized crops for exports to the Britain Empire. This was a dark side of colonialism its advocates rarely saw.

In 1857, introduction of a new rifle cartridge into sepoy units sparked the most dangerous colonial rebellion ever faced by Imperial Britain. Muslim sepoys feared that the paper cartridges, which had to be torn upon by their teeth, were greased with pig fat. Hindu sepoys were warned that fat from sacred cows had been used. Units mutinied, killed their officers, and proclaimed themselves part of a liberation army. Major cities, including the capital, Delhi, fell to the insurgents.

Indians call this uprising their first War of Independence. Britain's government and press, however, called the uprising "the Great Indian Mutiny," which was as much a misdescription of real events as President Bush's "war on terror" in 2001. Britain's jingoistic press went wild with stories of gruesome atrocities committed on British colonials in such notorious massacres as the Black Hole of Calcutta, Cawnpore, and Delhi's Red Fort.

India's sepoy insurgents were treated by Victorian Britain's press with the kind of fevered animosity and overheated language that often sounds like the western media's portrayal of today's Muslim radicals. In contemporary parlance, they would be branded terrorists. Victorian clergymen thundered that the Indian Hindu and Muslim insurgents were "Godless, evil followers of satanic gods." America's religious demagogues, like Jerry Falwell and Pat Robertson, echoed similar anathema against Muslims a century and a half later.

The Great Uprising brought calls from India's Muslims for jihad against the British, and restoration of the Muslim-dominated Mogul Empire, which the British invaders had previously overthrown. This was the first instance that calls for jihad had been widely heard in a modern context—but certainly not the last.

The Sepoy Mutiny was finally put down by reinforced British units and loyal native troops, notably Gurkhas and Sikhs, who would serve the British Crown until our own time. Repression and punishment by Britain was merciless, and soon became known as the Devil's Wind.

Captured "mutineers" were routinely strapped to the muzzles of cannon and blown to bits—a particularly nasty punishment for Hindus and

Muslims who hold in great sanctity proper disposition of deceased bodies through burning or immediate burial. Civilians in rebel cities stormed by the British were put to the sword or bayonet; women were raped; homes were looted and pillaged. In effect, the British behaved with much the same cruelty and ferocity as the Muslims and Hindus to whom they were ostensibly bringing the light of western civilization.

The 1857 uprising put an end to the East India Company. India fell under direct rule of the British Crown, henceforth known as the Raj. British soldiers, with loyal sepoys, kept the Queen Empress's peace; British administrators managed the daily affairs of India; British magistrates efficiently dispensed Anglo-Saxon justice and suppressed the curse of the ritual killers, of the Thugee cult; British bankers supervised the Raj's finances; and British merchants monopolized India's growing trade.

But the British Raj could not crush the growing desire of Indians for independence and unification of their patchwork nation. Nor could the Raj ever again suppress the belief among many Muslim Indians, who comprised about 15 percent of the population, that Great Britain, no matter how majestic, admirable and worthy in many ways of emulation, was also a foe of the Muslim faith.

The Great Mutiny had another important residual effect. It infused subsequent British literature, popular culture, and public belief with the lasting prejudice that brown-skinned men, and particularly Muslims of India's northwest frontier, were cruel, deceitful, fanatical people who were inherently violent and dangerous. Britain's Christian establishment began preaching crusades to "liberate" Asians and black Africans from the evils of "wicked, lascivious" Islam. These Islamophobic prejudices originating from the Indian uprising were passed on through British literature and popular culture to Americans, Canadians, Australians, and New Zealanders in the early years of the twentieth century.

During the nineteenth and twentieth centuries, Britain, as part of its policy of divide and rule, sought to drive wedges between India's Hindus and Muslims and exploit their profound religious differences. The separation of India in 1947 into Hindu and Muslim states produced a geopolitical earthquake that left one million dead and has kept nuclear-armed Pakistan and India with scimitars drawn ever since.

THE MAHDI ATTACKS

The next major Islamic insurrection against western colonialism took place far up the Nile in the heart of the vast, poorly demarcated region then known as the Anglo-Egyptian Sudan. It warrants close attention because in it we see all the seeds and many of the themes of our own era's war on terror.

In 1881, a prominent, highly respected religious teacher and Sufi mystic, Mohammed Ahmad, proclaimed himself the "Mahdi." According to some Islamic tradition, a Mahdi, or savior, will come to rescue Muslims from oppression and reinvigorate their faith.

Mohammed Ahmad attracted a sizable following. He declared jihad against the Anglo-Ottoman-Egyptian rulers of Sudan, and proclaimed a struggle of national liberation to free his country.

The Mahdi's declaration of jihad proved a watershed in modern Islamic history, marking the opening of a century-and-a-half struggle between Islamic peoples and western colonial powers.

His exhortations to Muslims to live very modestly, eschew nonessential material comforts, and share their incomes with needy coreligionists— just as the Prophet's original followers, known as "ansar," had done—proved enormously popular among all but the very wealthy.

More important, Mohammed Ahmad's clarion call for a return to early Islamic modesty, austerity, and altruism would reverberate through every subsequent Islamic revival movement right down to the twenty-first century when Osama bin Laden and his followers would claim they were emulating the simple lifestyle of the Prophet of Islam and his ansars.

At first, the Mahdi was dismissed as an obscure religious fanatic and either derided or ignored by the British. But he soon assembled an army of 30,000 ansars dressed in patched robes as a sign of their poverty. Britain's press and imperialists, in an effort to demean and trivialize the Mahdi, called his followers "Dervishes," after Turkey's famed whirling dervishes of Konya.

To Britain's collective horror, the Mahdi and his Dervishes, armed only with spears and swords, made quick work of two British-commanded Egyptian expeditions sent to crush them. The Mahdi proclaimed Sudan "liberated" and an "Islamic caliphate," just as Afghanistan's Taliban leader, Mullah Omar, did in 2002. The Mahdi announced his ambition to occupy other "godless" Muslim nations, notably Egypt and the Ottoman Empire, and proclaim himself caliph, or supreme religious and temporal ruler, of Islam.

Mohammed Ahmad's revolt was aimed as much at restoring the vigor and purity of original seventh-century Islam as it was at occupying territory and driving out European colonialists. He was the second great revolutionary reformer of Islam to appear in the modern era.

The previous century, another would-be reformer, Muhammed ibn Abdel al-Wahab, launched a powerful religious and social movement in Arabia dedicated to purging contemporary Islam of encrustations of superstition, idolatry, heresies, worship of saints, and many forms of deviation from the austere faith of the Prophet.

Wahab warned that Islam had grown weak, corrupt, and polluted under the rule of the dissolute Ottomans. The faith needed to be purged, and then returned to its original simplicity and vigor. The word of Allah, as expressed in the Holy Koran, was, according to Wahab, absolute and unquestionable. No deviations and no modernizing interpretations could be accepted. Allah's truth was revealed and immutable. Those Muslims who did not follow this strict path, known as "Salafist," were "takfir," or apostates.

The Wahabist creed, or more properly, Salafism, quickly spread among Arabia's tribes. When Abdul Aziz Ibn Saud conquered Riyadh in 1924 and established the modern state of Saudi Arabia, Salafism became the official creed that conferred temporal and spiritual legitimacy on the Saudi ruling dynasty. Dedicated followers of the Salafist creed became known as the "Ikhwan," or Brotherhood.

As we saw in the story of the dashing Glubb Pasha, the Ikhwan regarded many neighboring Muslims as heretics, but held special hatred for Shia Muslims, who were deemed dangerous apostates and idolaters polluted by Babylonian superstition and Zoroastrian fire cults.

Wahab's dour, puritan reformist movement failed to extend beyond the confines of Arabia until the end of the twentieth century when it spread to Afghanistan and North Africa, and shaped the thinking of Osama bin Laden.

However, other reformist movements were also emerging across the Muslim world—India, North Africa, the Balkans, Syria, Persia, and even in the moribund Ottoman Empire. They followed different paths, but all generally agreed that Islam had been gravely corrupted and debased under Ottoman and European colonial rule, and urgently required drastic purification. At the time, a revived Islam, not secular western-style government, was almost universally seen as the only force capable of freeing Muslims from colonialism, and from the stultifying torpor and backwardness into which Islamic societies had fallen.

It is uncertain whether the Mahdi was influenced by the Wahabi-Salafist creed. He may have simply developed a parallel philosophy on his own. Whatever the case, he too was determined to purify Islam, unite its disparate peoples, and re-create the idyllic early Islamic Caliphate of the seventh century, which is the closest Muslims had ever come to democratic government guided by traditional tribal values and Koranic law. During this near-mythic time, major decisions were arrived at by tribal conclaves through a process of consensus. Justice was harsh but swift. The young, weak, and elderly were protected and fed by the common purse. Great store was accorded to the wisdom of elders, and to learning. Social and economic equality were deemed high virtues. It is to this period of "Islamic democracy" that modern-day reformers and Salafist radicals like Osama bin Laden refer when they advocate a return to their political and moral roots.

In 1885, the Mahdi's Dervish army besieged and stormed Sudan's capital, Khartoum. The city was defended by a famed British imperial general, Sir Charles Gordon. He was better known as Chinese Gordon, having earned dubious glory by killing large numbers of Chinese during the 1850–71 Taiping Rebellion and enforcing Britain's campaign to promote opium addiction among the Chinese.

In spite of his brutality in China, Gordon had become something of a Christian hero for combating slavery, trying to convert Muslims to his faith, and fighting with a bible in his hand. The siege of Khartoum turned Gordon into one of Victorian Britain's virtual saints, an iconic figure and martyr who embodied all the imagined virtues of colonialism.

The Dervish army took Khartoum by storm after feeble British efforts to relieve it failed. Khartoum's fall produced in Britain much the same anguish, outage, and fury that the 9/11 attacks on the United States provoked. Gordon's death by a Dervish spear profoundly shocked and outraged British public opinion as no other event since the Sepoy Mutiny in 1857.

Remote Sudan, a vague geographical expression few Britons could find on a map, and even fewer had ever visited, became a national cause célèbre. A century and a quarter later, the alleged need to invade and liberate Iraq from a tyrant, who not long before had been a useful American ally, sparked another colonial expedition disguised as a humanitarian rescue mission. Few American could locate Iraq on the world map and fewer had been there.

Britain's press and publishers vied ferociously to produce new Jeremiads against the "evil Mahdi." His scowling, swarthy visage and white turban filled the pages of British newspapers. Unruly Victorian children were sent to bed atremble from dire parental threats that the Mahdi would come to get them if they didn't behave.

A steady steam of breathless books appeared about Britain's nemesis and became best sellers. Some good Britons even feared that the wicked Mahdi and his vast army of sword-wielding Dervishes and "Nilotic Fuzzy-Wuzzies" tribesmen might even reach the peaceful, green shores of Britain, there to lay waste, pillage, and ravish Christian maidens.

The Mahdi, in short, became Britain's public enemy number one. He was often referred to as "the Mad Mahdi," the supposition being that only a man driven to lunacy by the malevolent intoxication of Islam would deny the manifest benefits of British rule and Christian redemption. As the turbaned incarnation of alleged Islamic evil, the Mahdi was the Osama bin Laden of his day.

To Victorians, the devil figure of the Mahdi was allowed no human attributes, no rational thoughts, no purpose other than killing Britons. He was simply a madman, a medieval monster who had to be hunted down like a rabid dog. The malevolent, menacing figure of the Mahdi also blended perfectly into lingering folk fears from the Crusades of evil Islam that still colored British thinking about the East. It was inconceivable that the wicked Mahdi and his followers could have any possible legitimate claims. Extermination was the only way to deal with such mad dogs.

In 2001, precisely the same claims would be made by the Bush administration and Britain's Tony Blair against the Mahdi's modern reincarnation, the turbaned and bearded Osama bin Laden, and his terrifying but almost invisible al-Qaida.

Echoing Victorian Britain's crusade against Islam, in 2002 the US government's published National Security Strategy asserted, "Our responsibility to history is already clear: to answer these attacks and rid the world of evil."

Soon after liberating Sudan from Anglo-Ottoman-Egyptian rule, the Mahdi died in 1885. But his successor, known as the khalifa, or caliph, kept up the offensive against the British.

After an earlier false start, Britain finally sent a powerful army up the Nile in 1898 under Sir Herbert—later Lord—Kitchener, armed with quantities of quick-fire artillery and the new Maxim machine gun, which was to become one of the next century's premier killing machines.

At Omdurman, just outside Khartoum, 50,000 Dervish horsemen and bushy-haired Fuzzy-Wuzzies armed with spears, swords, and a few flint-lock rifles charged the British lines. A young subaltern, Winston Churchill, fought in the battle.

The quick-fire artillery and Maxim machine guns did their execution before the Dervishes could close to use their swords and spears. Omdurman was the first major employment of the revolutionary machine gun designed by American inventor Hiram Maxim, a pioneer of industrialized killing.

Over 11,000 Dervish warriors were mowed down at Omdurman, as wave after wave of horsemen and infantry kept trying to reach the British line. It was a grand massacre: only forty-eight British troops were killed. The Dervishes were crushed, Sudan annexed as a British colony, and the first great completely Muslim revolt against European imperial rule crushed.

Omdurman was a grim harbinger of future massacres of Iraq's forces and the paltry US losses in the 1991 Kuwait oil war, the 2003 US invasion of Iraq, and the Taliban's speedy defeat in 2001. Once again, hopelessly outmatched, poorly led Muslim Third World armies that were little more than mobs armed with obsolete weapons, were mowed down by western military power just as surely and ruthlessly as were primitive Dervish warriors at Omdurman.

Like Kitchener's epic victory on the Nile, the slaughter of Saddam Hussein's forces in 1991 and 2003, whose strength was vastly overblown to make the US victory appear all the greater, delivered a thunderous message to other Muslim miscreants thinking of challenging the might of the new Raj.

The British poet Hilaire Belloc perfectly summed up in a bit of verse what Britons called "the Dervish Insurrection" and, in fact, the succeeding course of western colonial history right up to the present:

Whatever happens we have got
The Maxim gun, and they have not.

NORTH AFRICA

The next major revolts against western colonialism erupted in North Africa, the vast immensity of sand, barren earth, rock, and mountains that sweeps west from Egypt across the Sahara Desert to the Atlantic Ocean. This region is barely known by non-French westerners, yet it has produced in our day some of the most violent, extreme, and dangerous Islamic militant groups.

Spain established colonies and outposts on Morocco's Mediterranean coast as early as the sixteenth century. In the late nineteenth century, Spain began pushing deeper into Morocco in hopes of colonizing that potentially mineral-rich nation. In response, the fierce Berber tribes of Morocco's Rif Mountains took up arms to resist Spanish colonization.

A Berber notable, Muhammed Abdel Krim, assumed leadership of the Berber mountain tribes. He quickly revealed himself to be a brilliant, charismatic military and political leader. In 1919, he declared jihad against the invading Spaniards. Abdel Krim convinced the fierce Rif tribes to unite to fight the European invaders rather than one another, and launched a series of mobile offensives against Spanish forces.

For the next five years, Abdel Krim's holy warriors, or mujahidin, defeated Spain's modern, 100,000-man colonial army in numerous battles, drove Spanish forces back to their coastal enclaves, and nearly pushed them into the sea. Abdel Krim gained renown across North Africa as "the Lion of the Rif."

In 1921, Krim proclaimed the independent Rif Republic. This by now forgotten state became the first independent Islamic republic of the twentieth century. Turkey would proclaim itself a nonsecular republic two years later. The Muslim emirates of post-czarist Central Asia also declared themselves independent states during the early 1920s, but they were quickly snuffed out by Bolshevik forces.

Krim in many ways personified, and sought to emulate, early Muslim leaders by making all major decisions through councils of notables known as "shuras," allowing free speech and open dissent, promoting austere personal habits, piety, and moderation. His skill and bravery were such that the Spaniards came to regard him as a modern version of their own national hero, El Cid.

In desperation, Spain called on its erstwhile colonial rival, France, for succor. This action deeply galled proud Spaniards who knew the imperious French looked down on them as backwards and only quasi-European, but they were desperate.

France dispatched 160,000 troops under General Philippe Petain, the future hero of Verdun and villain of Vichy, to join 100,000 Spanish troops in a joint offensive against the Rif forces. Outnumbered five to one and unable to withstand European aircraft, artillery, armored cars, and machine guns, Abdel Krim's Rif warriors were finally defeated in 1926 after fierce resistance and heavy losses. A young Spanish colonial officer, Francisco Franco, also went on from the Rif war to gain future notoriety a decade later.

Abdel Krim was sent with his family into exile to the remote French Pacific island Réunion. In 1947, legend has it that Abdel Krim managed to escape, hidden inside a coffin supposedly bearing his recently deceased mother. The old lion managed to get to Egypt, but he refused invitations from the puppet king of French-ruled Morocco to return to his homeland so long as French troops remained there. Abdel Krim died soon after in exile.

Not long after Krim's death, large crowds assembled in the Algerian cities of Algiers and Oran, demanding freedom from French rule and carrying banners emblazoned with Koranic inscriptions and the name Abdel Krim. In Morocco, demonstrations demanding independence from France carried similar banners, shaking the French puppet monarchy to its foundations.

The jihad in the Rif was crushed by western military technology, but its spirit has lived on and become part of North African folklore. Both the Moroccan Salafists and Algeria's Armed Islamic Groups, two of the most dangerous underground extremist groups, frequently invoke the memory of the Lion of the Rif in their bloody struggle to free North Africa from foreign influence. Abdel Krim is held as their role model for the leader of modern Islamic government.

THE GRAND SENOUSSI

During the nineteenth century, French troops began probing the raw mountains, barren hinterlands, and Saharan wastes that lay behind France's colonies on the fertile Moroccan and Algerian littoral.

In the early part of that century, Mohammed ibn Ali as-Senoussi, a noted Islamic scholar who had spent much of his life traveling and studying in Muslim lands from North Africa to India, settled in Mecca and began to formulate a new Islamic philosophy designed to counteract what he saw as the ummah's—or Muslim world's—backwardness and ruinous tribalism.

In spite of becoming an acclaimed and respected figure in Arabia, Senoussi moved to an oasis in what is today Libya, near the Egyptian border, and devoted the rest of his life to preaching the concept of Islamic brotherhood, tribal cooperation, and a reawakening of traditional Islam.

Senoussi's message calling for the political, social, and moral revival of Islam captured the spirit of North Africa's hitherto feuding nomadic tribes, and spread with remarkable rapidity from the border of Egypt to Morocco, and deep into the Sahara and the mixed ethnic and racial sub-Saharan region known as the Sahel.

Though he quickly became the most powerful and revered figure in North Africa, Senoussi did not seek personal political power for himself or his descendants. As the writer Muhammed Asad put it, "What he wanted was to prepare an organizational basis for moral, social, and political revival of Islam. In accordance with this aim, he did nothing to upset the traditional tribal structure of the region, nor did he challenge the nominal suzerainty over Libya of the Turkish Sultan."

Asad was an adventurous Austrian Jewish journalist, né Leopold Weiss, who converted to Islam after covering Palestine in the 1920s and became a key adviser to the founder of modern Arabia, King ibn Saud. Muhammed Asad fought in the Libyan jihad against Italian fascist colonialism, and went on to become Pakistan's ambassador to the newly founded United Nations in 1947. This brilliant thinker and adventurer fused in one person many of the finest qualities of Jews and Muslims. He was able to look deeply into men's hearts and never lost his moral compass or intellectual rigor.

Asad was perhaps the most insightful observer of Islam's travails. His 1954 book, *The Road to Mecca*, is an important political treatise of modern Islamic thinking; in fact, one far more worthwhile than the oft-cited primitive anti-western fulminations of the Egyptian Said Qutub which neocons routinely cite as a sort of Islamic *Mein Kampf.*

Senoussi battled against the plague of tribalism and regionalism that had afflicted and weakened the Muslim world for centuries. Even the ferocious Tuareg nomads of the Sahara put themselves under his authority and heeded his call. Unlike Senoussi, who urged obedience to the temporal powers of his time, modern Muslim radicals and revolutionaries see the rulers of Muslim nations as an essential part of the sickness afflicting the Islamic world, and a primary reason for its backwardness and exploitation.

France's relentless advance ever deeper into Algeria and the Sahara compelled Sayyid Ahmed, the second Grand Senoussi, as he by now was known, to reluctantly forsake the moral regeneration of his followers and draw his sword against the invading foreigners.

Thus began a new great jihad pitting the Senoussi desert warriors against the power of the expanding French Empire, with all its modern weapons and native auxiliaries. This half-century-long struggle is almost unknown to westerners, and only dimly remembered even in France. The sole hint most westerners had of this fierce but obscure struggle comes from the book and film *Beau Geste* and other Hollywood potboilers in which isolated French colonial garrisons fought off waves of attacking Arab horsemen.

In 1911, as the Ottoman Empire was dying, Italy invaded the Turkish-ruled region of Cyrenacia (modern Libya), and set about colonizing the region. The Senoussi mujahidin were now waging a multi-front war against two European powers.

Somehow, the desert jihadis managed to battle the French and Italians to a draw. Then, the Grand Senoussi committed a fatal error. As a loyal Muslim, when the Ottoman caliph in Istanbul declared war on Britain in 1915, the Grand Senoussi obediently followed him, thus pitting his mujahidin against a third European enemy.

At first, Senoussi camel columns almost reached Cairo, but British reinforcements brought back from the Sinai campaign repulsed them. British aircraft and armored cars attacked the Senoussi's desert oases and, after more heavy fighting, finally crushed the reformist movement, putting an end to the second major effort to reform and revitalize Islam. The Maxim guns had again triumphed.

LIBYA: LION OF THE DESERT

During the 1920s and early 1930s, Italy was rapidly expanding its control over Libya, importing large numbers of peasant colonists from Calabria, and remaking dreary Tripoli and Benghazi into sprightly little copies of Genoa and Naples.

Mussolini and his black-shirted fascists transformed the pedestrian process of Libya's colonization into a glamorous, operatic crusade to re-create in Italian Libya the Roman Empire of Scipio Africanus and Caesar Augustus. "Noi siamo imperatori!" thundered the Duce.

A revered elderly Libyan, Omar Mukhtar, rallied national resistance to the Italians, igniting the third North African jihad against European colonialism. Mukhtar, who was soon dubbed Lion of the Desert, was a master of fluid guerrilla warfare. His attacks threw the Italians off balance and forced them for a time to retreat to the coast, where they struggled to hold on to Tripoli and Benghazi.

But, as before, the weight of European military technology gradually but relentlessly overcame the courage and skill of Omar Mukhtar's lightly armed Libyan mujahidin, who were particularly vulnerable in Libya's barren, treeless terrain to attack by Italian aircraft, armored cars, and poison gas.

Unable to subdue Mukhtar's fighters, Mussolini's modern legions embarked on a ruthless strategy to crush Libyan resistance. A fortified line of barbed wire and watchtowers was erected along Libya's eastern border to cut off the flow of fighters, arms, and supplies from supporters across the Muslim world that were being smuggled in from Egypt.

Interestingly, two decades later, the French would erect a similar, but far more elaborate and deadly, barrier along the Algerian-Tunisian border. Half a century later, India would erect an even more elaborate and lethal line to stop mujahidin crossing Kashmir's Line of Control.

Mussolini sent his military favorite, the strutting Field Marshall Pietro Badoglio, who had distinguished himself by massacring spear-wielding tribesmen in Somalia and Ethiopia, to destroy Libyan resistance. Badoglio, the very model of a modern fascist general, quickly brought more aircraft and armored cars to Libya, as well as savage "askaris," or native troops, from Somalia. He created concentration camps in the desert, and herded a quarter of Libya's sparse population, then about two million souls, into them. This occurred when Stalin's gulag was still in its early stages, and more than a decade before Hitler's concentration camps were opened.

Libyan civilians were machine-gunned and bombed from the air. Fifty thousand Libyan civilians died of disease or hunger in the concentration camps. The Italian Air Force made extensive use of mustard gas against Libyan mujahidin and the villages that dared aid them. Omar Mukhtar's warriors could only fire their ancient, bolt-action rifles in impotent fury at Mussolini's marauding air force.

The Lion of the Desert was wounded in an Italian attack in 1931 and pinned under his dead horse. He kept on firing until out of ammunition, and was then captured by the Italians, who jubilantly proclaimed they had finally captured Libya's leading "Islamic terrorist."

Omar Mukhtar was publicly hanged with great fanfare by the gloating Italian fascists. So ended Libya's courageous but hopeless resistance to Italy's modern military technology. In a bitterly ironic tragedy, Mohammed Akkad, an accomplished Arab filmmaker who had immortalized Omar Mukhtar in his fine film *The Lion of the Desert*, was killed in 2005, along with his daughter, by one of Abu Musab al-Zarqawi's Iraqi suicide bombers in the lobby of an Amman hotel.

Libya remained an Italian colony until 1941 when the British drove out Mussolini's legions and the Afrika Corps.

While there had been great consternation in Europe and North America over Italy's invasion of Christian Ethiopia, Italy's savagery and genocidal actions in Libya, wide-scale employment of mustard gas, and its torture and execution of civilians, were largely ignored.

The Libyan jihad was extinguished, but its memory lingered on among Muslims. For the first time, funds had been raised for the Libyan jihad across the Islamic world, and even from as far away as India.

Small numbers of Muslims from Asia and other parts of Africa had come to Libya, crossing the Italian "Wall of Death," to wage jihad to defend their oppressed brothers.

The Koranic command to give aid to all oppressed Muslims in distant places echoed during the North African jihads. No one in the West took any notice or cared that Muslims in India and Afghanistan or Saudi Arabia were sending arms, gold, and fighters to help Omar Mukhtar's mujahidin.

In 1951, Britain made an aged member of the Senoussi family, ibn Idris, king. In the same year, oil was discovered in Libya. A year previously, the US had established a Strategic Air Command base for nuclear-armed B-47 bombers at Libya's sprawling Wheelus Air Base which held 5,000 US military personnel and families. The Americans began unceremoniously elbowing the British out of Her Majesty's former colony.

During the 1967 Arab-Israeli War, Idris's inaction and unconcern enraged his people, who called for his ouster. Realizing that the old king had lost legitimacy, the Central Intelligence Agency (CIA) cast about for a malleable replacement.

With an uncanny knack for picking the single Libyan most likely to displease, disobey, and bedevil the West, America's intelligence experts selected an untutored Bedouin soldier, named Muammar Khadaffi, who, as a boy, had studied the campaigns of Omar Mukhtar and had vowed to seek revenge for his execution. The CIA eased Colonel Khadaffi into power in a 1969 coup, confident one of "its boys" would henceforth be running a compliant, oil-rich Libya.

Omar Mukhtar would have his revenge.

Other Muslim peoples resisted western colonial expansion, but none of these conflicts had the pan-Islamic character seen in the Sudanese and North African jihads. These largely forgotten wars were limited in geographical scope, often conducted in the most remote areas, and driven as much by straightforward resistance to foreign occupation as by religious convictions.

Yet in all cases, Islam played a key role in energizing the resistance, and sustaining it in the face of overwhelming odds.

SHEIK SHAMYL

When the history of heroic but hopeless causes is written, the 400-year struggle of the Chechen people to resist Russian imperial rule will constitute the first and most heartrending chapter.

Russian Cossacks began moving into the Caucasus lowlands as early as AD 1559. Over the next four centuries, Russian armies relentlessly pushed into the Caucasus, subjugating the Muslim mountain tribes of Dagestan, Circassia, Ingushetia, Chechnya, and Abkhazia. All resisted fiercely, but the notoriously warlike Chechens and Dagestanis offered the most prolonged, determined resistance to the Russian invaders.

After a century of scattered resistance, in 1830, the Muslim peoples of the Caucasus halted their traditional feuding, banded together, and proclaimed the Imamate of Dagestan, the first Islamic nation declared in modern history. Russia immediately sent a large army to crush the revolt.

A Chechen chieftain and religious leader, Sheik Shamyl, rallied the Muslims of the Caucasus and waged an epic guerrilla war against extraordinary odds. Shamyl's Chechen warriors ambushed Russian armies in the Caucasus defiles, cut up relief columns, raided lowland Russian forts and settlements, and managed to hold off the czar's best generals for nineteen years. Such was Shamyl's courage, nobility of character, and tenacity that they captured the attention and admiration of Europe.

Russian generals followed their usual brutal custom of razing Chechen villages, killing captured mujahidin, taking hostages, and destroying farm animals and crops. In 1859, Shamyl was finally captured and sent in chains as an exotic trophy to the czar's court. Many Chechen and other Caucasian mountain peoples fled to Turkey and the Middle East.

The Chechen and other Muslim peoples of the Caucasus disappeared into the Russian Empire, which Karl Marx rightly termed "the prison house of nations," and then into the belly of its successor, the Soviet Empire. But the Chechens had not been defeated and would, as we will see in Chapter 12, again rise up when the doors of this great prison house were thrown open in 1991.

Somalia: "The Mad Mahdi"

Expanding European colonialism encountered Muslim resistance in other parts of Africa. At the very end of the nineteenth century, as the British, French, Italians, and Ethiopians were vying to grab Muslim Somali lands in the Horn of Africa, another remarkable Islamic scholar appeared.

Muhammed bin Abdullah Hassan preached an extremist, purifying version of Islam close to the Wahabi-Salafists, and was deeply influenced by the Mahdist movement in nearby Sudan.

Muhammed Hassan raised an army of Somali Islamic warriors and led resistance against the invading Europeans. At the same time, he managed to quell the traditional feuding between notoriously factious Somali tribes and clans that remains a scourge to this very day.

Hassan was quickly dubbed the "Mad Mahdi" by Britain's jingoist press, and his followers "Dervishes." As in Sudan, Britain's media and politicians depicted Somalia's Islamic movement as a horde of fanatical, blood-crazed savages intent on destroying the outposts of Christian civilization on the Horn of Africa.

The Mad Mahdi took pen in hand and wrote a message to the British, the gist of which is not very far from what today's Islamic mujahidin would say. In fact, Muhammed Hassan's warning uncannily foretokened some of the speeches of Osama bin Ladin and his deputy, Dr. Ayman al-Zawahiri, and may have served as an inspiration to them:

I like war, but you do not. I have no cultivated fields, no silver, no gold for you to take. I have nothing.

If the country were cultivated or contained houses or property, it would be worth your while to fight. The country is all jungle, and that is of no use to you. All you can get from me is war— nothing else.

I have met your men in battle, and have killed them. We are greatly pleased at this. Our men who have fallen in battle have won paradise. God fights for us.

We kill, and you kill. We fight by God's order. That is the truth. We ask for God's blessing. God is with me when I write this. If you wish for war, I am happy; and, if you wish for peace, I am content also. But if you wish for peace, go from my country back to your own. If you wish for war, stay where you are. Hearken to my words.

After two decades of struggle, Somalia's Mad Mahdi was finally defeated in 1920 by British airpower, just as American airpower later defeated Taliban and Iraqi forces in 2001 and 2003. But not before the baleful image of a second malevolent Muslim fanatic was firmly implanted in the psyche of Britain.

So evocative and resonant was the sobriquet Mad Mahdi, that Britain's press soon sought out and discovered yet another candidate, this time during the 1920s in the Afghan mountains above the great British Northwest Frontier garrison city of Peshawar.

There, a Pashtun (Pathan) Afghan religious leader, who was seriously vexing the British garrison, was dubbed the new Mad Mahdi. When he saddled up 20,000 wild horsemen, rode down the Malakand Pass, and proclaimed he would lay fire and sword on "impious" Peshawar, Britain's press went into paroxysms over the latest Islamic threat to the Raj.

No sooner had the Mad Mahdi retreated into the mountains under a barrage of artillery fire than another Muslim mischief maker arose in the Afghan hills and set about bedeviling the British.

This local imam, a religious prayer leader in the village of Ippi, was quickly dubbed with the delightful moniker the "Fakir of Ippi." Living up to his reputation as a ferocious Muslim fanatic, the Fakir of Ippi vowed to storm Peshawar and hand its Christian ladies over to his lust-crazed Pathan warriors. Or so the British press, now in full frenzy, proclaimed.

The Fakir and his holy warriors were finally driven back into their mountain fastness by the RAF and massed field artillery, but not before Peshawar's British ladies had a serious scare.

THE MORO WAR

America's collective memory of what was euphemistically termed the Philippine Pacification has vanished. Like other dark episodes in America's history, such as the Mexican War, and the relentless ethnic cleansing of native peoples, America's experiment in European-style colonialism in the Spanish American War, Central America, and the Philippines, had vanished down the memory hole.

After conquering the Philippine archipelago in the 1898 Spanish-American War, US occupation forces fought a hard, three-year counterinsurgency campaign against the renowned Filipino resistance leader Emilio Aguinaldo. In the mostly Muslim southern Philippines, US forces waged a difficult, thirteen-year war against Islamic tribal chieftains and the Sultanate of Sulu.

This forgotten "pacification" struggle was conducted against the historic background of the long struggle by Muslims of the southern Philippines to resist expansion of far more numerous Christian Filipinos from the north. As in so many other cases in the Muslim world, Filipino Muslim tribesmen, known collectively as Moros, were too busy fighting one another to effectively resist Christian encroachment into the regions of Mindanao and Sulu.

The Philippine Pacification was, in fact, a limited but brutal campaign of repression by US forces in which whole villages were wiped out and large numbers of civilians killed. Muslims fought ferociously, but hopelessly, since they were mostly armed with flintlock muskets, swords, and bolo knives.

America's only memento of this brutal little colonial war is the renowned Colt .45 heavy automatic, whose powerful bullet was expressly developed to knock down charging Moro warriors. From the fierce Moro came a new term, "to run amok."

While total casualties are unknown, estimates put the death toll at between 20,000 and 100,000 Muslim Moro fighters and civilians at the hands of US forces. Large numbers of Moros also died from cholera and other diseases, as is common in most wars, wherein sickness often kills far more than battle.

While this obscure war is forgotten in America, in the modern Philippines, vivid memories of the historic struggle of the Muslim Moros, and the continuing seizure of their lands by Christian settlers, sparked a modern uprising led by the Moro National Liberation Front that simmers to this day. In the lexicon of Manila and Washington, the MNLF is a "terrorist group," though a quiescent one. Washington believes it has deep links to the Jemaah Islamiyah Front of Indonesia and Malaysia, which is high on America's and Australia's terrorist blacklist.

Another far more extreme group, Abu Sayyef, which is closer to a bandit band than a resistance movement, continues to fight against government forces. US military advisers joined this remote counterinsurgency fight in the southern Philippines as part of President George W. Bush's war on terror.

Muslims across Southeast Asia have used the Moro War and Filipino Muslim resistance as the historical foundation of their modern opposition to western and Christian influence in the region, and demands for an Islamic sultanate. Similar demands came from Indonesia's Sumatran province of Aceh, whose Islamic sultanate staunchly resisted Dutch colonial forces for over a century.

In spite of ongoing peace talks in the Philippines that have dragged on over a decade, Muslim unrest in the south of that nation remains a significant regional problem and persistent destabilizing factor. On a positive note, in 2007, a two-decade-old rebellion by Aceh's Muslims against Indonesian rule was finally ended through an autonomy agreement.

To no surprise, these "little wars," as Victorian soldiers used to call them, have slipped away from western consciousness. But for Muslims, and particularly in their cultures where oral history plays a very important role, memories of the valiant, if hopeless, struggles of their ancestors against western imperial domination remain alive, and often vital.

Many Muslim peoples, like the Japanese, place great store and respect in those who wage hopeless but morally just struggles against impossible odds. Japanese term it "the nobility of failure." There is no braver warrior in Japan than one who willingly embarks on a battle that he knows cannot be won and will surely result in his death.

For Shia Muslims, steeped in the battle of Kerbala in which their beloved paragon Ali fought overwhelming odds and was slain, such self-sacrifice is the most profound and heroic of all acts.

Speeches of Islamic militants are filled with references to the West's thousand-year history of attacking the Muslim world and gobbling up its lands. Many Muslims, as a result, feel themselves the victims of a ruthless, continuing crusader campaign against Muslim peoples. They conveniently forget that before this era, from the late 600s until the fourteenth century, it was the Muslims who were assaulting or raiding Christian Europe.

Muslim radicals see fellow Muslims who urge cooperation with the West as traitors and quislings. The most militant among them believe the West's historic wars against Islam—the twenty or more large and minor Crusades, and nineteenth-century colonialism—have never stopped, but continue to the present.

Like many people of the Third World, Muslims tend to think backwards, recalling past glories and affronts as if they are current experiences, while westerners in their far more dynamic societies have abjured their history in favor of living for tomorrow's impending excitements. As a result, westerners are constantly bemused, and often angered, by Muslims' constant references to long-past events. "It's history. Forget it and move on!" they tell Muslims. But for many Muslims, yesterday remains today and tomorrow.

The legacy of these by now remote nineteenth-century colonial conflicts remains with us, both in the form of our highly negative mental images of Muslims and their leaders, and residual animosity against the West in the Muslim world. In fact, our collective thinking and view of the Muslim world too often recalls the primitive jingoism, crude prejudices, and religious bigotry of Victorian days. As for Americans, the shameless marketing of the 2003 Iraq War recalled the yellow journalism and crude, whiskey-inflamed patriotism of the Spanish-American War.

A century after the apogee of British colonialism, the North American media, and Europe's right-wing media, continue the practice of demonizing uncooperative Muslim leaders as dangerous, demented fanatics, and Muslims in general as backwards, malevolent, and violence-prone foes of western civilization. By contrast, Muslim leaders who cooperate with the West are termed moderates.

Almost invariably, highly complex issues are too often reduced to one-dimensional misrepresentations. Childish labels like "bad guys" or "terrorists" replace rational discussion. History and context must be avoided at all costs lest readers and viewers grow bored or confused. Muslims have also fallen prey to such childish characterizations, depicting westerners as "Great Satans" or "Zionist-Imperialists."

It has always been easier for the West to demonize and make crude caricatures of Muslim leaders who resisted their designs. Third World affairs were and remain too complex and turbid to be readily described to western audiences. It is much easier to turn foreign policy into morality cartoons than admit that foreign adventures were being waged for resources or to please domestic pressure groups.

It is no coincidence that over the course of the era after World War II, western governments and media have presented us with an unbroken progression of sequential Muslim malefactors who just happen to pop up every time the West pushes its influence ever deeper into the Muslim world, or when Muslim peoples seek to shake off western domination.

For western powers, it was far more convenient and effective to personalize issues by setting up an evil straw man, blaming all the Mideast's problems on him, then knocking him down to a thunder of applause.

This way, it could be denied that the West's problems with the Muslim world come from the lingering effects of European colonialism, poverty, corrupt, dictatorial, brutal regimes, or the need to buy oil cheap and sell arms dear.

The essence of the problem, went the western party line, was backwards Islam, wicked Muslim leaders, and their irrational, violent followers. Americans, Canadians, and Australians readily agreed. They just wanted to be told who the "bad guys" were. Don't confuse us with details, they seemed to ask. Like the Victorian British, we prefer our foreign affairs problems to be incarnated in one ubervillain whose elimination becomes a moral virtue. There are, of course, despots and tyrants who indeed demand to be removed from power. But the West has been notoriously selective in its choices of "regime change." Pro–US dictators, as we shall see, have special dispensation. "He's an SOB," as it was said in Washington of Nicaragua's despot Anastasio Somoza, "but he's our SOB."

The first postwar heir of the Mad Mahdi was Iran's democratic leader, the nationalist Dr. Mohammed Mossadegh. He was branded a dangerous Communist by Britain's MI6 and the CIA, and subsequently overthrown in an Anglo-American coup.

Next came Egypt's fiery Gamal Abdel Nasser. Scourged as "the Hitler of the Nile" by Britain's Anthony Eden, Nasser for a time incarnated the renewal of long-repressed Arab pride, the desire to be rid of lingering colonial domination, and, however quixotic, the quest for Arab dignity and unity.

Nasser was held up by London and Paris as a threat to the entire globe. In 1956, the British, French, and Israelis secretly colluded to invade Egypt and topple Nasser. Israel's prize was to be the Sinai Peninsula. Britain would regain the Suez Canal, and France wrongly believed overthrowing Nasser would fatally weaken the uprising in French-ruled Algeria. The Suez invasion turned out to be a comical fiasco that made the British and French look like toothless fools. A furious US president Dwight Eisenhower ordered the British, French, and Israelis to withdraw or face crippling economic sanctions. Soviet leader Nikita Khrushchev, fresh from invading Hungary, threatened the British and French "imperialist aggressors" with nuclear attack. Suez marked the end of Britain and France as imperial powers. Israel, by contrast, set to work making sure it could never again be pressured by a foreign power, particularly so the United States.

During the 1960s, the British press screamed headlines that Nasser was developing long-range missiles, dramatically code-named Operation Cleopatra, allegedly bearing warheads packed with germs and radioactive material. Like later claims about Saddam Hussein's nonexistent weapons of mass destruction, these accusations were false and part of the propaganda war being waged against Nasser by London and Paris. Britain and, later, the US launched unsuccessful plots to assassinate Nasser.

After Nasser died in 1970, the role of chief Muslim demon was conferred upon Palestinian leader Yasser Arafat. With his unshaved face, Bactrian features, and ever-present pistol, Arafat looked the very picture of a modern terrorist menace. The Israelis and US managed to turn Arafat into a world-class threat, ably aided by some of his more extreme followers, who took to blowing up aircraft, or like the windbag PLO "spokesman" Ahmad Shukairy, made bloodcurdling, but utterly empty, threats to "drive the Jews into the sea." Such childish bombast provided Israel with an ideal pretext to launch its devastating June 1967 surprise attacks on the Arabs.

Iran's 1979 Islamic revolution brought to power a large number of malevolent-looking mullahs, led by the always scowling and often demonic-looking Imam Ruhollah Khomeini, who became the poster-mullah for supposedly menacing Islam. The only message that non-Iranians ever heard from their medieval Islamic nemesis was "death to America." Iran's Islamic leadership scared everyone and, to westerners, provided ideal examples of just how nasty, backwards, and aggressive Muslims could be if not rigorously policed. But after Khomeini's death in 1989, attention again turned elsewhere.

Libya's zany leader, former CIA ingénue Muammar Khadaffi, then took center stage as the West's chief Islamic devil. The western media had a field day with Khadaffi's silly Italian-tailored opera buffo uniforms and ludicrous bombast. Comedy aside, his agents brought down two civilian airliners and bedeviled the western powers. Khadaffi's greatest outrage in western eyes, however, was shaming Arab oil producers into raising their prices instead of selling their oil to the West for next to nothing.

The West never forgave Khadaffi for this offense, nor for his uncritical support of any and all "anti-imperialist" groups, from Nelson Mandela's ANC to the Irish Republican Army. In retaliation for an alleged Libyan attack on a Berlin disco frequented by US troops, President Ronald Reagan tried to assassinate Khadaffi by bombing his sleeping quarters, but succeeded only in killing Khadaffi's two-year-old adopted daughter and around a hundred other hapless Libyans and some French diplomats.

After the 1987 attack, Khadaffi ceased goading the US and adopted a low profile. The notorious hired killer Abu Nidal briefly played Islamic villain. But he was soon replaced by Hezbollah's angry, bearded mullahs. But no one could remember or pronounce the name of their leader, Sheik Fadlallah, so the US media moved on and trained its big guns on a new Muslim malefactor, Syria's Hafez Asad. But Syria was too confusing, and the wily Asad did not play well as a villain in Peoria.

Iraq's Saddam Hussein, another Arab despot who had been helped onto his throne by the CIA's relentlessly bumbling political midwives, abruptly emerged in 1990 as the latest Islamic villain. A former intimate US ally in the eight-year war against Iran, Saddam was foolish enough to believe Washington's assurances it had no objections to him invading Kuwait.

Saddam, driven by his own megalomania and brutishness, made a wonderful villain and hate-figure for western audiences, eclipsing such as Libyan leader Muammar Khadaffi and the organization Hezbollah. Until 1991, when Saddam had been a close US ally in the Arab war against revolutionary Iran, his infliction of mass atrocities on Iraq's rebellious Kurds was largely ignored by western governments and media. After all, he was our SOB.

President Saddam Hussein's rash invasion of Kuwait in 1990, the result of a gross insult from its crown prince, turned Iraq's strongman from American-British SOBs into a new Mideast devil par excellence. The United States, Britain, Israel, and Saudi Arabia focused their wrath on Iraq's leader and determined to overthrow him. Saddam, who had an amazingly self-destructive sense of public relations, snarled at the world and acted every inch the ogre he was.

Then came the 9/11 attacks. At first, there was uncertainty about who had engineered them. But before long, a lanky Saudi exile named Osama bin Laden, who had fought as a mujahid in the 1980s Afghan struggle against Soviet imperialism, burst upon the world as the most wicked Muslim since Sudan's Mahdi a full century earlier. Like Saddam, Osama bin Laden fit the role perfectly. With his swarthy skin, long beard, lurid threats against the West, and religious fulminations, he perfectly fit the role of Mad Mahdi. Saddam's overthrow in 2003 left bin Laden the Mideast's unchallenged ubervillain.

Osama Bin Laden, however, proved maddeningly elusive in spite of a hunt for him by over 130,000 US and Pakistani troops and a small army of CIA agents. Unable to find bin Laden, the embarrassed Bush administration sought to downplay his importance by claiming he was of no further importance, "marginalized" and "on the run."

The Bush administration and US media soon shifted its wrath to a new, more convenient target they could at least locate. This time, the new Islamic devil turned out to be an Iranian blacksmith's son named Mohammed Ahmadinejad who had unexpectedly become president of Iran in 2005. This short, unimpressive-looking individual quickly came to compete with Osama bin Laden for the American title of Islamic Great Satan.

The first years of the twenty-first century saw America's government both obsessed by events in the Mideast and seemingly unable to eliminate the Muslim malefactors that threatened and vexed the United States. No sooner was one notorious "terrorist" eliminated than another sprang up to take his place. After the September 11, 2001, attacks on the US, and the ensuing wars in Afghanistan and Iraq, the cold war against Iran, and the joint Ethiopian–US invasion of Somalia, America appeared locked in conflicts in the Muslim world that raised the specter of an actual "clash of civilizations."

How did America's affairs become so tangled with those of the distant Muslim world? Why have so many of the world's 1.5 billion Muslims become so hostile to the United States? First, we must examine the troubling legacy that European colonialism left behind in the Muslim world.

CHAPTER FOUR
★ ★ ★

THE MIRAGE OF INDEPENDENCE

Nearly half a century has passed since Europe's colonial empires vanished and were replaced by a galaxy of new states across Africa and Asia. While many reminders of the colonial era's positive accomplishments remain, such as the worldwide use of English as a lingua franca, stately imperial edifices in Cape Town, bewigged jurists in steamy Kenyan courtrooms, or India's vibrant rough-and-tumble democracy, its negative aspects have vanished from our consciousness.

But even a cursory study of the Muslim world immediately encounters many of the colonial era's lingering political, economic, and social maladies that continue to damage and roil modern Muslim nations.

First among these is the well-known problem of favored minorities. The standard colonial practice of divide and rule was relentlessly utilized in Africa and Asia to detach tribal, religious, or ethnic minorities from the majority, shower them with special favors, plum jobs, and privileges, thereby turning them into loyal servants of the foreign rulers. The British were grand masters of this technique. This time-honored colonial tactic left minority groups holding an unfair, often intolerable share of political and economic power after independence. Prime examples are Lebanon's Maronite Christian elite and Iraq's Sunnis.

Tribalism, a far worse scourge, certainly did not originate with colonialism, but Europe's imperialists invariably played tribes against one another, producing chronic national instability and long-term centrifugal forces. Equally bad, they often divided tribes by artificial borders, as Britain did with the Pashtun people in Afghanistan, or lumped them into new colonial political creations with traditional foes or rivals. Sudan and Nigeria are striking examples.

The Mongol and Ottoman invasions, followed by subsequent centuries of misrule by petty rulers, and widespread economic collapse or social decline, left most of the Muslim world shattered and reduced to its basic components of tribe and clan. Trust and loyalty were reserved for blood relations and the tribe. In a chaotic, corrupt, often dangerous world, no other group could be trusted. Governments were almost always seen as thieving, cruel extorters of taxes and leviers of soldiers. The notion of government as a positive force providing security, laws, and social protection was almost unknown in the Muslim world.

In the Mideast, lackadaisical, corrupt, and usually incompetent Ottoman rule accentuated these problems and left many parts of the Muslim world without functioning national or even local governments.

Scrape away the political veneer of most Muslim nations, whether Egypt, Saudi Arabia, or Pakistan, and one will find family, clan, and tribal relationships dominating politics and national security, and dense webs of corruption and nepotism everywhere. Trust only your brothers, and your first cousins, and much less your second cousins, as an old Arab saying goes.

Today's Muslim nations, particularly those of the Mideast, have often and rightly been termed "tribes with flags." Development of genuine democratic government, based on the essential elements of consent of the governed, national political consciousness, compromise and power sharing, trust, laws, reliable institutions, and modern economies, is impossible in a system handcuffed by blood-and-clan loyalties, and total distrust of government at all levels.

Then there is the endlessly contentious problem of sub-elites—known as "brown Frenchmen" or "brown Englishmen"—that continues to seriously vex the Muslim world. Colonial rulers cultivated a native elite through favors, jobs, and education that provided it regiments of soldiers, bureaucrats, and plantation or mine overseers. The sepoy soldiers of Britain's Indian Raj, red-fezzed askari troops of British East Africa, and the hundreds of thousands of Algerian "harkis" who fought for France during the bloody 1950s independence war are well-known examples. These sub-elites came to closely identify with their colonial masters and distance themselves from the colony's native majority who, quite naturally, resented and grew to hate the collaborating class.

When the colonial powers left, these "brown Europeans" in many cases assumed control of their nations, often by default for lack of any other educated cadres, but in many cases because the departing colonists handed power to them. When Belgium granted Congo independence in 1960, there were only a handful of Congolese who were literate. One of them, Patrice Lumumba, a former clerk, became prime minister. He was soon murdered and replaced by a former sergeant in the Belgian colonial army, Joseph Mobutu, who became a faithful overseer for western mining interests, until he fell terminally ill, and was brusquely discarded.

During the 1960s, Europe's colonial powers quickly gave up their remaining possessions in a rush to decolonize. The Anglo-French disaster at Suez in 1956, and the Algerian Revolution in 1954, put an end to the last pretenses of direct European colonial rule in the Muslim world.

The Europeans were gone, but they were not really gone. To be sure, the white-helmeted colonial troops had returned home; the flags of Britain, France, Belgium, and Holland were furled; viceroys, proconsuls, and governors and their staffs sailed away. Only little Portugal fought a hopeless, rearguard action to preserve its ramshackle African Empire against the surging tide of history.

The physical symbols of colonial rule were no longer visible, but other equally effective instruments of control remained, notably the "brown Europeans" of the old native colonial elite and loans that effectively kept many Third World nations in financial fetters.

In former French Africa, for example, every new black government minister had a special French "adviser" whose word was law. Paris controlled these new African nations' currencies, central banks, extractive industries, transportation systems, plantations, power supplies, and large local businesses. Only French imports were permitted.

Next to the French president's office in the Élysée Palace sat a shadowy intelligence official, Jacques Foccart, known as the "Czar of Africa," who controlled the destinies of the "independent" leaders of French Africa. None of them dared make a serious move without prior approval from the "czar" in Paris. In the event of a coup, army mutiny, or civil unrest, the widely feared Foreign Legion, with its large contingent of former German ss troopers, could go into action from one of its West African bases within hours against rebels or rioters.

While claiming the mantle of noble liberator and independence-giver to West Africa, France remained just as much in charge of its former African colonies as it had been during the colonial era, but at a much lower expense. There was less glory, but much higher profits. In today's terminology, France had outsourced colonial administration and economic exploitation to much lower-cost Third World staff.

The same technique, with many local variations, was used by Britain in its former colonies. The administrators of Britain's East India Company, and later those of the Imperial Raj, learned that local rulers were best managed by granting them economic privileges, carefully calibrated flattery, and some limited social access to the British colonial elite, along with protection from their neighbors and unappreciative subjects.

The British followed the same pattern with their vassal Arab emirs in the Gulf's Trucial States. Any of these satraps who failed to comply with the imperial diktat would soon be overthrown in a palace coup staged by a more compliant relative. When, for example, Sultan Said bin Timur of Oman proved insufficiently responsive to London's plans for his nation, he was swiftly ousted in a 1970 coup mounted by Britain's foreign intelligence agency, MI6, and replaced by his more amenable son, Qaboos.

In more developed Muslim nations, such as Egypt, foreign influence was exercised through a royal family and its coterie of large landowners and corrupt businessmen. In the case of Pakistan, it was through the bureaucracy and army, whose Anglophile officer caste was notorious for acting more pukka than the stiff British themselves.

In the 1950s and 60s, Turkey's then 700,000-man army offered another striking example of foreign influence at work. Turkey's generals ruled the nation behind a thin facade of squabbling parliamentary politicians. The United States controlled the army's weapon's supplies and finances, and commanded the loyalty of Turkey's right-wing generals who were devoted to sustaining the anti-Islamic policies of Ataturk that assured their own privileges. They were strongly backed by Turkey's large landowners, government bureaucrats, and industrialists who acquired great wealth under the secular statist system created by Ataturk known as "Kemalism" and were for the most part in no mood to observe Islamic tenets calling for distribution of personal and national wealth to the needy. Whenever the squabbling politicians got out of hand, the generals would stage a coup and hang some, *pour encourager les autres*.

But perhaps the most striking example of a western-oriented elite that was totally alienated from its Muslim citizens was imperial Iran under Shah Mohammed Pahlavi. His dour father, Reza Shah, shared Ataturk's detestation of Islam and determination to uproot it from Iran. The Shah's extended court and royal family, Iran's social and intellectual class, big landowners and industrialists formed, as in Turkey, a westernized elite that sought to distance itself as far and fast as possible from Iran's Islamic roots, aping Europeans in every possible way, right down to speaking French at home.

This writer saw the same kind of cultural disassociation in Lebanon during the 1982 Israeli invasion. When I referred to a group of Lebanese Christians from the pro-Israel Phalangist Party as Arabs, they took great offense and huffily replied, "We are not Arabs, we are Phoenicians!"

The scorn and contempt in which Iran's elite held the nation's Muslims played an important a role in sparking the 1979 Iranian Revolution. Iran's rural poverty, the reign of terror of the secret police, SAVAK, and the orgiastic consumption of luxuries, thievery, and malfeasance of the foreign-backed royal family ignited fury against the ruling elite.

In Iran, and later in Anwar Sadat's Egypt, the United States pressed their leaders to adopt policies, such as overt support for Israel or for regional security alliances, that were strongly opposed by the people of these nations.

Both in Iran and Egypt, the pro-western elite came to been seen as not only corrupt thieves, but also as a class of traitors and fifth columnists doing the West's bidding. North African elites who cooperated with France, including today's regimes in Morocco, Algeria, and Tunisia, are also scourged as "brown Frenchmen," "foreign overseers," or "traitors" by anti-western nationalists, and "béni-oui-oui's."

The conflict between the Muslim world's westernized civilian and military elites on one hand and self-proclaimed authentic native Islamists on the other, keeps the entire ummah locked in a nonstop ideological battle that neither side appears to be winning.

In the western media, these pro-western elites are usually described as moderates, while those who oppose them and their western attachments are known, variously, as radicals, militants, extremists, or terrorists.

The intense hostility of Islamists to western cultural invasion has a great deal to do with their belief that those who succumb to it inevitably become agents of western political and economic influence. In the Islamist view, western films and TV play the same role of advancing colonial interests and subversion of traditional ways that Christian missionaries did in Africa during the nineteenth century.

One of the chief complaints by Islamists against westernized moderates is that they have poisoned the minds of Muslim peoples, and particularly the young, by perpetuating the falsity that Muslims are inherently backwards, and Islam is the reason. Secularism, claim many western "experts," is the only escape for the benighted Muslim world.

Most non-British today have no idea how much racism was a part of the British psyche and imperial ethos, at least until the more enlightened 1980s. In British-ruled Egypt and India, the "wogs" or "darkies," as natives were called by the English, were banned from sporting clubs and social functions. The British, masters of snobbery, were adept at imparting to their colonial subjects a deep sense of racial, social, intellectual, and historical inferiority which played a key role in sustaining their rule.

Britain's remarkable ability to project an aura of racial, intellectual, and moral superiority certainly played an important role in allowing only 100,000 soldiers and officials of the British Raj to rule 300 million Indians during the late nineteenth century. The French, by interesting contrast, promoted their intellectual rather than racial superiority to their colonial subjects, who often—but not always, as in the case of Algeria—responded with admiration, affection, and respect, even when they opposed France's political actions.

A profound sense of inferiority still hangs over the Muslim world. Some of it comes from the manifest failures of Islamic states to govern themselves honestly or well, to teach their children properly, or to provide food, clothing, and shelter to their own people. One is hard pressed to think of many Muslim states outside the Gulf emirates that are held up as a model of good government or fair distribution of wealth.

But fairly or unfairly, many angry or abashed Muslims blame their failures to keep up with the modern world, intellectual and technological backwardness, and inability to translate their resource wealth into social or political progress on the western world and pro-western elites who many believe are determined to keep Muslim nations in fetters. Similar views are held in parts of black Africa.

Iran's supreme leader, Ayatollah Ali Khamenei, successor to the late Imam Ruhollah Khomeini, summed up this line of thinking in an April 2006 address:

Today, Western liberal democracy is as much discredited and despised in the Muslim world as are the socialism and communism of the erstwhile Eastern Bloc. Muslim peoples seek to obtain freedom, dignity, progress and honor in the shade of Islam. Muslim peoples are tired of the two-hundred year domination of foreign colonial powers and are fed up with poverty, humiliation and imposed backwardness.

The phrase "imposed backwardness" is noteworthy. This concept courses through modern Islamist thinking. The West promotes backwardness and corruption in Muslim lands, claim Islamists, to prevent Muslims from electing clean governments that would demand fair deals for their oil and gas.

In the early 1970s, as noted, Libya's eccentric leader, Muammar Khadaffi, made himself the target of Anglo-American fury by accusing the Arab oil monarchs of squandering the birthright of the Muslim world. Later, Osama bin Laden would level the same charges against Muslim oil monarchies.

Iran claims the West keeps the Muslim world backwards, preventing it from developing any modern technology or industry, so that Muslim nations must import arms, consumer, and industrial goods from the West. This conspiracy to keep Muslims backwards, not fear of nuclear weapons, claims Iran's president, Mohammed Ahmadinejad, is the real reason why the western powers have ganged up on Iran to deny it the benefits of nuclear power. Most Iranians believe him.

In the same 2006 speech, Ayatollah Khamenei returned to the theme of the supposed dangers of westernization:

When (Islamic) principles are abandoned or overlooked, the Islamic world will lose its compass, as a result putting itself at the mercy of the rules made by the enemy, with obvious consequences. We have the right to respond to the humiliation and hubris of hegemonic powers.

But how? Most of the newly independent nations of Africa and Asia had no industries save those serving the economic needs of the former colonial power, and little infrastructure or education. Farmers were unable to compete with subsidized food exports from Europe, North America, Australia, and New Zealand. Politicians were quickly enticed into taking on huge loans from the former colonial powers, the International Monetary Fund, and the World Bank they could never hope to repay, thus keeping their nations in thrall to western bankers and their political masters. Large tranches of such loans usually ended up in discreet numbered accounts in Zurich and Geneva.

One positive accomplishment of the colonial era, the creation of well-disciplined armies that often served as vehicles of upward social mobility for lower classes, eventually turned into something of a curse for parts of the Muslim world. After the Europeans left, many of the local institutions they created, such as civilian governments, courts, and educational institutions, soon succumbed to corruption, nepotism, and incompetence. However, most military establishments remained intact and often retained the high quality and character they held under foreign tutelage.

Since the military was one of the only national institutions to function reasonably honestly and efficiently, consequently commanding widespread respect and support, it was inevitable that in the decades after independence, the Muslim world's soldiers would assume a leading role in political, social, and economic affairs and, sooner or later, seize control of their nations.

Pakistan is a perfect, if dolorous, example of this phenomenon. Since independence in 1947, it has been run for half its life by British-trained military officers and their successors. Pakistan's weak, corrupt civilian governments failed to gain traction and fell from power after corruption scandals and growing unpopularity.

Six decade after being established as a beacon of good government for the Muslim world, Pakistan—literally, "land of the pure"—was ruled by a military dictatorship until early 2008 when a coalition of democratic parties finally challenged the US–backed dictatorial regime of Pervez Musharraf. Today, military regimes directly rule Algeria, Tunisia, Egypt, and Sudan. In other Muslim nations, like Syria, Indonesia, or Yemen, the military establishment exercises extraordinary influence, if not disguised control. Put simply, the men with the guns make the rules.

Had colonialism not created these military establishments, they would in any event have come to be. But, ironically, it was the high standards imparted to their native officers and ranks by the British and French, and the

Japanese in Asia, that caused these military organizations to thrive and retain respect while so much else around them was foundering.

However much all this is true, for the Muslim world to continue to complain and ascribe its failings to colonial events that occurred half a century ago, resembles a 65-year-old blaming all his current lifestyle misfortunes and character defects on his parents.

Still, the pernicious legacy of colonialism—artificial states and artificial borders, divided peoples, troubled minorities, stunted economic development, and a sense of humiliation and inferiority continue to trouble relations between the West and the Islamic world. Of all these negative emotions, humiliation is the one that lingers longest and is least easily forgiven.

CHAPTER FIVE
★ ★ ★

DAWN OF THE AMERICAN RAJ

The end of World War II produced a wave of hope and euphoria across the Islamic world. From Morocco to Iraq, India and Indonesia, subjects of western colonialism believed genuine independence and self-rule lay just before them. A new era of prosperity, honest, representative government, and self-respect was about to dawn.

Archimperialist Winston Churchill had vowed never to preside over the dissolution of the British Empire. But the two wars against Germany he had championed ended up doing just that. By 1945, the British Empire, only a decade earlier supremely arrogant and still majestic, lay bankrupt and exhausted. Britain's colonial subjects saw how the mother nation had to be rescued from defeat by the United States, and began demanding independence. Unable to afford the cost of maintaining its vast empire, Britain's Labour government quickly moved to abandon its once-vast imperium.

France was in even worse condition, broken, bankrupt, and humiliated. A year after the liberation of Paris, demonstrations erupted in Morocco and Algeria demanding independence. In Indochina, Vietnamese Communists and nationalists led by Ho Chi Minh began fighting in 1946 for their independence from France.

Revolts against Dutch rule broke out in Indonesia in 1945. In India, members of the National Congress began openly calling for the independence of their ancient nation. Independence movements sprang up in Burma, Malaya, and Indochina.

Caught up in this wave of liberation, the Muslim world universally regarded the world's newest power, the United States, as a natural ideological and moral friend and ally, as a nation that championed and practiced ideals of liberty and justice, and as their natural liberator from the yoke of colonialism. Few people at the time seemed to take note of the irony that the United States, which claimed to have waged war against Germany for the sake of "liberty, freedom, and democracy," was allied to the world's two mightiest colonial empires, Great Britain and Stalin's Soviet Union.

However naive or Panglossian these sentiments were, they were felt with intensity and passion right across the Muslim world. America had fought a mighty war to defeat European fascism and Japanese militarism in order to bring the peace and democracy it preached to the world. Americans were honest, friendly, decent people who said what they thought, and did what they said, and knew how to make money.

In the prevailing Muslim view, Americans had none of the infuriating snobbism, racism, and facile insincerity of the British, none of the clever ruses and double-dealing of the French, and none of the exploitive nature of the Dutch. America was coming to rescue the Muslim world just as surely as it had liberated Europe. Americans could be trusted.

During this early postwar period, Americans already had long-standing oil and security arrangements with Saudi Arabia. But for America, the rest of the Muslim world was more or less terra incognita. Jewish Americans were mesmerized by events in Palestine, but aside from them, few Americans had any concept of the Muslim world beyond the camels, sand dunes, and sheiks they saw in silly Hollywood films.

In 1947, the government of President Harry Truman, entirely focused on the looming confrontation with the Soviet Union, showed little interest in the Mideast beyond trying to gain the backing of Jewish voters by supporting the partition of Palestine and Israel's independence.

This seemingly minor diplomatic act in a faraway place did not then appear much more significant than the usual conduct of American ethnic politics in throwing bones to Irish, Italian, and Polish voters. Half a century later, Truman's decision to support the creation of Israel would have the most profound impact on America's future relations with the Muslim world.

At the same time, almost unknown to Americans, and certainly without any master plan by their government, the United States was taking the first small, tentative steps into the Muslim world, drawn in by the business of oil, and by the growing desire to surround and contain the dangerous Soviet Union before it could advance into the defenseless Mideast and gobble up its precious resources.

Few empires in history have begun so hesitantly, so cautiously, and in such a haphazard manner. In the late 1940s, the Muslim world was a huge power vacuum. All power abhors a vacuum, and will invariably move to occupy it. But America did not rush into the Muslim world as a new conquering power. Its political, economic, and military influence slowly, almost hesitantly, tiptoed into the Muslim nations until a decade later Americans and their government suddenly realized they were deeply engaged in the Muslim world.

America had no East India Company such as drew Britain inexorably into the affairs of India, but it did have mighty Esso oil, which pumped, refined, shipped, and retailed Saudi Arabia's oil. What was good for Esso was good for the USA.

This writer had a taste of Esso's power in 1957 when I went to Cairo to live with the family of the then president of Esso. In Egypt it was said, "In heaven there is Allah; on earth, the president of Esso." In Beirut, a Lebanese customs officer was rude to me. Informed I was part of the Esso party, the chief of Beirut police personally apologized to me and had the miscreant officer sent to guard a frigid crag in the remote Chouf Mountains.

Assuring the steady flow of Saudi oil at the nearly giveaway price of $3.08 per barrel, maintaining new military bases, and keeping the menacing Soviets out of the Muslim world meant assuring other regimes in the region were friendly and pro-American. These needs, inevitably, led America ever deeper into the Muslim world in a process that a decade later would aptly be termed "mission creep."

It was a process that was often amateur, bumbling, and frequently comical. In his delightful book *Game of Nations*, veteran CIA Mideast agent Miles Copeland recounts how his "political action team" overthrew Syria's government in 1949 because it was regarded as insufficiently responsive to Washington's needs. They cultivated and groomed an army general, Husni Za'im, for the role of Syria's new leader. The CIA team developed a backslapping rapport with General Za'im, whom they always called "Husni."

As soon as the coup was over, the CIA men went to the presidential palace to congratulate their new protégé. To their shock, "Husni" ordered them to cease using his first name, stand to attention, and address him formally as "Excellency." Syria's newest dictator quickly announced he would reject CIA tutelage and follow his own policies, and America be damned.

In 1953, the US tried to bribe Egypt's new leader, Gamal Abdel Nasser, with $3 million cash (worth about $75 million today), to adopt an anti-Soviet policy. Nasser had an aide accept the money, then used it to build the Cairo TV tower, a phallic-appearing structure whose rude and pointed message to Washington was unmistakable in any language.

Political theater would soon give way to deadly serious business, as the CIA embarked on attempts to overthrow the governments of Iran, Iraq, Egypt, Indonesia and, once again, Syria. By the end of the 1950s, the United States found itself ever more deeply engaged in the Muslim world. Strategic Air Command bases were established in Morocco and Libya. Egypt's independent-minded Nasser became the focus of American attentions and frustration.

The US–fostered Baghdad Pact in 1955 was designed to draw Turkey, Iran, and Iraq into an anti-Soviet regional alliance. The United States was rightly worried that the Soviet Union might be tempted to send the Red Army to occupy the oil fields of Iraq, Iran, and the Persian Gulf. The southernmost Soviet military bases in the Caucasus were not much farther from the great Saudi oil complex at Ras Tanura than was Brownsville, Texas, from Guadalajara, Mexico.

But as the US was putting the finishing touches on its Mideast chain of strategic containment of the Soviet Union, nationalist, anti-western sentiments erupted in Iran and the Arab world that undermined Washington's plans to turn the Mideast into an anti-Soviet bastion.

In 1951, Iran's elected prime minister, Dr. Mohammed Mossadegh, nationalized the country's British-owned state oil company. Two years later, CIA and Britain's MI6 organized the coup that overthrew Mossadegh, restored the compliant ruler Shah Mohammed Reza Pahlavi to power, and returned control of Iran's oil to Britain. Two dashing CIA agents from the illustrious Roosevelt family, Kermit and Archie, were deeply involved in Iran. They marked the high point of the CIA's "gentlemen spies." Both gifted agents were highly informed about the Mideast and sympathetic to its ways. Ensuing generations of CIA agents would lack their knowledge and savoir faire.

At the time, Washington's strategists regarded the coup in Iran and restoration of the Shah as a future model for dealing with troublesome resource-rich Third World nations. Few then suspected that by overthrowing the popular Mossadegh and replacing him with a vainglorious puppet, Washington had actually planted dragon seeds that, twenty-six years later, would contribute to the geopolitical earthquake of Iran's Islamic Revolution.

But that was well in the future. After 1953, US military, political, and economic influence poured into Iran, which proclaimed itself "the West's policeman in the Gulf." A diluted British influence remained, but London discreetly ceded pride of place in Iran to the United States, while picking up the crumbs from the American Raj.

The 1956 Suez invasion fiasco spelled the end of Anglo-French domination of the Mideast. Egyptian forces crumbled before the tripartite onslaught. But the British and French, who still saw themselves as great powers, had failed to obtain US approval in advance for the invasion and did not know what to do after landing in the Canal Zone.

Unlike Britain and France, their Israeli partners had a clear plan: to seize and annex the Sinai Peninsula and thus dominate the Suez Canal. Israel's Sinai campaign was brilliantly executed. But the Anglo-French operation lacked strategic clarity. The invading generals did not know if they were expected simply to hold the Suez Canal or advance into Cairo and fight the civilian population.

President Dwight Eisenhower was livid. With remarkable insight, he worried the Suez invasion would inflame the Muslim world and turn it against the United States, which would mistakenly be seen as having encouraged the aggression.

Eisenhower also feared that Soviet threats to militarily intervene in the Mideast, or even shower London and Paris with missiles, as Nikita Khrushchev thundered, might spark a nuclear World War III. At that time, no one knew how militarily unprepared for foreign operations the Soviets really were.

President Eisenhower summarily ordered the British and French out of Egypt, sent the US Sixth Fleet into the eastern Mediterranean to back up his orders, and warned that US Treasury loans that were propping up Britain's weak currency would be cut off and London's debt foreclosed. Britain and France were forced into a profoundly humiliating retreat that delivered the coup de grâce to their former colonial empires in the Mideast and North Africa.

With no less determination, Eisenhower ordered Israel to withdraw from Sinai. In 1956, Israel had little political clout in the United States. The Israelis grudgingly withdrew from Sinai. But the lesson was not lost on them or their supporters abroad. Israel's basic security and future military victories could not be assured without a powerful political support apparatus in the United States. Its energetic American supporters set about organizing a political network that, by the time of the next war eleven years later, had become a major factor in US domestic politics and as potent a weapon as Israel's vaunted air force.

Most Americans today have forgotten, or simply do not know, that it was also President Eisenhower who both warned his people against the growing power of what he termed the military-industrial complex, and called for the reduction, then total elimination, of nuclear weapons.

In the year 2007, Eisenhower's decisive actions at Suez in 1956 and his warnings seem remarkably prescient. The US invasion of Iraq in 2003 in many ways resembled the Anglo-French-Israeli Suez debacle: a swiftly executed but poorly planned operation that turned military victory into strategic political defeat. The Iraq War may end up producing as great a political disaster for the United States as Suez did for Britain and France.

After Suez, the Muslim world rang with praise for the United States. President Eisenhower was called "the great liberator" who would free Muslim nations from foreign control as surely as he had freed Europe from German occupation. The United States had liberated Indonesia from Dutch colonial rule. America's standing in the Muslim world had reached its zenith.

Unfortunately, the United States became ever more focused on the growing strategic challenge of the USSR and never followed up on its triumph at Suez by seizing the moment to cultivate genuine democracy in the Muslim world. Soon after Suez, it was back to Cold War business as usual.

But only two years later, in 1958, Mideast nationalist passions burst forth anew, sending quakes through the entire region. Iraq's British-run monarchy was overthrown in a bloody coup by an obscure army brigadier, Abdel Karim el-Kassem.

Jordan's monarchy was nearly overthrown by its rebellious Palestinian subjects who comprised the majority in that nation. British paratroopers put down the uprising. That same year, 1958, Egypt and Syria united to form the United Arab Republic, which was to be the first step in Nasser's vision of pan-Arab unity. The union of two Arab states deeply alarmed Washington and London: they quickly set about undermining it.

In an effort to shore up Lebanon's wobbly Maronite Christian minority government, the US Marines were landed in Beirut for the first but, unfortunately, not the last time.

Iraq's new ruler, Brigadier Kassem, threatened to invade British colony Kuwait and "reunite it to the Iraqi motherland." He allied with Iraqi Communists and proclaimed Iraq a socialist state aligned with Syria's "brotherly" socialist Ba'ath Party. Kassem's threats against Iran and the Kurds helped lay the foundation for the calamitous 1980 Iraq-Iran War.

The CIA and MI6 organized a coup against Kassem in 1963. In a harbinger of reality TV, the mercurial brigadier and forty-seven of his allies were executed on live TV by submachine-gun fire. Washington and London engineered a pro-western officer named Aref into power, but he died in a suspicious helicopter accident.

In 1968, the CIA and MI6 organized another coup in Iraq that brought to power another supposedly pro-American officer, General Hassan al-Bakr. He turned out to be a figurehead. The real power behind his throne was a then little-known Ba'ath Party enforcer named Saddam Hussein. With US backing, Saddam soon pushed aside General al-Bakr and took over as president of Iraq.

In South Asia, American military aid poured into Pakistan, which was seen as a bulwark of western interests. CIA agents backed a separatist war in Indonesia against the regime of Sukarno, who was considered too close to Indonesia's large, very powerful Communist Party. CIA agents rallied and armed tribes to oppose Egypt's expeditionary forces in North Yemen's civil war.

All the while, US political and economic influence in Saudi Arabia and the Gulf grew. Even Saudi Arabia's takeover of the Arabian American Oil Company did not hinder the deepening of US influence in the kingdom. In 1941, at the outbreak of World War II, America had been the world's largest producer and exporter of oil. By the 1960s, America had become a net importer, relying on the Mideast and Venezuela for much of its oil. Europe and Japan were almost totally dependent on Mideast oil.

Washington's Cold War strategists, most of whom had served in World

War II, were keenly aware of the decisive role of oil in geopolitics. They realized that whoever controlled Mideast oil would dominate Europe's and Japan's economies, and influence that of America. Oil was one of the pillars of world power. American control of Mideast oil would allow it to hold sway over large parts of the globe and deny this vital resource to the Soviet Union.

The 1967 Arab-Israeli War proved a decisive turning point in US involvement in the Muslim world. When Israel launched what it called a pre-emptive surprise attack on its verbally threatening but woefully militarily unprepared Arab neighbors, the political ground had been well prepared in advance by Israel's American supporters. Ever since President Dwight Eisenhower had ordered Israel out of the Sinai, its American partisans had been building a political support network designed to prevent another American president from pressuring Israel.

So successful was the pro-Israel lobby that during the 1967 Arab-Israeli War, many US intelligence professionals were convinced that the Johnson administration provided Israel with US satellite-targeting information of Egyptian and Syrian airfields that allowed Israel's air force to wipe out Arab air forces on the ground. A brutal Israeli air and naval attack on the unarmed American intelligence vessel USS *Liberty*, in which the Israelis even machine-gunned crewmen in the water, was hushed up by the Johnson administration and its survivors forced to keep their silence for decades. Congress refused to investigate this assault.

America's prestige in the Muslim world quickly evaporated; respect and admiration were soon replaced by anger, then fury. Unable to comprehend how the armies of Egypt and Syria, equipped with modern Soviet weapons, had been so humiliatingly trounced by Israel, many Muslims chose to believe conspiracy theories that US warplanes had actually participated in Israel's surprise attack. Eventually, most Muslims were forced to admit that not only would Palestine not be "liberated" any time soon, but their nationalist regimes had failed to deliver on their oft-made promises to develop modern military power and improve standards of living.

The untimely death in 1970 of Egypt's Nasser—many Egyptians still believe he was poisoned—spelled the beginning of the end of militant secular nationalism in the Muslim world. Fiery speeches, thrilling slogans, and mass rallies had proved utterly ineffective in the face of modern reality and Israel's western-backed military power.

Israel's stunning victory in 1967 left the United States in a painful political dilemma it has been unable to resolve to this day: how to reconcile support for Israel with its own strategic and economic interests in the Muslim world.

Before the 1967 war, Israel had been a minor concern to most of the Muslim world, which cared very little for the plight of the dispossessed Palestinians. But as a result of Israel's stunning victory, its territorial expansion, and seizure of Jerusalem's Old City, Muslims grew increasingly angry and alarmed at Israel, and painfully conscious of Arab humiliation. Nevertheless, Palestine remained a political problem localized in the Levant. It had not yet become a primary pan-Islamic issue.

Even so, the region's American-supported regimes were caught squarely in the middle of this dispute. On one hand, they had to play to the street by appearing to do something to defend the Palestinians and oppose Israel. But on the other, they did not want to antagonize Israel's new patron, the United States, or anger its ardently pro-Israel Congress.

So the Arab monarchs of Saudi Arabia and Jordan played a double game, speaking against Israel, and making handouts to anti-Israeli Palestinian groups, while really doing nothing and sometimes even secretly colluding with Israel. Just before the "surprise" 1973 Arab attack on Israel, for good example, Jordan's King Hussein actually warned Israel of the impending assault. The Israelis, however, were too filled with self-pride and contempt for the Arabs to take the monarch's warnings seriously.

US financing of Israel steadily increased to the point where it officially reached three billion dollars annually—and perhaps close to five billion when secret "black" and other concealed programs were included. Israel's well-financed and influential American supporters had drawn a decisive lesson from Israel's forced retreat from Sinai in 1956. Support mechanisms in Congress and the media that made Israel's future position unassailable, even by the president, were absolutely essential. Twenty years of patient work produced decisive influence over US Mideast policy and widespread sympathy for Israel, with polls showing upwards of 70 percent of Americans expressing strong support for the Jewish state.

Egypt, now under former CIA "asset" Anwar Sadat, was paid one billion two hundred fifty million dollars annually to drop out of the Arab confrontation with Israel. Washington had to expend extensive other amounts of money and effort shoring up "moderate" Arab allies like the kings of Morocco and Jordan, both of whom maintained strong secret links with Israel.

But the US also benefited from billions of dollars' of arms sales to its clients in the Muslim world. In exchange for protection, autocratic Muslim rulers were expected to buy large amounts of arms and equipment that their feeble armed forces could not possibly hope to master. Earnings from oil sales were recycled through western banks and used to buy yet more arms from defense contractors in politically important American states. The Saudis alone were said to keep upwards of $100 billion in US banks. Similar deals were signed with British and French state-owned arms companies.

The constant tug-of-war between Israel and the Arabs, and the need to deal with the rising wave of nationalism in the Muslim world, kept drawing the US ever deeper into its turbulent affairs. In 1981, Anwar Sadat was assassinated by a radical Egyptian nationalist group, Gamma Islamiya, half of which would eventually merge in 2004 with al-Qaida. One of the Gamma Islamiya leaders, a mild-mannered eye doctor named Ayman al-Zawahiri, vowed to seek revenge on the United States for imposing the hated "pharaoh" Sadat on Egypt. He is believed to have been one of the primary planners of the 9/11 attacks on New York and Washington.

A year later, the US unwisely intervened in Lebanon's ferocious civil war in an attempt to maintain a minority, pro-Israel Christian Phalangist regime in power. The resulting deaths of 241 US marines in the bombing of their Beirut barracks has been seared in America's memory.

While Lebanon was burning, the US had become stealthily involved in the bloody Iran-Iraq War. President Ronald Reagan's then US special Mideast envoy Donald Rumsfeld and senior Pentagon official Dick Cheney went to Baghdad in 1983 to offer President Saddam Hussein decisive US military and financial support in his war to overthrow Iran's new Islamic Republic. The US quickly supplied Iraq with vital satellite intelligence on Iranian troop deployments, and facilitated, in cooperation with Washington's Arab allies, a steady flow of arms, munitions, spare parts, financial assistance, and food to Iraq. Jordan became the primary conduit of covert US aid to Saddam Hussein.

US Navy intervention in the "tanker war" in the Gulf finally brought

Iran to its knees. The Iran-Iraq War, which most Mideasterners believe was engineered by the United States to crush Iran's Islamic government, cost the two sides over a million dead and an estimated $80 billion over eight years of bloody fighting.

Iran blamed the United States for its defeat and vowed to one day exact revenge on the "Shaitan-i-Buzurg" or "Great Satan." Few westerners noted at the time Ayatollah Khomeini's statement at war's end in 1988 that Iran would not have been defeated had it possessed nuclear weapons.

The collapse of the Soviet Union in 1991 and end of the Cold War left those Muslims nations that had defied US guidance, like Syria, Indonesia, or Libya, totally stranded. Their main sources of arms, aid, and diplomatic support had vanished.

Three years later, Saddam Hussein's invasion of Kuwait provided US strategists with a golden opportunity to advance the rook of US strategic power into the Arabian square of the Mideast chessboard. The 1991 Gulf War crippled and made an example of upstart Saddam Hussein, a former US ally grown too big for his britches. His army was mowed down by high-tech US forces as quickly and decisively as the Mahdi's horsemen at Omdurman a century earlier.

The victorious Gulf War allowed the US to implant permanent air, land, and naval forces in Saudi Arabia and the Gulf emirates—athwart the world's greatest reserves of petroleum.

By the end of the First Gulf War in 1991, or, as I call it, the First Gulf Oil War, US domination of the Muslim world from Morocco to Indonesia was virtually complete. Israel was triumphant and, for the first time in its existence, decisively superior to any possible combination of Arab forces.

Those few Muslim "rogue" nations that defied Washington and Israel, like Syria and Libya, quickly pulled in their horns and adopted a low profile. At this very triumphant apogee of US power, a single man at the ragged periphery of the Muslim world emerged from obscurity to declare war on the United States and its allies, vowing to drive American influence from Muslim nations.

CHAPTER SIX
★ ★ ★

THE SUN NEVER SETS ON THE AMERICAN RAJ

As the new millennium opened, US military, economic, and political power appeared supreme and unchallenged around the globe, just as Imperial Britain's had been precisely a century earlier. The once-fearsome Soviet Union was about to collapse and be exposed as a Wizard of Oz.

Most Americans gave credit for the "Evil Empire's" disintegration to the Reagan administration's triumphant cold warriors. Few at the time understood there was also another major cause of the USSR's implosion.

First, during the early 1980s, the CIA and the Pentagon's Defense Intelligence Agency had grossly overestimated the USSR's offensive military power and economic strength. These were the days when the Red Army's 50,000 tanks and 100 divisions were believed capable in wartime of reaching NATO's key supply ports of Rotterdam and Antwerp after only six days of intensive combat.

As a result of the exaggerated intelligence estimates of Soviet strength, the conservative Reagan administration embarked on an enormously expensive conventional and nuclear arms buildup. Convinced by the White House's inflammatory rhetoric that the US was preparing to attack the USSR, the Kremlin ordered what proved to be a disastrous diversion of scant national resources into even more arms in a hopeless effort to equal US–NATO spending, though the West's GDP was more than twice that of the threadbare USSR.

Moscow's second catastrophic error was, of all things, in accounting: the obscure area of capital cost allowances and depreciation. I learned from KGB sources in Moscow that in 1975, a group of eminent Soviet scientists, led by Andrei Sakharov, wrote to the Kremlin warning that its policy of diverting funds from depreciation earmarked for industrial machinery replacement into the military would wreck the Soviet economy in fifteen years. Their prediction proved remarkably accurate.

The collapse of the Potemkin Village of the old USSR in 1990 due to the arms race with Washington and industrial mismanagement left the US the world's sole superpower, and one without any discernible military challenger. Losing one's longtime enemies can be almost as traumatic an experience as losing a loved one.

America's mighty and hugely expanded military-industrial colossus, against which President Eisenhower had so rightly and presciently warned, suddenly found itself without a major enemy, and bereft of a raison d'être. American cold-warrior conservatives were abruptly faced with being eclipsed from influence and public prominence by the shocking evaporation of the Soviet threat.

Even this writer, a veteran cold warrior who had seen combat against Soviet forces in Afghanistan and Angola, and had enjoyed many intelligence-related adventures in the old USSR, felt the loss deeply.

As the old saying goes, military glory is a function of the prowess of one's enemy. Germans, Japanese, and then Russians were splendid, worthy foes. Blasting a ragtag bunch of Arab jihadists or medieval Afghan tribesmen was hardly a triumph of arms.

By the first years of the twenty-first century, the US accounted for half the world's total military spending. Adding in America's major allies, the figure rose to two-thirds of world military expenditure. With the exception of the chronically insubordinate French, Washington's European and Asian allies were as closely integrated into US strategic requirements as the Soviet Union's Warsaw Pact allies had been.

In the words of one of America's most insightful strategists, Zbigniew Brezezinski, Washington's NATO allies, Japan, and South Korea were all integral parts of what he calls America's "imperial system," and "stepping stones" for the projection of US power onto their respective continents. It seemed impossible at the time for any combination of enemies to challenge the immense military and financial strength of America and its rich allies.

The summer of 2001 marked what may be viewed by future historians as the high-water mark of American influence in the Muslim world.

Washington held imperial sway over the region from Morocco to Indonesia as surely as the British Raj had ruled Egypt, India, Burma, and Malaya.

America's influence over the Muslim world has followed this tried-and-tested British pattern. The ummah's historic fragmentation, loss of national consciousness, and resurgence of primitive regionalism and tribalism in many ways mirrored India's political divisions during the British Raj. Like eighteenth- and nineteenth-century India, the Mideast and Muslim South Asia provided fertile ground for foreign domination.

The contemporary American Raj, however, exerts its power and influence over Muslim nations in far more complex ways than the old British Empire ever did. Save for Iraq and Afghanistan, neither US troops, governors, nor administrators are needed to control the modern Raj. Security and management is provided by pro-American cadres in the member states supported financially and, when necessary, militarily by the United States. In many member states, heavily fortified US embassies have become a parallel government. Soberly suited American ambassadors have replaced the resplendent British viceroys and governors of Victorian days.

The new American Raj is, if anything, discreet in exercising its power. The political, military, and financial links that keep its members attached to America's system of world power are largely invisible to the general public. For the most part, there are no imperial troops, no proconsuls, no foreign flags, and no foreign colonists. As noted with France's rule in Africa, the business of colonial management has been outsourced to local specialists.

But from beyond the horizon, powerful US naval and air forces stand ready, when necessary, to intervene within days or even hours. In the core region of the Raj, which extends from Morocco to Pakistan, US air and naval power is within convenient striking range of all major military and industrial targets. Israel's powerful, highly skilled air force, and its missiles, can also strike all major targets in the Arab world and Iran.

However, the American Raj is not primarily a military alliance, as was its forerunner in the 1950s, the US–created Baghdad Pact. First and foremost, the raison d'être of the American Raj is control of black gold—oil. No nation has ever understood the strategic imperative of oil better than the United States.

On the eve of World War II, the leaders of Germany, Italy, and Japan had shown a disastrous lack of understanding of their future need for oil in wartime. At the time, the United States was Germany's leading source of crude oil, lubricants, and high-octane aviation fuel. For the previous half century, the United States had been the world's leading producer of oil, a fact many Americans have forgotten.

In 1939, nearly all Japan's oil came from the United States or the distant Dutch East Indies. Japan's decision to go to war against the United States was primarily motivated by Washington's total oil embargo against Japan in retaliation to its occupation of Manchuria. This new danger produced a near panic in Tokyo that Japan's carefully hoarded, two-year strategic reserve of petroleum would be quickly exhausted under the US embargo. The military-dominated regime in Tokyo decided on an immediate attack against US Pacific forces in hopes of a quick victory before their oil reserves were depleted.

Once the war broke out, Germany's sole source of oil became Romania and ersatz synthetic oil made from coal. Astoundingly, Italy's sole source of wartime oil, it turned out, was Germany! As a result, Italy's fuel-deprived fleet remained sitting ducks in port, unable to challenge the Royal Navy's control of the Mediterranean, subdue Malta, or protect Axis convoys delivering desperately needed supplies to Rommel's Afrika Corps.

Adolf Hitler refused to heed warnings from the German General Staff that it could not wage war against the Soviet Union with its already scarce fuel supplies. When such warnings were confirmed in late 1941 by critical fuel shortages, Hitler made the catastrophic and fatal decision to try to seize the Caucasus-Caspian oil fields while still attacking Moscow and Leningrad. By late 1944, Germany had hundreds of jet-powered Me262s that should have turned the tide of the air war against the Allies, but these revolutionary aircraft were grounded due to lack of fuel.

As of June 1944, a US submarine blockade and extensive mining had cut off 100 percent of Japan's oil imports and most of its imports of strategic resources and food. Without oil, Japan's navy and air force became useless. The US strategic-bombing campaign against Japan amounted to a slow-motion coup de grâce for the already prostrate imperial Nipponese Empire. Japan went to war because of oil and lost the war because of it.

America's leadership was thus keenly aware of the paramount importance of oil, both in light of the experience of World War II and the gradual decline in America's once-enormous reserves. To maintain America's dominant strategic position, foreign sources of oil had to be obtained, secured, and protected. The Soviet Union must not be allowed to threaten the West's "oil jugular."

As a result, President Franklin Roosevelt signed the first of many protection agreements with the Saudi royal family. This deal, enlarged and reaffirmed many times after, stipulated that the Saudis would sell petroleum to US oil firms at extremely low prices and bar foreign competitors. In exchange, the US undertook to defend the ruling elite of the oil producers from both hungry, covetous neighbors and their own people should they be stirred to revolution by discontent or foreign provocations.

The US–Saudi basic pact became such a centerpiece of American foreign policy that even the Soviets never openly dared challenge this cornerstone of Washington's Oil Raj. Any nation that dared touch Saudi Arabia would face the full and immediate wrath of the United States. Attacking Riyadh would be tantamount to bombing Houston.

The US–Saudi pact was gradually extended to other Mideast oil producers in the Gulf: Kuwait, Bahrain, Qatar, and the United Arab Emirates. Britain also added its own layer of security guarantees onto Kuwait and Oman. Iran was also given some security assurances, though not of such amplitude as those offered to America's Arab allies. Vaguer but still significant American security assurances were given to Pakistan and to Indonesia in the improbable event of an amphibious invasion by Red China.

The first and most important tool of power of America's Muslim Raj was the offer of protection. The first priority of all the Muslim world's regimes was survival and defense against enemies, both external and internal.

The Arab oil sheiks, whose military forces were small and weak, were delighted by these deals. Many feared rebellion from within as much as invasion by their neighbors, and also worried deeply about the Soviet Union which was unnervingly close to their borders. American protection allowed members of the Saudi royal family to devote their lives to sumptuous ostentation and sybaritic self-indulgence that traditional Muslims considered profoundly un-Islamic.

In the event of serious trouble, US forces from Europe or North America could be brought in to rescue endangered allies. Reliable troops were hired from friendly nations like Pakistan, which at one point provided a full army division whose primary mission was to defend the Saudi royal family. The CIA and other US security organizations threw a protective intelligence-security blanket over friendly regimes. In Egypt, for example, the US FBI, National Security Agency, and CIA set up protective layers of security around President Anwar Sadat, then his successor, Husni Mubarak.

The Saudi royals were all acutely aware of what had happened in 1958 in Baghdad. Iraq's British puppet ruler, King Faisal, and his Anglophile strongman, Nuri as-Said, denied the Iraqi Army ammunition for fear of a coup at a time when nationalist passions were sweeping the Arab world.

An obscure Iraqi brigadier, the aforementioned Abdul Kareem al-Kassem, pleaded that his brigade, deprived of ammunition, did not know how to shoot their rifles, never mind hit distant targets. "How can we liberate Palestine," he asked, "if my troops cannot shoot their rifles?" Reluctantly, the Defense Ministry allowed Kassem's brigade six rounds of ammunition per soldier.

Kassem marched a few kilometers out of Baghdad, turned his men around, seized the capital, and proclaimed a republic with himself as the new leader. Mobs caught and tore apart King Faisal. His hated pro-British henchman, Nuri as-Said, who was trying to escape Baghdad disguised as a woman, was exposed and hanged from a lamppost. Even Nuri's bitter foe, Egypt's leader, Gamal Abdel Nasser, was horrified, calling Iraq's new rulers "the wild men of Baghdad."

Nasser's view of the Iraqis was to prove prescient.

Saudi Arabia's horrified rulers thereafter denied their small army ammunition or fuel, a restriction in force to this day. To counterbalance any dangers from the military, no matter how feeble, the Saudis built up a well-armed Bedouin tribal force, known as the White Army, with a substantial contingent of US and British Special Forces advisers and mercenaries.

Basic protection soon developed into other forms of symbiotic relations. One of the most important was the purchase of arms and weapons systems. Protection, in Washington and London's thinking, also meant buying arms, billions' worth, and civilian aircraft.

US defense firms account, according to the Stockholm International Peace Research Institute (SIPRI), for about 63 percent of total world arms sales of nearly one trillion dollars. Europe and Russia account for roughly a third. US exports of arms to the greater Mideast account, according to the authoritative London-based International Institute for Strategic Studies, for 40 percent of its total worldwide arms sales, and constitute its single-largest market.

Major American, British, and French defense contractors are important, high-salary employers that are often concentrated in politically sensitive regions. For example, many of America's leading defense plants are found in the key electoral states of Texas and California, and the Deep South.

America's Arab clients have a long-established practice of using targeted defense contracts to support the party in power in Washington. The oil Arabs have lavished special attention on Republicans, whose senior leadership has traditionally enjoyed intimate personal and business relationships with them. They have also lowered oil prices or boosted production to support Republicans at election time. A March 2008 visit to Saudi Arabia by US vice president Dick Cheney was believed designed to get the Saudis to lower oil prices in time for the November US elections.

Former Saudi ambassador to Washington Prince Bandar was a master at directing his nation's arms contracts to states where they would produce political dividends for Republicans, or where there was a risk of growing unemployment, termination of weapons production lines, or the closure of entire defense plants. He invested $60 million with the Bush family in the hedge fund Carlyle Group, the very epicenter of Washington's Republican-dominated military-industrial-financial complex, joining him at the hip with Washington's power insiders.

In mid-2006, the British media revealed that Prince Bandar had personally received secret payments of over two billion dollars from a ninety- to one-hundred-billion-dollar arms contract between Saudi Arabia and defense contractor BAE. The weapons contract went to Britain after the pro-Israel lobby blocked American arms sales to Saudi Arabia.

Reports of this and other kickbacks on British arms contracts with numerous Muslim nations had been hushed up for a decade by British authorities. Prime Minister Tony Blair had shut down a major investigation of such illegal payoffs. But the truth finally came out and caused huge embarrassment to the Saudis and Blair, a self-appointed paladin of moral rectitude. The scandal further underlined Islamists' claims that western powers corrupted Muslim nations. Other BAE stipends went to pay for operating Bandar's private A-320 jet, which was painted in the colors of the Dallas Cowboys and his $137-million Aspen mansion.

Arab oil monarchs have routinely rewarded or bought the support of British and French politicians through orders of warplanes, tanks, naval vessels, artillery, antiaircraft systems, and military-construction programs. European arms suppliers rarely placed restrictions on their products, in contrast to the United States, which limited the offensive capabilities, avionics, range, and weapons loads of the F-15s and F-16s it sold to Saudi Arabia and the Gulf emirates due to strong pressure from Israel's partisans in Washington.

After Iraq's 1991 invasion of Kuwait was ended, the Kuwaitis went on a shopping spree, ordering billions' worth of US, British, French, and Russian weapons systems in an effort to reward these nations' support against Iraq and ensure their future support. Sales of spare parts also proved a highly profitable business for western defense contractors. Over the life of an aircraft, like an F-16 or Tornado, spare parts could amount to three times the original cost of a twenty-eight- to thirty-five-million-dollar aircraft, assuring a steady flow of high-margin sales for the manufacturer.

Arab oil monarchies would commit to buy advanced weapons systems from US and European suppliers for which they lacked trained operators or, equally important, maintenance personnel. They also bought massive, multibillion-dollar infrastructure projects like ports, new military cities, roads, hospitals, universities, and petroleum complexes. These purchases, worth some fifteen to $20 billion per year, also meant lucrative training, consulting, and engineering projects for private contractors with the right political connections to the party in power and, of course, discreet donations of soft funds by Mideast rulers to the political war chests of American and European politicians.

Nonmilitary purchases from the West also played an important role. The largest were, of course, commercial airliners. The airlines of Saudi Arabia and the Gulf emirates often bought more transport aircraft from Boeing and Airbus than they could profitably operate as part of the vast recycling of oil funds to strategic western industries. Other high-ticket purchases like power plants, port equipment, trains, and vehicles soaked up more billions in oil revenue.

As a key part of this strategic entente, the US was allowed to establish military bases in Saudi Arabia and along the Gulf in Qatar, Oman, Kuwait, and Bahrain that covered the oil-producing regions of the Arab world and projected power as far east as Pakistan and Afghanistan. They were kept strictly off limits to residents of their host nations and their personnel ordered to keep the lowest profile possible. These "stealthy" bases played a major role in both wars against Iraq and the conflict in Afghanistan. They also perform an overwatch role in monitoring Iran's activities and protecting tanker routes in the Gulf and Arabian Sea.

In 1992, the nervous Saudis asked the US to vacate the Taif, al-Khobar, and Prince Sultan bases, where the USAF maintained around one hundred warplanes and, at the latter, housed the main command-and-control center for all Mideast air operations. Washington wisely consented. Its air units and about 7,000 troops had become a major irritant to Saudis and were providing ammunition to Osama bin Laden and other Islamic militants who claimed the US military presence was defiling the holiest land of Islam and militarily occupying the kingdom.

The US Central Command reconstituted its main air operations center in neighboring al-Udeid Air Base, Qatar, and moved troops into other Gulf states. But important US military-training and liaison missions still remained in Saudi Arabia and kept a grip on the kingdom's modest armed forces by controlling information, maintenance, and spare parts.

While arms played a dominant role in US–Arab relations, money came a close second. The cheap-oil-for-protection deal between the petro-Arabs and their western mentors had other important financial dimensions. The lion's share of funds earned by the Saudis and other Gulf oil producers are invested in US, European, and Asian banks and government securities or public equities, effectively recycling these oil funds and providing a huge inflow of cash to western financial institutions.

Figures on Saudi investment in the United States are difficult to ascertain as they have been purposely obscured to mask their size and influence. The Washington-based Institute for Research of Middle East Policy estimates that 60 percent of Saudi Arabia's worldwide investments of $700 billion, or some $420 billion, are invested in the United States, in addition to $120 billion in US commercial banks. Some sources put the figure at close to $1 trillion. A century earlier, the wealth and finances of India's princely families were lodged at the Bank of England and London's financial institutions.

Whatever the precise figure, it is obvious the enormous sums that Saudi Arabia and other Arab oil producers have invested in the US and Europe have become an indispensable part of the western financial system. The new state-owned sovereign wealth funds of nations like Saudi Arabia, the United Arab Emirates, Singapore and, most lately, China, are rapidly becoming 800-pound gorillas in the world of international finance.

While such huge investments give the Arabs some limited political and financial clout in the West, at the same time they make the oil Arabs extremely vulnerable to political pressure from the West as so much of their money is literally held to ransom by US and British treasuries and banks. Threats of an oil embargo, such as the Arabs launched in 1973, would swiftly be met by a freeze on their vulnerable bank and share assets. The West could also embargo its food exports to the Mideast upon which many Arab states depend for half their daily sustenance.

Egypt, which accounts for at least a third of the Arab world's total population, offers another striking example of the multi-layer control mechanisms of the American Raj. When Egypt's late strongman, Anwar Sadat, broke with the Soviet Union and allied his nation to the United States, a volte-face that led to his historic visit to Israel and the ensuing 1978 Camp David Accords, he put his nation in long-term economic and military thrall to America.

Egypt, with too many people and too little arable land, could then only produce enough grain to feed half its people. So more than 50 percent of Egypt's food had to be imported. Since Egypt lacked enough hard currency to buy grain, it had to rely on foreign aid to feed its surging population, which has relentlessly grown to 68 million people crammed into arable land no larger than the size of the small US state of Maryland.

When Egypt was led by Gamal Abdel Nasser, the USSR had made up the grain shortfall. Sadat turned to his new American benefactor, and, after his peace accord with Israel, secured congressional approval and funding for a long-term aid program to supply free or below-market-price wheat to Egypt. Besides becoming rife with corruption, the wheat program put Egypt's food supply under the control of the US Congress which was then, and remains, strongly influenced by the US–Israel lobby. It did not take a second Metternich to figure out that Sadat had, in effect, put his nation indirectly under the control of Israel, a fact that sent Islamists into paroxysms of fury. But, of course, Egypt had to eat and there were not many other sources of millions' worth of food aid.

Cementing its influence over Egypt, the US threw a cordon of protection around Sadat and ensured his armed forces, the regime's power base, remained loyal and unable to wage war against Israel. Sadat had been a

CIA "asset" since the 1950s. US agents protected him and kept a weather eye on local opponents as well as on any generals who harbored Bonapartist ambitions. The same system continued, though with more assiduous application, after Sadat was assassinated in 1981 and Washington eased into power another longtime ally, air force general Husni Mubarak.

The CIA and the Pentagon's Defense Intelligence Agency had agents sprinkled throughout Egypt's armed forces right up to senior-command level. They worked closely with Egypt's secret police, the Mukhabarat, to identify and eliminate dissenters and the growing Islamic opposition that accused Sadat of being a traitor who had sold out Egypt to the Americans and Israelis. The Islamists charged Sadat and his family with extensive corruption and malfeasance, accusations that were almost universally believed by Egyptians.

Egypt's large armed forces were slowly reequipped with US aircraft and heavy weapons to replace their aging Soviet material. But Washington ensured that Egypt's armed forces did not have enough munitions or spare parts to sustain more than a few days of combat or much movement. Any threat of a US cutoff of military aid would paralyze Egypt's armed forces. Washington made sure the Egyptian military was supplied just enough modern weapons to keep the generals happy and loyal, but not enough to wage war with Israel. In fact, Egypt's armed forces were configured and armed for combat with other Arab regimes, not Israel.

Washington's final lever of control over Egypt was financial aid: the over two billion dollars' of military and economic aid Egypt received from the US for abandoning the Arab confrontation with Israel and making peace with the Jewish state. This figure did not include generous annual secret CIA stipends to senior members of Egypt's elite. Not surprisingly, a lot of this American annual aid, or "baksheesh" (bribes, tips), as Egyptians called it, found its way into the pockets of Egypt's ruling elite, their friends and families.

Egypt's regime has become dependent on this American aid and would be hard pressed to function without it. Islamists and nonreligious opposition groups accused the government of selling out to America and Israel for personal gain. They did not, however, explain how they planned to feed Egyptians if the hated Americans were expelled and their aid terminated. Some Islamists hoped China would make up their nation's food deficit.

The other members of the American Raj are controlled in similar fashion. The US and France provide military and intelligence protection to the feudal ruling family of Morocco and to the military dictator of Tunisia. Both of these North African nations and their armed and security forces receive extensive US arms and financial aid. Morocco's royal family receives extra protection from Israel's Mossad.

France, and more lately, the US, finance Algeria's brutal military junta. Even Libya's mercurial leader, Colonel Muammar Khadaffi, finally bowed his knee to the Raj after decades of punishing sanctions and serious fright at the prospect of being invaded by US forces. Western oil firms are now moving into newly sanctified Libya to exploit its high-grade oil. Western arms merchants are right behind them.

Iran's armed forces under the Shah were largely equipped by the US and Britain and, once again, were held in thrall by Washington's control of their general staff, spare parts, munitions, and training. Supply of US arms has also played a crucial role in Pakistan, whose armed forces had been largely dependent until recent times on American weapons, spare parts, munitions, and financial assistance. The same can be said of Turkey, whose powerful army, NATO's second largest, was run by politically influential right-wing generals who more often than not took their marching orders from the Pentagon rather than from their own weak politicians.

The West, particularly the United States, also exercises various forms of soft control over the Muslim world. The ummah sends the sons and daughters of its elite to American high schools and universities. Wealthy Muslims flock to American hospitals and clinics for advanced medical treatment. Los Angeles and Miami, London, Nice, Cannes, and Marbella remain premier playgrounds for the Muslim world's moneyed class. Even those young Muslims who profess to despise America and everything it stands for seem to have no problem enjoying the many delights of its "decadent, Godless culture." Militant western Communists behaved similarly in the 1930s and 1940s, advocating violent Leninist revolution while sipping cocktails at fashionable soirees in New York, London, and Paris.

The United States also extends its influence into the Muslim world by means of Hollywood films, pop music, fashion, the American-English language, cars, sexual marketing, junk food, computer games, and rampant consumerism. Young Muslim men grow up on western films, legal or bootlegged, and are often infused by American cultural values. The dour mullahs have been little more successful in keeping out America's cultural inundation than were South Africa's Boers or the late, unlamented East Bloc.

America's pervasive military, economic, and cultural influence in the Muslim world is a fact. Many Muslims simply accept it as a natural state of affairs and enjoy its rich culture of consumerism. But America's political domination of the region's repressive governments causes the most antagonism towards the United States. This fact is routinely cited by militant Islamists as their primary motivation for violence: "We cannot create democracy or end corruption until we get rid of the tyrants who rule us ... and they will not be overthrown without a fight to the death."

While Imperial Britain and France made excellent use of "brown Englishmen" and "brown Frenchmen," to promote their colonial interests, the United States turned the long-distance management of its tame Muslim rulers into a high political art form. Like all loyal satraps and fine servants, Washington's Muslim rulers have become adept at swiftly anticipating its wants and needs, and implementing them without direct orders from the White House, Pentagon, or CIA. They know how to head off actions that will anger or annoy their patron.

Self-policing and self-censorship have become the political autopilot of most of the Muslim world's rulers. A few stern punishments of malefactors or insubordinates by Washington, such as the overthrow of General Manuel Noriega in Panama and Saddam in Iraq, were enough "pour encourager les autres."

One of the sadder ironies of our era is that the United States, once the world's leading advocate and example of democracy, rule of law, and good government is today seen by many Muslims as a primary promoter of despotism, bad government, and corruption in the Muslim world. America did not create or export these evils to Islamic nations: they abounded long before America was born. But in the course of expanding and sustaining its Raj, and preserving the status quo, America has ended up supporting many of the world's most brutal, nasty, and repressive regimes, all in the name of stability, moderation, and fighting terrorism. These are precisely the autocratic or oligarchic regimes that have squandered the Muslim world's riches, terrorized its peoples into sullen quiescence, stunted economic and intellectual growth, and fostered a culture of all-pervasive corruption, nepotism, cronyism, and moral squalor. Add to this equation the regressive, sometimes obscurantist influence of hidebound, self-serving religious establishments across the Muslim world, and one easily sees why it appears to be slipping backwards while the rest of the world, sub-Saharan Africa excepted, is racing forward.

In early 2003, a time when President George Bush and his éminence grise, Vice President Dick Cheney, were preaching a military crusade whose alleged goal was to bring democracy to Saddam Hussein's Iraq, a "rogue nation" they did not yet control, but soon would, the White House was doing absolutely nothing to foster genuine democracy or good government in the Muslim nations over which America exerted paramount influence, such as Morocco, Tunisia, Egypt, Jordan, and Saudi Arabia. Instead, Washington was involved in the attempted crushing of the only democratically elected government in the Arab world, Hamas in Palestine. In Pakistan, the US was busy shoring up the Musharraf dictatorship and trying to block restoration of parliamentary democracy in that nation.

Unfortunately, when faced by the rising demands of Islamists and democrats alike for an end to despotism and corruption, and introduction of genuine democracy, the US intensified its support for the Muslim world's repressive regimes and their brutal security forces.

Another brief *tour d'horizon* of the Muslim world paints a dismal picture of the target of George Bush's purported "crusade for democracy."

MOROCCO

Morocco is a key American ally, ruled by a hereditary king kept in power by the army and secret police. A parliament and tame opposition parties provide democratic window dressing. Though the political climate has improved under the nation's new monarch, dissidents who cannot be bought off still face arrest, torture, and confinement in underground prisons in the Sahara. The CIA has sent many Islamist suspects to Morocco for "harsh interrogation."

A permanent charm campaign skillfully mounted in Washington by the Moroccan government, junkets to Marrakech and Fez for American legislators and journalists, and close but discreet links to Israel, ensured that few troublesome questions would be asked by Congress or the media about Morocco's human rights record.

ALGERIA

Few nations have undergone a more horrifying and bloody recent history than Algeria. In fact, compared to Algeria, Morocco's monarchy looks like a model of enlightened government.

After a decade of fighting to free Algeria from French rule, in which up to one million Algerians died, the nation fell under the control of revolutionaries turned corrupt socialist bureaucrats who exploited the oil-rich nation for their personal profit. In 1991, Algeria's military junta ran out of ideas on how to solve the nation's mounting problems, and allowed the Arab world's first free elections to take place. The parliamentary vote produced a landslide victory for the opposition Islamic Salvation Front. The army, encouraged by France, immediately annulled the election, arrested opposition leaders, and instituted martial law.

Protests, then uprisings broke out and spread across Algeria. Muslim militants, led by the Islamic Salvation Front and other militant groups battled the military junta. The nation nearly dissolved in an orgy of slaughter and bombings in which at least 200,000 died. Entire villages were wiped out, their inhabitants were beheaded or had their throats cut. Horrific crimes were committed by both sides. In many cases, according to defectors, government agents disguised as Islamic militants staged massacres that were blamed on Islamists.

After eleven years of ghastly mayhem, the US and French-backed military junta, which proudly called itself "the eradicators," largely suppressed the rebellion using ubiquitous torture, savage reprisals, armies of informers, and the most brutal methods imaginable.

With the exception of France, the outside world paid little attention to Algeria. But the violence there eventually spilled over into Europe. A breakaway faction from Algeria's Islamic resistance, the Armed Islamic Groups (known as GIA by its French acronym), joined a Moroccan extremist group to form the North African Salafist Group for Teaching and

Combat, forming a notoriously violent jihadist underground in Europe that would later be accused of the 2004 Madrid train bombing and attempt numerous other attacks.

Algeria's military junta became a full member of President Bush's war on terror and a recipient of significant US financial, military, and intelligence aid. US–French support for Algeria's junta has become a major driving force behind North African extremists' violent hatred of the West. In many ways, these North African Salafists, as they are now known, are even more extreme and dangerous than the members of al-Qaida, though far less understood by western security authorities.

TUNISIA

This country still remains a military dictatorship that holds occasional rigged elections. Its regime rejects all calls for democratic reforms as acts of "Islamic terrorism," and routinely arrests anyone who opposes the regime.

LIBYA

Once America's bête noire, Libya abjured its revolutionary past and, after 2003, became an American ally. Its eccentric dictator, Colonel Muammar Khadaffi, claims to head a "people's democracy," but, in fact, leads a fairly repressive regime with an active secret police.

EGYPT

Egypt is a military dictatorship behind a make-believe facade of parliamentary government, run since 1981 by former air force general Husni Mubarak. A staunch ally of the United States, which defends and sustains his regime, Mubarak has been an iron-handed but reasonably intelligent leader who has sought to keep Egypt out of pan-Arab troubles, comply with American wishes, and focus his nation's daunting economic problems while brooking no meaningful internal opposition. Egypt's ubiquitous security forces have crushed both violent Islamists and moderate democrats and Islamists. President Mubarak is said to be grooming his son, Gamal, to succeed him.

JORDAN

Ruled by the kings of the Hashemite dynasty since its creation after World War I, pro-American Jordan is one of the Arab world's better-run nations, but it still remains a feudal kingdom defended by a well-trained army and highly effective secret police ruling a restive majority Palestinian population.

SAUDI ARABIA, KUWAIT, THE GULF EMIRATES, AND OMAN

America's closest Arab allies retain their feudal political structure, though the progressive rulers of the Gulf emirates have been experimenting with various forms of local and parliamentary government. Perfunctory, half-hearted American efforts to get the Saudis to implement democratic reforms failed dismally.

YEMEN

Another key US ally, Yemen has been ruled by the same strongman, Ali Saleh, since 1978. Rigged elections, buying off opponents, and intimidation keep the regime firmly in power. President Saleh is said to be grooming his son to succeed him.

PAKISTAN

A former semi-democracy, Pakistan was run since a 1999 coup by military strongman General Pervez Musharraf, one of America's closest and most lauded allies. Rigged elections, bribery, intimidation, and threats of prison kept Musharraf in power and the democratic opposition scattered or in exile. In 2008, after the murder of Benazir Bhutto, Pakistan's traditional democratic parties united in a coalition to oppose Musharraf's continued dictatorship.

BANGLADESH

This Muslim nation of 150 million, the former East Pakistan, is one of the world's poorest, most distressed nations. It has suffered political instability and bitter feuding between rival political dynasties since its creation, leading to endless turmoil and military coups. In 2007, the army ousted Bangladesh's civilian rulers and staged a bloodless coup.

LEBANON, SYRIA, AND IRAQ

A trio of special cases: Lebanon is an ethnically fractured semi-democracy misruled by corrupt, US–backed Christian, Sunni, and Druze politicians locked in political tribal warfare with the Shia Hezbollah movement; Syria continues to be ruled by the Asad dynasty and is a bitter enemy of Washington; Iraq remains under US military occupation and is currently in political chaos as warring ethnic and political militias battle for power.

Washington's new Central Asian allies, the former Soviet republics of Kazakhstan, Uzbekistan, Turkmenistan, Tajikistan, and Kyrgyzstan, remain dictatorships under the control of their Communist "Red Sultans" and local KGBs. Communist Uzbekistan, a US ally, has a frightful record of human rights abuses and medieval torture, most notably boiling opponents alive. These grim "petrolistans" are becoming important suppliers of energy to the West and remain fierce foes of Islamists and other would-be democratic reformers.

The only Muslim nations closely aligned to Washington that can be called democracies are Turkey, Malaysia, and Indonesia, though the latter two have had dodgy elections in the past. But both now seem headed on a positive democratic course. Aside from highly strategic Turkey, they remain out of the ambit of the American Raj. The Mideast heartland of the American Raj remains steeped in autocracy and political repression.

A final important point needs be made about corruption. A primary goal of all militant Islamists is to cleanse the Muslim world of endemic corruption. The Holy Koran repeatedly warns against all forms of corruption and enjoins good Muslims to honest dealings. Islamists see the Muslim world's ubiquitous corruption, and particularly that of its regimes, as moral chains that keep their nations in bondage. Corruption, in the Islamist view, begins at the top and cascades down to the lower ranks of society. The monarchs and generals who rule the ummah, and the swarms of political and business parasites that feed off their power, are the progenitors of corruption, using it as a weapon to buy off honest men and keep thieves and fraudsters in power.

When peoples of the Muslim world are asked why they support militant Islamist parties, their inevitable response is that they do so because of the honesty and genuine concern by these movements for the common man. In a world of self-serving governments, rampant corruption, malfeasance, and double-dealing, where everything and everyone has a price, Islamic parties, with the exception of those in Pakistan, are seen as comparatively incorruptible and dedicated to promoting the common good rather than lining their own pockets. This point cannot be overemphasized.

Most people living in the Muslim world believe almost all their leaders can be bought by foreign powers or groups. The case of Sudan's late dictator, Jaffar al-Numiery, who took millions in bribes from international Jewish groups to permit Ethiopian Jews to transit through his nation on the way to Israel, is well known. Egypt's Anwar Sadat became the poster boy for corrupt rulers when it was revealed that his family and business associates had grown extraordinarily rich from the Camp David Accords while the average citizen lived on rice and beans. Revelations about secret CIA stipends paid to many other Muslim rulers only deepened the conviction that the ummah's rulers had been bought and sold like so many sacks of dates.

Egypt's Muslim Brotherhood, the rootstock of current Islamic movements, established the pattern for moral and financial rectitude. This creed of good government was taken up by its offshoot, the Hamas movement in Palestine, which provided education and social services to its members and, unlike the western-backed PLO–Fatah Party was not rife with corruption.

In Lebanon, the Hezbollah movement established a reputation for honesty and public welfare. Both Hamas and Hezbollah provided bribe-free government, and civic and social services. After highly destructive Israeli bombing in the brief 2006 war, Hezbollah astounded everyone by swiftly setting about the rebuilding of shattered buildings and bridges, cleaning up rubble and caring for homeless civilians while the US–backed regime in Beirut dithered and did nothing.

In the view of Islamists who make up 10 to 15 percent of Muslim political opinion, western powers have always fostered corruption as a device to control and weaken their colonial subjects, and continue to do so without relent. Accordingly, the struggle to oust western, and particularly American, influence is intimately linked to the Islamists' war against all forms of corruption.

America, as one overwrought militant Islamist claimed to this writer, "injects corruption into our veins like heroin." The only way to extirpate corruption from the Muslim world, say Islamists, is to purge the corrupt regimes that rule it, expel western influence, including banks, harshly punish all those who deal in bribes and kickbacks, and restore the moral and financial purity of early Islam. Americans would call it draining the swamp.

The western powers reject charges that they foster corruption. They insist they are merely dealing with moderate Muslim governments, encouraging economic and social development, and maintaining stability. Bribery and kickbacks are an essential part of doing business and diplomacy in the Muslim world. Resorting to them is not the West's fault, but that of the societies that produce such malfeasance and tolerate corruption.

From the Atlantic to the Java Sea, the sun never sets on the American Raj. The cruel old line about the Muslim world's rulers having to call Washington for permission to go to the toilet is even more painfully true today than it was thirty years ago when I first heard it in Amman. The president of the United States in the White House has replaced the queen empress in Windsor Castle as the imperator of the Raj.

The nations that comprise America's Raj are all hard-wired into the US system of international military and financial alliances. Their exports often depend on access to the US market, their military forces depend on US arms and spare parts, their political parties or leaders on secret finance from Washington, their regimes on US political support against domestic foes, and much of their money sits in US financial institutions. Many depend on the US for subsidized food, without which their people would riot. The leaders of the Raj are keenly aware that displeasing Washington could invite American political, financial, or military support for their domestic rivals and unfriendly neighbors. The US–engineered Ethiopian invasion of Somalia in December 2006 was the most recent example of the Raj's raw power at work.

Unlike most modern Americans, the Victorian British understood and accepted one important fact about their empire: their colonial subjects would occasionally rebel and fight back. Britain's imperialists called it "the price of empire." Such resistance was normal and expected. Mad Mahdis, spear-waving Dervishes, and Zulu war parties were popping up all the time across the vast expanses of Britain's empire. There would always be unenlightened savages and religious fanatics who would oppose the civilizing mission and wisdom of the empire. Just as a certain amount of crime in London's streets was inevitable, so was "criminal" resistance by various bands of angry misguided natives in the far corners of the British Imperium.

Most Americans, by contrast, have yet to understand they control a vast empire that rivals the former British Empire. It is hardly surprising they are startled, dismayed, and usually outraged when their subjects occasionally rebel and bite back, acts which are now commonly described away as terrorism.

Most Americans would probably be surprised to learn their nation has been involved in at least nine major military actions against the Muslim world since the 1980s alone, or that it has overthrown governments in the region and sustained or installed new dictatorial regimes with regularity. Or that polls show the United States is now seen by 70 percent of Afghans and Iraqis as an unwelcome foreign occupier rather than a liberator.

The attacks of September 11, 2001, did not come out of the blue. They were a huge, overdue installment payment in the costs of empire. Five days before the attacks, I predicted in my syndicated column that America's heavy-handed actions in the Muslim world would very soon provoke violent retaliation against the United States.

The natives are fighting back and America, like the old British Empire, finds itself waging a series of "little" colonial wars in exotic, faraway places for, of course, the advancement and defense of western civilization.

The element that makes the American Raj different by a whole order of magnitude from its British predecessor is that America's rebelling subjects are motivated not just by a nationalistic desire to throw off foreign rule, as in past colonial uprisings, but by an additional new force: collective anger and calls to action generated by a series of tragic, incendiary conflicts across the Muslim world that have ignited an extraordinary and unprecedented level of pan-Islamic fervor and anti-western violence. These crises, growing resistance to the American Raj, and opposition to western-backed dictatorships are the fuel powering much of the anti-western violence known as terrorism. To examine the roots of anti-western animosity and attendant violence, it is important to look at each of these tragic and deeply emotive events through Muslim eyes.

CHAPTER SEVEN
★ ★ ★

PALESTINE: THE FOUNTAINS OF RAGE

Today, the misfortunes and long agony of the Palestinian people are, along with resistance to dictatorships, the primary cause of the Muslim world's current anger against the West. But it was not always so.

During the creation of the state of Israel in 1947–48, some 750,000 to 850,000 Palestinians lost their ancestral homes and became refugees. Fierce debate has raged ever since over whether they voluntarily quit their homes, as most Israelis and their supporters claim, or, as Arabs insist, were driven out at gunpoint, or fled for fear of being massacred.

The official Zionist view that became widely accepted in America and Britain held that Palestine was "a land without people for a people without land." European Jews who had survived the Holocaust, went the official line, came to an empty land, a tabula rasa, devoid of any real population other than small numbers of nomadic Bedouin. These settlers made the desert bloom.

Israeli prime minister Golda Meir famously declared, "There are no such people as Palestinians." In fact, some Zionists claimed, Palestinians were a made-up nationality that had never existed. This was a rather rich claim coming from Israelis, many of whom hailed from Poland, Russia, and other parts of Eastern Europe, who assumed biblical identities and a reborn language, and asserted they were the direct descendants and rightful territorial heirs of an historic Israel that had existed over two millennia earlier.

Recent works by a number of leading Israeli historians have established that most of the Palestinian refugees were the victims of what today is called ethnic cleansing. The old canard that the Palestinians abandoned their homes at the behest of their leaders to clear a path for advancing Arab forces has been thoroughly debunked by respected Israeli historians like Ilan Pappe, Simcha Flapan, and Benny Morris, though Israel's right-wingers resolutely defend the cherished old myths about Israel's birth.

One fact is indisputable. These 750,000 to 850,000 Palestinians (some Arab sources put the number at a million) lost their homes and property, which were confiscated by the Jewish state as "abandoned property." Hundreds of Arab villages, particularly in Galilee, were bulldozed and all traces of their former inhabitants eradicated. Arab residential neighborhoods in towns and cities were denuded of their inhabitants. The forgotten Palestinian refugees ended up subsisting in tents and shacks in Jordan, Lebanon, Syria, and Egypt, where they were fed by the United Nations Relief Agency and the United States.

Israel's supporters have long portrayed its 1948 War of Independence as a desperate struggle against overwhelming Arab forces determined to drive Jews into the sea. "Israel versus 100 million Arabs." In fact, Israeli and foreign historians have shown that throughout the war, Jewish military and paramilitary forces outnumbered and outgunned local Palestinian irregular forces and, later, the feeble Arab contingents from five states that were sent to help Palestinian militias stop Jewish forces from expanding their areas of control.

Aside from Israel's immediate Arab neighbors, the rest of the Arab world, and indeed the wider Muslim world, were largely indifferent to events in Palestine, confining themselves to protests at the UN and a few demonstrations. The Muslim world was too fragmented, inward looking, and absorbed by local and provincial matters to care much about confused events in Palestine.

The small, poorly equipped, and even worse-trained forces sent by Syria, Egypt, Iraq, and Lebanon, and a small, ragtag unit grandly styling itself "the Army of Arab Liberation" proved pathetically inept. Rifles bought by Egypt from Italy had been sabotaged by Jewish agents so they would explode in the shooter's face. Grenades detonated when their pins were pulled. Supplies were stolen by officers and resold.

Egyptian and Syrian forces lacked artillery and rifle shells because the funds to buy munitions had been stolen by their corrupt generals. The Lebanese army ran away, while a small Iraqi force's sole contribution to the war effort was biting a number of Jewish fighters in close combat. The

Egyptian contingent ended, as so often in their wars with Israel, surrounded near Gaza in the Faluja Pocket. A young Egyptian officer named Gamal Abdel Nasser trapped at Faluja decided that when the disastrous war was over, he and his fellow junior officers would cleanse their nation of its shame and overthrow its corrupt, western-imposed rulers.

Only Jordan's British-trained Arab Legion acquitted itself with competence and honor in the conflict. A more humiliating disaster would be hard to imagine—at least until the Arabs' catastrophic defeat in 1967. The botched war left many thoughtful Arabs furious and deeply shamed; it led directly to the overthrow of Egypt's monarchy and Syria's government.

One of the most shocking events of the 1948 war did not come into public view until decades later. While ostensibly backing the Palestinians in the 1947–48 war, Jordan's British-supported King Abdullah secretly colluded with Israel's David Ben Gurion to strangle in the cradle the infant Palestinian state mandated by the United Nations, and divide up its territory with Israel. To this day, many Arabs believe that had Abdullah not reined in his Arab Legion and halted its offensive, the postwar state of Israel would have been closer to the original UN partition plan, and would have been unable to uproot so many Palestinians. Ironically, the Arabs had totally rejected the 1947 UN partition plan for Palestine, which envisaged a Jewish state that was much smaller than the one whose ultimate borders were formed by the 1948 war.

Abdullah was assassinated by Palestinians after the 1948 war and reviled by his foes as the "first Arab traitor." In the eyes of Arab nationalists and, later, the jihadist movement, Jordan's Hashemite dynasty is the fruit of a poisoned tree.

World War II and the ensuing years had seen huge dislocations of entire peoples and nations. Six millions Jews had been exterminated or died; millions more were uprooted. Over fifteen million Germans were ethnically cleansed from portions of Germany seized by the USSR and Poland, and from their ancestral homes in Eastern Europe; two and a half million were killed in this mass expulsion, and two million German women raped. Millions of Poles, Ukrainians, and peoples of the Baltic, and millions more Chinese, had become refugees during World War II. On Stalin's orders, Cossacks, Volga Germans, and many small Muslim peoples of the Soviet Union, notably the Chechens and Tatars, were either slaughtered or sent en masse to Siberian concentration camps.

Compared to these titanic numbers, the plight of less than one million Palestinians seemed relatively minor. There was widespread sympathy in North America and, to a lesser degree, in Europe, for Jewish suffering, and almost none for a people few had ever heard of, even in the Muslim world. But Palestinians were to pay the price for Europe's attempt to exterminate the Jewish people.

In a cruel twist of history, while nearly all of World War II's uprooted peoples had been peacefully resettled by the 1980s, the Palestinian refugee problem remained unresolved, becoming sand in the eye of the Mideast and, increasingly, a cause célèbre for the Muslim world.

A primary reason for this surprising development was the Arabs' callous indifference to the uprooted Palestinians and Israel's adamant refusal to allow at least some of them to return to their homes, or, at minimum, offer them fair compensation for their lost property. Israel, feeling itself besieged by the Arab world, missed its best chance to resolve what would eventually become an historic curse for all concerned; so did the Arab states, by failing to conclude a peace with Israel on the lines proposed by the UN partition plan.

However, it should also be noted that because of the creation of Israel, large numbers of Mideastern Sephardic Jews were compelled or elected to leave their ancestral homes in the Arab world, or were stampeded into flight to Israel by exaggerated warnings by the Jewish Agency of impending persecution. The exact numbers of this Jewish flight from the Arab world are uncertain, but 500,000 to 600,000 appears a reasonable estimate. Morocco, Egypt, Syria, Yemen, and Iraq were denuded of their Jews, who had been at the center of their commercial and intellectual life for a thousand years. Jewish property was nationalized; the Jewish refugees never received compensation. This exodus of large numbers of Sephardic Jews from the Muslim world, where they had been given refuge from the Inquisitions and pogroms of Christian Europe, and had enjoyed full integration and high respect in Muslim society, was the second Mideast tragedy of the 1940s and 1950s.

Jews who left or fled their homes in the Arab world were quickly, if not comfortably, settled in Israel, Europe, and the United States. Israel desperately sought more Jewish inhabitants and, with extensive US aid, made a huge effort to quickly integrate the newcomers.

By stark contrast, the majority of Palestinian refugees refused to be dispersed or resettled, believing they would soon return to their lost homes. Arab leaders of all stripes fatuously assured them that restoration of their rights would shortly be achieved. Arab nationalists built careers calling for the "liberation of Palestine." While this childish exercise in bombast went on, the growing numbers of Jewish settlers from Eastern Europe coming to Israel took over former Arab land, making it increasingly less likely that the original Palestinian inhabitants would ever be able to return.

All the while, the fecundity of the Palestinians made their problem ever larger. By the end of the twentieth century, the 750,000 to 850,000 Palestinians driven from their homes, and 500,000 more displaced by Israel after the 1967 war, had grown to seven million to nine million refugees scattered across the West Bank, Gaza, Jordan, Lebanon, Syria, the rest of the Mideast, and around the globe, including 214,000 in the United States. Israeli demographers warned the government that even accounting for the influx of a million Russians to Israel, as early as 2010, Arabs might well outnumber Jews in the land between the Jordan River and the Mediterranean Sea.

The 1967 Arab-Israeli War abruptly had changed the Mideast's political landscape. A triumphant Israel captured and annexed the West Bank, Jerusalem's Old City, Gaza, Sinai, and the Golan Heights, from which at least 50,000 forgotten Syrians were ethnically cleansed (Syria claims 250,000). The loss of so much Arab land and the third holiest city of Islam shook the entire Muslim world and brought the first significant calls for pan-national action to liberate Jerusalem and succor the Palestinians.

In spite of such sentiments and a great deal of fiery oratory, Palestine remained a secondary, or even tertiary, issue to most of the Muslim world so long as its people got all their news from their nations' state-run media. Arab and other Muslim rulers had personal sympathy for the Palestinians, but they also feared them as a potentially destabilizing influence and a source of unwelcome revolutionary zeal. Armed Palestinian militants, it was feared, might easily get out of control and bite the Arab hands that fed them table scraps.

So the most frequent response was to pay the Palestinian cause lip service, and shower kisses and small favors on their leader, Yasser Arafat, while confining PLO fighters to their bases and making sure they did not infect the local population with dangerous, revolutionary ideas.

No Arab leader wanted another Black Friday, such as had occurred in

Amman in 1970, when Palestinian fighters rose up against King Hussein and were crushed by the Jordanian army's US-supplied tanks. When Syrian troops and armor intervened to help the Palestinians, King Hussein got Israel to launch devastating air strikes that crippled the advancing Syrian forces and forced them to retreat.

Arab leaders, like Nasser, Anwar Sadat, Hafez Asad, and Saddam Hussein all used the cause of Palestine to rally their followers, and the "threat" of Israel as the excuse for many of their endemic problems. By the 1970s, thanks to billions in US military and economic aid, and an extensive nuclear program, Israel had become invulnerable and was so strong it could quickly defeat all of the Arab armies combined. But Israel's 1982 invasion of Lebanon, and its bungled campaign there in 2006, also starkly demonstrated that while Israel could readily defeat Arab regular armies and capture Arab land, holding on to it was another thing.

The Muslim world's heavily censored media kept the issue of Palestine at a low simmer until the first intifada erupted in late 1986. This spontaneous uprising by so many Palestinians against perceived Israeli repression could not be ignored or downplayed. The first and second intifadas also coincided with another event of profound importance: the Muslim world's growing access to uncensored cable and satellite TV, and that greatest of all modern liberating revolutions, the Internet.

Each evening, entire families across the Muslim world ate their dinner while watching harrowing scenes of Palestinian suffering on TV. They saw Israeli tanks shelling residential neighborhoods, Arab children throwing rocks at armored vehicles, Israeli troops brutalizing civilians, and, without relent, scenes of shrieking women, hysterical with grief, weeping for their dead husbands, brothers, and sons. They listened night after night to Palestinian widows crying out, "Who will help us?" and "Who will avenge us?"

Such intense scenes were new to most TV viewers in the Muslim world, and, of course, profoundly disturbing. Until the advent of satellite and cable TV, and the Internet, the conflict over Palestine had seemed a distant issue to many people in the Muslim world. The iconic TV footage of a Palestinian man trying to shelter his young son with his body from a hail of Israeli bullets became etched with acid in the memory and hearts of Muslims.

It is difficult to convey to westerners the impact of TV footage from the Palestinian intifadas on opinion in Muslim nations where illiteracy was high and newspaper readership very limited. In the West, we regard Mideast violence as a faraway event that is inherently part of the region's violent scenery. By contrast, most Muslims watch these same scenes with horror and anger, with an outraged sense of injustice, with shame and disgust, reacting in much the same way as Jews when they see the horrifying, grainy films of the Warsaw Ghetto uprising. The two events are not in any way comparable, but the emotional effects on their viewers are similar. Americans watching TV pictures of survivors in New York fleeing ground zero during the 9/11 attacks have a similar deeply disturbing reaction.

The intense reaction to these scenes of bloodshed and mayhem in Palestine has been identical right across the Muslim world, from North Africa to Pakistan or Indonesia, as this writer has witnessed on his travels. There was fury at Israel and, disturbingly, increasing anger against Jews. Until the 1990s, I had rarely encountered any anti-Semitism in the Muslim world in almost fifty years of residence and travel.

Until then, Muslims had been careful to say "Israelis" or "Zionists" to draw a distinction between proponents of Israel and Jews in general. But the growing belief across the Muslim world that Israel had taken charge of US Mideast policy and engineered the US invasions of Afghanistan, Iraq, and, most lately, Somalia, quickly fueled the rankest, most ugly, and irrational forms of anti-Semitism. Old European conspiracy theories that Jews ruled the western world through their control of finance and the media were reborn in the Muslim world and widely disseminated. The discredited anti-Jewish forgery "Protocols of the Elders of Zion" was reprinted and distributed in many Arab countries.

As the agony of Palestine continued, Muslims everywhere began to drop this careful distinction and simply use the term "Jews." At precisely the same time, and in a disturbing mirror image of this process, many influential Jews in North America—particularly the so-called neoconservatives—began to adopt an overtly hostile, even racist view towards Muslims, as distinct from their old foes, the Arabs. They regarded Islam as a deadly new enemy of the Jewish people and of the West, a position they energetically promoted in the media and in the US Congress. This Islamophobia was readily adopted by the neoconservatives' new allies, America's Christian evangelicals about whom, it was said, "their foreign policy is Greater Israel."

As much as Muslim anger was in spate against Israel and, increasingly, Jews, it was also directed with equal intensity at the United States.

Muslims blamed the United States, and to only a slightly lesser degree, Britain, for the creation of Israel, which was widely seen as a western colony implanted in the heart of the Mideast that was clearly designed to prevent Arab unity.

The geographical fact that Israel blocks all land communications between the two most important parts of the central Mideast—Egypt and Iraq—was not lost on the Arabs who often portray Israel in the shape of a dagger thrust into the bosom of the Muslim world. Israeli strategists were well aware that in spite of their nation's small size, its central position in the Levant gave Israel decisive tactical and strategic power, allowing rapid concentration of forces from interior lines and preventing Arab forces from Iraq, Syria, and Jordan from linking up with the most important Arab power, Egypt.

To no surprise, the surging anger of the Muslim world over events in Palestine became directed as much at its US-supported regimes as at Israel and the United States. As the first and second Palestinian intifadas flared on, Muslims everywhere kept asking why their governments could do nothing to help the Palestinians, and why their leaders refused to put pressure on their patron, the United States, to resolve the Arab-Israeli conflict.

The response of Egypt, the Arab world's leading military power, was to counsel Palestinians whose children were being shot down in the streets of Hebron and Jenin to "negotiate with patience," and to use "moderation." "How can we be moderate," retorted one Palestinian militant, "when the Israelis are using tanks and artillery against our homes?"

Egypt held endless ministerial meetings with the United States and Israel, the Arab League, various Islamic groups, and Yasser Arafat's Fatah Party. President Husni Mubarak issued platitudinous declarations urging Arab-Israeli cooperation and confidence building while, as the Cairo regime claimed, "working behind the scenes to bring a lasting peace." All of this verbiage was simply a thin smoke screen masking the fact that Egypt's military regime was, as its opponents claimed, working hand in glove with the US and Israel to maintain the status quo, prevent the Palestinians from getting their own state. Egypt feared Palestinian agitation would arouse nationalistic militancy inside Egypt, or, equally perilous, drag Egypt into another war with Israel that it would undoubtedly lose.

In the West, Egypt was hailed for its moderation in all things having to do with Palestine, and lauded for its ruthless repression of dissidents who, whether democrats, leftists, Nasserites, or Islamists, were all branded "Islamic terrorists."

By contrast, in the Muslim world, General Mubarak's military regime in Egypt was held up by nationalists and Islamists as the very model of western-imposed despotism that was betraying every aspiration of those seeking to free the Arab world of western control and corrupt, repressive rule. Egypt's image as a hypocritical enforcer of the American Raj reached new depths after Hamas's victory in the 2006 elections in Palestine. First the American publication *Vanity Fair*, then Arab media, revealed that Egypt and ally Jordan had colluded with the US to overthrow by force the democratically elected Hamas government.

Similar Islamist anger was directed at the regimes in Saudi Arabia, Morocco, and Tunisia, which, while paying lip service to Palestinian rights, were also working with Israel to thwart Palestinian aspirations and to cut down any Islamists that showed their heads. Israel's intelligence service, Mossad, had long played a discreet but highly important role in protecting the monarchies of Jordan and Morocco against internal opponents and various jihadi groups.

To Islamists and many nonreligious Muslims, it was the same story all over again: betrayal of the Palestinians in 1948 by the Jordanian monarchy. Now, it was the same Jordanian monarchy, plus the Egyptians, Moroccans, Tunisians, in league with other traditional foes of the Arabs, such as Turkey, Ethiopia, and Russia, who were again conspiring against Palestinians and the greater Muslim world.

The Arab member states of the American Raj, notably Saudi Arabia, Egypt, and Jordan, were badly shaken by the steady upsurge of anger over Palestine coming from their own people. Censoring media, staging do-nothing summits and feckless "liberation committees," getting the state-run Islamic clergy to issue soothing edicts, and naming streets after Palestinian martyrs no longer assuaged their citizens' ire. Increasingly, the cry was heard, "Our leaders are traitors and our generals are cowards." Riots broke out across the Muslim world, but were usually brutally suppressed and their organizers jailed and tortured. The US–backed Muslim regimes may have been hopeless failures at providing effective, honest government and human rights, but they were always highly efficient when it came to repressing dissent.

Washington rightly took alarm, fearing its Muslim satraps from Rabat to Islamabad might be swept away by popular fury or military coups. The Bush administration came up with what it believed was a solution: a "campaign for democracy" aimed at providing a vent for rising Muslim anger against the US–backed dictatorships, and, equally important, showing voters at home that the administration was indeed determined to bring the light of democratic government to every dark corner of the Muslim world. The meaningless slogan "Exporting Freedom" sounded very nice to many Americans. The final act of this surreal drama that alternated between black comedy and arrant hypocrisy was Bush's dispatch in 2005 of his friend, Undersecretary of State Karen Hughes to promote administration policies to the Muslim world. This lady from Texas, whose knowledge of world affairs did not extend much beyond the International House of Pancakes, was humiliated and scorned everywhere she went. Her doomed voyage was the worst diplomatic fiasco since Colin Powell preached war at the United Nations.

US Secretary of State Condoleeza Rice took over as standard-bearer for Bush's "democratic" crusade. She did not become an American Joan of Arc. Far from it, this weakest national security adviser and secretary of state in memory was received by heads of Muslim regimes with polite condescension and treated just as the president's daughter would have been if she had been sent her college junior year abroad on a whistle-stop tour of the Mideast.

Bush's democracy crusade sold for a while in the United States, where it was vigorously promoted by neoconservatives as a new justification for active military intervention in Muslim nations. One could almost hear the strains of "Onward, Christian Soldiers." But in the Muslim world and Europe, George Bush's latest brain wave was greeted with acid cynicism and contempt. In fact, while Condoleeza Rice was preaching democracy, at precisely the same time, the security services of Morocco, Algeria, Tunisia, Libya, Egypt, Jordan, Saudi Arabia, Yemen, and Oman were all intensifying efforts to root out any form of dissidence, trying to block satellite broadcasts, censoring the Internet, intimidating journalists, and locking up advocates of democratic elections.

In the Mideast, a few naive advocates of democracy, misled into believing that Secretary Rice's crusade might afford them some sort of cover, were audacious enough to make public criticisms of their US–backed regimes. They were quickly arrested on trumped-up charges and bundled off to prison where they were thrown into vermin-infested cells and promptly wired up to electric generators, beaten with electrical cables, or raped with broomsticks.

The seemingly endless agony of Palestine quickly came to symbolize for the Muslim world the many failures and wrongs of the western-supported regimes that ruled them. Palestine defined the weakness, incompetence, subservience, and moral failure of many Muslim leaders. It was a nightly slap in the face and a humiliation without relent. Palestine underlined in fire the political, moral, and religious illegitimacy of many of the Muslim world's regimes. According to Islamist opponents, not only did the ummah's regimes despoil, brutalize, and misgovern their own people, while virtually giving away their energy riches to the West, these rulers could not fulfill the primary Islamic duty of going to the aid of fellow Muslims suffering severe persecution.

Israel's use of US weapons such as armored vehicles, F-16 fighters and Apache attack helicopters, tanks and heavy artillery, Hellfire missiles, and 1,000-pound laser-guided bombs against Palestinian fighters and civilians generated intense anti-American animosity in the Muslim world. Muslims constantly accused the United States of a double standard in supporting and provisioning Israel's mini-war against Palestinians and Lebanon that employed US heavy weapons in clear violation of the US Arms Export Control Act which banned the use of US–made weapons against civilian populations. Congress has never enforced its own law in the case of Israel. Yet the United States condemned Saddam Hussein for using heavy weapons against Kurdish and Shia rebels after President George H.W. Bush encouraged them to revolt during the 1991 US–Iraq War.

Israel maintains it is fighting terrorism, defending its national security, and insists it always tries to avoid attacking civilians. There would be no civilian casualties, Israel contends, if Palestinian fighters stopped hiding among the civilian population and launching attacks from urban areas.

Of course, the Muslim world had its own double standards aplenty. There were few protests in 1971 when Pakistan's army massacred hundreds of thousands of rebellious Bengalis in then East Pakistan, or in 1982 when Syria slaughtered some 10,000 Sunnis in Hama who rose against the Alawite-run military regime of President Hafez Asad, or when the regime of Saddam Hussein allegedly killed over 100,000 Kurds when they revolted during the 1980–88 Iraq-Iran War. There were no protests at the murder of more than 200,000 Algerian civilians in the course of ferocious counterinsurgency operations by that nation's western-backed military junta against equally murderous Islamic insurgents.

In fact, the worst that could be said against Israel, which held itself up to be a paragon of western-style democracy in the Mideast, and thus due special consideration, was that it often mistreated its Palestinians with the typical brutality and cruelty of many Muslim regimes. It must also be said that however harsh Israel's repression and torture of rebellious Palestinians, many of them would likely still opt for an Israeli prison rather than one of Algeria's nightmarish prisons or Egypt's torture mills.

In a sad commentary on human nature, it has been this writer's observation when covering fourteen wars and civil conflicts that people will fight to the death against oppression and abuse by foreigners, but they seem to accept exactly the same kind of mistreatment from their co-citizens. In my idealistic youth, I organized demonstrations for Algeria's rebels, then known as the National Liberation Front, or FLN, who were fighting what seemed to be a noble struggle for independence from brutal French rule. Once in power, the Algerian Revolution, like its French predecessor, turned ugly and began devouring its young. Leader after leader was murdered in a gruesome power struggle. In the end, a cabal of socialist officers took power and has misruled and despoiled that wretched nation ever since. Algeria's current military rulers act with even more brutality than the French ever did, but somehow this is accepted by the Muslim world.

While acutely aware of the sufferings of Palestine, many in the Muslim world had little understanding of the complex Israeli-Palestinian negotiations that have struggled on for decades, of Israel's own internal political problems in trying to reach peace with the Palestinians, or of the Palestinians' chronic feuding, intriguing, indecision, and factionalism that made dealing with them an exercise in profound frustration. As Israel's witty Abba Eban wryly observed, "The Palestinians never miss a chance to miss a chance to make peace." All that most Muslims knew was that Palestinians were victims of Zionist aggression, ethnic cleansing, and persistent treachery by Washington, Jerusalem, and the "traitor" regimes of the Muslim world. The United States was blamed for everything. Since it was so all-powerful, at least in the Arab mind, everything that happened was due to Washington.

Though hardly the first to point out the shameful record of Muslim

governments over Palestine, Osama bin Laden became the most vociferous and widely listened-to exponent of the theory of betrayal. Palestine, the
bleeding heart of the Muslim world, the sacred land that held its third
holiest city, cannot be liberated, thundered bin Laden, until the Muslim
world's corrupt, treasonous regimes are swept away and replaced with
legitimate governments of the people. "The liberation of Palestine," he
preached, "begins in Cairo, and Rabat, and Amman, and Jeddah."

Bin Laden's thunder cast a baleful light on the basic political illegitimacy of the Muslim world's unelected, nondemocratic regimes. Few could
claim to have come to power legitimately, either by Islamic or western principles, or to retain it by popular mandate. None, save Hezbollah, the elected,
de facto government of half of Lebanon, could claim any military victories
over their foe, Israel. Even fewer could claim a genuine Islamic mandate to
rule, though the Saudi royal family's long embrace of the Wahabi-Salafist
movement conferred some religious respectability on it, at least in the eyes
of its tribal supporters in the remoter wastes of the desert peninsula.

In the Muslim world, and most of Europe, Palestinians were viewed as
inmates in a giant, open-air prison run by Israeli guards. This depiction
was reinforced by the so-called "security wall" Israel was building to enclose
areas designated as Palestinian enclaves, and to continue expropriating
more West Bank land and artesian water. This grim concrete barrier was
even taller than the notorious East German wall, and just as heavily
guarded. The difference was, of course, that no American president would
ever come to Israel and demand, "Mr. Prime Minister, tear down this
wall!," as Ronald Regan had done so dramatically before Communist East
Germany collapsed.

Israel's plans for the West Bank and Golan seemed clear: retain control
of all its high ground and water resources, as Prime Minister Ariel Sharon
had repeatedly urged the settlers' movement, keep the Jordan River valley,
surround Jerusalem with fortress-like Jewish settlements, and slowly
squeeze out its remaining Arab population. Those West Bank Palestinians
who stayed put would be compressed into a group of enclaves that would
be isolated from one another and surrounded by Jewish settlements,
checkpoints, Israeli-only roads, and Israeli troops.

The inhabitants of these "Arabistans" would have no direct contact
with the outside world. All their internal borders would be controlled by
Israel. They would be forced to rely on Israel for telecommunications,

water, tax revenue, fuel, food deliveries, and medical supplies, and kept under 24-hour Israeli surveillance by means of informers, listening devices, drone aircraft, and direct observation. Their inhabitants would be required to obtain Israeli permits to travel, to use designated Arab roads.

Sizable chunks of the West Bank—some estimates said 15 to 20 percent—that contained large Israeli settlements would be annexed to Israel. Troublemakers and their families would be exiled to the Gaza Strip, which had been designated by Israel as the major dumping ground for unwanted Arabs. "Let them cut each other's throats in Gaza," as one Israeli told this writer. He was not far wrong. Once Israeli troops pulled out of Gaza in September 2005, after a 38-year occupation, Palestinian factions fell on one another in an increasingly bitter struggle for political domination and control of lucrative rackets and payoffs.

In January 2007, the Muslim world was horrified to witness a mini civil war in Gaza between the US–backed Fatah faction and the democratically elected Hamas government. But what should it have expected? Gaza and the West Bank remained prisons for millions of Arabs. Much of the inter-Arab violence that raged through the West Bank and Gaza was simply a normal prison riot writ large. At the same time, the CIA was arming and encouraging Fatah fighters to launch a civil war against Hamas. The Arab media called these enclaves "bantustans" after the native reserves created by South Africa's former apartheid government. But as I observed when covering conflicts in the region, South Africa's white government never exercised the same degree of intense control over its autonomous bantustans that Israel does over its Palestinian enclaves.

Israel vigorously rejects any comparison to South Africa, insisting that the Arab enclaves it created—and those it intends for the future—merely recognize Arab population concentrations and are policed for the security of Israel proper and Jewish settlers on the West Bank. Israelis point to the fact that their expanding "security barrier" has resulted in a sharp drop in suicide bombings and armed attacks against Israel.

Jerusalem is a unique problem. The beating heart of the Jewish faith, this ancient hill city is also considered Islam's third holiest place, though some Jewish historians strongly challenge this assertion. Israel captured the Arab eastern portion of divided Jerusalem, called the Old City, during the 1967 war. Since then, Israel has been expropriating Arab property, building huge settlements around the city, and making life extremely difficult for its Arab inhabitants in hopes they would leave.

A key provision of the 1993 Oslo Peace Accords that were to provide the framework for settling the long Jewish-Palestinian conflict was that Israel would freeze all settlement activity in the West Bank and Gaza, and the Palestinians would cease all attacks on Jewish targets. Tragically, both provisions were violated, fatally undermining what had so far been the best chance at a comprehensive peace in half a century.

Israel's governments, both Labor and Likud, ignored the Oslo Accords and kept expanding existing settlements and building new ones, while dragging their feet on talks about a Palestinian state. At the time the Oslo Accords were signed, there were about 187,000 Jewish settlers on the West Bank. After the Accords, Israel moved 185,000 settlers into a ring of new settlement blocs it had created in an arc to the east of Jerusalem's Old City. These were huge, thick-walled reinforced-concrete apartment blocks designed as much as fortifications as permanent residences. By 2007, the number of Jewish settlers on the West Bank had grown to 260,000, plus another 200,000 in the Jerusalem blocs, for a total of 460,000. However, Israel denied it had brought in new settlers in violation of Oslo by claiming that the newcomers were not actually in the West Bank but were residents of Jerusalem, or had simply moved into existing settlements and were part of "natural growth."

The whole issue of demographics had become supercharged with politics and propaganda. Arab scholars and demographers claimed there were 3.8 million Palestinians on the West Bank and Gaza, 1.3 million in Israel proper, 2.6 million in Jordan (half its population), 395,000 in Syria, 388,000 in Lebanon, and 288,000 in Saudi Arabia. The total number of Palestinians, including the worldwide Diaspora, was over 9 million, according to Palestinian sources. As noted, Palestinians claimed they would soon outnumber Jews in the land between the Jordan River and the sea, mirroring estimates by some Israeli sources. Today, say Arab demographers, Jews outnumber Arabs in the West Bank, Gaza, and Israel combined by 47 to 53 percent, but the far higher Arab birthrate is expected to soon erode this difference and put Arabs into the majority.

Zionist groups, their US allies, and Israel's government insist these Arab figures were inflated, and that there are only 2.4 million Palestinians in the West Bank and Gaza, 1 million in Israel, and 1.6 million scattered elsewhere, a total of 5 million.

The real numbers most likely lie at the midpoint between the two sides' estimates—7 million Palestinians. Whatever the case, too many people are already packed into the West Bank, a mere 5,860 square kilometers of semi-arid land that is smaller than the tiny US state of Delaware.

The squalid Gaza Strip is only 360 square kilometers, twice the size of Washington, D.C., into which 1 million to 1.3 million wretched Palestinians are crammed, a population density three times more than Manhattan. In both cases, the Palestinians have been under economic siege by Israel for decades as their orchards and farmlands are relentlessly annexed, their natural markets and water resources cut off, their movements restricted, and permits to start new businesses denied. About half of the Palestinians of the West Bank, and about 75 percent of those in Gaza subsist on handouts from foreign donors. Recent studies show that over half of all Palestinian children suffer from malnutrition and most are deficient in education. Before 1948, Palestinians were among the most prosperous and best-educated members of the Arab world. Today, they have fallen near the bottom.

The story of one Palestinian man named Anwar pathetically captures the long series of national and personal tragedies this industrious but ill-fated people has suffered during the 1980s. I met him in the course of business in Amman, Jordan. Anwar was a markedly dour man who wore a perpetual frown and gave forth a perpetual air of the deepest melancholy. Most Arabs are cheery people, given to quick laughter and merriment. I never saw him laugh or even smile. In fact, I soon took to calling him "the man who never smiles." One day, a colleague of his explained why Anwar looked so melancholy.

He had grown up in Jaffa, Palestine, where his family were prosperous orange growers. At the end of the 1948 Arab-Israeli War, he and his family lost everything, were driven from their home by Israeli forces, and became refugees in the Old City of Jerusalem. There, Anwar started a modest business in the bazaar, selling fabrics. After two decades of very hard work, Anwar had managed to build up a successful business in a small building he had purchased in the Old City, and to support and educate his growing family.

Then came the 1967 Arab-Israeli War. The conflict provided Israel the opportunity to finally seize Jerusalem and the West Bank, long the goal of the Zionist movement. Israeli troops quickly stormed the Old City and declared it permanently annexed to Israel. Anwar's property was expropriated by the Israelis and his business ruined. Devastated, Anwar fled with his family to Amman, Jordan.

There, he used all his savings to set up another small textile business in a rented shop. He worked seven days a week. Three years later, violent combat erupted in Amman between King Hussein's Bedouin army and Palestinian militants that raged for a week. His modest shop was burned out during the fighting, and all his inventory destroyed.

In despair, Anwar took his family to the one place he was certain had to be safe, Beirut. Once again, he worked without cease and, with help from a relative, managed to get a business started in Beirut. By 1975, he had again built up yet another profitable small enterprise and seemed finally to have found peace and security. That summer, however, civil war erupted between Lebanon's Maronite Christians, Muslims, and Druze. Beirut became a battleground, and along with it Anwar's business, which was again destroyed.

Half-crazed and desperate, Anwar fled back to Amman, where he found work as a clerk in a cosmetics-import agency. When I met him, he had been resettled in Amman for a few years, but he still had about him the look of a hunted animal, and he never, ever smiled. His story is, more or less, that of the Palestinian people. Their suffering in no way equals that of the Jewish people, but then again, no people has a monopoly on suffering, and for Palestinians, their modern era is called "the disaster," or "naqba."

Palestinians were not only unwanted by their fellow Arabs, they had become an irritant to the Mideast, one that would not go away. Each time Palestinians believed they had found a savior—Nasser, Khadaffi, Arafat, Saddam—their hopes were dashed, and their "Arab brothers" exacted revenge on them.

The most tragic example came after the Iraqis were driven from Kuwait by the United States in 2001. In the run-up to that conflict, Yasser Arafat and many Palestinians saw Saddam Hussein as their potential savior; in reality, he proved their undoing. Saddam cynically claimed he had invaded Kuwait to force the West to pressure Israel into allowing millions of Palestinian refugees to return to their lost homes. Arafat foolishly lauded Saddam and backed his invasion of Kuwait.

After regaining power, Kuwait's royal family ordered 400,000 Palestinians, a full 30 percent of that state's total population, the core of its commercial and managerial class, expelled. The Kuwaitis, it should be noted, expelled almost half as many Palestinians as the new state of Israel did in 1948. So much for Arab brotherhood.

Seven years after the Oslo Accords, the second Palestinian intifada erupted in 2000 after it became clear to angry, frustrated Palestinians that Israel had no intention of halting settlement activity and was, in fact, accelerating it. Israel's ongoing assassination of Palestinian militants, known as "targeted killing," provoked revenge attacks by Palestinian bombers and guerrilla groups that were, inevitably, answered by more Israeli revenge operations. This cycle of violence, in which the death toll averaged ten Arabs for each Israeli, became impossible to halt.

It was also clear that powerful members of Israel's defense and security establishment allied to its right-wing parties, settlers' movement, and their neoconservative American supporters were determined at any cost to thwart Oslo and thus prevent the return of the occupied Arab territories and Golan. For them, retaining Greater Israel was their nation's paramount strategic and emotional objective.

Meanwhile, Palestinian militants such as Islamic Jihad and, later, Hamas, were just as determined to block implementation of Oslo, which they denounced as a US–engineered sellout that would leave Arabs with less than a quarter of original, pre-1947 Palestine, forever eradicating the rights of millions of Palestinian refugees to their lost homes, and making Jewish settlements permanent. Palestinian suicide bombers set about blowing apart the Oslo Accords.

Making peace was excruciatingly difficult; breaking it was extremely easy. In spite of the best efforts of peacemakers on both sides, the Oslo peace accords slowly eroded and then finally collapsed. Each timid step forward in the Arab-Israeli peace process could be halted by a single suicide bombing, targeted killing, or more retaliation bombing.

Outsiders constantly wondered why Palestinians did not cease their violent acts and rely on negotiations. They were often urged to follow Gandhi's splendid example. But the tough Israelis were not the British. Pacifism did not work in the internment-like camps of the West Bank and Gaza, and, unlike the clever, worldly Gandhi, the Palestinians had very little understanding of how to win sympathy abroad.

Armed resistance was hopeless. Palestinians had only small arms and

were chronically short of ammunition. Israel's highly efficient security service, Shin Bet, had informers everywhere, tapped all communications, and
maintained 24-hour overhead and ground-based surveillance of the Occupied Territories, which, after decades of pressure on the North American
media, are now most often referred to there as the Disputed Territories.

Palestinian militants could be picked off like fish in a barrel by Israeli
assassination teams, missile-firing drones, helicopters, and fighter aircraft.
Yet Palestinian groups like the al-Aqsa Martyrs' Brigade, Islamic Jihad,
and Hamas kept fighting back in spite of the fact that the only result of
their feeble efforts was to make the Israelis all the angrier and bring more
demands by Israelis for a harsher line towards their Arab neighbors.
Militants in besieged Gaza kept firing homemade rockets that killed or
injured a handful of Israelis and brought heavy bombardments and air
strikes by the Israelis that killed hundreds of Palestinians, both fighters
and civilians.

Some Palestinian militants believed they could emulate Hezbollah's
fighters in southern Lebanon by waging a guerrilla war that would eventually drive out the Israeli occupiers. But Hezbollah had rigid discipline,
infantry training, a secure hinterland, and modern heavy weapons like
antitank missiles and medium-range rockets, and room to hide from Israeli
counterattacks. Palestinian militants had only AK-47 rifles, homemade
rockets, suicide bombers, and rocks. The efficient Israeli security forces
swept aside Palestinian militants like flies and did not hesitate to punish
Palestinians for such attacks by liberal use of tank fire, bombs, and missiles, and by routinely demolishing Palestinian homes, a flagrant violation
of the Geneva Conventions.

The use by Palestinians of suicide bombers proved to be a catastrophic
mistake. Their ranks were filled with hot-blooded young militants who
sought revenge against Israel for the killing of their relatives and friends.
"If we had tanks and jet fighters, we would use them instead of our bodies,"
as one Palestinian militant put it, "but we do not. So our bodies become
our only weapons." Palestinian suicide attacks had a profound effect on Israel that their prior ambushes and occasional raids did not. Attacking settlers
and military posts was one thing, but attacks on innocent shoppers in
malls, markets, in cafés, and on buses was intolerable. Suicide bombers
terrorized Israel's civilian population and, for the first time, made it feel
vulnerable at home. The randomness and destruction of these suicide

attacks demoralized and frightened Israelis and inevitably brought furious demands for the government to exact fearsome revenge.

The waves of suicide bombers had another unanticipated effect: they silenced Israel's peace movement and the 50 percent of Israelis who had been favoring a permanent settlement with the Arabs. The gruesome carnage caused by the bombs made Israel's moderates and leftists run for cover, leaving the field to the Greater Israel Likudniks and their even farther-right allies who damned the Arabs as bloodthirsty beasts and called for ethnic cleansing of the West Bank.

The Palestinian suicide bombings provoked revulsion and horror around the world, inflicting enormous damage on their cause. Suicide bombings were ideal news stories for television: they were gory, horrifying, and confined to small, easily covered locales. When the African National Congress (ANC) bombed café and burger bars frequented by whites in South Africa, there was no international condemnation of these crimes. Yet when they were foolishly duplicated by Palestinians, the world was quick to denounce them as acts of terrorism. The US only removed Nelson Mandela from its 'terrorist list' in July 2008.

Israel lost no time in telling the world that the Palestinians were a bunch of evil, mad-dog terrorists with whom no civilized discourse could be possible, and who could not have any legitimate political grievances, being motivated only by blind hate and religious fanaticism. This image of bestial Palestinian terrorist bombers would later be adopted by the Bush administration in its wars against the Muslim world.

As so often in their recent history, Palestinians again demonstrated a stunning lack of understanding of media relations and the need to win public support in the West. In fact, they proved remarkably adept at wrecking their own cause and projecting the most negative possible images of themselves. While Israel promoted itself with images of tall, beautiful, female settlers making the desert bloom, the symbol of Palestine became the homely, unshaved, pistol-toting Yasser Arafat, who looked curiously like 1930s Nazi caricatures of Jews. Between the untelegenic Arafat, black-hooded marchers, and suicide bombers with their scary videotapes, and scenes of Israelis blown to bloody bits, the Palestinians broadcast an image to much of the non-Muslim world that their worst foes would have been hard pressed to create.

A few cynics might have wondered if Israel's always clever and resourceful intelligence service was not somehow behind some of these

Arab outrages. Surely the Palestinians could not be stupid enough to commit such barbarities that were promptly beamed to America's TV watchers? The Israelis were indeed master of "false flag operations,"[1] something they learned from the Soviet KGB, but all the negative public relations was being done by the Arabs themselves. They were playing to their own audiences who were demanding action, revenge, and emotional release, heedless of the damage to their cause and immaturity of their behavior. As so often in the Arab and greater Muslim world, empty gestures and histrionics came to replace reality.

In 1975, I recall talking to Syria's then minister of information. I told him, "For the price of one squadron of MiG fighters, you could run a highly successful public relations campaign in the United States that would help Americans understand your side of the story." He laughed and agreed, but, of course, did nothing. Seven years later, the Israeli Air Force shot down four or five squadrons of Syria's MiGs in one day.

Thanks to the Palestinians' failure to get their story across to the world, and their absolutely self-defeating suicide-bombing campaign, they went from being regarded as victims to terrorists. One is inevitably reminded of the wonderfully cynical Tallyrand's observation about Napoleon's murder of Louis de Bourbon, Duc d'Enghien: "a crime, to be sure; but even worse, a mistake."

Most of the Muslim world also reacted negatively to the suicide-bombing campaign, but with considerable sympathy for its motivation. Some Muslims called the bombers heroes and martyrs, but many understood that such ghastly behavior was wrong and self-defeating, and called into question the intelligence and maturity of the Palestinian leadership.

Israel struck back harshly at the Palestinians. At least 10,000 of them were held at any given time in Israeli prisons, including a few hundred children. Marwan Barghouti, seen as the successor to Yasser Arafat and often called "the Palestinian Nelson Mandela" by his supporters, was jailed on trumped-up murder charges in order to deprive the Palestinian movement of its most effective figure. His jailing, and Arafat's mysterious death,

---

1. False flag operation: an intelligence operation appearing to be mounted by one
    nation or group but actually mounted by another.

cleared the way for the pliant Mahmoud Abbas, the man selected by the US and Israel to lead the Palestinians.

Israel, backed by Washington, branded the imprisoned Palestinians terrorists. However, to the Muslim world and many Europeans, the captives were political prisoners and freedom fighters. Israel developed specialized techniques of physical and psychological torture designed by its doctors and scientists to break the will of Palestinian prisoners and make them reveal information or, very often, collaborate. Israeli and international human rights groups routinely protested Israel's mistreatment and torture of prisoners, but few in the United States or Britain cared, and Washington routinely blocked international efforts to censure Israel for human rights violations.

These interrogation, dehumanization, and torture techniques were reportedly later taught to US forces in Iraq and Afghanistan by Israeli "technical advisers" and "private contractors," forming a model for the later notorious human rights violations at Abu Ghraib, Bagram in Afghanistan, and Guantanamo. When I warned in early 2003 that if the US invaded Iraq it would end up duplicating Israel's occupation of the West Bank and Gaza, I did not imagine just how closely the two occupations would come to resemble one another. In the eyes of the Muslim world, the two occupations were seen as identical repressions. There was no difference at all, to most Muslims, between Israeli soldiers kicking down doors in Jenin and herding blindfolded Palestinian prisoners, and American soldiers in Iraq doing precisely the same thing in Falluja and Baghdad.

In fact, one of the more hotly debated questions among Muslim intellectuals and political leaders was whether the Israeli tail was wagging the American dog, or vice versa. The consensus was that Israel's right-wing politicians and their powerful American supporters had indeed managed to totally align US foreign policy with the interests of the Jewish state's right-wing parties. In the Muslim view, the US Senate, White House, and media had been co-opted by Israel. While this view is simplistic and takes little account of the complexities and nuances of the US political system, most people in the Muslim world became convinced that America and Israel were indistinguishable, two peas in a pod—and thus, a single enemy.

President Bill Clinton's administration was hailed as the most pro-Israel ever. During the Clinton years, Israel's center-left Labor Party had commanded considerable influence in the Democratic administration through pro-Israel Mideast experts aligned with it, such as Dennis Ross and Martin Indyk. At times, it was difficult to tell whether they were speaking for the US or Israel, but they favored a workable peace with the Palestinians based on territorial compromise. But their more moderate voices were quickly replaced when the Republicans who came to power included pro-Israel hawks like Richard Perle, Paul Wolfowitz, John Bolton, Douglas Feith, "Scooter" Libby, Elliott Abrams (convicted in the Iran Contra scandal), who bitterly opposed Oslo and favoured a Greater Israel that would dominate the Mideast, and, of course, Vice President Dick Cheney himself, godfather of Washington's neoconservatives. All of them were very close, emotionally and politically, to Israel's expansionist right-wing Likud Party. Perle and Feith had written a strategic plan in 1996 for Israel's hard-line prime minister Benjamin Netanyahu. Entitled "A Clean Break," it called for an end to the Oslo Accord, no concessions to Palestinians, and the overthrow of the regimes in Syria and Iraq. This notorious document would later become the strategic Mideast road map for the Bush administration.

Critics—even leading traditional Republicans—accused the Bush administration of having been "Likudized." Indeed, it was difficult to discern where Israel's Likud left off and the Bush administration began. Israel's American supporters had learned the lesson of 1956 when Washington ordered the Jewish state out of Sinai. In the ensuing five decades, they had come to dominate and guide American Mideast policy, and exercise a veto over it. No one in Washington cared or dared stand up to the Israel lobby. Those few legislators, academics, and journalists who got onto its blacklist were soon out of jobs or marginalized.

The supremacy of American neoconservatives aligned with Israeli conservatives effectively left them as the sole voice of Israel. American Jews who did not support the goals or methods of Israel's rightists were shut out of political discourse. Worse, Israel's moderates and its pro-peace left, who counted for half the electorate, became isolated, powerless, and were wholly ignored by Washington.

At the same time, Palestinians continued to grow more radical. The glaring corruption and ineptitude of Yasser Arafat's Palestine Liberation Organization (PLO) evoked widespread dismay and disgust among Palestinians. Hamas was founded in early 1980s by a highly respected religious figure, Sheik Ahmed Yassin, as an alternative to Arafat's discredited Fatah movement. Unlike Arafat's wholly secular party, Hamas emerged from a group of Islamic charities and the conservative Muslim Brotherhood. The new movement was dedicated to the twin goals of recovering lost Palestinian lands—which clearly meant removing the Jewish state of Israel—and creating a state based on Islamic law and run under the principles of Islamic governance and social justice.

There is very strong evidence that Israel's internal security service, Shin Bet, discreetly aided the formation and spread of Hamas. It did so by taking no action to curtail Hamas activities or funding. Some claim Israel even secretly financed Hamas in its early days. Israel hoped Hamas would divide Palestinian loyalties and undermine Arafat's Fatah and PLO. But like Israel's discreet early help for Lebanon's Hezbollah, its initial encouragement of Hamas backfired badly when the new movement gained widening popularity and was soon perceived as a stronger, more capable foe of Israel than Fatah.

Hamas's rapid spread, and attacks launched by some of its members against Jewish targets, assured a virtual state of war with Israel. The organization's venerated founder, Sheik Ahmed Yassin, was assassinated by Israeli forces in 2004, an act some believe was intended to foreclose in advance any hope of future peace negotiations between his movement and Israel. Just before his assassination, Yassin had called for an eventual peace with the Jewish state.

The main appeal of Hamas was that it was comparatively honest and efficient compared to the PLO, and provided social and civic services. The same attributes made the Hezbollah so popular and respected in Lebanon. The corrupt governments of Arab nations and the Palestinian territories failed to provide adequate or even minimal social services for their citizens. Education, medical care, housing, care for the elderly, and a range of other basic social programs were widely neglected across the Arab world, with the exception of the ultra-rich oil states of Saudi Arabia, Qatar, and the United Arab Emirates.

The new Islamist movements in Palestine, Lebanon, and Egypt set up and ran their own schools and medical clinics, built homes, and provided pensions and municipal services like garbage collection, clean water, sewage, and local transportation. They became, in effect, functioning sub-governments that gave rather than took from the people. Every block and village had a Hezbollah or Hamas official whose job was to look after the residents and help them in time of extraordinary need. To no surprise, these Islamist movements soon commanded ardent support, loyalty, and affection.

In 2006, Hamas won a landslide parliamentary victory in one of the Muslim world's only two free and honest elections, beating the Fatah Party of Mahmoud Abbas by 132 seats to 76. The United States, Britain, and the rest of the EU were shocked by the results, believing that the more pliant Fatah would easily win and thus earn final validation as the voice of Palestinians. Palestinian voters spoke, but not with the message the West wanted to hear.

On taking power, Hamas, to the West's consternation, reaffirmed its refusal to recognize Israel. Not surprisingly, Israel declared it would never deal with a movement that called for its destruction. Whether Hamas was really dedicated to Israel's destruction or merely using nonrecognition as its opening bargaining position remained uncertain due to conflicting statements by its leadership.

The Bush administration and Canada's new conservative Harper government quickly followed Israel's lead in seeking to isolate and crush Hamas. All three denounced Hamas as a dangerous "terrorist organization" linked to suicide bombings that was determined to "destroy Israel." Ottawa and Washington went out of their way to insist they would never talk to Hamas until it dropped its refusal to recognize Israel.

Beside offering good governance, minimal corruption, and a strong social conscience, Hamas appealed to Palestinians precisely because if its adamant refusal to recognize the state of Israel. This hard-line, rejectionist position created endless crises within Palestinian society, and brought a western economic siege of the Palestinian territories. The western-donated funds on which the Palestinians depended were cut off, imposing great hardship and causing malnutrition in the West Bank and Gaza, from which Israeli troops had only recently withdrawn.

Why, asked many westerners, did Hamas cling to a policy that was not only patently illusory, but also self-destructive? It did not take a military expert to see that Hamas, with a few thousand followers armed with AK-47 rifles, could hardly pose an existential threat to Israel. Israel's superb military had a half century's experience fighting feeble Palestinian irregulars, a large nuclear arsenal, and was the world's fifth most powerful armed force. Why throw away whatever Palestinians could gain from negotiations by holding fast to the preposterous notion that Israel could somehow be removed from the map?

Hamas's position made no sense to Americans, Canadians, or Britons, but a great deal of sense to Palestinians and their supporters in the Muslim world. Palestinians who had lost their original homes were being offered back only unwanted bits and pieces of what was to have been their state. Israeli settlers had taken the best land and water resources. The Arabs, Hamas said, were being offered only sand, rock, and humiliation. Hamas was speaking for seven million or more stateless Palestinians whose ancestral homes and property had been taken from them without even token compensation. Hamas would not let the world forget their plight, much as it was convenient for others to do so. Hamas accused Fatah of having sold out to the Americans, and claimed it was the only authentic voice of millions of Palestinian refugees.

The only weapon the Palestinians had, reasoned Hamas and other militant groups, was its refusal to recognize Israel. Recognizing Israel, warned Hamas, would forever and irrevocably nullify the land claims of the millions stateless Palestinians. Recognition would legitimize the usurpation of their lands and violation of their human rights and international law. Once the Palestinians recognized Israel—even if only within its pre-1967 "Green Line" borders—their rights and claims would evaporate and be forgotten. For this reason, Hamas repeatedly condemned the PLO/Fatah for recognizing Israel and "selling out the Palestinian cause" before agreement was reached on the rights of the Palestinian Diaspora.

Such was Hamas's maximum position. Behind the scenes, however, numerous of its senior officials, notably Sheik Yassin, had dropped broad hints that a peace with Israel would be conceivable, provided Israel recognized the rights of the dispossessed Palestinians and paid some form of compensation, or resettled at least some evictees, even if these were to be mostly symbolic measures. Israel utterly refused to consider any compensation or, far worse, resettlement of some Palestinian refugees, claiming to do so, even in reasonably small numbers, "would threaten the very existence of the Jewish state." Besides, Israel insisted, Palestinians had "abandoned" their lands and were due nothing from the Jewish state. This was a morally questionable and rather ironic position for a nation that continues to this day to demand compensation or restitution for Jewish refugees who lost properties in Europe during the 1930s and 1940s.

Israel's rightists insisted the state of Jordan was already a mostly Palestinian state. They had a point. Jordan's population was 50-60 percent Palestinian. "Let the Palestinians move to Jordan and make it their homeland," Ariel Sharon repeatedly asserted. But Palestinians had had no desire to be pushed into the arid wastes of Jordan. The desert was no compensation for the fertile lands of Jaffa and Galilee.

"Look at Oslo," Hamas leaders pointed out. "The Israelis made a deal and then violated it immediately by continuing to build settlements. Once we play our only card and recognize them, they will continue to colonize our lands. Who will stop them? America? It's been financing their settlement projects. Washington lets Israel do whatever it wants. Palestinians will be quickly forgotten." Israel, for its part, insists Hamas is a terrorist organization with whom negotiations are both impossible and unethical. In the words of President George Bush, Hamas is "pure evil," a disease that must be eradicated without mercy.

Furthermore, many Israeli rightists subscribed to the position originally enunciated by founding father David Ben-Gurion that the state of Israel was a work in process and its borders should not be fixed or even defined. Some on the hard right even favored a very large Jewish state encompassing parts of Egypt, Lebanon, Syria, and all of Jordan, hence the old, pre–World War II slogan "from the Nile to the Euphrates." But such grandiose ambitions were harbored by only a small number of militants of the extreme right whom Ben-Gurion and his allies branded fascists.

Addressing Israel's impending sixtieth anniversary, the brilliant Israeli thinker, veteran political critic of the right and former Knesset (parliament) member Uri Avnery wrote:

> That is the reason for David Ben-Gurion's refusal to include in the Declaration of Independence of the new State of Israel any mention of borders. He did not intend for a minute to be satisfied with the borders fixed by the United Nations General Assembly resolution of November 29, 1947. All his successors had the same approach. Even the Oslo agreements delineated "zones" but did not fix a border. President Bush accepted this approach when he proposed a "Palestinian state with provisional borders"—a novelty in international law.
>
> In this respect, too, Israel resembles the United States, which

was founded along the Eastern seaboard and did not rest until it had reached the Western shores on the other side of the continent. The incessant stream of mass immigration from Europe flowed on westwards, breaching all borders and violating all agreements, exterminating the Native Americans, starting a war against Mexico, conquering Texas, invading Central America and Cuba. The slogan that drove them on and justified all their actions was coined in 1845 by John O'Sullivan: "Manifest Destiny."

The Israeli version of Manifest Destiny is Israeli military leader and politician Moshe Dayan's slogan: "We are fated." Avnery cites an important speech Dayan delivered in August 1968, after the occupation of the Golan Heights, before a rally of young kibbutzniks. Dayan had this speech inserted into the parliamentary record, a very unusual act according to Avnery.

Avnery continues:

This is what he [Dayan] told the youth: "We are fated to live in a permanent state of fighting against the Arabs...For the hundred years of the Return to Zion we are working for two things: the building of the land and the building of the people ... That is a process of expansion, of more Jews and more settlements...That is a process that has not reached the end. We were born here and found our parents, who had come here before us...It is not your duty to reach the end. Your duty is to add your layer...to expand the settlement to the best of your ability, during your lifetime... (and) not to say: this is the end, up to here, we have finished."

Dayan, who was well versed in the ancient texts, probably had in mind the phrase in the Chapter of the Fathers (a part of the Mishnah, which was finished 1,800 years ago and formed the basis of the Talmud): "It is not up to you to finish the work, and you are not free to stop doing it."

That is the hidden agenda (of Israel's rightists). We must haul it up from the depths of our unconscious minds to the realm of consciousness in order to face it, to reveal the terrible danger inherent in it, the danger of an eternal war which may in the fullness of time lead this state to disaster.

The extreme Palestinian and Israeli positions certainly appear irrec-oncilable, but one must remember that this is the Mideast, where bazaar haggling was old when Babylon was young; when buying a carpet, spice, baklava, or baubles in the souk, or holding high-level political talks, negotiations always begin with maximalist positions. One usually offers half of what one finally expects to pay; the shop owner begins by demand-ing twice what he expects, then gradually reduces his price over little cups of cardamom-flavored coffee.

Most Israelis and Palestinians understand fully that they will eventu-ally have to work out a modus vivendi. The question is, how much will each side end up paying? And how painful will these concessions be?

In spite of a worrying growth in the number of Holocaust deniers in the Muslim world, there still remains a general perception and under-standing that the Jewish people suffered genocide in the 1930s and 1940s and deserved special treatment. But Muslims keep asking the following awkward question: Since Europeans committed this historic crime, why were they not the ones to pay? Why was a part of Germany not turned into a Jewish state? Why did Palestinians have to pay for the sins of others?

Furthermore, Palestinians find themselves in a political trap. Their plight would have remained unknown to the world were it not for the 1970s aircraft hijackings. I met the author of this first major act of terror-ism, Palestinian militant George Habash, in Tripoli, Libya. He was a Christian and a Marxist. "If we had not committed this act," he told me, "who would have ever listened to us? Our people were living in tents and slums thirty years and no one cared." Unfortunately, this man who was billed as an archterrorist by the West and Israel had a point.

Without the two intifadas against Israeli occupation, the Palestinian cause would have languished. Palestinians keenly remember the much-ballyhooed Camp David Accords that were supposed to bring them a homeland but ended up ignoring it. The Palestinian issue had simply been included to keep the rest of the Arab world off Egypt's back after Anwar Sadat sold out his Arab allies in one of modern history's great acts of cynical political bribery in which Egypt got over one billion dollars annually, and the Palestinians nothing.

To many of the Palestinians and their Muslim supporters, it seemed that once they ceased making trouble and accepted the undeniable reality of Israel, they and their cause would surely be forgotten. Palestinians thus seemed condemned to a permanent position of rejection and violence, at least so long as they lacked a viable state and some form of compensation for their losses.

In the view of Israel's dominant rightist and center-right political leaders, their nation already had what it had long coveted: Jerusalem, the West Bank, and the Golan Heights with its water resources. Holding on to these territories was problematic and expensive, but infinitely preferable to returning to Israel's narrow, pre-1967 borders and, horror of horrors, handing back the Old City of Jerusalem to Arab control. What's more, Egypt had been removed from the Arab confrontation with Israel, Iraq crushed by the United States, and old foe Syria was just about surrounded. Israel was clearly in the best position it had ever been. Why change?

Suicide-bombing campaigns conducted by Palestinians convinced even many peace-minded Israelis that they could never afford to return to the old borders. In fact, the reason long given for Israel holding on to the West Bank and Golan—the need for strategic depth under threat of land offensives from Syria and Iraq—had vanished. Iraq was occupied by the US and Syria's forces were obsolete. The only serious military threat to Israel after Iraq's defeat came from Iran's medium-range Shahab missiles.

So, in the right wing's view, it was very much in Israel's interest to maintain the status quo. Empty peace talks would be held to please Washington, whose Arab allies were under rising pressure from their own restive citizens and were hounding the US to do something about Palestine. While the meaningless talks droned on, settlements would continue to be expanded; the security barrier, when completed, would wall up the Palestinians, keep them away from Israel, and carve out large chunks of the West Bank containing Israeli settlements. As long as Israel avoided serious peace talks with Syria, its continued hold on the Golan Heights was assured. Some members of Israel's right even feared that once the process of Zionist expansion ceased, Israelis would lose their national ethos and turn into a bunch of soft bourgeois unable to withstand the dangers posed by the Arabs around them.

To the rest of the Muslim world, Palestine remains a bleeding wound, a reminder of past humiliations by western colonialists, a symbol of their weakness and shame. Palestine remains a symbol of Muslim moral, political, military, and technological failures, of backwardness, and inability to deal effectively with the modern world.

Most Muslims long ago concluded that the agony of Palestine was the fault of the United States and Britain. They would like to see the US press Israel into a durable peace settlement, open relations with Iran and Syria, and implement a nuclear-free zone in the Mideast. But, of course, this plan is unlikely to ever see the light of day so long as US Mideast policy remains in the grip of influential lobbies aligned to Israel's expansionist rightist parties and to militant Christian Evangelical fundamentalists—aka Christian Zionists—who now make up some 40 percent of Republican voters, and have come to dominate the party. Under the leadership of Senator John McCain, the Republican party appears headed even further to the right than under George W. Bush and, if that is possible, even more supportive of Israel's rightists.

Meanwhile, the Muslim world is so busy directing its anger and desire for revenge over Palestine against the western powers that it fails to face its own heavy responsibility for the continuing tragedy of Palestine. In a final irony, many of the Muslim nations that continually profess such outrage over Israel's harsh subjugation of Palestinians mistreat their own people with even more brutality. Indeed, Israel's Palestinians, though second-class citizens often enjoy more human and civic rights than do citizens of neighboring Arab nations.

A half century after being evicted from their homes, Palestinian refugees and their millions of descendants are today no closer to regaining their lost rights than they were in 1948. For them, the clock has stood still. For the rest of the world, and particularly the United States, they continue to be a dangerous problem that will not go away.

CHAPTER EIGHT
★ ★ ★

OSAMA BIN LADEN

The headquarters and international nerve center of what was to become the world's most dangerous terrorist organization was a tiny storefront in a dilapidated, two-story building in the teeming bazaar of Peshawar, Pakistan.

The shabby, poorly lit shop with dirty windows, grandly titled the Afghan Information Center, was piled high with stacks of cheaply printed political tracts and pamphlets in Urdu, Pakistan's national language, Arabic, and English. Dust hung thick in the air. An elderly blue mimeograph machine occupied one corner.

This modest undertaking, known as the Mujahidin Service Bureau, I was told by my Pakistani hosts, with more than a touch of sarcasm, was the official voice of the Afghan resistance, or mujahidin, charged with telling the outside world, and particularly the Muslim nations, of the then little-known struggle being waged against the Soviet occupation of Afghanistan. The year was 1986.

At one end of the crowded room was a flimsy desk, also piled high with publications, behind which sat a small, scholarly-looking middle-aged man in a tattered sweater, wearing old-fashioned, round glasses. He rose as I came in, introduced himself as Abdullah Azzam, greeted me warmly, and offered me tea. The diminutive, intense man, who would later be recognized as creator of the Muslim International was a displaced Palestinian who held a doctorate in law from Cairo University and was one of the leading advocates of unrelenting jihad to liberate the Muslim world. For the next three hours the man who came to be known as Sheik Abdullah spoke to me in a measured but forceful voice of the suffering of the Muslim world, and particularly of his fellow Palestinians and the Afghans.

He kept handing me political tracts to illustrate his point that Muslims everywhere were still victims of western or Soviet imperialism. One read, "Soviet Crimes in Afghanistan"; another, "The plight of Philippines Muslims"; another, "The Occupation of Palestine," and so on. Azzam had assigned himself two daunting missions: to tell an uncaring, heedless world the story of the bloody struggle to liberate Afghanistan, and to keep track of the growing numbers of men coming to Peshawar from the four corners of the Muslim world who were seeking to go north and fight the Soviets in the Great Jihad. The sheik would record their names and information so that if they failed to return from battle in Afghanistan, he could notify their families.

Sheik Abdullah also ran a dingy little rooming house next to his office for Muslim mujahidin headed for Afghanistan that came to be known as "the base" or "the center," and in Arabic, "al-Qaida." Rarely in history has an international revolutionary movement sprung from such modest origins.

I vividly recall the moment when Azzam stood up, paused for moment, took a deep breath, pointed at a large school map on the office wall, and then said slowly, and with the deepest certitude, "We the mujahidin are going to defeat the godless Soviet Communists and their Afghan Communist dogs." How could the lightly armed mujahidin defeat the world's greatest land power? I wondered, dismissing the sheik's claim as typical Arab braggadocio.

His next statement stunned me. "When we have finished driving the Soviet imperialists from Afghanistan, we mujahidin will then go and drive the American imperialists from Arabia, and then liberate Palestine." I had never before heard America's dominant role in the Muslim world equated to Soviet imperialism.

Such epic ambitions from a little man armed only with some ballpoint pens and mimeographed pamphlets in a little shop in the Peshawar bazaar seemed preposterous. At the end of the Afghan war, just as the defeated Soviets were pulling out of Afghanistan, Abdullah Azzam was killed near Peshawar by a car bomb. His assassins have never been identified. Most Pakistanis, however, believed they came from the CIA, though the KGB was also suspect. Azzam's quixotic cause appeared to have been buried with his shattered body.

But this was not so. Among the tens of thousands of young men of the Muslim International Brigades who came to fight the Soviets in Afghanistan—the Communists branded them Islamic terrorists—was a young engineer from one of Saudi Arabia's wealthiest families, the bin Ladens. Unlike his youthful contemporaries who went off to Europe to drink, whore, and squander their princely allowances, Osama bin Laden, who had always been a very serious, intense young man, went to wage the Great Jihad in Afghanistan. He quickly became a role model for other young Saudis who were increasingly disgusted and disillusioned by the westernized lifestyles and grotesque self-indulgence of the Saudi elite.

Bin Laden joined the mujahidin in their fight against the Soviets and puppet Afghan Communist army. Bin Laden was wounded six times in combat, earning wide renown and deep admiration in Afghanistan and Pakistan for his courage, tenacity, and Islamic modesty. It was during this period of combat that bin Laden developed what was to become one of his hallmarks, emulation of the ansar.

The tall, very thin Saudi multimillionaire earned respect and admiration for following the early Islamic ideal of a virtuous, ascetic lifestyle that included subsisting on beans and bread, sleeping on the ground or in insect-infested caves, and deporting himself with genuine modesty, self-restraint, and respect for his companions.

Bin Laden spent a good portion of his personal fortune importing bulldozers and Arab engineers into Afghanistan. His men and machines dug deep caves for the mujahidin and their supplies that sheltered them from incessant Soviet air strikes. Bin Laden's "cave war" played an important role in the final Islamic victory. The young Saudi's renown soared in Afghanistan and Pakistan, and he became well known around the Muslim world as a sort of new Arab—dynamic, focused, determined to fight injustice and follow the principles of the Koran. In short, the very antithesis of the image of the timid, debauched, lazy Saudis whom Bin Laden and his men sneeringly dismissed as "fat women."

During the later 1980s, bin Laden also worked with Abdullah Azzam to organize his guesthouse and record-keeping operation. He quickly fell under the spell of the Palestinian revolutionary, and became one of his most ardent disciples. It was from Sheik Abdullah that Osama bin Laden adopted his strategy and worldview of a transnational jihad to drive American and British influence form the Muslim world. The dreamer and the engineer joined forces, turning a run-down little guesthouse into an organization that would come to profoundly challenge the might of the United States and its allies.

I crossed paths once with bin Laden, who had become widely known by the honorific Sheik Osama. It was during fighting outside Jalalabad, the Afghan city that commands the route from Peshawar to Kabul. I had been in battle with mujahidin against Afghan Communist troops, backed by armor and artillery. As is the Afghan custom, the battle ended before dusk and all sides repaired to their various homes or camps. I was taken to the sprawling, mud-walled compound of my host, local warlord Hadji Abdul Qadeer, who later became vice president of US–occupied Afghanistan and was assassinated by unknown assailants in Kabul in 2002.

We were about twenty men in a long, rectangular room covered in colorful Persian and Afghan carpets, reclining on round bolsters set against the wall. After about half an hour of smoking, drinking tea, and chatting, we all rose and prepared to go our various ways. I later recalled one man from the group because he was much taller than the others, remarkably thin, even gaunt, and did not look Afghan. I guessed he was a Yemeni. He had the expressive eyes and pale, thin, angular face of one of Velasquez's martyrs, and exuded an aura of profound calm and dignity, as well as an almost religious solemnity. The warrior smiled at me gently. He offered me traditional greetings in Arabic and I replied in the same tongue.

I asked one of my companions who he was.

"Ah, Mr. Eric, he is a Saudi mujahid who has come from far away to perform his jihad with us, Allah be praised."

At the time, I took no further notice of him and soon left the group. Why should I have? He was then only one of tens of thousands of foreign mujahidin who had come to fight the Communists. At that time, these Islamic militants were hailed by the Reagan administration and the western media as freedom fighters. It was only when Osama bin Laden and other veteran mujahidin freedom fighters undertook Sheik Abdullah Azzam's goal of liberating Arabia, Palestine, and North Africa from western domination that they came to be reviled by the West as terrorists.

After the end of the war in Afghanistan, Osama bin Laden and a handful of followers returned to Saudi Arabia, where they began agitating against the royal family, accusing the oil kingdom's 7,000-plus princes and princesses of misgoverning, virtually giving away Islamic resources, and being lackeys of the United States and Britain. Not surprisingly, the rogue scion of one of the kingdom's wealthiest families was deported in 1992, and stripped of his citizenship two years later. His family's influence, and his Afghan fame, protected him for a time from jail, or assassination by Saudi intelligence.

Bin Laden moved to Sudan where he set up an agricultural business. In the process, he reportedly lost millions of dollars dealing with the deeply corrupt Khartoum regime. In 1996, he packed up and returned to Afghanistan, where an avowedly fundamentalist Islamic regime, the Taliban, had taken power after defeating a coalition of Communist-dominated Tajiks and Uzbeks. Bin Laden was welcomed by the Pashtun Taliban as a returning hero of the Great Jihad and offered facilities, dubbed liberation camps, to train new mujahidin to fight the remaining Communists in northern Afghanistan, Central Asia, and the Indians in Kashmir.

In 1996, Osama bin Laden promulgated a remarkable document from his lair in the wild Hindu Kush that was to exert enormous influence over the coming decade. It was a "fatwa," or religious decree, grandly entitled "Declaration of War Against the Americans Occupying the Land of the Two Holy Places."

According to usual Islamic religious practice, only religious scholars and leading prayer leaders could issue a fatwa. Bin Laden was widely derided in the Muslim world for having the effrontery to do so. But, as he rightly insisted, during the early days of "pure Islam," any pious Muslim could issue a fatwa or lead prayers. Like other purist Sunni Muslims, bin Laden opposed any form of clerical establishment coming between believers and God. Bin Laden's fatwa was cleverly designed to anoint himself with the aura of an Islamic redeemer, or Mahdi, and to apply a moralistic, religious veneer to his political movement.

At that time, hardly anyone in the western world paid attention to the defiant gesture of a then-unknown man in the mountains of Afghanistan. The few experts on the region that read Osama bin Laden's declaration of war dismissed it as the ravings of an obscure Islamic *enragé*. A little over a half century earlier, Sir Winston Churchill had also dismissed another world-shaker, India's Mahatma Gandhi, as "a half-naked fakir."

What hardly any westerners understood at that time, including US and British intelligence, was that Sheik Osama, as he had come to be known, was the most recent incarnation of the long line of Muslim redeemers, discussed in Chapter Three, who had led resistance to western occupation and colonization. Like his predecessors, the Mahdi in Sudan, Abdel Kader and Omar Mukhtar in North Africa, and more recent Afghan tribal insurgents, Osama bin Laden had appointed himself to the role of religious guide, redeemer, and savior.

As occurred in the case of his predecessors, some of the "ulema," or assembly of Muslim notables, gave bin Laden support and religious approval, but the majority of the religious establishment did not, considering him an upstart and parvenu. Bin Laden remained an independent figure, answerable to no one, and operating beyond the bounds of any state, organization, or formal religious establishment. He was sui generis.

Like his jihadist predecessors, Osama bin Laden took upon himself— critics said arrogated to himself—the mission of freeing the Muslim world from what he termed oppression, plunder, and humiliation. Bin Laden's call for an international uprising was not at all understood in the West, which was unused to independent actors operating outside the normal political framework in which states held a monopoly on violence. Perhaps the only precedent to bin Laden was the Argentine Marxist revolutionary Che Guevara, who also launched what was essentially a one-man jihad against America's pervasive influence in Latin America. But Guevara was backed by Cuba; bin Laden was a warrior with no state support and, after the US invasion of Afghanistan, no place to even call home. He became the quintessential man without a country.

While the West reviled Osama bin Laden, to his many admirers in the Muslim world he appeared a second Che Guevara in a turban. Like the dashing Che, bin Laden's crusade, and its quixotic, idealistic nature, sparked the imagination of Muslim youth, to whom he directly and repeatedly appealed, and who formed the foundation of his expanding movement.

Bin Laden's November 2002 jeremiad against the West, "Letter to America," fully promulgated his cause and formed the ethos of his movement and other like-minded jihadist groups that bedevil the West today. It is thus worth careful consideration, not the least because it was largely suppressed by western media and rarely reproduced in full.

"Why are we attacking you?" bin Laden rhetorically asked. "Because you attacked us and continue to attack us."

The United States, he asserted, has sustained the "military occupation" of Palestine for the past fifty years. The creation of Israel was a "criminal act" committed by the United States. According to bin Laden,
Arabs—not Jews—are the true descendants of Abraham and Moses, and
thus entitled to Palestine!

Bin Laden accused the West of attacking Muslims in Somalia, of
supporting Russia in its brutal repression of the Chechens and India's
occupation of Kashmir, and the 1982 Israeli invasion of Lebanon.

Muslim regimes installed by the West "steal our *Ummah's* wealth and
sell them to you at a paltry price," the "biggest theft in history." Pro-
American Muslim regimes collaborated to create Israel. The West "occupies
our countries" and installs military bases in the Muslim world.

In Iraq, charged bin Laden, US sanctions caused the deaths of 1.5
million Iraqi children (the UN figure is 500,000). "Yet when three thousand
of your people died (referring to 9/11), the entire world rises and has not
yet calmed down."

Since Americans pay the taxes that buy the bombs dropped on Arabs
and finance Israel, since they have "killed our civilians," bin Laden proclaimed Muslims had the right to kill Americans, both soldiers and
civilians. It should be noted that bin Laden's murderous summons to
primitive, eye-for-an-eye retribution and blanket responsibility of all civilians was denounced by almost the entire Islamic religious establishment
and most ordinary Muslims as un-Islamic. Polls across the Muslim world
showed that while a majority of Muslims supported bin Laden's defiance
of the United States, they rejected his claims that killing western civilians
could in any way be justified.

Not content with declaring open season on Americans, bin Laden,
sounding rather like an Arab version of the late evangelist Reverend Jerry
Falwell, who blamed the 9/11 attacks on homosexuality and moral laxity,
went on to excoriate the United States as a nation of lies, debauchery,
homosexuality, fornication, drunkenness, gambling, and usury. America,
bin Laden thundered, is the world's largest consumer of drugs and leading
producer of alcohol.

Bin Laden took special aim at President Bill Clinton's Oval Office
escapades as a prime example of American immorality. He claimed the
West exploits women as sexual tools to sell consumer products, and debases
women while claiming to be a champion of women's liberation in the Third

World. America created and spread AIDS, claimed bin Laden, offering no proof whatsoever.

Osama Bin Laden even donned the mantle of an outraged environmentalist, accusing the United States of "destroying nature with your industrial waste and gases more than any other nation in history. Despite this, you refuse to sign the Kyoto agreements so that you can secure the profits of your greedy companies and industry."

Bin Laden's anti-American litany terminates with an accusation that captured one of the principal grievances of the Muslim world against the United States, its double standards.

"All (your) manners, principles and values have two scales: one for you, and one for others. The freedom and democracy that you call to is for yourselves and for white (sic) race only; as for the rest of the world, you impose upon them your monstrous, destructive policies and governments, which you call the 'American friends.' Yet you prevent them from establishing democracies."

According to bin Laden, America allows its friends to keep nuclear weapons while denying them to others. Washington flouts international law, and has permitted Israel to do so for fifty years. The US refuses to join an international criminal court while committing war crimes across the Muslim world. "What happens in Guantanamo is an historical embarrassment to America and its values."

Osama bin Laden's call to arms specifically mentioned the loss of Jerusalem, the murder of his mentor, Sheik Abdullah Azzam, and the jailing of Sheik Ahmed Yassin, founder of Hamas, by Israel, and the blind Egyptian cleric Sheik Omar, in New York. Bin Laden modestly proclaimed his intent to "correct" the ills and injustices that had befallen the Muslim world.

Bombing attacks in Saudi Arabia for which bin Laden appeared to take responsibility were a warning, he said, that the Arab clients of the US were sitting atop a "volcano." Arabs were suffering "severe oppression, humiliation, poverty, iniquity and injustice."

This catalogue of anti-Americanism is worth studying because it embodies the intellectual and emotional motivation of nearly all current anti-American and anti-western groups across the Muslim world. It has also to varying degrees become the prevailing view of many non-Muslims who dislike or even detest the United States, notably so in Europe. For westerners asking "why do they hate us," studying bin Laden's theses provides the most accurate, if unwelcome, answer. Unfortunately, bin Laden's accusations will likely survive him long after his death and become the credo of new anti-western movements in Asia, Africa, and Latin America.

Osama bin Laden was the Arab oil sheik's and military ruler's worst nightmare. He shouted what others only dared whisper. Libya's Muammar Khadaffi had also scourged Arabia's oil monarchs as western puppets who were giving away the Muslim world's riches, but after narrowly escaping assassination by the US Air Force in 1986, the Libyan firebrand quickly quieted down. When I interviewed Colonel Khadaffi in his Tripoli headquarters a year later, he took me by the hand and led me through his bombed-out residence, showing me where his two-year-old daughter was killed in her bed by a US 1,000-pound laser-guided bomb meant for him. He was still deeply shaken by the attack a year later. He kept asking me, "Why did the US attack me, Mr. Eric?"

Bin Laden kept preaching exactly what the US and British–backed oil sheiks, monarchs, and generals did not want their people to hear. The Arab world's despots, charged bin Laden, who sounded increasingly like an Old Testament prophet preaching from the desert, were stealing the ummah's God-given oil. In his war declaration, bin Laden asserted that the Arab oil monarchs were "fixing" the price of oil and adjusting production levels to support the US economy. Oil, bin Laden thundered, should sell for $144 a barrel, a position not inconsistent with that of some of the more militant environmentalists. When bin Laden made this demand in 1992, oil was selling around $25 a barrel. By early 2008, oil had reached over $100 a barrel, bringing its price ever closer to that sought by bin Laden and further enriching oil producers.

Oil equaled Islamic wealth and had to be protected. Those who "gave away" this finite resource to the West and Asia in exchange for protection and mammoth wealth were traitors to their people and to Islam, according to bin Laden. So, too, the Saudi and Gulf rulers who squandered tens of billions on US, British, and French arms they could not use, raking in billions in secret commissions and payoffs. Bin Laden called for a boycott of US arms and consumer goods, insisting that such purchases, notably by the Saudis, helped finance the ongoing occupation of Jerusalem and Palestine.

Osama bin Laden reserved particular venom for the Saudi dynasty, which he branded corrupt, thieving, degenerate, and an enemy of Islam, and for whose overthrow he has incessantly called. The Saudis, claimed bin Laden, abused human rights and had betrayed the Palestinians as far back as 1936.

The only way to rid the Muslim world of such destructive rulers was through guerrilla war and acts of violence that struck at the symbols of western power. He cited jihadist attacks in Beirut, Aden, and Somalia as examples of correct resistance.

"Terrorizing you," said bin Laden ominously, "is a legitimate right and moral duty."

Bin Laden's fevered orations increasingly found an audience across the Muslim world, particularly among the vast majority of its people who shared none of Arabia's oil billions. Even many comfortable or well-off Saudi citizens, disgusted by their ruler's grotesque extravagance and subservience to the US, harkened to bin Laden's calls for jihad. His words found particular resonance with young Muslims steeped in feelings of inferiority, humiliation, and frustration, who saw little future in their backwards, stifling Muslim societies. Bin Laden also appealed to many ardent Islamists who demanded that the oil Arabs share their vast wealth with the poor, as the Holy Koran commanded.

The Muslim world's regimes had done nothing to help the beleaguered Palestinians, or stop anti-Muslim outrages in Bosnia and Kosovo, repression in Kashmir, the US invasion of Afghanistan and Iraq; nor had they done anything to prevent genocide in Chechnya. In fact, many Muslim nations were complicit in these events. Increasing numbers of young Muslims believed that their nations had shamefully ignored their responsibilities to the ummah, and the desires of their own citizens.

If "traitorous" leaders of the Muslim nations refused to defend afflicted Muslims in their direst hours of need, went the thinking of bin Laden and fellow jihadists, then it was up to ordinary citizens to go to the rescue of their coreligionists. Islam demanded a defensive jihad. "Apostate" regions of the Muslim world should be overthrown. Accordingly, the violence traditionally monopolized by states was privatized by groups of Muslims who had witnessed in Afghanistan how individual jihadis could combine to defeat foreign occupation and injustice.

It was *le moment juste* for Osama bin Laden's calls for jihad against western domination. His speeches and writings were widely disseminated throughout the Muslim world and found immediate, even urgent, response from young people disgusted at their corrupt western-backed regimes. Suddenly, here was a leader who managed to put all their turbulent, confused, burning thoughts into sharp focus, to promulgate a creed of resistance to foreign oppression, and advance a clear strategy to liberate Muslim nations from western domination.

The grand strategy proposed by bin Laden was simple and effective. No combination of Muslim peoples or nations could militarily challenge the mighty United States, which spent as much on its armed forces as the entire world combined and commanded the world's skies in the same way Britain's Royal Navy had once ruled the waves. The United States and its principal allies accounted for two-thirds of world military spending. America and Britain, said bin Laden, had only one vulnerability. The only way to hurt them was by attacking their economies. This would be bin Laden's target. The next step, he preached, would be to tie down US forces in a series of small but expensive wars, and relentlessly bleed America of men and resources until it would one day give up and withdraw, as it had done in Vietnam.

Muslim jihadis were to form small, autonomous groups and take up arms against US and British forces, and against allies of the American Raj. While bin Laden's organization, al-Qaida, had a formal framework of executive and legislative councils, or shuras, its primary role was one of inspiration and strategic guidance. The western response, bin Laden warned, would be ferocious and ruthless. Therefore, it was essential that the resistance be sufficiently dispersed, compartmentalized, self-sustaining, and self-directing so that it could operate without central direction and in isolation from its other members; in short, the classical cellular organization long favored by underground revolutionaries.

The struggle envisaged by bin Laden was to pit the American Gulliver against swarms of angry Muslim Lilliputians. In the end, he prophesied, the AK-47 semiautomatic rifles and RPG rockets of his jihads would eventually overcome the West's high-tech weaponry and advanced technology. This was a dangerous promise; the Mahdi had given his Dervish followers similar assurances before they were mowed down in 1898 by British artillery and Maxim machine guns at Omdurman.

In words that echoed those of the Somalia's rebel Mad Mahdi, Osama bin Laden warned, "You love life. We love death, and fear it not." He promised his followers that Muslim jihadis who fell in battle would be forgiven all their sins and go directly to paradise. This was a vow that all of his predecessors, such as the Mahdi, or the Grand Senoussi in the Sahara, had also made to their followers.

Such claims sound bizarre and antique in our secular age, but they do not seem so far-fetched when compared to the ardent belief of tens of millions of America's evangelical Christians that God will soon destroy the earth and, in a process called "the Rapture," transport only the born-again directly to heaven, leaving the unfortunate rest to slowly roast to death or be dismembered.

The fame, or infamy, of Osama bin Laden quickly spread around the world as a result of the September 11 attacks on New York and Washington. The mighty United States had been deeply humiliated and its tough-talking Republican administration caught sleeping on guard duty.

Repeated warnings of the administration's national security experts, like Richard Clarke and the CIA's bin Laden expert Michael Scheuer (see his excellent book, *Imperial Hubris*) were ignored by President George Bush, Vice President Dick Cheney, and national security adviser Condoleeza Rice. Just before 9/11, the then US attorney general, the latter-day Savonarola, John Ashcroft, had actually cut spending on counterterrorism. Caught so embarrassingly unprepared, the Bush administration sought to deflect or channel Americans' equal parts of fear, fury, and demands for revenge by declaring war on all those "who are against us," in the words of the president. Afghanistan became the first target for retribution, shortly followed by Iraq.

To this day, some uncertainty remains whether Osama bin Laden was truly the architect of the 9/11 attacks that killed 2,973 people, not including the aircraft hijackers. In the past, bin Laden, who cultivates a reputation for veracity, has repeatedly denied being behind the attacks. But he has also even more frequently approved of and lauded the 9/11 attacks in various speeches and tapes.

US intelligence was convinced the attacks were planned and executed by the Pakistani Khalid Sheik Mohammed, who admitted to planning them before a military tribunal at Guantanamo, Cuba, in March 2007, after two years of physical and psychological torture. Whether it was Khalid Sheik Mohammed or Osama bin Laden who was the main force behind the attacks, or both of them, remains unclear.

In one 2004 tape "discovered" by US forces in Afghanistan, which I believe used an impostor to represent bin Laden, he is seen chortling over the attack and showing with his hand how one of the aircraft dove into the World Trade Center tower. Having met the real Osama bin Laden, I am convinced that the man in the tape, who was far heavier and broader of face than bin Laden, was a fake. The objective of the tape was to convince American audiences of bin Laden's guilt.

Yet in other tapes, bin Laden appears to accept responsibility for the attacks. In an October 2004 tape, bin Laden is seen talking to three of the hijackers. In other speeches, bin Laden applauded the 9/11 attacks and vowed to "bleed America to bankruptcy," and warned, "Americans will have no peace until there is peace in Palestine."

Faked tapes and forgeries were a much-loved specialty of the Soviet KGB and its successor operating in Afghanistan, the FSB. The tape reportedly was given to the CIA by members of the FSB–backed Northern Afghan Alliance of the late Ahmed Shah Massoud, a longtime "asset" of the old Soviet KGB.

Though bin Laden's direct culpability for the 9/11 attacks remain to be proven, there could be no doubt about his message; nor any doubt that even if bin Laden did not directly plan the attacks, he was well aware of them and close to some of the men who executed them. But in another confusing note, a Spanish court indicted a group of North Africans for complicity in the 9/11 attacks, which was developed by a jihadist cell in Hamburg, Germany, and executed by a US–based suicide commando of whose nineteen members, fifteen were Saudis. This, of course, raises the question of just how much bin Laden, who was holed up in Afghanistan, was actively engaged in the plot. Or did he merely try to take credit, after the fact, for the attacks?

Soon after 9/11, Secretary of State Colin Powell vowed to issue a white paper detailing bin Laden's guilt in the attacks. Curiously, the white paper was never released.

According to the US 9/11 Commission, the Pakistani Khalid Sheik Mohammed was the attack's key planner. The source of funding for the operation has never been discovered, the commission concluded, which went on to whitewash the Bush administration and the president's national security adviser, Condoleeza Rice, for ignoring or dismissing a steady stream of warnings of impending attacks. As noted, just before 9/11, the administration had reduced the Justice Department's antiterrorism budget. The commission, made up of Republicans and Democrats, failed to hold any senior administration officials responsible for the attacks and agreed with the White House that they could not have been foreseen.

For the Muslim world, the question of Osama bin Laden's culpability remains unresolved. In the days after the attacks, there was widespread, deeply felt sympathy across the Muslim world for America's losses and suffering, and outrage that Muslims had committed such a horrible crime against civilians. There were many who simply could not believe it was so, and believed conspiracy theories about Israeli-engineered attacks, or a false flag operation staged by American neoconservatives.

Polls show a disturbingly large number of Americans also continue to give credence to such conspiracy theories. A September 2006, Scripps Howard/Washington Post poll found 36 percent of over 1,000 respondents believed the US government was behind the 9/11 attacks, or had allowed them to happen.

Shortly after 9/11, President George Bush went on air and told Americans that they had been attacked by Muslims "who hate your freedoms, our democracy." The president and his senior aides made it clear that America's new enemies were Muslims, not simply Arabs and Pakistanis who violently opposed US political policies in their region. The media immediately picked up the theme of "Islamic terrorism." This was the first of many big untruths to come and a clear call to religious conflict. Bush misled many Americans into believing they had been plunged into a religious-cultural war, a clash of civilizations, or had been assailed by Muslim lunatics. However much Osama bin Laden hated most things about America, the rest of the Muslim world certainly did not. In spite of virulent opposition to the U.S.'s political polices, American culture, natural beauty, and friendly, generous people remained widely admired and liked across the Muslim world.

The hijackers, in their valedictions, made quite clear they were about to go to their deaths not for religious reasons but to punish the United States for its support of Israel and the suffering inflicted on the Palestinians. As the CIA's Michael Scheuer, no friend of the jihadist cause, observed, the attacks were the result of what the US had long been doing in the Muslim world—in short, "what we've been doing to them." In short, revenge. While most Muslims strongly condemned the 9/11 attacks on civilians, there was widespread rejoicing across the Third World that America had been punished for its political acts.

This was a harsh political truth that neither the Bush administration, the media, nor most Americans either understood or cared to face. So the White House, the national media, and, of course, the neoconservatives unleashed a hurricane of exculpatory excuses for why the attacks had occurred. The neocon media, such as Fox News, the *Wall Street Journal*, and right-wing publications like the *National Review* and *Weekly Standard*, gave the impression that Muslims were innately violent, neo-Nazis, intent on world domination under an Islamic caliphate. In short, almost every reason was cited save the obvious one: the natives in America's Raj were biting back.

President Bush's aggressive rhetoric, his ill-chosen use of "crusade," the invasions of Afghanistan, then Iraq, quickly dissipated the widespread but ephemeral sympathy felt for post–9/11 America across the Muslim world. Polls in Egypt, Indonesia, Pakistan, and other important Muslim nations showed a majority of Muslims remained appalled by the attacks on New York—though hardly anyone was distressed by the attack on the Pentagon.

Bush's militarized response to what was essentially an international criminal act and proclamation of a war on terror were quickly taken by most Muslims to be a war against Islam. Fulminations against Muslims by demagogic American Protestant evangelists, which were widely reported across Africa and Asia, and mistakenly depicted as official US government policy, left many Muslims fearing that yet another Christian crusade had been declared against them.

Once the shock of 9/11 wore off, many Muslims—and probably a majority of Europeans—were left with a feeling that America had finally "gotten what it deserved." After all, claimed anti-American groups everywhere, the United States and Israel had been bombing Muslims for decades and grabbing their land and wealth. That almost 3,000 innocent civilians had died in New York as a result of the attack did not seem to matter.

After the 9/11 attacks, former US secretary of state Madeleine Albright's notorious comment on May 12, 1996, on the CBS TV program *60 Minutes* that the death of 500,000 Iraqi children "was a price worth paying" to punish Iraq was resurrected and echoed across the Muslim world. After the US invasion and destruction of large portions of Iraq, any residual sympathy in the Muslim world over 9/11 quickly evaporated.

Even many dependent Muslim allies of the United States, like Egyptians and Saudis, were secretly delighted that the superpower they saw as a swaggering bully had finally gotten a bitter dose of the same medicine it had inflicted on Syria, Iran, Iraq, Libya, Somalia, Lebanon, and Afghanistan, as well as payback for successful or unsuccessful attempts to overthrow regimes in Iran, Syria, Egypt, Libya, Tunisia, Indonesia, Sudan, and Pakistan. US heavy weapons—tanks, helicopter gunships, and missiles—were being routinely used by Israel against Palestinians. How could Americans not expect that someday America would suffer some return fire?

The majority of Americans were unaware of the extent or details of their nation's past and present machinations in the Muslim world. Many were equally unaware that Muslims everywhere blamed America for Israel and the plight of the Palestinians. Poorly informed about the Muslim world by their media and often misled by politicians catering to ethnic voters, Americans found it hard to believe that anyone, save madmen and far leftists, could have reason to hate the United States. All but a tiny minority of Americans felt themselves innocent victims of incomprehensible, malign outside forces.

It was far easier to believe George Bush's childish explanation that the nation was facing "evil," clearly something for which Americans were not at all responsible. To combat the looming menace of evil, the Pentagon's budget doubled and the US military-industrial complex, of which the prescient president Dwight Eisenhower had so eloquently warned, went into high gear turning out new, high-tech weapons systems that were of little use against jihadi guerrillas—and even less against "pure evil"—but that returned soaring profits for their manufacturers. Over the six years after 2001, the profits of America's leading defense contractors doubled.

One of the most striking aspects of Osama bin Laden's anti-western campaign was that while he portrayed himself primarily as a religious leader, his followers largely rejected or ignored his theological advocacy and teachings, and saw him instead as a secular revolutionary using the idiom of Islamic life and custom. The main objective of bin Laden's active and passive followers was ousting western influence from the Muslim world and overthrowing its foreign-backed regimes. Religion was strictly a secondary matter, and even here there was intense debate between fundamentalists seeking to impose traditional Sharia or Koranic law on Muslim societies, modernists who wanted more western-style democratic governments with legislatures and secular courts, and the silent majority who were too preoccupied trying to feed and house their families to worry about abstruse questions of religion and government.

Osama bin Laden's calls for the restoration of early Islamic government were ignored. The religious uprising and reformation he had called for did not happen. Traditional religious establishments were not overturned. Most disappointing of all for this revolutionary, he was not called upon by the ummah to give it spiritual and temporal direction. Osama bin Laden failed to become a new Muslim redeemer. There was no general Muslim uprising to support his religious agenda, no upsurge of Islamist religiosity. But bin Laden succeeded beyond doubt in projecting his image onto the world stage and laying the foundation for an international jihadist movement.

The Saudi militant became a lightning rod for all sorts of angry discontents and West-haters everywhere. More important, his adroit articulation of a worldview and his philosophy of active Muslim resistance against western influence found ready followers from Morocco to Indonesia. Translated into English, his speeches sound obscure, orotund, and often downright bizarre, but in their original, highly refined, literary Arabic, they are carefully crafted and seeded with historic and religious references designed to arouse Muslim emotions and sensibilities. Bin Laden's harangues are often couched in the elegant language of the Holy Koran and the mythic days of early Islam, and are clearly antimodernist in tone and intent.

This was ironic because bin Laden and his fellow jihadis made excellent use of modern western and Asian technology in the form of audio- and videotape cassettes, transistor radios, fax, and, later, the Internet to spread their message of rebellion and resistance. Another profound antimodernist, Iran's late Grand Ayatollah Khomeini, had earlier made highly effective use of videocassettes to spread his revolutionary message among Iran's illiterate masses.

The American and British media also played a major role in elevating Osama bin Laden to the role of archvillain. As previously noted, it was much easier to personify a complex foreign issue in the nature of a new Mad Mahdi than to confuse and bore westerners with the multilayered complexities of the Muslim world. Bin Laden's inaccessibility and aura of exotic Oriental mystery propelled his persona as a modern combination of Dr. Fu Manchu and the fabled Hassan-i-Sabbah, the Old Man of the

Mountain, chief of the medieval cult of Hashishin, better known as the Assassins.

However, during the 1990s, bin Laden's goals were far more modest than establishing a world caliphate that his enemies would later claim to be his true ambition. Bin Laden concentrated on building a small, tightly knit organization of around 300 veteran jihadis from the 1980s Afghan war into an ideological cadre to form and train Islamic guerrillas from the rest of the Muslim world. He eventually set up six training centers in Afghanistan that the West would later call terrorist training camps. Any Muslim that had attended these camps would automatically be branded a terrorist.

In reality, these camps, which, as this writer saw, were very rudimentary affairs designed to provide young Muslim volunteers with basic military and physical training, were run to prepare mujahidin for combat in a number of regional anti-Communist conflicts, not to attack the West. Their primary mission was to prepare Muslim volunteers to go fight Afghanistan's Communist-dominated Northern Alliance, and the neo-Stalinist regimes of Uzbekistan, Tajikistan, Kyrgyzstan, and Kazakhstan, and to aid Muslim Uighurs in Chinese Xinjiang. Meanwhile, bin Laden's own men played a key role in aiding Taliban forces battling the Russian and Iranian–backed Northern Alliance in Afghanistan. (See Chapter Nine.)

After invading Afghanistan in 2001 and scattering the Taliban, the United States believed it had all but eradicated al-Qaida, though it failed dismally to locate bin Laden or his Taliban ally, Mullah Omar. Still, the invasion and occupation of Afghanistan were held up by Washington's neoconservatives as the model of how to deal with Muslim troublemakers who disturbed the Pax Americana.

Osama bin Laden had indeed vanished, but his incendiary philosophy had not: thanks to the miracle of modern communications technology, it had already spread from one end of the Muslim world to the other. In some ways, bin Laden's 1996 and 2002 call to arms addressed to the Muslim world had the same explosive effect as did Martin Luther's nailing of his ninety-five theses to the door of Wittenberg Cathedral in 1517. Luther, of course, was a great Christian reformer. Bin Laden will far more likely be remembered, at least in the West, as a promoter of mass murder and the apotheosis of Muslim negativism rather than as a religious or political figure. But both acts of astounding defiance and heresy ignited a wildfire that inflamed disparate groups across both Christendom and Islam, each of whom adopted the new revolutionary principles and modified them to suit their own particular local, political, or religious needs. Just as pockets of Protestant rebellion against Rome broke out in sixteenth-century Geneva, Sweden, southwestern France, and northern Germany, each with its own unique character, so disparate jihadist groups across North Africa, Saudi Arabia, Yemen, Pakistan, Central Asia, Afghanistan, and Indonesia, who had little in common, save Islam and a desire to drive western influence from their lands, quickly joined the cause of Osama bin Laden.

Osama bin Laden gave a name and intellectual framework for the previously formless anti-Americanism that had long swirled through the Muslim world. Equally important, as we have seen, Muslims throughout their history have harkened to messianic leaders, and bin Laden amply filled this role. He certainly lacked any competitors. During the mid-1990s and after, the Muslim world, and particularly its youth, was completely bereft of heroes and inspirational figures. With perfect timing, Osama bin Laden entered, stage center.

But the biggest boost to bin Laden's fortunes came when the US government and western media made great fanfare over al-Qaida, portraying it as a murderous, far-reaching international organization devoted to terrorism and anarchy, a sort of Muslim version of international criminal/terrorist organization SPECTRE found in James Bond novels. This fevered depiction fulfilled the need to come up with a palpable, well-defined enemy. The Bush administration simply could not tell its citizens that they were facing a motley collection of small, anti-American groups from all over the Muslim world who were staging acts of violence aimed at driving out western influence or domination.

Al-Qaida, with only 300 core members, was in no way an international organization, though it would later have supporters aplenty around the globe. It was, as bin Laden had intended, an ideological core devoted to what the Soviets used to call "agitprop," or agitation and propaganda.

An extremely violent, radical Egyptian extremist group, Gamma al-Islamiya, which became notorious for the murder of fifty-eight European tourists at Luxor in 1997, attached itself to al-Qaida. One of its leaders, a former ophthalmologist named Dr. Ayman al-Zawahiri, had became a bloodthirsty radical after being arrested on false charges by Egypt's notorious security police, imprisoned, and tortured. After the Luxor terror attack sparked outrage and revulsion across Egypt, the group split. Most of its members renounced violence, but a minority, led by Zawahiri, decamped for Afghanistan and joined al-Qaida. Zawahiri became bin Laden's second in command, chief operating office, and in-law.

The reason western intelligence and security services had so much trouble eliminating al-Qaida was that outside Afghanistan it really was not an organization at all, but a loosely linked collection of like-minded jihadists from Morocco to Indonesia who had few, if any, direct operational links. The operational and organizational methods of al-Qaida could be compared to Israel's Mossad. The Israeli intelligence service was small in numbers, both at home and abroad. Mossad has reportedly always relied on Jewish supporters, known as "sayanim," across the globe for information, funds, safe houses, and other forms of operational support. A rare Mossad defector, Viktor Ostrovsky, claimed the Israeli service had 2,000 active sayanim in London alone, with many more in reserve.

In a similar manner, al-Qaida could call on anti-western individuals and groups across the Muslim world for assistance, shelter, and protection. At the heart of this nebulous network of jihadists lay personal relationships in most cases established during the Great Jihad of the 1980s in Afghanistan. Some of the foreign jihadist veterans, known as "men of honor," who returned to their homes in Asia and Africa, became the vital connections and mooring posts of al-Qaida. They could be trusted and called upon when necessary.

Al-Qaida operated as a movement rather than formal organization. Sheik Osama issued general strategic and religious directives, which were then transmitted to allied groups across the Muslim world. Al-Qaida's communications with fellow jihadists, and even its own very small operational elements, were limited to courier and occasional disguised Internet messages. The jihadists were well aware that they were blanketed around the clock by US and western electronic surveillance and communications intercepts. Osama bin Laden was so paranoid about the dangers of US electronic intelligence (ELINT) that he forbade anyone in his presence to even wear a wristwatch, for fear it might be a homing beacon. His caution was well justified after the assassination of Chechen leader Dzhokar Dudayev. (See Chapter Thirteen.)

Anti-western groups across the Muslim world did not need detailed orders from al-Qaida headquarters in Afghanistan to undertake attacks. It should also be noted that in spite of the continuing furor over al-Qaida, and hysterical stories in the US right-wing media that vividly recalled the 1950s "reds under our beds" panic, these anti-western attacks, though dramatic, were surprisingly limited in scope and lethality after 2001. With the exception of the 2004 Madrid train bombing, which was done by North African Salafists, not al-Qaida, it is surprising that with such a target-rich environment, violent anti-western groups have staged so few successful attacks. Sharply increased western security is certainly one reason for this decline, but one must also seriously suspect that the danger and extent of al-Qaida's supporters has been considerably exaggerated. One should also recall that the majority of attacks by extremist Islamist groups occur against their fellow citizens, not westerners.

It should also be noted that the so-called "al-Qaida in Iraq (AQI)," a particularly murderous group, had nothing to do with the original al-Qaida. Its late leader, Abu Musab al-Zarqawi, simply expropriated Osama bin Laden's brand name to bring his group international publicity and enhance its standing. Some veteran Mideast watchers even suspected "al-Qaida in Iraq" did not really exist at all but was a false flag operation staged to convince Americans they were fighting terrorism in Iraq. The Bush administration waged a highly successful media campaign to mislead Americans into believing their troops in Iraq were fighting Osama bin Laden's al-Qaida instead of twenty-two Iraqi national resistance groups. By 2008, virtually all US military operations in Iraq were described by the White House, Pentagon, and cooperative US media as "fighting al-Qaida." Once again, Americans were misled into believing Iraq was somehow involved with 9/11. In March 2008, a Pentagon study of 600,000 captured Iraqi government documents concludes there never had been any links between Saddam's regime and Osama bin Laden. The White House ordered the Pentagon not to release the study.

Alleged Iraqi collusion in the 9/11 attacks was the second justification given by the White House for invading Iraq. Like the weapons-of-mass-destruction canard, it proved to be another big lie. First it was weapons of mass destruction, then links to al-Qaida, and, in the spring of 2008, a new rational: the danger posed to Iraq by Iran.

The most dangerous jihadist groups to emerge in the 1990s originally had nothing whatsoever to do with Osama bin Laden or his original al-Qaida. They arose in the North African nations of Morocco, Algeria, and Tunisia, collectively known as the Maghreb. Other radical, but less dangerous, Islamist groups also sprang up in Colonel Khadaffi's Libya, Mauritania, Mali, and Nigeria. The most lethal of these groups was the Armed Islamic Group (GIA), a breakaway faction of Algeria's Islamic Salvation Front leaders. The Salvation Front, as noted, won a landslide election in Algeria in 1991. The vote was annulled by the Algerian Army, backed by the US and France, which imposed draconian martial law, and which remains to this day.

The Islamists quickly took up arms against the military regime in what became a disorganized, bloody guerrilla war. Over the ensuing decade, Algeria was plunged into a nightmare bloodbath of massacres, assassinations, reprisals, counter-reprisals, and torture that killed 120,000 to 140,000 people and profoundly traumatized the nation. The military junta, which actually called itself "the eradicators," used special security units disguised as rebels to massacre entire villages. Slitting throats and cutting off the heads of victims became the norm for both sides. The Algiers regime resorted to mass reprisals and medieval tortures against the insurgents, who reacted with almost equal barbarity.

The Islamists were finally repressed, but from their ranks emerged former GIA fighters, and then the even more lethal offshoot, the Salafist Group for Preaching and Combat, or GPSC, that continued to wage war against the Algiers junta. The GPSC spread into Morocco, joining native Islamists who had long opposed that nation's brutally repressive, medieval monarchy. These militant Islamists also spread into Tunisia, and then deep into the Sahara. Collectively known as Salafists, these small, underground groups, forged in the crucible of Algeria's civil war, proved extremely violent, utterly bloodthirsty, and ruthless.

The Maghrebian militants were particularly disposed to the dangerous creed of declaring other Muslims who followed less austere or different religious paths as unbelievers or heretics, or "takfir." The Taliban also viewed other non-Salafist Muslims as takfir. Nor was there anything new about this belief. Readers will recall from Chapter Three Glubb Pasha's defense in the 1930s of the shepherds of Iraq from the depredations of the Saudi Ikhwan (Wahabis) who deemed their immediate Shia neighbors takfir. In fact, the entire history of Islam has been rent by conflict between Sunni, Shia, Sufis, smaller sects like Alawis, Ismailis, or Ahmadiyah, and subsects or different schools within these sects. But only recently has there been such a sharp upsurge in religious rivalry and hatred, thanks in large part to the rise of religious-political militancy in the Muslim world. The gruesome mayhem in Iraq between Sunni and Shia ignited by the US occupation has increasingly become driven by takfiri extremists on both sides. Some extreme, fanatical members of al-Qaida in Iraq acted so murderously against other Muslims that they were denounced by Osama bin Laden and Ayman al-Zawahiri.

Many North African extremists driven from Algeria and Morocco sought refuge in western Europe, particularly Spain, where they eventually became involved in many terrorist attacks, most notably the 2004 Madrid train bombing that killed 190 innocent commuters. Other Maghrebian groups were behind planned attacks on Spanish enclaves in North Africa, targets in Spain and France. A Canadian–North African Salafist associated with the GIA, Ahmed Ressam, tried to mount a failed 1999 attack on Los Angeles International Airport. French, Algerian, and Moroccan security forces have worked closely to destroy the Maghrebian Salafists.

The Pentagon and CIA also began strongly supporting and financing Algeria's and Morocco's ruthless security forces, which only produced more hatred of the United States and its sometime ally and partner, but also rival in the region, France. Washington created a new African military command and spent over $500 million on "regional security" to combat Salafist groups and dispatched US Special Forces to Algeria, Chad, Mauritania, Mali, and Morocco where they waged small, obscure operations against local Islamist groups. Washington's growing involvement against Islamists in North Africa and the Saharan region threatens to open a new front of anti-American operations in the region, further straining already overextended US forces. In Nigeria, Africa's most populous nation, a local version of the Taliban, the Sunnah wal Jammah, has sprung up, dedicated to imposing Sharia law.

In late 2006, the Algerian GPSC, which had been partly founded by veterans of the 1980s Afghan jihad, known as Afghani, proclaimed its merger with Osama bin Laden's original al-Qaida, renaming itself "al-Qaida in the Maghreb." But again, as in the case of Iraq, this was a local group with no direct operational links to Afghanistan or Pakistan, that simply adopted the brand name of bin Laden's growing universal terrorist-franchise operation.

After six years of worldwide counterterrorist operations, expenditure of nearly $700 billion, with another $300 billion due to follow by the end of 2008, and the invasion of three sovereign nations, President George Bush's vaunted war on terror had not crushed al-Qaida, neutralized its allies, nor caught the elusive Osama bin Laden, Ayman al-Zawahiri, or Taliban leader Mullah Omar.

In Afghanistan, the supposedly defeated Taliban has returned to the offensive. Close to forty thousand US soldiers and a small army of CIA operatives had failed to find bin Laden and his allies after seven years of chasing shadows in the Hindu Kush. What made this ghastly embarrassment even more appalling was that these Islamic fugitives remained at large in spite of huge rewards on their heads. The $25-million reward offered for bin Laden is an unimaginably large sum of money in a region where the average annual income is under $600. It is astounding that bin Ladin and his allies have not yet been betrayed. The reward was doubled to $50 million in 2007. In Afghanistan and Pakistan, many whispered that the US really did not want to capture bin Laden and Zawahiri since their continuing presence justified the US occupation of Afghanistan and its future oil corridor.

Unable to find the renegade Saudi, Washington simply claimed he was no longer of any importance, and just as good as dead. But this claim convinced no one in the Muslim world, where bin Laden's continued defiance and freedom stood as a powerful symbol of resistance to America's power. It was very much as if George Bush's turbaned nemesis was sitting atop a crag in Afghanistan making rude gestures at the American president.

Humiliation also fell on America's massed, $40-billion annual intelligence services who, for all their hypermodern technology and armies of informers and agents, could not find one man in a relatively small area. Had not the hunt for Osama bin Laden and al-Qaida been so serious, the whole business would have been an immensely rich farce.

Adding to the mounting humiliation, President Bush's claims that he was still winning the war on terror were belied by his own combined intelligence agencies in the April 2006 National Intelligence Estimate (NIE). Their conclusions were shaking. According to the NIE, "The jihadists, although a small percentage of Muslims, are increasing in both number and geographic dispersion. If this trend continues, threats to US interests at home and abroad will become more diverse, leading to increasing attacks worldwide."

The report goes on to note that encouraging "greater pluralism and more responsive political systems in Muslim majority nations would alleviate some of the grievances the jihadists exploit." But that, of course, means replacing the subservient Muslim regimes the US has long kept in power. "We assess the Iraqi jihad is shaping a new generation of terrorist leaders and operatives; perceived jihadist success there would inspire more fighters to continue the struggle elsewhere." The US invasion of Iraq, notes the NIE, energized the jihadist movement and has become a cause célèbre for the Muslim world.

Four underlying factors, according to the US intelligence report, are fueling the spreading jihadist movement: 1) corruption, injustice, humiliation, and fear of western domination; 2) US occupation of Iraq; 3) slow economic, social, and political reforms in the Muslim world; and 4) pervasive anti–US sentiment among most Muslims. "Anti-US and anti-globalization sentiment is on the rise and fueling other radical ideologies. This could prompt some leftist, nationalist, or separatist groups to adopt terrorist methods." The NIE concludes that only al-Qaida could pose a potential future nuclear, chemical, or biological threat to the US homeland. Other jihadist groups will only threaten US interests around the world.

US intelligence services finally got things right. What a tragedy that their senior officials, notably then CIA director George Tenet, did not make these accurate assessments available to the public and Congress before George Bush embarked on his "crusade" against the Muslim world and his war on "evil."

What the NIE report tells us is that Osama bin Laden's carefully enunciated strategy of goading the US into numerous small, draining wars in the Muslim world has so far worked flawlessly. Bin Laden could not have found a better or more helpful ally than President George Bush, whose strutting arrogance and boundless ignorance made him a figure of deep hate, derision, and contempt in the Muslim world, as well as across Asia, Africa, and Europe.

The Bush-Cheney worldwide campaign against manifestations of Islamic political activity, whether benign or aggressive, led US military and intelligence operations ever deeper into North and sub-Saharan Africa, and across the rest of the Muslim world from the Mideast to the Philippines. America's knee-jerk reaction to Islamists of all types and persuasions was reminiscent of its similarly Pavlovian reaction during the

Cold War to all leftists movements. The Bush administration's moves to suppress even moderate, democratic Islamic groups, as in Egypt, Jordan, Pakistan, and Southeast Asia, convinced most people in many Muslim nations that America had indeed embarked upon a worldwide war against Islam. To the neoconservatives who shaped administration foreign policy, all Muslims were potential enemies of the United States and Israel, and, to paraphrase Winston Churchill's gibe against Germany, "either at your feet, or at your throat."

Bush and his mentor Dick Cheney fell right into the trap laid for them by the wily bin Laden who analyzed their psychology with amazing accuracy and foresight. He had goaded the US into what seemed to many Muslims a war against Islam, inflicted huge costs on the US Treasury that would not be paid off for generations, got the US Army bogged down in Iraq and Afghanistan, and generated worldwide anger against the United States.

The success of bin Laden's plan—or, conversely, the disastrous results of Bush's war on terror—were starkly revealed by an international survey conducted in twenty-five nations around the globe for the BBC that came out in early March 2007. Nearly two-thirds of the 26,000 respondents in these twenty-five nations held an unfavorable view of President George W. Bush. That was hardly a surprise. What was startling and dismaying: according to the survey, the three nations seen as having the most negative influence on the world were Israel, Iran, and the United States, in that order—a remarkably ironic twist to George Bush's "axis of evil."

Israel was viewed negatively by 56 percent of respondents, and positively by only 17 percent. Iran's image was 54 percent negative, 18 percent positive. The United States, which spends hundreds of millions annually on public relations and self-promotion, came in at 51 percent negative and only 30 percent positive. Unloved North Korea was actually less disliked than the US, with 48 percent negative and 19 percent positive. Without the inclusion in the survey of India and Nigeria, where the US is wildly popular, the results would have been even worse.

Canada, often the object of sneering attacks by US neoconservatives and the Christian religious right, ranked in the survey as the world's most respected nation and most positive influence. It was closely followed by France, Japan, and the European Union, another favorite target of America's hard right. Interestingly, American survey respondents were often as negative about their own government's behavior as were non-Americans.

Superpowers rarely win popularity contests, but America's image and reputation has never before sunk so low in the world's view. Fifty years ago, America was regarded across Europe, the Mideast, Africa and much of non-Communist Asia as a liberator, savior, the acme of all that was good and desirable. Today, the almighty United States evokes the same level of hatred, disrespect, and fear that the old Soviet Union did during the Cold War. As the US National Intelligence Estimate rightly warned, the rising tide of anti-Americanism around the globe is likely to lead to more violent attacks against US interests abroad and even the continental USA.

It seems inevitable Osama bin Laden will eventually be captured, killed, or die in hiding. But the international movement he created and energized will go on and grow without him until the United States and its allies make substantial changes to their self-defeating policies in the Muslim world. In fact, in death, Osama bin Laden is likely to become even a greater symbol of resistance to American domination than he was in life. The British Raj managed to eventually crush the various Mahdis and Mad Mullahs that challenged its imperial Raj. But in those days the Internet, satellite-TV cell phones, and fax did not exist.

Today, Britain's imperial successor, the American Raj, must not only chase the elusive bin Laden and his henchmen through the wilds of the Hindu Kush and Waziristan, it must also try to block his revolutionary message as it courses around the world through the Internet and airwaves. History has shown over and over that an idea whose time has come cannot easily be stopped.

America's debacle in Iraq, and its at best stalemated war in Afghanistan, unfortunately seem to validate Osama bin Laden and Ayman al-Zawahiri's once absurd-sounding claims that the United States would face the same kind of defeat in those two nations as the Soviet Union did in Afghanistan.

The big question now is will these twin defeats expose the United States as a paper tiger, as bin Laden has long insisted, and begin unraveling the American Raj, as defeat in Afghanistan began the collapse of the Soviet Union? And will this latest Raj one day join those of the defunct British Empire and the equally defunct Soviet Empire on the scrap heap of history?

The next decade will provide the answer. In the interim, one should not sell short the United States. For all its hubris, ignorance of world affairs, and often self-destructive foreign policies, the great American imperium is far more powerful, rich, resourceful, and technologically advanced than any empire in history. The United States still dominates the globe through military and economic power, cultural dynamism, innovation, and sheer size. In addition, America, which seems perpetually engaged in some sort of political, social, cultural, economic, or technological revolution, still retains élan vital, that motive force, according to the philosopher Henri Bergson, that keeps great empires and great nations potent and dynamic.

The power of empires always ebbs and flows. Right now, America's power is in decline, thanks in part to Sheik Osama bin Laden and the Bush administration's reckless bungling in the Muslim world. But tomorrow could as easily bring a recrudescence of America's world power and self-confidence. The Age of America is far from over.

CHAPTER NINE
★ ★ ★

THE LONG AGONY OF AFGHANISTAN

When I first began covering the then almost unknown anti-Soviet war in Afghanistan in the early 1980s, neither editors nor readers were interested in this obscure topic. At the time, "an Afghanistan story" was newspaper jargon for a particularly boring article of no earthly interest. When my book about Afghanistan, Kashmir, and the India-Pakistan conflict, *War at the Top of the World*, first came out in 1999, media interest was restrained. "Why should we care about Afghanistan?" was the usual response. My reply was that the region of South Asia, including Afghanistan, was about to become the new millennium's first major crisis zone.

The dismissive term "Afghanistan story" vanished after three hijacked airliners crashed into New York and Washington on September 11, 2001. The Bush administration named Osama bin Laden as perpetrator of the attacks and launched a long-range invasion of Afghanistan, vowing to wipe out this "nest of terrorism."

The United States thus became the latest great power to invade Afghanistan, succeeding Alexander the Great and his Macedonians, the Mongols, the British Raj, and the mighty Soviet Union, then the world's greatest land power. All these previous invaders had been eventually defeated by the ferocious Afghan tribes, for whom warfare was a passion. However, such historical caveats had no cautionary influence whatsoever on the Bush administration.

The primary targets of the invasion were Osama bin Laden, purported author of the 9/11 outrages, and his ally, Taliban leader Mullah Omar. However, there was also an unstated strategic goal of the invasion: to "secure" a long-sought pipeline corridor from Uzbekistan, through Afghanistan, to Pakistan's Arabian Sea port of Karachi. There were only two ways to get oil and gas out to the sea from the landlocked Caspian Basin, the world's newest major energy source: through Iran or Afghanistan. Since the US pro-Israel lobby had blocked any dealings with Iran, Afghanistan was the only alternative.

The US oil firm Unocal had been in intense negotiations with Afghanistan's ruling Taliban regime in the years before 9/11. Zalmay Khalilzad, an Afghan-born American, was working as a senior consultant for Unocal in 1997, advising them on their planned Afghan operations. Khalilzad, the only known Muslim neoconservative, went on to become US ambassador to Kabul and, later, Baghdad, and then UN ambassador.

Chevron was another major US energy corporation with a potent influence in Washington and ambitions in Afghanistan and Central Asia. Another English-speaking Afghan who had long been associated with the CIA, Hamid Karzai, and was later made president of Afghanistan, had been on Chevron's payroll, engaged in seeking new oil fields in Kazakhstan.

In December 1997, Unocal invited a senior Taliban delegation to Houston, Texas, to discuss a major oil deal. Unocal, with Washington's blessing and support, wanted to build the oil pipeline across Afghanistan linking the Caspian Basin oil fields of Central Asia with Pakistan's coast. This new trans-Afghanistan pipeline would form the principal export conduit for the newly discovered energy resources of Uzbekistan, Kazakhstan, and Turkmenistan and put even more of the world's energy supplies under US control.

But Osama bin Laden reportedly advised the Taliban's Mullah Omar to reject the Unocal contract in favor of a better deal from an Argentine consortium, Bridas. This infuriated the Clinton administration, which had been previously advised by Khalilzad to improve relations with the Taliban. As a result, the Taliban was put on Washington's blacklist.

In August 1998, two US embassies in East Africa were bombed, with a heavy loss of lives and thousands injured. From his vacation retreat in Martha's Vineyard, President Bill Clinton ordered retaliatory missile strikes on Afghanistan and Sudan. Embarrassingly, the bombing destroyed Sudan's main pharmaceutical plant that produced 50 percent of its medicines, and some shacks in Afghanistan, but had little further effect other than to put Osama bin Laden squarely in America's gunsights.

Curiously, the US government continued to give millions in aid to the Taliban until just four months before 9/11. To understand why, we have to go back to the Taliban's birth in the early 1990s.

After the Soviets finally admitted defeat after a decade in Afghanistan and withdrew in 1989, that nation fell into chaos and civil war. The seven mujahidin groups supported by the United States, Britain, and the Saudis fell upon each other like hungry wolves. Their sporadic wartime cooperation against the Soviets quickly dissolved under the force of revived tribal, clan, and ethnic rivalries. A secret campaign by the KGB during the 1980s to weaken the resistance by fomenting ethnic and tribal turmoil also worked all too successfully, contributing to much of Afghanistan's ensuing turmoil and chaos.

Pashtun tribes of the south, who comprise about 50 percent of Afghanistan's population of 31 million, had formed the core of the anti-Soviet struggle. Many of their traditional foes from the north, the more urbane Tajiks, who spoke Dari, a version of Persian, and the notoriously violent and backwards Uzbeks, had allied themselves with the Soviet occupiers and the Afghan Communists. During the ten-year jihad against the Soviets, the Tajik military leader Ahmad Shah Masood was lionized in the West as an heroic anti-Communist mountain warrior—the "Lion of the Panjshir." In reality, he had long secretly collaborated with the Soviet KGB, a fact recently revealed in the memoirs of retired Soviet intelligence officers from KGB and GRU military intelligence.

While pretending to fight the Soviets, Masood actually devoted his main efforts to combating the Pashtun mujahidin, thwarting their efforts, backed by Pakistani intelligence agents, to blow up the strategic choke point of Soviet logistics, the Salang Tunnel. Masood also intrigued to convince Moscow to ditch its current Communist puppet ruler, Najibullah, and make him ruler of Afghanistan.

The brutal civil war between mujahidin leaders and Afghan Communists, who were still supported by the Soviets/Russia and, later, Iran and India, was characterized by double-dealing, betrayals, and rapidly shifting alliances that inflicted huge damage on Afghanistan's cities, wrecked its feeble economy, and forced farmers to switch from cultivating cash crops to growing opium. Until then, Iran and Burma (Myanmar) had been the world's principal source of the poppies from which opium, morphine, and heroin are produced.

Anarchy engulfed most of war-ravaged Afghanistan. According to popular legend, one day in 1992, a number of women in a southern Pashtun village were raped. Rape is an unspeakable outrage in Islamic society, and punishable by death under Islamic law. But in Afghanistan, the total breakdown of law and order resulted in a wave of banditry and rapine. A Pashtun village mullah, or prayer leader, named Omar, who had been seriously wounded numerous times in the anti-Soviet jihad and lost an eye, rallied some armed villagers, captured the rapists, and shot the bandits.

Omar, now hailed as a hero and savior, quickly recruited tribesmen and young seminarians from madrassas known as Talibs. Mullah Omar and his young warriors soon came to be called "Taliban." During 1993–94, they marched from one Pashtun village to the next, armed with AK rifles and copies of the Holy Koran, wiping out banditry and rape, and imposing law and order through a combination of Islamic law and tribal custom. It was frontier justice at its harshest and most medieval, but Mullah Omar's cure worked, bringing peace and security to southern Afghanistan.

Pakistan traditionally regarded Afghanistan as its sphere of influence and "strategic depth" in any conflict with India. Islamabad was anxious to end the chaos caused by civil war among its former mujahidin protégés, combat-lingering Soviet/Russian and Communist influence, and keep the Indians out, so Islamabad quickly supported the new Taliban movement. The humble Talibs suddenly came into possession of heavy weapons, some artillery and even a few tanks, all thanks, they claimed, to the "Grace of All-Generous Allah." However, the real source of their military windfall was Pakistan's Interior Ministry and later its intelligence service, ISI, rather than divine intervention.

The Taliban rapidly cemented its control over southern Afghanistan and, in 1996, took the capital, Kabul, driving out the Tajik forces of Masood and my old comrade (see *War at the Top of the World*), Professor Burhanuddin Rabbani. At first, the Muslim world, shocked and disgusted by Afghanistan's post-liberation civil war, was elated to see an Islamic movement take power and impose law and order. The new Taliban government was recognized by Pakistan, Saudi Arabia, and the United Arab Emirates, but no other nations. However, as noted, Washington sent aid and maintained discreet links with the Taliban, in part through its old boys' network of mujahidin from the Great Jihad.

The new Taliban government in Kabul turned out to be a bizarre combination of ninth-century Islamic political and legal thought mixed up with the most backwards and primitive customs of isolated Pashtun mountain tribesmen. Even worse, nearly all were illiterate, had never been to a city before—which their mullahs warned them were dens of the vilest corruption and debauchery—and most were teenagers with more hormones than brains. It was as if an army of illiterate, holy-roller adolescent hillbillies from the Ozarks suddenly took control of Washington.

Even so, Pakistan's fundamentalist Muslim parties were overjoyed by the Taliban's victory and declaration of an Islamic emirate in Afghanistan. Many idealistic young Pakistanis went north to join the ranks of what was called "the first pure Islamic state." Afghanistan came to be called "the only free Islamic space" in the Muslim world, a refuge where true Muslims could practice their faith free of the restrictions and hostility of the Muslim world's repressive regimes. But most other Muslims outside Pakistan were increasingly dismayed by the antics and aggressive oafishness and obscurantism of the young Talibs.

In Islam, education is considered sacred, a gift from God. The closure by the Taliban of many girls' schools in Kabul shocked the Muslim world and ignited outrage in the western world, where increasingly vociferous feminist groups had singled out Islam as a persecutor of females. The Taliban's retro-medievalism was far more a reflection of traditional Pashtun tribal custom than Islam, but it was also a direct reaction to the Communist era. What almost no one outside Afghanistan understood was that during the 1970s, the Soviet-directed Afghan Communist Party had successfully infiltrated the small Afghan middle and intellectual class by championing modernization, education, and women's equality. For the Taliban, such reforms equaled Communism.

By the end of the 1970s, almost the entire Afghan teaching establishment was in the grip of the Communists, who also formed the most urbanized, "modern," and progressive part of the population. The Taliban temporarily closed schools to weed out lingering Communist influence, but this clumsy act brought worldwide anger and condemnation onto their heads.

In the West's demonization of the Taliban, the fact that it was a religious movement based on a very narrow, medieval interpretation of Islamic law, and an equally fierce anti-Communist movement, has not been understood.

During the 1979–89 Soviet occupation, Soviet forces and their Afghan Communist allies killed two million Afghans. Villages were razed in reprisals, livestock slaughtered, ancient irrigation systems destroyed, and millions of mines, some in the form of exploding toys, were scattered across Afghanistan. Another 2.5 million Afghans fled to refuge in Pakistan, where many remain to this day.

Some of the leaders of the anti-Taliban Northern Alliance, notably former Afghan Communist Secret Police chief General Mohammed Fahim and Uzbek warlord Rashid Dostam, had been responsible for frightful massacres and the most abominable crimes against real and fancied opponents, included flaying, impalement, burning and burial alive, acid baths, freezing to death in refrigerators, as well as more conventional tortures of electrocution, beatings, drownings, and the ripping out of eyes, beards, and fingernails.

Revenge lies at the very heart of the Pashtun ethos, and the Taliban were determined to exact revenge on the Communist criminals who had inflicted untold suffering on their nation. Ironically, these very same Communist war criminals would, after 9/11, become the leading Afghan allies of the United States.

After imposing order, Islamic Sharia law, and largely rooting out corruption, the Taliban's next objectives were to oust the remaining Afghan Communists in the north, and eradicate the poppy trade, which had spread like wildfire. By 2001, the Taliban's ramshackle forces and hundreds of foreign volunteers, including fighters from Osama bin Laden's al-Qaida, had managed to push the Communists, composed principally of Masood's Tajik forces, and those of General Rashid Dostam, almost out of Afghanistan. The Tajik/Uzbek Northern Alliance was sustained from neighboring Tajikistan by the Russian military and intelligence services, and by aid from Iran and India, both of whom sought to undermine Pakistani influence in Afghanistan and assert their own.

Under the Taliban, poppy production, according to the UN's Office for Drug Control and Crime Prevention, fell to nearly zero in 2001. The only places where the drug trade continued to thrive was in areas controlled by the Northern Alliance, whose leaders became the nation's leading drug kingpins.

However successful the Taliban was in bringing peace to Afghanistan and suppressing the drug trade, the rest of its agenda turned into a disaster. The country bumpkins of the Taliban swaggered around Kabul, intimidating its far more sophisticated residents, imposing primitive restrictions, beating unveiled women, stoning malefactors, and generally acting like ruffians. The backwoods Taliban, who could rarely speak any tongue except their own Pashtu, looked sullen, and grim, and were inarticulate and, too often, simply dim-witted.

The foreign media, which rarely ventured beyond the modest comforts of Kabul, sent a flood of outraged reports about the loutish behavior of the Taliban without ever seeing or recounting the benefits the Taliban brought to the countryside. Western press reports gave the impression that only the Taliban abused women, while, in reality, everyone in Afghanistan's tribal culture acted similarly. Women were no better off in Saudi Arabia, the tribal regions of Pakistan, or, for that matter, in rural India, where killing female babies and lynching lower-caste women for daring to marry higher-caste men was a frequent practice.

The Taliban's treatment of women became a hot-button topic among women's groups across the United States. Books were written, films and fiery seminars were directed at the Taliban's oppression of women. One million Afghan women were killed by the Soviets and their local Communist allies from 1979–89, but none of America's angry women's groups were moved by this fact or even bothered to mention it. Their ire was reserved for the Muslim Taliban.

The US would use the Taliban's mistreatment of women as one of its justifications for invading Afghanistan. When Canada sent combat troops to support the US occupation of Afghanistan, it actually claimed that a primary reason for its mission was to protect women's rights. These claims, however cynical and preposterous, sold very well at home, particularly to female voters, many of whom seemed to equate the Taliban's ruffians with all they found undesirable in men.

The Taliban soon became a growing embarrassment to Muslims everywhere, and to those Muslin nations that had recognized Mullah Omar's regime. Commentators across the Muslim world argued that what they were seeing in Afghanistan was pure primitive tribal behavior that had next to nothing to do with Islam. They were quite right, but the Talibs didn't give a fig for what anyone thought, a common trait among the famously stubborn Pashtuns. As a result, the Taliban suffered the first of a string of major public relations disasters that would eventually turn the world against them.

Once order was established, Osama bin Laden emerged as a close ally of Mullah Omar in the ongoing struggle against the Afghan Communists, providing the Taliban with both some finance and a few hundred veteran foreign mujahidin. Bin Laden's goal was to extirpate the remnants of the Afghan Communists and then embark on his long-cherished project of turning Afghanistan into a training ground for international jihadists.

In these pan-Islamist ventures, bin Laden was eagerly supported by Mullah Omar and his Taliban chiefs, as well as by powerful Islamist elements in Pakistan's armed forces and intelligence service. Their common ambition was to form cadres of Islamic fighters who would continue to wage jihad against the Afghan Communist Northern Alliance, and to liberate fellow Muslims in Central Asia and China's Xinjiang from Communist oppression, and Saudi Arabia, Egypt, Jordan, Chechnya, and Kashmir from American or Russian or Indian domination.

Small groups of would-be jihadists came from across the Muslim world to bin Laden's makeshift camps. Many were teenagers or young men elated by the victory over the Soviets and imbued with fervor to liberate their fellow Muslims from Communist rule. Contrary to what western security forces would later claim, their attendance was not motivated by anti-western hatred, but by a desire to fight Communism or develop a rigorous Islamic lifestyle.

Various Central Asian resistance groups came to the camps for combat arms training and comradeship. The most important was Jumma Namangani's Islamic Movement of Uzbekistan. Its goal was the overthrow of Central Asia's most brutal and savage Communist dictatorship, that of "Red Sultan" Islam Karimov, and the creation of a democratic Islamic government in that blighted nation. Other groups of jihadists came from Kazakhstan, Tajikistan, Kyrgyzstan, and Turkmenistan. Small numbers of would-be jihadists also arrived from the southern Philippines, Pakistan, Bangladesh, Thailand, and Chechnya.

The most exotic group were Uighurs, the Muslim Turkic people numbering some 7 million people who lived in the independent republic of East Turkistan. In 1949, China and the Soviet Union invaded and extinguished the independent Muslim republic. This unknown aggression came a year before China invaded and annexed neighboring Tibet. While the world continues to lament the plight of the Tibetans, it has totally ignored the fate of the Uighurs. Their resistance movements were cynically branded terrorist by the Bush administration in exchange for Chinese support against the Taliban and other Islamic resistance movements.

However, the largest contingent in the Afghan camps was foreign jihadists who were being trained to fight in Indian-ruled Kashmir by Pakistani intelligence. After 9/11, when Pakistan abandoned the Taliban under American threats, its involvement in the Afghan camps was hushed up or eradicated, and the jihadists dispersed. So many of what the US would later call "Osama bin Laden's terrorist camps" were, in fact, training bases for Kashmiri guerrillas run by Washington's close ally, Pakistan.

At the time of the US invasion of Afghanistan, there were only a few hundred anti-American al-Qaida jihadists. The rest of the 5,000 to 7,000 foreign-jihadist contingent were training to fight in regional causes, not against the West. They had been invited by the Taliban as a gesture of pan-Islamic solidarity. These fighters were not al-Qaida followers, though the US always lumped them into the al-Qaida total.

But screaming headlines in the US, British, and Canadian media about forty to sixty "terrorist training camps" and a great deal of disinformation that persists to this day, left nearly all westerners with the impression that Afghanistan was a hotbed of anti-western terrorists, aided and protected by Mullah Omar's Taliban. When the US invaded Afghanistan, it branded all these disparate jihadists as al-Qaida, and hunted them down ruthlessly. In fact, it is very likely that in the years before 9/11, the CIA considered making use of both bin Laden's group and the other assorted jihadists in Afghanistan, just as it had used the 100,000 volunteers from across the Muslim world during the great anti-Soviet war.

The US certainly had its eye on the post-Soviet republics of Central Asia, which were estimated to have 40 percent of the world's gas reserves and at least 6 percent of its oil. Perhaps another Muslim army could be assembled to overthrow the Communist regimes of Central Asia and bring these newly strategic "petrolistans" into America's political and economic orbit. The Taliban, which preached the liberation of Central Asia from godless Communist rule, looked like an ideal candidate to provide a proxy army for the CIA for use against Iran, Central Asia, and China. Shortly before his assassination, Pakistan's late leader, President Muhammad

Zia-ul-Haq, told me he planned to use the Taliban to liberate Central Asia from Communist rule.

The Taliban was also a very bitter enemy of neighboring Iran, which had repeatedly undermined the anti-Soviet Afghan jihad. The Taliban's Salafists regarded Iran's Shia as heretics, idolaters, and apostates. Tehran detested the Taliban and came close to invading Afghanistan after the Talibs killed a number of its intelligence agents. The Persian-speaking Tajiks were natural allies to Iran, which had its own designs on western Afghanistan.

To even the most sluggish minds at the CIA, it seemed clear that the Taliban might prove to be a very useful tool to use against Iran. Saudi Arabia, another bitter foe of Iran and competitor for the loyalty of Central Asian Muslims, came to the identical conclusion, and strongly backed the Taliban. The Saudis also funded hundreds of Salafist missionaries to spread the word of militant Islam in Afghanistan and Pakistan to counter Iran's dispatch of missionaries to preach Shia militancy and revolution. This writer has learned that the CIA also actively considered arming and using the Afghan-based Uighurs against China, with whom relations at the time were frosty. In the event of war with China over Taiwan, a Muslim Uighur uprising in Xinjiang could prove a useful diversion.

As a result, the US government continued providing substantial overt and secret payments and diplomatic support to the Taliban until four months before 9/11. In April and September 1996, US assistant secretary of state for South Asia, Robin Raphael, made a high-profile official visit to the Taliban leadership in Kabul aimed at cementing relations and showing Washington's support for Afghanistan's new rulers. The last overt US payment, $41 million in May 2001, was officially earmarked for anti-drug operations, but, according to this author's intelligence sources, was intended to keep the Taliban in the US camp just in case it could prove useful in the future against Iran or China. The Taliban's hatred of Iran was particularly noted and appreciated in Washington.

This US aid to Taliban contrasts sharply with Washington's fierce denunciations of the Islamic movement only four months later as a bunch of terrorists, thugs, and women beaters.

Shortly after the 9/11 attacks on New York and Washington, for which no group took responsibility, the US government accused Osama bin Laden of having masterminded the attacks, even though no proof of his complicity was ever offered. Washington, caught flat-footed in the worst surprise attack since Pearl Harbor, needed a target for its revenge and had no time for legal formalities. Ultimatums were delivered to Pakistan and the Taliban. Pakistan, as previously noted, was ordered to abandon the Taliban, open its bases to the US, and turn Inter-Services Intelligence (ISI) against the Talibs or face a US invasion and very likely coordinated attack by India. Islamabad quickly caved in. The Taliban was ordered to hand over Osama bin Laden or face immediate war.

But Mullah Omar and his tribal council refused. The Taliban told Washington it would not hand over Osama bin Laden until it supplied Kabul with proof of his guilt in a proper extradition process. In any event, retorted the Taliban, bin Laden could not get a fair trial in post–9/11 America; it would only deliver bin Laden, after proper extradition proceedings, to a court in a Muslim nation. Washington immediately rejected Kabul's offer and accelerated plans to mount an invasion. Why, one must ask, would the Taliban's leaders court a US invasion certain to bring their destruction? Ever since the 1998 bombing of two US embassies in East Africa, which were very likely staged by al-Qaida, the Taliban's leadership had been increasingly uncomfortable with bin Laden's presence in their country. Halfhearted efforts had been made to convince bin Laden to leave, but to no avail.

The primary reason the Taliban's leaders refused to hand over bin Laden to the Americans was "Pushtunwali," the ancient Afghan tribal code of conduct, among whose most sacred tenets is the defense, to the death, of a guest. Bin Laden, remember, was a renowned national hero of the Great Jihad, wounded six times in battle, an honored guest, and, eventually, became a son-in-law to Mullah Omar. Handing him over to the enraged Americans or expelling him would dishonor the Pashtun. In the western world, the concept of personal, family, and group honor has mostly vanished. But in Afghanistan, the Mideast, and other parts of the Muslim world, honor still often takes primacy over financial wealth or gain, a reality frequently lost on the many Americans who believe everyone has his or her price and money can buy anything.

The Taliban would not stain its honor, no matter how dire the outcome. This was a typical Pashtun decision. Anyone who knows these fierce, stubborn tribesmen also knows they cannot be backed into a corner or given an ultimatum. So, for an antique code of honor, the Taliban, in a supremely quixotic act, decided to resist the greatest power on earth. The results were predictable. While US B-52s carpet bombed Taliban fixed positions, Pakistani agents of the ISI fanned out to rent the loyalty of Afghan chieftains with bags full of US$100 bills. The Communist-dominated North Alliance suddenly received an arsenal of Russian arms, armored vehicles, and equipment, as well as military aid from Iran. Soldiers from Communist Tajikistan and Uzbekistan, and some Russian units, disguised as members of the Afghan Northern Alliance, drove south. On November 13, 2001, Northern Alliance forces, discreetly commanded by a Russian lieutenant general, entered Kabul. This was a rich moment for connoisseurs of irony. The largely Pashtun mujahidin, backed by the US and Pakistan, had combined to defeat the Soviets and local Communists, and drove them from Afghanistan.

Now, twelve years later, the US had allied itself with its former foes, the Russians and their Afghan Communist allies, to crush former allies, the Pashtun Taliban. After the Taliban was overthrown, Russia ended up with all of northern Afghanistan—essentially the Uzbek and Tajik regions—as its sphere of interest run by the KGB (now the SVR/FSB), thus in part reversing their lost war in 1989. The United States and the Communists had become allies against Islamic forces, and Russia gained a major role in exploiting the new Silk Road, the energy export route south from the Caspian Basin.

General Rashid Dostam's Uzbeks massacred thousands of captured Taliban fighters under the eyes of US Special Forces. Hapless, would-be jihadists who had come from abroad to fight Communism, Pakistanis on family visits, religious students, tourists, and even a few real al-Qaida were rounded up by local bounty hunters who were paid up to $1,000 a head for "terrorists" by US forces. Many ended up in secret CIA prisons in Afghanistan, or the notorious US prison camp at Guantanamo, Cuba, where they suffered frightful physical and mental abuse.

The Bush administration, and particularly its neoconservatives who, after 9/11, had seized control of foreign and military policy, was triumphant. The two-week invasion and occupation of medieval Afghanistan was vaunted as a new model for high-tech US military intervention around the world, and a highly efficient and effective example of how to deal with Muslim malefactors. Americans were told the "terrorist" Taliban, one of the authors of 9/11, had been eradicated and the war won. In reality, the Taliban was not a terrorist organization, as Washington claimed, had had nothing to do with 9/11, and most likely knew nothing in advance about it. The mullahs in Kabul were likely as surprised by the attacks as the Americans.

In 2001, this writer, to considerable derision from newly minted "Afghan experts" and pundits, warned that the Taliban had not been defeated, as the White House exulted, but had merely dispersed in the face of overwhelming firepower and would likely resume fighting in three or four years. Mullah Omar had merely ordered his men to replace their black Taliban turbans with white ones, blend back into the Pashtun civilian population, and wait. Serious resistance by Afghans after the 1979 Soviet invasion did not get under way until 1983. The Afghans move slowly and wage war at their own leisurely, medieval pace. They are well aware they can outlast any foreign invader.

Exactly four years after America's "total victory" in Afghanistan, the by then forgotten war suddenly came shockingly back to life as reformed Taliban fighters, who were much more proficient at waging a guerrilla rather than conventional war, began attacking American forces and their local rented Afghan allies. Caught by surprise, the US had to rush more troops to Afghanistan to supplement the division-sized forces that had been fruitlessly hunting Osama bin Laden and his chief of staff, Ayman al-Zawahiri. Washington also began to exert intense pressure on its NATO allies to beef up the token contingents they had sent to Afghanistan after the US invoked the alliance's mutual defense treaty after 9/11. In effect, the United States had ordered its tributary states to supply troops for a new war, an act as familiar to Emperor Xerxes in ancient Persia as to Napoleon or Chairman Leonid Brezhnev.

Britain, France, Italy, Australia, Canada, and a score of other nations sent minor contingents, many over the protests of their voters. Canada provided a vivid example. Under not-so-subtle threats of trade restrictions, Canada's then prime minister, Paul Martin, was given the Hobson's choice of either sending its soldiers to Iraq or Afghanistan. Ottawa at first agreed to send a small contingent of troops to the relatively quiet Kabul command. For reasons never made clear, it then agreed to send some 2,200 combat troops south, into the heart of Taliban territory. Canada's newly elected Conservative politicians, totally ignorant of Afghanistan and eager to curry favor with their ideological political mentors in the Bush administration, foolishly agreed for Canadian troops to be stationed in the middle of Taliban territory.

At the same time, Washington desperately struggled to create a compliant Afghan regime that had at least some popular support and appearance of legitimacy. The CIA's first choice for a new Afghan leader had been an old comrade in arms of this writer, former renowned mujahidin leader Abdul Haq. But Haq's famous impetuosity led him to rush off with some men to liberate Afghanistan from the Taliban. He was caught by the Taliban and swiftly hanged. This misadventure forced the CIA to turn to its number-two Afghan asset, the urbane, eloquent, but almost unknown Hamid Karzai. He was made interim leader by national tribal council that was surrounded by US troops and heavily bribed.

The decent, amiable Karzai was a political nullity and had no significant tribal or clan power base in Afghanistan, a fatal weakness. But with his excellent English, earnest speaking style, and trademark green cap (something Afghans did not wear), he proved very popular abroad and an eloquent, telegenic spokesman for the US–run "crusade for democracy." To outsiders, he was a welcome relief to the Taliban's glowering, hirsute turbaned wild men, who epitomized the quintessence of menacing Islam. But Karzai had no troops or tribal levies and no influence whatsoever outside the capital. He was widely scorned by Afghans as an American puppet and dubbed "the mayor of Kabul."

Karzai's true measure of popularity may be best judged by the fact that he remains surrounded by two to three rings of 100 to 200 American mercenary bodyguards at all times, his own countrymen being deemed insufficiently loyal for the mission. His Communist predecessor during the Soviet occupation, Najibullah, never had to rely on Soviet bodyguards for protection and often mixed with the public. The real power behind the figurehead of Karzai remained the drug-dealing Tajik and Uzbek warlords of the Northern Alliance and their Russian patrons. This, in turn, created a major dilemma for the United States. Afghanistan is like a three-legged stool. Stability required cooperation of all three major ethnic groups: Pashtun, Tajiks, and Uzbeks. Alienating the Pashtun, who comprised half the population, and excluding them from power, insured permanent instability in Afghanistan.

But that is just what the Bush administration did. It first demonized the Pashtun Taliban as mad-dog terrorists responsible for 9/11 with whom no discourse could be possible, and then got into bed with the Communist Tajiks and Uzbeks. To the angry Pashtun, the American invaders had simply replaced the Soviet invaders, in both cases allying with their traditional Tajik and Uzbek enemies. By refusing to deal with the Pashtun Taliban, the US and its allies ensured that Afghanistan's majority would be permanently alienated and remain deeply hostile.

Quite amazingly, in spite of Washington's offer of a $50-million bounty for Osama bin Laden and Ayman al-Zawahiri, and an army of intelligence agents, soldiers, informers, and a galaxy of electronic and aerial surveillance, al-Qaida's leaders remain at large and, according to the 2006 US National Intelligence Estimate, had rebuilt and reinvigorated their movement. Even if al-Qaida's chiefs were apprehended or killed, the conflict between the Pashtun Taliban and the foreign occupiers of Afghanistan, known by the Orwellian name the Coalition, would not have gone away. In fact, every bombed village in Afghanistan adds a score of new recruits to the Taliban and its allies.

After seven years of low-level warfare in Afghanistan, the United States and its dragooned Canadian and other NATO allies, could report almost no real progress in their war to pacify the unruly Afghans in spite of a steady stream of rosy reports from military public relations officers ready to fight to the last Xerox copy for their cause.

One of the more reliable monitors of the war, the French/Belgian/ Afghan–based Senlis Council, reported in 2006 that the Taliban effectively controlled or influenced half the nation and was moved northeast to begin threatening Kabul's surrounding region. This unwelcome news, which was generally ignored by western media, came as NATO commanders in Afghanistan were making increasingly desperate pleas for more combat troops.

Those western-oriented nations with right-wing governments, like Canada, Australia, Poland, and Denmark, or a retro-imperial-minded leader like Britain's Tony Blair, viewed sending troop contingents to fight in Iraq and Afghanistan as earning merit badges for their conservative principles. Canada's minister of foreign affairs even claimed it was essential to keeping troops in combat in Afghanistan to boost his nation's prestige in international meetings.

Among western and Australian right-wing politicians, hostility to Muslims had become a key element of their political platforms, just as anti-Semitism had been a common element in the 1930s among members of the hard right. Islamophobia had replaced anti-Semitism as a new, acceptable prejudice and an effective way of earning political benefit from rousing nationalism, prejudice, and war fever, the traditional staples of the right. However, the war in Iraq played a significant role in the defeat of Australia's right-wing Howard government in November 2007.

These conservative-ruled nations were happy to prove their ideological fraternity with the Bush administration, as well as demonstrate their leader's machismo. Being a war leader was intoxicating and appealed to the least-educated male voters, even if the war in question was a tiny, unequal one being waged against medieval tribesmen in the wastes of Afghanistan. Turkey's ultra-right generals, who still constitute something of a shadow government, were delighted to send troops in a war against their blood enemy, the Islamists, even though the mission was wildly unpopular among the rest of the country. A few tiny nations, like Albania and the Baltic states, sent handfuls of troops to Afghanistan out of sheer gratitude to the United States for freeing them from Communism.

Other allies of Washington, like France, Germany, and Japan, reluctantly sent troops, though with the caveat they remain in quiet garrison areas and avoid confrontation with the Taliban. All fulfilled their feudal duty to Washington, but with a minimum of zeal and effectiveness. Their voters, who mostly disapproved of the war in Afghanistan as a hopeless and unnecessary colonial misadventure, had demanded such a minimalist policy of token engagement.

In the Muslim world, the US invasion of Afghanistan was initially viewed by many as a legitimate response to a horrible crime. There was little or no sympathy for the Taliban, particularly after its brutal public punishments and after its extreme elements dynamited two ancient statues of the Buddha at Bamiyan, a barbarous act of vandalism that rightly outraged the entire world—though the same world, it should be recalled, that ignored the equally wanton destruction of Muslim mosques and shrines across Bosnia by Serbs a few years earlier.

But as the little Afghan war dragged on, and increasing numbers of Afghan civilians were killed by US bombing or shelling, what had initially seemed to be a justified retaliation for a criminal act was increasingly viewed as naked, oil-fueled western aggression against yet another Muslim nation, thinly disguised as an antiterrorist operation. These misgivings in the Muslim world were deepened by lack of proof of direct involvement by Osama bin Laden or the Taliban in 9/11, and the belief, however mistaken, that the 9/11 attacks were staged by Israel, the US government, or were a gigantic hoax.

By 2005, when the Taliban began resuming serious resistance, little sympathy remained in the Muslim world for the US occupation. The consensus held that the US had taken advantage of the 9/11 attacks to implement long-prepared plans to seize the Muslim world's energy wealth and establish new bases in its most strategic regions. The British Raj had done precisely the same thing a century earlier, provoking incidents with local monarchs whose territory it coveted, then invading and installing puppet rulers, all under the banner of establishing order or bringing the light of Christianity to the misguided heathen. Substitute the slogan "campaign for Democracy" with "Christianity," and the voices of the two Raj's were often identical. Which reminds us of Citizen Robespierre's noteworthy maxim during the French Revolution that "all the world hates armed missionaries."

Once again, as in the case of Palestine and Iraq, television carried coverage of the continuing misery and suffering of the Afghans to the outside world. Afghanistan came to be regarded as another noble Muslim struggle against western domination. Equally significant, jihadists in Iraq began bringing their combat techniques, honed in the struggle against US occupation, particularly deadly roadside explosive and suicide bombers, to Afghanistan, where the use of such devices was previously unknown. Afghanistan joined Iraq as the two poles of the Islamic "resistance struggle." A new, younger generation of jihadis went off to war in Afghanistan, just as they had to occupied Iraq.

To Washington's ire, Osama bin Laden and Dr. Ayman al-Zawahiri both gloated in video- and audiotapes that the United States was falling right into the trap they had laid. A good number of western Mideast and South Asia experts agreed with them.

By the end of 2008, the US and NATO were stalemated in Afghanistan. The US had over 40,000 troops, numerous CIA teams, and thousands of local mercenaries operating in Afghanistan; NATO and other nations seeking Washington's favor, contributed some 23,000 troops. This number, many of whom were engaged in static defense of their bases or supply lines, was simply too small to pacify southern Afghanistan.

During the 1980s, the Soviet Red Army deployed at least 160,000 regulars, contingents from the Warsaw Pact, and some 260,000 troops of the Afghan Communist regime. In spite of the unspeakable cruelty of the Afghan Secret Police, the KHAD, and a ruthless, scorched-earth campaign, Communist forces were unable to defeat the mujahidin resistance, which received large amounts of arms and supplies from Pakistan. Soviet chairman Mikhail Gorbachev was wise and humane enough to recognize the futility of continuing military operations in Afghanistan and in 1989 ordered a withdrawal.

How can the US and NATO expect to defeat resistance forces in Afghanistan that the ruthless Soviets, with far more numerous forces, could not? Washington's answer is airpower, and building up the Karzai regime. No force on earth can rival America's airpower, which is to our modern world what Britain's Royal Navy was in previous centuries. Airpower is the supreme expression of America's might and its most lethal application. The Soviets were never able to maintain constant air patrols over Afghanistan; their response time to attacks by mujahidin was usually 30 minutes, but sometimes much longer, allowing resistance fighters to escape after attacking.

By contrast, the US Air Force, supported by navy and marine aviation, is able to maintain 24-hour combat air patrols over southern Afghanistan that include B-1 and B-52 bombers loaded with precision-guided munitions, strike aircraft with similar weapons, helicopter gunships, deadly AC-130 Spectre gunships, and missile-armed drones. These permanently circling hunters can respond day or night to enemy attacks within minutes, showering the assailants with intense cannon fire and devastating cluster bombs.

Because of the effectiveness and lethality of such air counterattacks, both Iraqi and Afghan resistance forces have been forced to rely on roadside bombs and suicide bombers rather than traditional ambushes and infantry attacks. Were it not for the lethality, ubiquity, and immediacy of US airpower, overstretched American forces and their allies in both nations would have been unable to defend their vulnerable supply lines, and likely defeated.

Airpower, however deadly, remains a blunt instrument. The immediate reaction of US airpower to ground attacks too often ends up blasting villages and killing innocent farmers and travelers, generating ever-greater hatred for the occupiers and more recruits for the resistance. In both Afghanistan and Iraq, air attacks have also become a weapon of terror: villages that shelter Muslim fighters are routinely bombed in reprisal. Slain civilians are routinely described in Coalition reports as "suspected Taliban fighters."

The 1980s war turned against the Soviets once the US supplied effective Stinger man-portable antiaircraft missiles to the mujahidin. These deadly, low-level antiaircraft weapons quickly brought a halt to Soviet close air support, helicopter attacks, and supply missions. One must suspect that among the former KGB agents and retired soldiers now running Russia there are some Cold War veterans who would like to exact revenge for America's defeat of their nation in Afghanistan by quietly supplying today's mujahidin resistance with a modern generation of highly effective Russian portable antiaircraft missiles like the SA-16 and SA-18 IglaM.

American airpower may hold off the mujahidin, but it cannot win the war against them. If the US were to lose basing rights in Pakistan, Tajikistan, and Uzbekistan, its air war over Afghanistan would be severely curtailed. A major portion of the cost of this two-billion-dollar-a-month war comes from keeping large numbers of warplanes over Afghanistan around the clock, burning huge amounts of fuel, and maintaining aircraft carriers and other warships on station in the Gulf and Arabian Sea.

The restoration of democratic government in Pakistan in February 2008 may also prove a major blow to the US war effort in Afghanistan and pro-Taliban regions of Pakistan. The new democratic alliance of the People's Party and Muslim League that won power in a landslide election left former military dictator Pervez Musharraf isolated and increasingly besieged. The democratic coalition pledged to restore the judicial system purged by Musharraf with US backing, begin reducing Pakistan's support of US military operations, and cut way back the role played by Pakistan's military in supporting the American campaign. At the same time, anti-American militants sharply increased their attacks on US and NATO supply lines from Pakistan into Afghanistan, threatening fuel supplies for the occupation forces.

Senior members of the democratic coalition called for peace talks with the Taliban in Afghanistan and its Pakistani Pashtun tribal allies, and an end to Musharraf's war against his own people that was supported and paid for by Washington. Ham-handed attempts by US deputy secretary of state John Negroponte to intimidate the new coalition into changing its avowed plans were met across Pakistan with outrage and derision. However, in May 2008, attempts by the US and Washington to split the PPP-ML(N) coalition, and the divergent interests of their respective leaders, caused the alliance to fall apart. MN(N) leader Nawaz Sharif broke the coalition after PPP leader Asif Zardari refused to reinstate 60 leading judges that Musharraf had previously fired.

The ousted judges had vowed to declare Musharraf's second term as president illegal and to investigate his role, and that of Washington, in the disappearance of up to one thousand Pakistanis on charges of "terrorism." PPP chief Zardari sided with Musharraf by refusing to reinstate the judges. His motivation was obvious. The Supreme Court justices had also threatened to take up extensive corruption charges against Zardari. So, as of the spring of 2008, Pakistan's democratic opposition remained splintered and confused while dictator Musharraf still clung to power with US financial and political support.

Washington's second hope of imposing its will upon Afghanistan is creating a large Afghan sepoy army that will deal on the ground with the Taliban. This is traditional colonial war strategy, perfected by the British Raj, where native troops are raised to fight local insurgents. But after seven years, the US has been unable to cobble together a reliable Afghan national army loyal to its man in Kabul, Hamid Karzai. The best Washington has been able to achieve is to assemble a potpourri of unruly, unreliable regional mercenaries whose loyalty is to their local warlords.

At least there was some scattered ideological commitment among the Soviet's Afghan Communist troops. America's Afghan sepoys serve only for money. This is hardly surprising considering Afghanistan offers almost no other employment; it's either that, or growing opium. It was just such combat-averse Afghan mercenary soldiers that allowed Osama bin Laden and his followers to escape to Pakistan from the Tora Bora massif in 1991. The US did not want to risk its own troops against bin Laden's combat-hardened mujahidin.

During their decade of occupation of Afghanistan, the Soviets were routinely betrayed and double-crossed by their Afghan allies. The same phenomenon is happening to US, British, Canadian, and other NATO troops. In Afghanistan, blood, clan, and tribal loyalties trump all others. The US can use its wealth to rent temporary obedience, but it will never be able to generate genuine loyalty or true support from the Afghans, who have a time-honored tradition of readily taking money from foreigners, then stabbing them in the back.

While many Afghans served the Soviets, and, later, the Americans, they made sure to maintain discreet contacts with their relatives and fellow tribesmen on the opposite side. Every Soviet, and now NATO, operation is telegraphed well in advance to the resistance by the legion of Afghan translators, cooks, guards, drivers, and camp followers that the US and NATO cannot do without. Even the Communists of the Northern Alliance maintain backdoor contacts with the Taliban. Everyone is aware that one day the Americans and their auxiliaries will, like all previous invaders, go home, leaving the Afghans to sort out the ensuing mess. So just about everyone is hedging their bets in what will inevitably be a deadly game of post-occupation survival. Revenge remains a hallmark of the Afghan tribal code.

For the US and its allies, political stability in Afghanistan has proven even more elusive than military victory. Hamid Karzai has no real power and remains in office only thanks to the bayonets of foreign troops and a steady stream of cash from his patrons. The Communist and Russian-dominated Northern Alliance of Tajiks and Uzbeks is the real power behind Karzai, ensuring his continued unacceptability to the nation's Pashtun majority.

Outside Kabul, power is dispersed among a score of regional warlords whose loyalty is assured by regular delivery of bags of US$100 bills. Imperial Britain bought the loyalty of local tribal chiefs in Oman and Aden in the same manner. Many of these local Afghan despots are also deeply involved in the drug trade, which provides 85 percent of Afghanistan's GDP and grew an astounding 20 percent from 2005–8. Even the US government had to admit that opium production in its protectorate was surging, providing 93 percent of the world's supply of heroin. Before the 1990s, Southeast Asia's Golden Triangle had been the primary supplier of opium and morphine base. This narcotics trade in turn fuels massive corruption in Pakistan, where Afghan morphine base is refined into heroin and smuggled to the outside world. Pakistan's police, antinarcotics squads, customs and port officers, and scores of senior politicians all became infected by drug corruption.

In short, by 2008, Afghanistan had become the world's second-most highly developed narco-state, surpassed only in drug revenue by Colombia. Embarrassingly, the US and NATO found themselves as the proud new owners and defenders of the world's primary source of heroin. The US and NATO routinely blamed the Taliban for the drug trade. The small farmers in the south who supported the Taliban indeed raised opium. It was that, or starve, But the collection, transport, refining, and export of opium-morphine base was controlled by US–backed warlords and high government officials in Kabul. As in the case of the two Indochina wars, and Nicaragua, drugs became the sole viable currency of war-shattered economies, and the US soon found itself drawn into the narcotics business in order to fund its local allies. In the Indochina wars, first the French Secret Service, then the CIA, had ended up flying opium out of the remote mountains to refiners in Saigon.

In Afghanistan, President Bush's once-vaunted war on drugs ran head-on into his war on terror. The war on drugs lost, as the US Drug Enforcement Agency (DEA) was ordered to curb its operations in Afghanistan and turn a blind eye to the rising flood of heroin from that nation. So far, the extent of involvement of CIA and other US agencies in the Afghan drug trade remains unknown. It is, hopefully, minimal, but if experience in Indochina is any guide then damaging revelations of CIA involvement with Afghan narcotics may surface in the near future.

Efforts by Washington to enhance the political legitimacy of Karzai's regime failed in Afghanistan, but proved successful abroad, where the routinely ill-informed US and Canadian media relied exclusively on euphoric press releases from the US embassy in Kabul. Since hardly any reporters could speak an Afghan language, and even less dared venture beyond the secure confines of Kabul and US or British army bases, they naturally produced news that had been spoon-fed to them by official sources. As a result, Americans and Canadians were advised that democracy had triumphed in Afghanistan, thanks to the wisdom and guidance of the western occupying forces. By contrast, the cynical French stationed troops and aircraft in quiet zones of Afghanistan while cultivating discreet links with the Taliban, thus pleasing all concerned.

US–run elections in Afghanistan in 2004 and 2005 were as crudely rigged as votes held by America's other "democratic allies," such as Egypt, Morocco, or Pakistan. Any would-be candidate deemed insufficiently supportive of US policy was branded a supporter of terrorism and banned from the elections, thus removing the entire opposition. Huge amounts of bribes were dished out to ensure Karzai was confirmed as leader, and glowering, heavily armed US troops ensured that voters understood what they were expected to do, since ballots were carefully examined for signs of deviation from the party line. On top of all this, vote tallies were often doctored, and many voters denied access to the poles. UN observers validated this electoral charade.

Not surprisingly, the "triumph of democracy" in Afghanistan was bally-hooed by the White House and duly celebrated by the fawning North American media. Ironically, compared to these US–run elections, the national votes the Soviets had held in Afghanistan in 1986 and 1987 were far freer, more open, and more honest. Even many genuine anti-Soviet candidates were at least allowed to run. The final tallies were, of course, rigged, but the Soviet-installed ruler, Najibullah, proved much more popular and respected—and feared—than the green-caped Hamid Karzai. Eruptions of large anti–US demonstrations that were harshly suppressed did little to enhance Afghanistan's new image as a liberated nation relishing its newfound democracy.

These fixed elections underlined the unsettling similarities between the Soviet and American occupation of Afghanistan. The Soviets invaded Afghanistan in 1979 citing internationalist duty and the need to fight Islamic terrorists. Washington's slogan was fighting terrorism and spreading democracy. Both allied with the minority Tajiks and Uzbeks. Both were interested in carving out a corridor to and from the Arabian Sea coast in Pakistan (see *War at the Top of the World*). Both claimed they were fight-ing medievalist Islam, nation-building, liberating women, and bringing the benefits of modern education and democracy. Both claimed victory was just around the corner.

Having covered Moscow in the 1980s, I am struck by the many uncanny and ironic parallels between the Bush administration and the Brezhnev Polit-buro, but that is a topic for another book. Suffice it to say that once the US bested the USSR in the Cold War, and saw its old enemy collapse, it lost little time in assuming the role and aggressive behavior of the former Soviet Union, recalling the Taoist dictum "you become what you hate." More about this later.

As the twentieth century's finest military thinker, Major General J.F.C. Fuller pointed out, military victories are meaningless unless they create the groundwork for ensuing favorable political settlements. Or in his words, "The object of war is peace, not military victory." The US and its allies proved utterly incapable of forging any sort of political agreement in Afghanistan that would bring desired stability. The West could not cow the Pashtun, stop the run-amok drug trade, curb warlordism, or make the feeble Karzai into a credible, respected, or legitimate leader.

Equally vexing, the US was well and truly stuck in Afghanistan. The ostensible reason for the US invasion of Afghanistan was to capture Osama bin laden and "drain the swamp" of terrorism. Withdrawing its troops before these goals were accomplished would be a massive humiliation and defeat, resulting in the triumphant reemergence of Osama bin Laden and Ayman al-Zawahiri. They would inevitably crow to all the world that the mighty US had indeed been defeated, as they predicted, by the mujahidin. After the national humiliation of 9/11, the debacle in Iraq, defeat in Afghanistan by a bunch of medieval Muslim warriors was an intolerable prospect for both Republican chest-thumpers in Washington and even for most of their less bloodthirsty Democratic opponents. The best the Americans could hope for was the death of bin Laden and Zawahiri, followed by declaration of victory and mission accomplished, followed by a discreet pullout from Afghanistan, which would then lapse into the obscurity it had previously enjoyed.

But this seemed unlikely as the leaders of both of America's parties, Britain, and France called for sending more troops to Afghanistan, "to fight al-Qaida and terrorism." Even among antiwar Democrats there were calls for redeploying US combat troops from Iraq to Afghanistan. Few of these politicians seemed to understand that the elusive Osama bin Laden and his scattering of supporters were most likely not in Afghanistan at all but under deep cover in Pakistan; that their troops in Afghanistan were not waging an antiterrorist struggle, but had inadvertently become involved in a nineteenth-century-style colonial war against the Pashtun tribal people on both sides of the border; or that deeper involvement in Afghanistan was spreading the conflict farther into Pakistan, a nation of 165 million, anti-western people.

Meanwhile, the Muslim world bought none of the US claims about bringing democracy and social betterment to Afghanistan. The Taliban's brutal, stupid behavior was quickly forgotten, and replaced by gripping TV images of shattered villages, weeping survivors, and that new symbol of our imperial age, US troops in sunglasses kicking down doors and terrifying cowering civilians.

It was no coincidence, and certainly no error, that al-Jazeera's Kabul bureau was bombed by the US Air Force. Like the Soviets before them, the US was determined to control all news coming out of Afghanistan, and ensure that dead or wounded civilians did not make the evening dinner news around the globe. Much of the bad news from Afghanistan was in- deed suppressed, particularly in the United States, where the media too ea- gerly cooperated with the Pentagon's "see no evil" policy. This writer was advised on numerous occasions that the chiefs of major US television net- works had ordered there be no showing of American casualties or dead civilians and nothing that could be deemed anti-American.

But the facts did leak out, and viewers across the Muslim world were vividly aware of Afghanistan's ongoing suffering. Observing the world's mightiest power bashing a small, backwards nation was a deeply disturbing sight, one that increasingly roused anger and open fury in the ummah. September 11 was forgotten. Afghanistan, two and a half million of whose people had been killed, and an even larger number made destitute refugees, was now being ravaged by another foreign power and its allies. Britain, which had twice previously invaded Afghanistan in two bitterly fought colonial wars, was back again as an occupying power. The French also sent more troops to bolster NATO forces in Afghanistan.

In April 2008, Russia even agreed to supply US and NATO forces in Afghanistan, whose supply lines were coming under increasing attack by pro-Taliban tribesmen in Pakistan, confirming a view held by many Afghans that the old colonial powers were in league to permanently impose their rule over Afghanistan.

To many Muslims, Afghanistan was a martyr nation. Jihadists shouted that it was the sacred duty of all good Muslims to go to the aid of its afflicted people. As for the Afghans, they had defeated all previous foreign invaders since the fourth century BC. The Pashtun would fight on for another century, if necessary, or even two, until they were free of foreign occupation and able to resume their favored pastime, feuding among themselves.

CHAPTER TEN
★ ★ ★

DEBACLE IN THE GARDEN OF EDEN

On my first visit to Iraq in 1976, I was welcomed by the spectacle of alleged Israeli spies being hanged in the large square in front of my hotel. An attractive, blonde American neophyte CIA agent befriended me in hopes of gleaning information about Iraq's Soviet-supplied arms. Every room in our hotel was bugged by the Mukhabarat, or secret police. I was petrified the listeners would overhear the lovely young lady from CIA headquarters in Langley asking me about Iraq's ZSU-23 mobile antiaircraft guns.

Iraq was a grim, terrifying place in those faraway years, and so it remains to this day. When I was covering Iraq just before the 1991 war, the Iraqi secret police threatened to hang me as an Israeli spy. A curse seemed to hang over Iraq. Like its ill-fated European double, Yugoslavia, the Iraqi state cobbled together by British imperialists from fragments of the defunct Ottoman Empire, included the oil fields of Kurdistan in the north, a connective Sunni core in the middle, and the oil-rich southern Basra region, proved to be a geopolitical monstrosity.

The new state had no sense of national identity, no common purpose, and no raison d'être—except to provide the Royal Navy with oil. Iraq's main ethnic groups—Shia, Sunni, Kurds, Turks, and Jews—had little in common. As soon as Britain set up Iraq and imposed a puppet Hashemite monarch on the throne, Kurds, Sunnis, and Shia rose in revolt. British forces crushed the rebellion ruthlessly. Winston Churchill, then home and war minister, authorized the RAF to use poisonous mustard gas against rebellious Kurdish tribes. Eight decades later, Britain's prime minister, Tony Blair, would brand President Saddam Hussein a monster and war criminal for doing to the Kurds precisely what the sainted Churchill had earlier done.

When Saddam Hussein became president of Iraq in 1979, he followed a long line of inept rulers who were either puppets of the British or of a crazed dictator like Abdul Karim el-Kassem. Saddam, who ruled through fear, often compared himself to his hero, Stalin. Like the Soviet despot, Saddam used an iron fist and terror to mobilize his fractious people, rapidly develop a backwards nation, and turn it into a regional power. Saddam's Ba'ath Party had been helped into power by CIA and Britain's MI6. Iraq became a close ally of the United States and Britain. In 1979, Washington concluded that the new revolutionary government in Iran posed a grave threat to its Mideast interests and determined to overthrow it.

Iran's fiery clerical leaders were preaching Islamic revolution that called for the overthrow of the Mideast monarchs and generals who served as overseers for Anglo-American interests. Worse, the angry mullahs in Tehran were demanding the entire region's oil wealth be shared according to Koranic principles, with all Muslims, particularly so the poor. Tehran's demands for a higher, fair price for Mideast oil and the overthrow of "medieval Arab oil despots" deeply alarmed Washington and America's Big Oil. Here was a new danger that rivaled Communism.

Iraq, egged on by Washington, London, and the Saudis and Kuwaitis, and assured of their wholehearted military and financial support, invaded Iran in 1980. Saddam's forces were provided with western arms, secretly financed by the CIA through middlemen banks, and foodstuffs financed by the US Department of Agriculture (USDA) through Italy. The Saudis, Kuwait, and other Gulf emirates provided around $80 billion in loans to finance Iraq's war. Equally important, the US Defense Intelligence Agency supplied Saddam's military with daily satellite photos of Iranian troop dispositions that proved of decisive importance in the ground war. The US Treasury imposed a punishing financial blockade against Iran. In the later stages of the war, the US Navy went into action against Iran to thwart its efforts to close the Gulf.

While the US and western allies were arming and financing Iraq, Israel was quietly selling five billion dollars' worth of US arms and spare parts to Tehran, and continuing to arm Iraq's ever-rebellious Kurds. The Reagan administration and Israelis were delighted to see both Iraqis and Iranians locked in a long, debilitating war that proved a bonanza for western arms producers.

An attempt by a former Iranian schoolmate of mine, Sadegh Ghotzadegh, to overthrow Imam Khomeini was thwarted when an Israeli agent of influence on the US National Security Council revealed the plot to Israel. The Israeli government immediately warned Khomeini, who had Ghotzadegh arrested and executed, so preserving its leading arms-export customer. This was doubly ironic, since in 1979, Israel had reportedly planned, according to French intelligence sources, to intercept and shoot down the aircraft carrying Khomeini from his French exile home to Iran, but relented because of the large number of international journalists aboard.

After eight years of largely World War I static trench warfare, Grand Ayatollah Ruhollah Khomeini was forced in 1980 to sign a peace treaty with Iraq that he called "the bitterest day of my life." Iran was *in extremis*, its western cities laid to waste, and its dead in the long conflict numbered 500,000—more men than the US or Britain lost in World War II. A similar number of Iranians were seriously wounded, maimed for life, or blinded and hideously burned by Iraqi mustard gas.

While covering Baghdad in 1990, I discovered a group of four British scientific technicians who revealed they had been seconded to Iraq by the UK Ministry of Defense and MI6 foreign intelligence to work at a top-secret biological weapons laboratory at Salman Pak. Their mission was to weaponize the toxins anthrax, Q fever, tularemia, and botulism for use in battlefield munitions against massed Iranian infantry forces. The feeder stocks for these germ weapons had been supplied by a laboratory in the US state of Maryland, with Washington's full export approval.

The raw materials and technical expertise Iran used to produce the mustard and nerve gas it employed against Iranian formations, and, later, Kurdish rebels, came from Germany, Britain, Italy, and Holland. It should be noted that none of the germ weapons—which were never perfected or deployed—nor poison gases were genuine weapons of mass destruction (wmds). They were exclusively tactical weapons designed for battlefield use and delivery by 155mm artillery shells, artillery rockets, or bombs. By 2001, all old stocks of chemical weapons had been destroyed by Iraq or had become inert.

The only real weapons of mass destruction were large-yield nuclear weapons and, theoretically, germ weapons. The latter, however, were extremely difficult to produce or store, and even more difficult to disperse in quantities sufficient to cause mass casualties. The only nations with stores of germs weapons were the United States, Britain, the Soviet Union/Russia, and Israel. Many of their old stockpiles were judged militarily useless and are being destroyed. The West thus secretly supplied Iraq with some of the very weapons President George Bush and Prime Minister Tony Blair would later falsely claim threatened the entire globe with imminent destruction. In 2003, a sardonic joke went around the media: "Of course Saddam has weapons of mass destruction. We have the delivery receipts to prove it!"

Saddam's invasion of Iran, a nation with three times Iraq's population and great strategic depth, proved a military and economic disaster that left Iraq exhausted, unable to produce enough food, and deeply in debt to its Arab brothers. But the war also left Saddam Hussein as the US–backed policeman of the Gulf, and the cork in the bottle that confined the menacing Iranian genie. In the eleven years between assuming dictatorial power in 1979 and going to war with Iran, Saddam had used rising oil revenue to transform Iraq from a backwards agricultural nation into a modern state. He exercised his unfettered powers to promote universal education, comprehensive health care, women's rights, irrigation, and electrification, and to develop the region's most advanced industrial base. In spite of the losses and punishing expense of the war with Iran, Saddam managed to turn Iraq into one of the Arab world's most advanced nations—until much of Iraq's infrastructure was shattered by US bombing during the first Gulf oil war in 1991.

Iraq became a model for rapid national economic and social development—and savage political repression. In contrast to his neighbors, Saddam's regime was relatively free of corruption and less inclined to use state coffers as the ruler's private money, at least prior to the 1991 war. So long as Iraqis avoided politics or opposition to Saddam's all-powerful Ba'ath Party, they were assured an increasingly comfortable lifestyle, reliable medical care, and advanced education. Historically, Iraq had always been the Arab world's second pole, after Cairo, for learning, culture, and intellectual life.

Just as Iraq seemed destined for more future prosperity and influence once the damage of the Iran war was repaired, Saddam Hussein wrecked it all by his calamitous invasion of Kuwait. The Kuwaiti royal family detested and feared Saddam, sentiments which he generously reciprocated. Kuwait kept demanding billions of debt repayment from bankrupt Iraq; they slant drilled under the border to steal Iraq's oil, and hiked up its own oil production in order to lower Iraq's petroleum revenue. At a heated brotherly Arab conference in Riyadh, Saudi Arabia, on July 31, 1990, Crown Prince Sa'ad al-Abdullah is said to have sneeringly told the Iraqis that his nation would take Iraq's war widows for their harems as payment for Baghdad's overdue war debt. When Saddam heard this stinging, very Arab insult, he flew into a rage and immediately ordered his army to invade Kuwait. What ensued was an Arab tribal raid writ large that went horribly wrong.

Just before the invasion, April Gillespie, the US ambassador to Iraq, met with Saddam to deliver a very curious message from Washington: the US "took no position" in Arab border disputes, she informed Saddam. Iraq's ruler seems to have interpreted this message as a green light to deal with the insolent Kuwaitis. The near-universal view across the Mideast is that President Bush Sr. lured the too independent-minded Saddam into a trap in Kuwait in order to cut him down to size.

Washington reacted with deep anger, demanding that Saddam pull his army out of Kuwait. But Saddam had stuck his head into a trap. Like other dictators, he could not risk the dangerous political damage to his authority a forced pullout from Kuwait would have brought. Hitler committed the same lethal error at Stalingrad. Saddam dug in his heels, expecting the Russians or French would somehow get Washington to allow him a face-saving way out of the trap. But the first Bush administration had decided its sob had grown too powerful and needed to be gelded. The US presented Saudi Arabia's rulers with satellite photographs, purportedly showing that Iraq's forces were preparing to invade their nation. This was untrue, but the Saudis panicked and for the first time allowed a large US military force and other foreign troops into their kingdom. Ironically, this act convinced Osama bin Laden to begin his crusade against the Saudi royals and the western powers.

Saddam's last-minute offers made through the Russians to pull out of Kuwait were ignored. Washington unleashed a war designed to destroy much of Iraq's military power and provoke uprisings against the regime by always restive Kurds and Shia. President George H.W. Bush and his top advisers, led by James Baker and General Brent Scowcroft, were wise enough to know that invading and actually occupying Iraq would be an unnecessary, enormously expensive, counterproductive undertaking. Even Dick Cheney agreed—at the time.

The draconian sanctions imposed on postwar Iraq by the US, Britain, and their allies ravaged that already demolished nation. Everything from machinery for making powdered milk to medical supplies and X-ray equipment were denied; even lead pencils for schools were embargoed. During the war, the US had destroyed much of Iraq's water purification and sewage treatment plants. Parts to repair these essential facilities and chlorine necessary for water purification were barred. As a direct result, hundreds of thousands of Iraqis, in large part children, died from entirely preventable waterborne diseases. United Nations officials in Iraq put the toll at some 500,000 dead; some foreign experts claimed 800,000 to one million dead Iraqis in what anti-American groups claimed was a form of targeted biological warfare. The wildly inflated figure of 1.5 million Iraqi dead has unfortunately become common currency in the Muslim world.

As mentioned earlier, Secretary of State Madeleine Albright's cruel claim that the death of 500,000 Iraqis was "a price worth paying" was repeated across the Muslim world, reinforcing the widely held view that Iraq was savagely punished, if not outright destroyed, for daring challenge the American Raj. Washington had made an example of Saddam to discourage any others who dared defy the Raj.

Until the 2001 Kuwait war, there was almost no support or admiration for President Saddam Hussein in the Muslim world. He was viewed as just another brutal dictator working for the West. Saddam's terrifying police state inspired shame and loathing among Muslims. For Islamists, notably Osama bin Laden, Saddam was the archetype of the secular, western-backed dictators who they were struggling to overthrow. Bin Laden bitterly denounced Saddam Hussein as a tyrant and apostate. This fact was covered up by the Bush administration when it unleashed its pre-invasion war of words against Iraq in 2002, mendaciously seeking to convince Americans that Saddam had conspired with al-Qaida to launch the 9/11 attacks.

But as the US–led siege of Iraq intensified, the defiant, unapologetic Saddam began to gain some respect and sympathy across the Muslim world as one of its few rulers who dared stand up to the West. American efforts to promote insurrections against Saddam's Sunni-dominated regime by Kurds and Shia failed miserably, but they did plant the dragon's teeth for what would, after 2003, become that nation's bloody civil war.

Eric Margolis with Afghan Pashtun Mujahid on the front line.

тоM: At the Battle of Jalalabad firing at communist positions.

TOP: Margolis and Albania's first post-communist prime minister, Dr. Sali Berisha, in Tirana.

BOTTOM: Margolis dicussing Mideast politics with Libyan leader Muammar Khadaffi in his tent Tripoli, Libya.

ah Mohammed Omar, reclusive leader of the Taliban of Afghanistan. GETTY IMAGES

TOP LEFT: Osama bin Laden, founder of the jihadist organization Al-Qaeda. GETTY IMAGES

TOP RIGHT: Saddam Hussein, executed on December 30, 2006. GETTY IMAGES

BOTTOM: Margolis with Afghan warlord Haji Qadir in this tribal compound in Jalalabad, Afghanistan. Kadir became vice-president of Afghanistan, but was assassinated, July 2, 2002.

Margolis in Pakistan with Pashtun tribal "maliks" (elders).

TOM: Margolis in Rawalpindi, interviewing Pakistan's president, Pervez Musharraf, soon after he
d power in a coup.

LEFT: Ayatollah Ali Khamen[
Iran's Supreme Leader, speak[
at 19th anniversary of death [
Ayatollah Ruhollah Khomen[
in Tehran, June 3, 2008.
GETTY IMAGES

BOTTOM: Mahmoud
Ahmadinejad, president of Ir[
GETTY IMAGES

ıg girl carrying picture of Hassan Nasrallah, secretary general of the Lebanese Islamist party ollah. GETTY IMAGES

Benazir Bhutto and Eric Margolis. She was assassinated on December 27, 2007, shortly after her return to Pakistan.

It has by now become evident that the original plan for a US invasion of Iraq was developed and promoted in the late 1990s by a faction on the extreme right of the Republican Party which came together under the banner of the Project for the New American Century (PNAC). Funded by conservative foundations, PNAC included such leading conservatives as Dick Cheney, Donald Rumsfeld, former CIA director James Woolsey, Jeb Bush, John Bolton, and Zalmay Khalilzad (later ambassador to Iraq and Afghanistan). These hard-liners unashamedly advocated US military, economic and political global domination.

A second, quite differently motivated group of rightists allied themselves to these reborn cold warriors. Known as neoconservatives, they were primarily concerned with the expansion of Israel and its regional power. Their objective, which has not changed to this day, was to employ US power to destroy Israel's enemies, most notably Iraq, Iran, and Syria, in that order, and to maintain the United States as the world's sole superpower. They were intellectual descendants of the early Zionist far-right leader Vladimir Jabotinsky, who asserted that the Arab world was a fragile mosaic that could be smashed into fragments by sharp blows, leaving Israel the unchallenged master of the Mideast and its oil resources. His strategic worldview became the guiding ideology of the Israeli right, as sharply as former Israeli Knesset member and peace activist, Uri Avnery, warned in his sixtieth anniversary of Israel essay.

The neoconservative ranks included former Pentagon officials Richard Perle, Professor Paul Wolfowitz, writer Norman Podhoretz, senior officials Elliott Abrams, Abe Shulsky, Douglas Feith, Michael Ledeen, Dov Zackheim, and columnists William Kristol, William Safire, and Charles Krauthammer. All were closely aligned intellectually, politically, and emotionally with Israel's right-wing Likud Party and its leaders, Ariel Sharon and Benjamin Netanyahu, and shared the same worldview as Israel's hard-liners.

The conservatives and neoconservatives had one thing in common: with the exception of Don Rumsfeld, these chest-beating champions of waging global war against America's supposed foes had managed to dodge real military service to their nation during wartime, earning them the sobriquet "chicken hawks."

A 1992 Pentagon post–Cold War planning guide, *Defense Planning Guidance*, authored by then undersecretary of defense Paul Wolfowitz for his mentor Dick Cheney, was leaked in 1992 and provided unprecedented insight into the thinking of these hard-liners. Wolfowitz called for establishing a "new world order" that would "discourage challenging our leadership" and "deter competition" by establishing global "military dominance." The document called for invading Iraq as "necessary to assure access to vital raw materials, primarily in the Persian Gulf." Never in recent decades had a nakedly imperialist agenda been so exposed to political view. Had it issued from London or Moscow, one could have at least understood its historic context. But coming from Washington, which officially espoused multilateralism, arms control, and free trade, and opposed any form of aggression, the leaked report was shocking, even to hardened cynics.

Until 9/11, many of the men who promulgated this Soviet-style policy had been on the extreme, far-right fringes of the Republican Party, and dismissed as latter-day John Birchers, or former Trotskyites, howling in the wind. But 9/11 concussed America, producing a psychosis that allowed the hard right's leader, Dick Cheney, to seize effective control of the government and fill many of its most important positions with his allies and neoconservative ideologues.

President George H.W. Bush's highly respected former national security adviser, General Brent Scowcroft, actually went public with warnings that neoconservatives were exercising too much influence over administration policies, even stating that Bush Jr. "was wrapped around Ariel Sharon's little finger." Scowcroft was speaking for the traditional Republican moderate East Coast establishment that increasingly believed US foreign policy had become unbalanced and no longer reflected America's traditional vital national interests in the Mideast. Washington's best mind on international strategy, former national security adviser Zbigniew Brezezinski, echoed Scowcroft's warnings. Both were subsequently branded anti-Semites by the neocon agitprop machine.

Though most neoconservatives were pro-Israel hawks, polls showed an overwhelming majority of Jewish Americans, who tended to be liberal Democrats, were strongly opposed to the US invasion of Iraq and the Bush administration's aggressive, unilateralist policies, which many feared might unleash renewed anti-Semitism in America. But neoconservatives arrogated to themselves the sole right to speak for all American Jews and determine what was good for Israel. In the end, however, the Iraq War proved no more beneficial to Israel than it was to the United States.

However, the Bush administration's skillful media campaign to generate support for war against Iraq proved extremely effective among many Americans who were poorly educated in geography and foreign affairs. The United States and even parts of the Canadian media promoted war fever with a crass jingoism not seen since World War II. Certain members of the US media became a too-willing platform for the White House and the neocons. Even highly respectable newspapers like the *New York Times* and the *Washington Post* fueled war fever by running spurious reports about the alleged Iraqi threat to the world. Other self-serving US allies, like Egypt, Kuwait, and Britain, spoon-fed more disinformation to the Pentagon, CIA, and the US media.

The role of America's media in promoting the war has been insufficiently understood and constitutes one of the most disturbing episodes in modern US history. Scholars have uncovered the fact that almost all of the 400 or more major stories about Iraq run by the mainstream media in the lead-up to war actually originated with the Bush administration. Senior White House officials would plant false stories in major US newspapers, then cite these same stories as irrefutable evidence of fact.

Following a similar tactic, the White House would appoint generals to wage the war in Iraq and Afghanistan who were reliable yes-men. They would support the war, and the president would be able to say, "I'm just listening to the professional advice of my generals." When a senior officer who headed the US Central Command, Admiral William Fallon, had the audacity to oppose a US attack against Iran and other Muslim nations, he was forced to retire, as had been some of his other too-honest colleagues.

According to the always authoritative March 17, 2008, issue of *Aviation Week and Space Technology* magazine, a senior air force general says Fallon was "siding with the Joint Staff (meaning Joint Chiefs of Staff, the supreme US military command) in particular the Army and Marines, in urging the President to get out of Iraq faster because it's undermining the US military.... Top Army and Marine Corps leaders know the military is not designed to carry on a long-term war. It's tearing itself apart and quality is dropping fast."

Growing unrest in the US military establishment went woefully underreported by the US media. Not since I had covered Moscow in the late 1980s had I witnessed such a tame media establishment that licked the hand of power. Prominent members of the US media violated their vital role of fourth estate in keeping government honest and properly informing Congress and the public. Put simply, the media allowed itself to be used.

Leading establishment pundits and journalists like George Will, William Safire, Charles Krauthammer, Jim Hoagland, Judith Miller, William Kristol, and Fox News led the charge for war, insisting Iraq was a grave and urgent threat to the globe. "Experts" like Michael O'Hanlon and Kenneth Pollack, and former CIA chief James Woolsey, made fools of themselves on CNN by incessantly warning of Iraq's weapons of mass destruction. A battalion of retired generals portentously misinformed viewers about the danger from Iraq and the ease of its conquest. Today, the very same commentators remain on TV or in the print media, continuing to push the government party line on Iraq, while those dissenting journalists who were right all along became, in best Soviet style, media non-persons.

One of the unexpected consequences of the Iraq War was to turn younger people away from the traditional media, which many rightly saw as mouthpieces for the government or special interests, and divert them to the Internet, which, if not always reliable, was at least not censored and allowed divergent views. The trend towards lower TV viewership and newspaper readership among younger consumers was evident before the 2003 war, but it sharply accelerated after all the falsehoods and propaganda that accompanied the US invasion of Iraq.

American national security professionals and journalists who protested the blizzard of disinformation were threatened with loss of jobs and pension. The CIA was forced by George Tenet, its sycophantic chief, to toe the party line. Embedded American journalists with US military forces in Iraq or Afghanistan were reduced to reporting only what the military chose to tell them. The big TV news networks quickly adopted all the official slogans—war on terror; rebuilding Iraq; fighting for freedom; spreading democracy; liberating Iraq—that played a key role in the domestic campaign to market the invasion of Iraq and legitimize other military operations in the Muslim world.

The mainstream media, with a few notable exceptions like the Knight Ridder chain and *Christian Science Monitor*, simply closed its eyes to evidence that the Bush administration was misleading the nation into an unnecessary war. Britain's media, in contrast, was far more critical, but even it faced serious, unprecedented intimidation from that other self-appointed apostle of democracy and free speech, Prime Minister Tony Blair, who purged the British Broadcasting Corporation, probably the world's most respected news organization, after it dared criticize his lie-fueled rush to war. Canada's media echoed the White House party line.

A series of sensational leaks from 10 Downing Street in 2003 and 2005 were barely mentioned by the US media, or simply ignored. Bush and Blair met in London in July 2002, eight months before the invasion of Iraq, to finalize political and military strategy for the planned conflict. At the time, both leaders insisted they were seeking a diplomatic solution to the Iraq crisis, which they had, in fact, manufactured.

Britain's prime minister had pressured scientific and intelligence experts to make inflammatory claims about the alleged dangers of Iraq's nonexistent wmds. Sir Richard Dearlove, known as "C," the former head of British MI6 intelligence, later stated that "facts" about Iraq had been "fixed to suit the policy." US and British officials had coordinated the effort to spread the canard about Iraq's so-called weapons of mass destruction and to seek ways of provoking Iraq into war. The memo recorded that Bush and Blair had settled on twin fabrications about Iraq's alleged wmds and links to terrorism as the best way to sell the war to their citizens and the world.

According to further leaks from the prime minister's office, President Bush reportedly told Tony Blair just months before invading Iraq that when he was done with Saddam, he would "go on to deal with Saudi Arabia, Syria, Iran and Pakistan." This explosive leak—never denied by 10 Downing Street—should have been banner headlines in the United States. Yet it went largely unreported in one of the most scandalous failures of modern American journalism.

According to another official cabinet memo leaked from 10 Downing Street shortly before the 2003 war, Bush actually proposed to Tony Blair that a US Air Force plane be painted in UN colors and buzz Iraqi antiaircraft sites in hopes it would be fired on, thus providing a casus belli for invading Iraq. One is disturbingly reminded of Dr. Joseph Goebbels's proposal to create a pretext for invading Poland in 1939 by disguising German soldiers in Polish uniforms, and having them attack a German border post.

Many Americans would have been deeply shocked by such revelations and demanded immediate explanations from the president and vice president. They would also have opposed the impending invasion of Iraq. The smoking gun provided by these damning memos clearly showed Bush and

Blair had concocted a brazen war of aggression against Iraq behind a tissue of lies. These revelations might also have convinced the US Congress not to rush to give Bush carte blanche for aggression.

The fact that the London smoking gun did not become widely known in the United States points to a conspiracy of silence by America's mainstream media, which favored the war and feared that any serious questioning of the war effort might cause anger among its consumers of news, and bring accusations of anti-Americanism. In the end, however, those sectors of the US media that cooperated in this conspiracy of silence bear heavy responsibility for the Iraq disaster and all its negative consequences for their nation.

By contrast, the Downing Street memos received wide currency abroad, both in Europe and across the Muslim world. They added fuel to the bonfire of anger over the White House's fabrications about Iraq, many of which would have made Soviet agitprop specialists blush with shame. They also played a major role in convincing the Muslim world that the United States had become its determined foe and was planning to invade Iraq to seize its oil wealth. Those Americans and foreign leaders, like France's president Jacques Chirac who opposed the war against Iraq, or warned it would be a disaster, were branded anti-American, a standard tactic used by all rightists to discredit their critics.

To the Muslim world, the Bush administration's untruths about Iraq became the Father of All Lies and discredited America's word for at least a generation to come. Pentagon hawk Paul Wolfowitz, who assured the nation that the war's total cost would not exceed $40 billion (by 2008 it was headed towards $1 trillion) and would be fully amortized by plundering Iraq's oil, finally admitted that weapons of mass destruction had been selected as a pretext for war as the easiest story to sell to the public.

Americans were indeed fooled. Even 83 percent of evangelical Christians, whose faith taught to turn the other cheek, supported Bush's invasion of Iraq. The ultimate big lie came from Condoleeza Rice, who warned that Americans faced a possible mushroom cloud unless it invaded Iraq. This was at a time when the Bush administration knew full well that Iraq had neither nuclear arms nor any long- or even medium-range delivery systems. In the end, the demonized Saddam Hussein turned out to be telling the truth while the self-professed leader of the free world, George Bush, who assured his nation the invasion of Iraq would usher in a "shining age of human liberty," was lying.

The US invasion of Iraq in 2003 began with an attempt to assassinate President Saddam Hussein in a nighttime bombing attack against a private residence in which he was believed to be holding a meeting. Attempted murder of a head of state of an internationally recognized nation is a crime.

Soon after the attack, George Bush sought to justify the attempted murder of President Saddam Hussein because of the Iraqi leader's alleged plot to "kill my dad." Bush did not apparently know that the Kuwaitis concocted this story and peddled it to the Americans to help provoke the US into war against Iraq. These were the same Kuwaiti allies whose Washington public relations agency had faked the infamous stories about Iraqis throwing babies out of incubators in Kuwait. In March 2008, an exhaustive search of Iraqi government records by the US Joint Forces Command concluded no such plot had existed. This was the same search group that sifted through 600,000 Iraqi documents and found no links between Baghdad and al-Qaida.

The rapid defeat of Iraq's dilapidated armed forces by a high-tech US blitz was hailed in North America as a titanic victory, but much of the outside world, and particularly Muslim nations, saw a Goliath aided by its British ally mercilessly stomping on a small, ruined, Muslim nation of only 25 million—precisely the outcome against which General Colin Powell wisely warned in 2001 when he opposed invading Iraq, and allowed Saddam's best divisions to escape from the Kuwait pocket.

By 2008, Osama bin Laden's master plan to bleed the US in little wars seemed to be advancing well. President George W. Bush and Vice President Dick Cheney had sent half of all US combat forces into Iraq, where they became hopelessly overextended and bogged down in a hugely expensive classical guerrilla war combined with communal mayhem between the newly enfranchised Shia majority and disenfranchised Sunni minority. The self-proclaimed war president, George Bush, had destroyed Iran's two leading enemies, Saddam Hussein and the Taliban, leaving Tehran free to extend its influence into Iraq and Afghanistan.

Prewar assurances by the neocons and their chief Arab ventriloquist's dummy, the fraudster Ahmed Chalabi, that US forces would be greeted by flowers proved a black joke for Americans. Elsewhere, the US "liberators" were greeted by either sullen hostility or armed opposition, except for the pro-American Kurdish enclaves where they were indeed rapturously welcomed. Polls routinely showed 80 percent of non-Kurdish Iraqis wanted US troops out. Only the secessionist Kurds urged the US to keep forces in their mini-state to protect them from the wrath of Iraq and Turkey.

The US invasion and occupation, and Washington's subsequent decision to side with Iraq's Shia leadership, sparked a civil war that Mideast experts had warned was inevitable. The US invasion and subsequent internal conflict caused at least 100,000 civilian deaths, perhaps as many as 250,000. Ethnic cleansing drove 2 million mostly Sunni Iraqis abroad, and left another 2 million more internal refugees.

The United States bore a heavy measure of responsibility for this civil war by blatantly siding with the Shia Supreme Council for the Islamic Revolution (SCRI) and using its Shia Badr Brigade militia, which had been trained in Iran, as death squads to hunt down Sunni resistance forces. The Pentagon's employment of these Shia irregulars in Iraq mirrored the use of similar bands of anti-Communist mercenaries in Central America and Colombia. In both cases, the result was near anarchy, gruesome massacres, and frightful atrocities against civilians. Most of what the US media called the Iraqi Army, was really the Shia Badr Brigade militia, which was believed to be heavily infiltrated by Iran's intelligence service.

Saddam Hussein had not been exaggerating in 2001 when he proclaimed, to great universal mirth at the time, "the Mother of All Battles." Before the 2003 US invasion, which he knew was inevitable, Saddam ordered his best regular Sunni units and fedayeen commandos to disperse, cache arms and munitions, and prepare to fight a decade-long guerrilla war against American occupation. The profoundly stupid decision by the US proconsul in Iraq, Paul Bremer, to disband the Iraqi armed forces and Ba'ath Party bureaucracy, ensured there would be hundreds of thousands of angry, unemployed Iraqis available to oppose the US occupation. The White House eagerly backed Bremer's catastrophic decision.

The Bush administration sought to confer political legitimacy on its Shia puppet government, and secure foreign recognition for it, by staging a series of predetermined elections that were designed to produce victory for America's local satraps. But, appearances to the contrary, Iraq and its

American mentors never managed to produce a real, functioning central government beyond the US-fortified Green Zone in Baghdad. Real power outside the Kurdish mini-state remained in the hands of the heavily armed, Iranian-influenced Shia militias, Sunni tribal sheiks, and local warlords. The Iraqi Humpty-Dumpy was well and truly broken.

The UN, which had increasingly become more responsive to the needs of US foreign policy, was brought in to anoint the preordained elections, as it also did in Afghanistan. Democracy in Iraq was proclaimed to great fanfare. Some 67,000 "terrorism suspects"—i.e., Iraqis who resisted the new Iraqi order—were thrown into prisons that rivaled or surpassed those of Saddam for squalor, brutality, and numbers of inmates.

It did not take long for some Iraqis to yearn for the quiet, prosperous days of Saddam's rule. For all his cruelty, at least Saddam had been efficient. For many, his regime of fear was far preferable to the repression, anarchy, civil war, and banditry they now endured.

Left-wing parties across the globe had a field day—and a new cause célèbre—denouncing US occupation forces in Iraq. For Muslims, Iraq came increasingly to symbolize legitimate, even noble, resistance to western domination. Washington's enormously embarrassing but perfectly predictable failure to discover weapons of mass destruction in Iraq not only dishonored the United States, it convinced Muslims everywhere that Americans were untruthful, untrustworthy, and no better than those past accomplished Fathers of Lies, the perfidious British.

Over a score of Sunni resistance groups emerged after the US–British invasion. Some were composed of former soldiers or commandos from the disbanded Iraqi Army. Others, by Ba'ath Party members. But there were also Communists, socialists, Nasserites, and religiously motivated groups. There was little cooperation between these groups, which made them much less effective militarily than they could have been. But this fragmentation also made it far more difficult for the confused Americans to understand their order of battle or roll them up. In all cases, the new mujahidin would attack, then blend back into the civilian population.

Most of Iraq's Shia, tasting power after centuries of marginalization, at first eagerly cooperated with the US occupation. Iraq's supreme religious leader, Ayatollah Ali al-Sistani, directed his followers to collaborate with the occupation in exchange for securing a Shia-dominated regime. Sunnis accused Sistani, who was very close to Iranian intelligence, of treason. But a Shia faction of younger men, under the leadership of the perpetually scowling Muktada al-Sadr, chaffed at Sistani's collaboration and the occupation. His ragtag "Mahdi army" eventually clashed repeatedly with US forces, suffering heavy casualties. The Shia were now split, and Muktada offered a serious challenge to the aged Sistani and his pro-American strategy. However, in 2007, Muktada declared a truce and ordered his fighters to cease combat against the Americans. It is probable that he bowed to pressure from Tehran, which was anxious to avoid an American air attack. But in mid-2008 his fighters were again locked in battle with government troops who were, in fact, the rival Shia Badr militia.

The United States proved unable to fully dominate Iraq and impose its will across the nation. As the former US Army chief of staff Eric Shinseki had rightly predicted, the 140,000 to 160,000 troops it then maintained in Iraq, half of all US combat brigades, were stretched far too thin to control that fractious nation. Shinseki was forced into retirement by Secretary Donald Rumsfeld for his candor.

Much of the US military effort was devoted to protecting bases and vulnerable supply lines. As in Afghanistan, without the ubiquitous presence of US airpower, the American occupation of Iraq would have been untenable. The steady expansion of the use of roadside bombs (IEDs, in US military jargon) made road travel by US forces and their supply trains increasingly perilous, and the resistance force's preferred mode of action. The bombs badly dented US troops' morale and led to reprisals against civilians by frustrated, frightened American soldiers—an inevitable byproduct of all guerrilla wars.

After having successfully linked Saddam Hussein to al-Qaida and 9/11 in the minds of confused Americans, the Bush administration continued its campaign of disinformation by trying to build up the minor Islamist resistance figure Abu Musab al-Zarqawi into a second Osama bin Laden. The publicity-seeking Zarqawi, who had never had anything to do with al-Qaida, played right along, reveling in his new notoriety. This allowed the White House to expand its fatuous claim that Iraq was indeed the "frontline in the war on terrorism." A conveniently intercepted letter ostensibly gave bin Laden's blessings to his new disciple, Zarqawi. It was all a charade, but the US media, as usual, gobbled it up and echoed the

White House/Pentagon party line about arch al-Qaida terrorist Zarqawi. His subsequent death, hailed as the tuning point in the Iraq War, made not a whit of difference.

Americans bought this deception, at least until the 2006 elections, but the Muslim world, and, in fact, most of the non–North American world, did not. Iraq was increasingly seen by many Muslims as a freedom struggle, and the second Great Jihad after the original one in Afghanistan in the 1980s. Iraq quickly became a magnet for young mujahidin from the Mideast, Pakistan, and, of particular interest, from small numbers of Europe's millions of "forgotten" Muslims. Various Islamic groups set up covert underground channels to send young European Muslim fighters to Iraq, via Syria, Saudi Arabia and, more rarely, Iran. Many of Iraq's lethal, much-feared suicide bombers come from Europe or South Asia. Intense efforts by the US, Britain, and their European allies to interdict the flow of foreign mujahidin to Iraq sharply decreased but did not end the arrival of new fighters. Osama bin Laden and his supporters have repeatedly expressed their profound satisfaction over the turn of events in Iraq. Equally pleasing to bin Laden, Iraq's and Iran's "heretical" Shia have revealed themselves as enemies of the Sunni and tools of American policy, as he long claimed.

Most important, however, the Bush administration's debacle in Iraq could bring a major military and political reverse for the world's sole superpower. American troops may yet remain in Iraq for a long time, as US Republicans urge, kept there by the need for oil and Washington's desire to avoid losing face. In the course of his campaign, Presidential candidate John McCain vowed to keep US troops in Iraq "for 100 years, if necessary." He later appeared to backtrack from his pledge. Meanwhile, it was revealed in July, 2008, that the US was negotiating with the Baghdad regime to keep over 60 bases in Iraq and have absolute control of that nation's air space, ports, and oil fields. But it is also increasingly clear that the US has failed to attain its strategic objectives in Iraq and seems fated to eventually retreat. American voters made clear in 2006 that they wanted a withdrawal within a year. In response, the White House plunged ever deeper into the morass called Iraq by sending more troops, known as the surge, and allocating tens more billions of dollars for the war, funds mostly borrowed from Japan and China.

Wars, as we have noted, are waged to achieve political ends. Washington's political goals in Iraq have proven illusory. A stable, legitimate, popular Iraqi government with a reliable sepoy army ready to do Washington's bidding has not been fashioned. Ethnic cleansing of some four million Iraqis, and the temporary truce declared by the Mahdi Army, lessened the level of violence in 2008, a fact trumpeted by the White House. But Iraq remains fragmented and in a state of near civil war and ridden by crime. The United States remained stuck there like the proverbial little Dutch boy with his finger in the dike.

Given the clamor in the US to end the war, and the apparent futility of the occupation, it is only a matter of time before American troops in Iraq suffer a grave collapse of moral and fighting spirit, just as I witnessed while serving in the US Army during the Vietnam War after President Lyndon B. Johnson announced that his goal was a negotiated settlement (code for withdrawal and retreat) rather than military victory. No one wants to die or be dismembered in a war that is already lost. The logical course for the United States is to face facts, declare victory, end the hugely expensive war—"we have overthrown the tyrant Saddam and created democracy"—then quickly decamp.

America's abrupt retreat from Southeast Asia's wars was indeed humiliating, but the world did not end and the dominoes did not fall. In fact, just about everyone was happy to forget about Vietnam and turn to more pertinent matters. (More on this in the final chapter.) An American failure in Iraq will be an entirely different story. Superbly trained and equipped US forces have won all the battles. But America appears set to lose the war by failing to win a political victory and create a pliant vassal state. The US managed to pull out of Vietnam without endangering its vital interests in the region. The split between the Soviets and China removed the danger of all Indochina falling to the Communists. By contrast, a retreat from Iraq is likely to have serious negative political and military consequences for the American Raj and its other worldwide interests.

Today, it seems inconceivable that a lightly armed force of Iraqi irregulars could worst the mightiest military power on earth. Iraq, after all, is a ruined little country of only 25 million feuding inhabitants. The Sunni resistance which has so bedeviled US occupation forces numbers no more than 3,000 full-time fighters using small arms and bombs, and an estimated 20,000 supporters. The grandly styled Mahdi Army has about 16,000 amateur, part-time gunmen, most of whom cannot shoot straight.

Against them, the US has arrayed its finest military units, like the Marine Corps and elite airborne and Special Forces. A veritable cornucopia of the most modern and lethal weaponry has been used against Iraq's resistance, ranging from M-1 Abraham heavy tanks, Bradley armored fighting vehicles, and helicopter gunships, to robots, armed drone aircraft, night-fighting equipment, and a galaxy of electronic sensors, all backed by ever-present US airpower.

Yet, in this Mother of All Battles, Saddam's left-behind forces have so far fought the US to a stalemate and denied Washington any hope of political victory in Iraq. The Shia Mahdi Army of Muktada al-Sadr stands ready at any time to turn its guns against the occupiers, seriously endangering US supply lines south to Kuwait. In short, the world's greatest military power appears to be facing defeat—or at least non-victory—at the hands of lightly armed Muslim mujahidin—the same ignominious fate that befell the Soviet Union in Afghanistan.

The psychological ripple effects of this fact are difficult to predict and will be even more difficult for Americans to accept. A bunch of "Eye-raki towel heads" defeat the US Army and Marines? Preposterous, but true: western powers have been almost invariably defeated by Third World guerrilla forces. Equally, western forces are simply too costly to be used to wage counterinsurgency wars. They are ideally suited for breaking and entering, that is, invasion and battle with enemy main force units, but unsuited to waging prolonged wars in the midst of a hostile civilian population. The US military is mighty in war but strikingly ill suited to occupation duty with its essentially political tasks.

Still, it seems almost inconceivable that the world's most modern, high-tech armed force, the United States military, could not swiftly defeat ragtag Iraqi or Afghan guerrilla forces in largely bare, open countryside or cities. There are numerous reasons for the failure. First, the US did not deploy an adequate number of troops in either conflict. In early 2008, as noted, the commander of US forces in Afghanistan, General Dan McNeil, stated in a speech to NATO delegates that to follow standard US military doctrine for fighting an insurgency, he would need the classic troop ratio of ten Americans to each enemy. To win the war in Afghanistan, he said he would require 400,000 US troops, not the 40,000 he had been allocated. A similar-size force would be needed in Iraq, where the deployment of only 140,000 to 160,000 US troops strained the military to the point of crisis. Second, the US has not had Britain's former skill in raising large numbers of sepoys, or native troops. Those it has raised in Iraq and Afghanistan are largely mercenaries or local militias masquerading as a government army, and are thoroughly unreliable, usually combat averse, and often secretly in cahoots with the enemy. Third, guerrilla wars are not about occupying territory but about dominating civilian populations, either through bribery, fear, or their voluntary support. US forces in Afghanistan and Iraq have largely failed to achieve this goal, though they are supported by ethnic minorities in both nations. Fortunately, Americans have failed to show the ruthlessness and savagery that allowed Russia to crush the life out of Chechen independence-seekers.

For America, the failure to achieve victory in the war it started means defeat on many levels and some very painful self-analysis. Whatever happens to Iraq after the US pulls out or greatly thins its forces there, Iraq's religious and secular mujahidin will proclaim a mighty victory to all the world. An American defeat in Iraq will reverberate across the Muslim world. From Iraq's resistance groups will come a new generation of Islamic and secular nationalist leaders who want to sweep away the Mideast's old political order. They will very likely fall on one another in a typical postrevolutionary, fratricidal power struggle, or continue war against the Shia, who may engage in their own internecine conflict. Even so, Iraq's resistance may eventually emerge from the crucible as the Muslim world's revolutionary vanguard, as did the foreign mujahidin from Afghanistan a generation earlier. Having withstood the worst that the world's greatest power could throw at them, Iraq's jihadists will present themselves as a role model for the rest of the ummah.

A renewal of the spirit of transnational jihad, which burned so fiercely in Afghanistan in the 1980s, can be expected to emerge from Iraq, invigorating a whole new generation of Muslims seeking to throw off western domination. Saudi Arabia, Egypt, Morocco, Tunisia, and Pakistan offer fertile ground for new jihads against western-backed regimes. The Saudi royal family would be a primary target for a renewed jihadist revolution, launched and sustained from next-door "free" Iraq, the new hotbed of the world jihadist movement.

In military terms, the new, post-Iraq jihadist will benefit from holding the important psychological initiative. The mighty US will be in retreat, and its allies in the Muslim world seriously weakened. If a few thousand

Iraqi mujahidin could best the US, Britain and their allies, which other Muslim nations could not be "liberated," similarly, provided the anti-western mujahidin were sufficiently aggressive and resourceful?

Psychology in war, as Napoleon noted, is to the physical as three to one. A dispirited America may be loath to soon embark on any more liberations or regime changes, and less inclined to shore up its clients and allies with US military forces. By the time Washington admits defeat in Iraq, it will have poured at least $1 trillion or more into the sands of Mesopotamia. Some recent academic studies say the figure could rise to above $2 trillion when full costs of veterans' care, pensions, and equipment are accounted. Since much of the Iraq War was funded through emergency, Enron-style off-budget allocations, assessing the true total cost of the Iraq misadventure remains very difficult. The White House has consistently sought to conceal the war's true costs.

The monster one-to-two-trillion-dollar bill for Iraq will be passed on to the next generations of Americans. Worn-down US military forces will have to be replaced: the average age of US Air Force warplanes is now 27 years. An estimated $66 billion is needed to replace tanks, armored vehicles, and motor transport alone worn out in Iraq, not to mention upkeep on the naval units kept on station to support them or the huge costs of heavy, long-range airlift from the US to Iraq and Afghanistan. However, Afghanistan may be an exception. In the event of a US troop pullout or reduction in Iraq, some of these units might be transferred to Afghanistan, a war that still finds support among Americans as a legitimate antiterrorist operation, though all the real terrorists long ago decamped.

An American reverse in Iraq could also have profound effects upon America's role as world hegemon. There seems little doubt that the European Union, China, Russia, Iran, and India will move quickly to start picking up the pieces of America's shattered Mideast power. Vladimir Putin's Russia is already reasserting its former influence in the Mideast and Mediterranean. In August 2007, Putin announced Russia would reopen the former Soviet naval base at Tartus, Syria, and resume regular naval patrols in the Mediterranean.

The EU will very likely accelerate its efforts to break from America's postwar alliance system, establishing its own integrated military forces and adopting a competitive rather than cooperative foreign policy. China will waste no time in inserting its influence in the Mideast, as will neighboring India, which craves access to the Gulf's oil. Both are already seriously vying with Europe for Africa's natural resources. Japan will certainly reevaluate its compliant position under America's security umbrella. New revolutions are likely to break out in Latin America. Such is the fate of empires suddenly seen as clawless paper tigers.

In fact, President George W. Bush's historic blunders will probably vitalize and energize America's enemies—particularly radical Islamic forces and international leftist movements around the globe. The dominoes will begin to fall, but not, as once feared in the 1970s, in Southeast Asia. They will be in the Mideast, one of the pillars of America's global dominion. One may easily imagine how Japan, China, the EU, and India will react if some or all of their primary sources of oil are no longer dominated by regimes beholden to the United States.

In the shorter term, whether or not the US and its allies pull out of Iraq, it will continue to serve as an incubator for the international jihad and generator of anti-western movements. However undeserving, the late President Saddam Hussein will very likely come to be seen by many as a martyr. Ironically, five years after invading Iraq, not a few officials in Washington and London, and some of Iraq's neighbors have come to almost miss the days of Saddam. I predicted in 2002 that after the Americans and British overthrew him, they would eventually end up putting another iron-fisted general, a new SOB, in power in Baghdad.

This raises the following question: What if the US and Britain had not invaded Iraq and overthrown Saddam Hussein? By 2003, Iraq was completely bottled up and toothless. Its armed forces had decayed to the point where aircraft were grounded due to lack of spare parts, and tank barrels were so badly warped they could not fire. Even assuming that Iraq was somehow an actual world threat, which it was not, keeping it isolated was the more humane and certainly far less expensive way of dealing with a "rogue regime." By contrast, the US shied away from invading nuclear-armed North Korea, which was capable of defending itself however obsolete its military equipment, and elected sanctions and isolation as the most effective strategy. A Pentagon study estimated the US would suffer 250,000 casualties in a major ground war with North Korea. But decrepit Iraq was an easy target, and, of course, it had the Mideast's second-largest oil reserves.

Neocons still keep making the argument that Saddam would have one day produced nuclear weapons. However unlikely, given the international sanctions imposed on Iraq and its total lack of medium- or long-range missile-delivery systems, Saddam's original attempt to build a crude nuclear weapon was driven by two ambitions: enhanced prestige in the Arab world and self-defense. Like North Korea, Iraq saw a few nuclear weapons as life insurance against a possible US or Iranian invasion, and a limited counterforce against threats of nuclear attack by Israel. The idea that Iraq, or, later, Iran might try to obliterate Israel in a surprise attack is illogical. No leader in Baghdad or Tehran would risk the nuclear annihilation of his nation for the chance to make a hit-or-miss nuclear strike against Israel that would also kill large numbers of neighboring Arabs.

President Saddam Hussein was not the mad tyrant portrayed by US and British prewar propaganda, but a nasty, brutal Mideast dictator who had once been a valued American ally. It was perfectly conceivable for Washington to have restored its alliance with Iraq before or after the 1991 Oil War. After his rash, foolhardy invasion of Kuwait, Saddam sought a face-saving way to retreat, but President George H.W. Bush would not accept anything less than destruction of Iraq's army and infliction of a supposedly mortal political blow on President Hussein. Bush Sr. rejected Moscow's efforts to arrange a peaceful Iraqi retreat from Kuwait.

Before the 2003 US invasion of Iraq, Saddam was again desperately seeking a diplomatic exit from his confrontation with western powers. But efforts by Russia and France to deter the oncoming US–British attack were spurned by Washington, just as European and Soviet/Russian efforts had been rejected in the first war. The US had declared Saddam a world threat who had to be removed. Diplomacy was out of the question. We now know from former senior White House officials that President George W. Bush and Vice President Cheney had begun planning the invasion of Iraq in early 2001.

When US forces captured Saddam Hussein after invading Iraq, they put on a show trial for him in Baghdad that was blatantly illegal under international law and a mockery of justice. The trial's conclusion was clearly foreordained. This was most unfortunate, since Iraq and the entire Mideast would have benefited from a fair trial, conducted by an independent legal authority, like the UN's International Court of Justice in the Hague, which would have examined Saddam's many crimes against his own people. Instead, the US–directed kangaroo court denied Saddam a fair defense and sentenced him to death. US troops also cornered and killed Saddam's two brutish sons, Uday and Kusay.

Saddam was handed over to a Shia lynch mob by his US captors. Saddam, who claimed he was dying for his nation, went to his death on the scaffold with great courage and dignity that made him a martyr to many Arabs. But Washington was happy. Dead men tell no tales. Saddam was silenced before he could reveal embarrassing details of his long, covert alliance with the United States. His execution again validated Henry Kissinger's famous dictum that being America's ally was much more dangerous than being its foe.

Today, much of Iraq lies in ruins. Twelve thousand doctors fled the country, unemployment is at 69 percent, and oil and electric production are still below pre-invasion levels. More than 200 of Iraq's top scientists have been mysteriously murdered since 2003. Many Iraqis believed the US allowed Israel to send Mossad assassins to Iraq to eradicate that nation's scientific cadre, thus preventing it from ever re-creating a nuclear infrastructure. In past decades, Israel had used similar lethal tactics against Iraqi and Egyptian scientists.

Iraq also produced a sea change in Muslim opinion about the UN, or, more specifically, its Security Council. Until 2003, the UN was generally seen as benevolent, playing a positive role in world affairs, and defending the rights of Palestinians. After invading Iraq, many believed the Bush administration took revenge on UN secretary-general Kofi Annan for gently criticizing the war as illegal and unjustified. Annan was publicly humiliated over his son Kojo's involvement in a scandal and senior UN officers threatened with criminal charges over a corruption-plagued food-aid program to Iraq that had been blessed by the US Congress and the White House. The chastened UN quickly fell into line behind Washington, which provided the lion's share of its income, and became a facilitator of attempts by the US to legitimize and solidify its occupations of Afghanistan and Iraq, and to punish and isolate Iran.

The media in Egypt, Saudi Arabia, Pakistan, and Indonesia kept rightly asking, "Why does the Security Council keep passing resolutions supporting the ongoing US occupation of Iraq and Afghanistan, and punishing Iran for its nuclear program? What about Israel's occupation of Arab lands or its covert nuclear arsenal? Why didn't the Security Council condemn the US–British invasion of Iraq as a brazen violation of the UN Charter, and demand the western powers end their occupation? Why were not India and Israel censored for their nuclear programs?

Canada, long esteemed as the world's premier provider of peace-keepers and sagacious conciliation, became widely discredited in the Muslim world after gradually being sucked into Afghanistan as a combatant, then into Iraq as a major provider of aid to its US–backed regime. Iraq's US$667-million debt to Ottawa was forgiven, another $300 million was earmarked for aid to Baghdad's Shia regime, and $1.1 billion was budgeted for Afghanistan, including an order for new heavy German tanks at a time when Canadians could not get adequate care from their broken-down medical system. The total cost of Canada's military, political, and humanitarian involvement in Iraq and Afghanistan are a carefully guarded government secret.

By 2008, the fighting and sectarian mayhem in Iraq had become a major danger to the entire Mideast. The US invasion opened a veritable Pandora's box, as many Mideast observers had predicted prior to the war. Washington's overthrow of Iran's principal enemies, the Taliban and Saddam, left Tehran the dominant power in the region and the major influence over the majority of Iraq's population. Iraq's future seemed to lie in Iran's hands. Iran's creeping domination of oil-rich Iraq was a danger that the neocon imperialists who led America into this calamitous war never apparently contemplated. What the neocons did contemplate and hope for was to achieve Vladimir Jabotinsky's dream of fragmenting this important Arab nation into three important parts, thus taking it permanently out of confrontation with Israel. An independent Kurdish republic in Iraq's north was singled out as a possible future Israeli ally, military base, and supplier of oil.

Iran's fast-growing influence in Iraq was amply illustrated in March 2008, when Iran's president, Mahmoud Ahmadinejad, made a triumphant visit to downtown Baghdad, becoming the first Mideastern leader to visit that nation. His very public visit stood in stark and embarrassing contrast to those of President George Bush, Vice President Dick Cheney, and British prime minister Tony Blair, who had to slip unannounced into Iraq and remain in the safety of US or British military bases. To Washington's chagrin, the US–installed Baghdad government gave a very warm reception to its bête noire, Ahmadinejad. Adding insult to injury, Iran's leader gave a fiery Jeremiad in which he claimed that the US had been defeated in Iraq and should withdraw.

Iraq's neighbors, Jordan, Saudi Arabia, and Syria, have felt the rising tensions of Sunni-Shia strife. Jordan and Syria suffer the heavy burden of sheltering most of the two million Iraqi-Sunni refugees. To Washington's great annoyance, they have been discreetly supplying Iraq's Sunni resistance groups with arms and money.

Saudi Arabia, already simmering with unrest and, on occasion, violent antigovernment attacks, faces the return of large numbers of veteran Saudi jihadis who had been fighting in Iraq. For some of Iraq's Sunni and Shia militants, and certainly for al-Qaida and its allies, the Saudi royal family would be the next target if the Americans and British are eventually driven from Iraq.

Iraq's instability also threatens Syria, a fragile mosaic of ethnic groups and religions that is run by a tiny Allawi religious minority, comprising only 12 percent of the population. Syria's long-repressed Sunni majority (the mirror image of Iraq's Shia) and its underground Islamists would almost certainly be emboldened by a victory of Iraq's Sunni mujahidin to renew attempts to overthrow the Allawi regime. The main reason the Bush administration hesitated to go ahead with the neoconservatives' plans to overthrow the Syrian government was the well-justified fear, after the Iraq disaster, that the Asad regime would be replaced by militant Islamists.

Failure of the US war in Iraq would undermine the entire superstructure of its Mideast Raj and start a run on the strategic bank of American influence and power. Washington's allies, like Jordan, Tunisia, Morocco, and perhaps even the Gulf emirates, would be shaken by any perceived diminution of American power in the Mideast. The knock-on effects of an American defeat would have even more potent negative consequences in that pillar of the Raj, Egypt, where Islamist revolution simmers just below the surface as the regime of General Husni Mubarak nears an end.

All the governments of these nations depend to varying degrees on US political, military, or financial support. Their armies use US–supplied weapons and spare parts. Their intelligence agencies have become virtual extensions of the CIA, just as Warsaw Pact intelligence services were called little brothers by KGB Center in Moscow. Their leaders are often protected by US security specialists and their borders assured by American guarantees. This entire superstructure of US influence—the American Raj—would be shaken to its foundations by a perceived American strategic defeat in Iraq.

Turkey, one of Washington's most faithful allies, would be politically buffeted by a failure of American arms in Iraq. First, an unstable Iraq, particularly one divided into Shia, Sunni, and Kurdish mini-states, is anathema to Turkey, which fears secession by its own Kurds, who comprise over 20 percent of the population. In February 2008, Turkey sent some 3,000 troops into Iraqi Kurdistan to fight guerrillas of the Kurdistan Workers Party (PKK), a violent Marxist rebel group that has battled Turkey for the past two decades. The Turks' operation was aimed at both punishing the PKK for killing Turkish troops and staking a claim on Iraq's northern oil region.

Turkey has repeatedly stated its determination to intervene militarily in Iraq to prevent the emergence of an independent Kurdish state. If Iran were to annex the oil regions of southeastern Iraq, Turkey would be seriously tempted to seize Iraq's northern oil fields around Kirkuk and Mosul, which, after all, used to lie within the Ottoman Empire until torn away by Imperial Britain. Any triumph by anti-American nationalist and Islamist forces in Iraq would strengthen Turkey's own Islamists and bring demands to close the important US air base at Incirlik and undermine the power of its ardently pro-American, anti-Muslim generals who still run a secret government behind the scenes. The long-term tensions between Turkey's secularists and Islamists could very well burst into open confrontation, tearing that nation apart. In the 1970s and 1980s, hostility between leftists and right-wing nationalists almost plunged Turkey into civil war.

The massive exodus of two million Iraqis from their strife-torn nation, and the creation of another two million internal refugees, is the largest movement of refugees in the Mideast since the 1948 Palestinian tragedy. Having seen the extent to which the Palestinian Diaspora roiled the Mideast, one can only imagine what problems and tensions huge numbers of Iraqi refugees will cause in the future if it becomes permanent. Only small numbers have so far returned. Massive ethnic cleansing of Sunnis from Shia regions took place in Iraq under the eyes of its American occupiers. Many Sunnis have no homes to which to return.

As US power in Iraq wanes, that of Iran will wax ever stronger. Iraq's Shia eastern regions are already being drawn into Iran's economic and political orbit. The largest and richest chunk of oil-rich Iraq seems destined to eventually fall to Iranian control unless a viable national government in Baghdad can somehow be created.

So what lies in store for Iraq? It is very difficult to conceive of how it can be stabilized or reassembled into a viable nation. Continued US military occupation appears likely. But, as noted, Washington's inability to engineer a regime that has political legitimacy and the support of a majority of Iraqis means that its soldiers and the giant US embassy in Baghdad, the world's largest, will remain the real government. History shows that the longer occupying powers remain, the more their presence generates opposition and violence. It also seems inevitable that the US Army in Iraq will be corrupted and brutalized by having to maintain a repressive occupation against a sullen, hostile population. So instead of being an oil Eldorado, Iraq has turned into a staggeringly expensive albatross for its American occupiers and an ongoing generator of anti-Americanism in the Muslim world.

CHAPTER ELEVEN

IRAN: REVENGE OF THE MULLAHS

Iran has always been the Muslim world's odd man out.

To understand how this once isolated nation that was long despised and feared by its Sunni neighbors emerged as the Muslim world's new champion and leading opponent of the American Raj, one must have a look at Iran's turbulent modern history.

Sunni Muslims traditionally have regarded Iran's brilliant, rich artistic and intellectual culture with awe and admiration. But, in a manner similar to Rome's conflicting feelings of admiration and contempt for classical Greece, Sunnis also scorned Iran, or Persia, as it was known until the modern era, as a font of hedonism, effeminate ways, self-indulgence, and lack of proper Islamic austerity.

Far more important, for many Sunnis, the Shia faith was and remains a grave perversion of Islam, and a dangerous heresy. The traditional western view of Persians was equally negative, coming almost exclusively from ancient-Greek historians who were naturally hostile to their principal enemy.

The newborn faith of Islam suffered an historic split over the succession of its temporal and religious leadership a decade after the death in AD 632 of the Prophet Mohammed. One faction, led by Ali, the son-in-law of the Prophet, claimed the title of caliph—the temporal and spiritual leader of all Muslims. Another faction, led by Mu'awiya Ummayad, contested the leadership. The widely respected Ali and a small band of followers were outnumbered and killed in an heroic but hopeless battle against Mu'awiya's men outside the Iraqi city of Kerbala.

Ali's death produced the deep schism that afflicts the Muslim world to our day. His followers, concentrated in what is modern Iraq, Bahrain, Yemen, and Iran, with outposts in Afghanistan, India, and Pakistan, became known as Shia, or followers of the law. They believe only the 11 imams who followed Ali are the rightful interpreters and leaders of the true, or legitimate, Islam. Ali became a virtual Shia saint. For some Shia, Ali even became a deity in his own right, though Imam Ali himself condemned this idea as a heresy.

Sunnis, who today make up 85 percent of all Muslims, believe the caliphate was rightly due to the Ummayad rulers. They rejected the Shia as apostates with almost the same antipathy that Catholics held for Protestant reformers during Europe's sixteenth-century religious wars. Sunni Islam abjures a formal clergy or church, holding there should be no intermediary between man and God. In the Shia doctrine, a formal clergy of imams and mullahs came to play a dominant role in matters of faith, politics, and society. The charge by Reformation Protestants that Catholics were priest ridden were echoed by Sunni accusations that Shia were slaves of their mullahs.

Equally offensive to Sunnis, Shia Islam quickly became influenced by older Persian Zoroastrianism, including the worship of saints, shrines, and holy relics—intolerable idolatry to austere mainstream Islam. In many ways, the Shia faith, which spread rapidly across the Persian plateau, became an expression of Persian resistance to Arab political and religious domination. Persia, an ancient, highly cultured civilization of Indo-European Aryan stock, dates back to 2000 BC. In spite of their rapid, universal acceptance of Islam, Persians regarded the invading Semitic Arabs from the wastes of Arabia as ignorant Bedouin, a view still held by modern Iranians 1,500 years later.

As a result of this great schism in Islam, Persia remained mostly aloof from the affairs of the Sunni Muslim world except for waging frequent wars against its principal rival, the Sunni Ottoman Empire. In fact, around AD 1500, a war between Persia's Safavid dynasty and the Turks saved Renaissance Italy from Ottoman invasion.

By the mid-1800s, the expanding British and Russian Empires reached Iran's borders and, through military action and brazen intimidation, gobbled up almost half of its territory. In 1921, a Cossack officer, Reza Shah, overthrew Persia's decrepit Qajar dynasty in a revolt similar to the ousting of moribund dynasties in China and Turkey. Reza was a rough, brutal soldier, who, like Mustafa Kemal Ataturk in neighboring Turkey, sought to drag his backwards nation by its hair into the modern age.

Then came World War II. In 1941, Britain and the Soviet Union jointly invaded Iran in an act of wanton aggression every bit as illegal and rapacious as the Soviet-German partition of Poland in 1939. While everyone remembers Germany's unprovoked aggression against Poland, the British-Soviet invasion of Iran has largely vanished from our memory.

The British and Soviets claimed their invasion was provoked by Reza Shah's pro-Axis sympathies, but the real reason was to seize Iran's extensive oil fields. The Allies overthrew Reza Shah and put his weak young son, Mohammed Reza Pahlavi, on the peacock throne. The "baby Shah" became a useful and valued western satrap (a Persian word meaning loyal vassal ruler) whose reign would extend, with one notable interruption, until 1979.

Iran, as it had come to be known, served as a docile and dependable supplier of oil to Britain. But in 1951, a venerable, quirky Iranian centrist democratic political leader, Dr. Mohammed Mossadegh, became prime minister and shocked everyone by nationalizing the British oil firms that pumped Iran's oil, claiming he would use its huge profits to modernize Iran and help its rural poor. The Shah fled to Rome. Her Majesty's government immediately began plotting Mossadegh's overthrow and convinced the United States to join the conspiracy by claiming the Iranian leader was a secret Communist.

Two years later, a combined task force of Britain's MI6 Secret Intelligence Service and the brand-new CIA mounted a daring coup in Tehran that overthrew Mossadegh and put the shaken Shah Reza back into power. The Tehran coup was one of the last totally successful intelligence operations of the era, covering legendary CIA agents Archie and Kermit Roosevelt with glory. But this apparent brilliant intelligence success proved a mirage. The Anglo-American coup in Iran convinced its Shia religious establishment and most ordinary Iranians that their nation had become a puppet of the British and Americans, and victim of their exploitation.

At the same time, Iran's royal family and its army of parasitic relatives and retainers strained every sinew to distance themselves from Islam and its culture, pretending that they were white Europeans or, at least, Aryans, who had nothing to do with their benighted, superstitious Muslim countrymen. "We are Persians, not Muslims," went the refrain. Iran's nou-veau-riche imperial elite put on grotesque pretensions, and sneered at Islam. Ladies of Iran's gilded elite flew to Paris to have their hair done for dinner parties and sent their soiled laundry to France for hand washing while many Iranians went without enough food. The Shah's family alone absconded with billions of dollars from Iran, using front companies to invest these funds in American, British, and French real estate.

By the 1970s, the Shah had grown from a timid, frightened youth who had been mercilessly bullied by his brutal father, into a preening megalomaniac. Courtiers and American advisers convinced Reza Shah that he was truly, as he styled himself, the "Light of the Aryans," and the "Shah of Shahs," the worthy successor of great emperors Xerxes and Darius. The Nixon administration encouraged these imperial pretensions, selling the Shah billions' worth of arms and sending a small army of US intelligence and military advisers to build up Iran into America's "policeman of the Gulf." The Shah began secret talks with Israel to acquire nuclear warheads and medium-range missiles to carry them in exchange for Iranian oil.

Behind the preposterous ostentation and pathetic imperial pretensions of the Shah's court, Iran was effectively ruled by a rapacious bureaucracy and tiny oligarchy, backed by the secret police, known as Savak. This agency, which was funded and "advised" by the CIA, became the Mideast's most notorious, feared, and sadistic security organization. In a region notorious for brutal secret police, Savak's primacy of place was truly remarkable. Political opponents of the Shah, Shia clergy, nationalists, Communists—in fact anyone suspected of opposing the royal family in any possible way—was hunted down, tortured, and often executed or simply disappeared.

While Washington hailed the Shah's regime as a model of democracy, economic development, and Islamic good government, Savak was terrorizing Iran with a ferocity that would have shocked East Europe's Communist secret police and their KGB big brothers in Moscow. Savak and Israel's Mossad cooperated closely against their mutual foe, the Arabs and Islamists.

Opposition to the Shah's anti-Islamic regime turned to anger, then to fury as the excess of the thieving elite grew and its members outdid themselves pretending they were French aristocrats who had been unaccountably transported to Tehran by some unfortunate mischance. Washington, which wholly relied on Savak for all its information about Iran, had no inkling that pressure was building towards an explosion. Meanwhile, under urging from the US and Israel, the Shah increased his support for Kurdish rebels in Iraq and began a dangerous confrontation with Baghdad over the disputed Shat al-Arab waterway. These actions helped ignite the calamitous 1980 Iran-Iraq War.

In 1979, revolution finally erupted in Iran, led by the most unlikely figure of an aged, white-bearded, exiled ayatollah (senior cleric) named Ruhollah Khomeini. The vainglorious Shah's Imperial Persian Empire collapsed almost overnight; the "Light of the Aryans," abandoned by his former American mentors, fled ignominiously into exile in Egypt, then to a rundown resort hotel in seedy Panama, and finally to Egypt, where he died in 1980 of cancer and sorrow.

Iran's Islamists seized power, heading off a coup by the country's powerful underground Marxist group the Mujahidin-i-Khlaq, or People's Mujahidin. Islamist students seized the US embassy in Tehran, claiming it was a "nest of spies." Inside, they found a treasure trove of hastily shredded CIA documents, which, when patiently reconstructed, revealed the extent of CIA influence over the Shah's regime and a long list of its Iranian agents.

The new government proclaimed it would champion an Islamic revolution to overthrow the American Raj's oil monarchs and military dictators. Oil, thundered Tehran, would become the common property of all Muslims and be shared according to need. Islamic government, based on Sharia law and "democratic consultation" would replace feudalism and dictatorships. The Muslim world would return to its religious and cultural roots, and expunge the deleterious influences of western exploitation and rampant consumer culture.

Needless to say, alarm bells sounded all over Washington. The powerful military-industrial complex was losing one of its best foreign customers. The White House saw its Mideast Raj seriously threatened for the first time. Big oil feared that nationalization would spread across the Mideast. The influential Israel lobby saw one of the Jewish state's strongest allies suddenly transformed into a bitter foe. All agreed that the Islamic regime in Tehran had to be overthrown. But various attempts by the CIA, MI6, and Mossad to do so failed miserably. Washington and London and their Arab oil allies next turned to their new Gulf policeman, Saddam Hussein, and sent his army into Iran. As discussed in Chapter 10, Iran suffered 500,000 dead and about 500,000 seriously wounded in eight years of bitter,

World War I–style trench warfare. Iraq's use of deadly western-supplied cluster munitions, mustard and nerve gas convinced Iranians their nation had been marked for destruction. The ruthless Saddam would make an example of the Iranians who had dared challenge the American Raj.

Iran managed to hold the far better armed and supplied Iraqi Army by means of raw courage and suicidal attacks. Teenagers went forward to clear dense Iraqi minefields with their young bodies. Fifty thousand or more Iranians were blinded outright by mustard gas or had their noses, mouths, throats, armpits, or groins hideously burned and scarred. Iranian men of the Basiji militia, aged from 12 to 70 years, launched human-wave attacks against Iraqi defenses. Iran's border cities were destroyed and its economy ravaged; its losses in the war were equivalent to America suffering four million casualties.

Iranians without exception blamed this frightful conflict on western machinations, and particularly on the American "Great Satan." The cup of Iranian wrath was overflowing: first the 1941 Anglo-Soviet invasion; the overthrow of the democratically elected Mossadegh government; the Shah and his murderous Savak; and then the eight-year war with Iraq and its western and Arab sponsors. The United States was determined, Iranians believed, to destroy the Islamic Republic, regain control of Iran's oil wealth, and restore to power Iran's exiled royal family.

Westerners watched Iran's "death to America" demonstrations and concluded that Iranians were violently anti-American because of their Shia faith and the fiery mullahs who inflamed their passions. Few Americans or Britons took the time or effort to understand the historical factors that had driven Iranians to such hatred for the western powers. Once again, westerners failed to comprehend that it was the political actions of their governments against Iran, rather than some clash of cultures, that had turned former admiration and friendship to searing hatred. As much as ordinary Iranians liked and admired the United States, many could not avoid seeing America as an exploiter and author of their immense suffering in the Iran-Iraq War. For similar reasons, Britain also became an icon of hatred for Iranians.

To no surprise, Iran's leadership, surveying its one million casualties in a war imposed on it, its ruined cities, armies of widows, and persistent subversive efforts by the US and Britain, concluded that their nation had to have the ultimate weapon of self-defense.

Most of the Muslim world witnessed the vicious, eight-year conflict with Iraq with mixed emotions. Sunnis felt natural sympathy for Iraq as a bulwark against Shia expansions and traditional Persian incursions into the Fertile Crescent. A growing number of Sunnis, and nearly all Shia, saw Iran as a clear victim of western imperial policy. But the war was obscure and there was little reliable reporting about it in the media. Besides, Imam Khomeini and Tehran's angry mullahs scared many Sunnis almost as much as they did the Americans, the British, and their Mideast satraps.

But when the war ended in 1988 after the US openly intervened on Iraq's side, the Muslim world came to understand that it had witnessed a conflict conceived, financed, and abetted by the US, Britain, and Israel, whose primary objective was to exhaust Iraq and Iran, thus facilitating its continued western influence over the region. Such ruthless cynicism shocked even jaded Muslims and profoundly altered their view of Americans, who, hitherto, had been generally seen as straightforward, unsubtle thinkers, as well as a decent, humanistic nation in spite of its support for Israel.

Iran emerged from the devastating war gripped by a profound national sense of martyrdom and self-sacrifice, the two attributes of the martyred Ali that form pillars of Shia doctrine. Iran's post-Khomeini theocratic leadership became all the more determined to challenge US–British hegemony over the Mideast and Israel's expanding power. The miserable failure of Arab leaders to defend the Palestinians, and their obeisance to the American Raj, left Tehran as the de facto voice of resistance to foreign domination.

Still, the terrible Iran-Iraq War had depleted a good deal of Tehran's revolutionary ardor, as it was designed to do. After the death of Imam Khomeini in 1989, Iran's fragmented government structure, power, and authority were widely dispersed under the new Supreme Leader, Ali Khamenei, through a system of checks and balances that often led to paralysis or endless debate. Iran's leadership was torn between advocates of rebuilding the battered economy and firebrands who wanted to export Islamic revolution, both as a matter of religious duty and as a way of keeping Iran's regional opponents on the defensive. The reconstruction faction finally won out and Iran switched from offensive revolutionary agitation in the Mideast and Central Asia to a more defensive stance in light of continued threats of attack from the US, Britain, and Israel, and efforts by Saudi Arabia to counter Shia revolution.

During the 1970s and 1980s, Iran began supporting Lebanon's long-marginalized, impoverished Shia, who accounted for a third of that small nation's population. Many Lebanese Shia clergymen had attended seminaries in Iran, so it was no coincidence that links between them and Iran's mullahs were close. As Lebanon slipped into civil war and then was invaded by Israel, Iran's Revolutionary Guards Corps (IRGC) began training and arming Shia militias, who eventually coalesced under the banner of the new Hezbollah movement.

While the Muslim world regarded Hezbollah as a legitimate organization fighting Israeli occupation of Lebanon, the United States once again adopted Israel's viewpoint and lexicon, branding Hezbollah terrorists. At the same time, Tehran, which strongly rejected any attempts at a Palestinian-Israeli compromise settlement and demanded the total liberation of Palestine, also provided funds and light arms to a variety of militant Palestinian groups that rejected the PLO's call for an eventual compromise with Israel. These Palestinian rejectionists included the Popular Front for the Liberation of Palestine, Popular Front for the Liberation of Palestine General Command, the Palestine Islamic Jihad, and a new resistance organization, Hamas.

Since most of these Palestinian groups had been involved in attacks against Israeli civilians and soldiers—in retaliation they claimed for the deaths of Palestinian civilians—they were branded terrorist organizations by Israel and the US. As a result, Iran was put on Washington's blacklist as a "sponsor of international terrorism."

Proof of Iranian involvement in what the US branded terrorist attacks remains elusive. Iranian officials were indicted by a court in Argentina for a series of deadly bombings of Jewish and Israeli targets in Buenos Aires. Washington blamed the attack on a US military housing complex at the al-Khobar base in Saudi Arabia on Iran, but the action could as well have been the work of Saudi jihadists aligned to al-Qaida.

In spite of the fact that Iran was a major victim of the kind of attacks Washington called terrorism, it was held up as a leading state sponsor of such acts. In 2006, Secretary of State Condoleeza Rice, fresh from promulgating the infamous mushroom-cloud big lie about Iraq, called Iran the "central bank for terrorism." She, of course, made no mention of secret US support for the violent Marxist Mujahidin-i-Khalq, which, while officially on America's terrorist list, was allowed to maintain an office in Washington and lobby Congress. Nor, in speaking about terrorism, did Rice mention funds openly voted by Congress to overthrow Iran's elected government, a clear violation of international law. Neither did she mention the CIA's arming and funding of violent groups inside Iran who were shooting off bombs and killing Iranian soldiers, police and officials, or secret US funding of radical Pakistani Sunni groups to stage cross-border raids into Iran.

In 1980 and 1981, the Mujahidin-i-Khalq assassinated much of Iran's leadership, including its president, prime minister, transportation and justice ministers, members of parliament, and many other prominent citizens. Large numbers of Iranians were killed by the People's Mujahidin. Today, combat units of this organization operate against Iran from Iraq, with the full cooperation, military assistance, and likely financial support of US occupation forces. The People's Mujahidin is also close to America's neoconservatives. So it seems, at least in Washington's view, that Iranians who staged attacks in occupied Iraq are terrorists, while Iranian Marxists who staged attacks inside Iran are legitimate antigovernment forces. In the old days of the Reagan era, they would have been called freedom fighters.

During the late 1990s, the CIA also claimed a bombing campaign it mounted against Saddam Hussein's Iraq that killed large numbers of civilians was legitimate "regime change operation." These attacks were led by a CIA "asset," Iyad Allawi, who the US later installed as Iraq's interim prime minister.

It was an open secret that Washington was trying to stir up revolts among Iran's very large Azeri-Turkish minority, said to account for 20 percent of its population, arming Iranian Kurds, or aiding ethnic Arabs of the western Iranian province of Khuzistan to stage attacks on government targets. During the same period, various senior Israeli military officers and right-wing politicians began making open threats to attack Iran's nuclear infrastructure. As reports of Iran's progress in enriching uranium multiplied, Israel and its American supporters intensified calls for war against Iran, further deepening Tehran's siege mentality.

Iran's steadfast defiance of US and Israel won it praise and growing admiration across the Muslim world, even among many ardent, anti-Shia Sunnis. Increasing numbers of Muslims began seeing Iran as the sole legitimate defender and champion of the growing Islamic resistance against western domination. They had little choice. No other Muslim nation was standing up to the West and Israel. The only other defiant Muslim notable was Osama bin Laden and he, though widely admired, was not regarded as a viable alternative to having an oil-rich state resisting the Raj.

Though bitter foes, Osama bin Laden and Iran shared one single thing in common: both had tried to export their religious creed to fellow Muslims, and both had failed. Most of the Muslim world wanted no part of bin Laden's angry, aggressive, fundamentalist version of Islam. Nor did Sunnis want Iran's medievalist Shia theology or restrictive society. But while both bin Laden and Iran failed in their religious crusade, each succeeded remarkably well in exporting their political and revolutionary beliefs and making themselves the twin poles of anti-Americanism.

Iran's ascendancy was, ironically, aided by the Bush administration's historic blunder of invading Iraq. Besides overthrowing Iran's blood enemy, Saddam Hussein, continuing resistance to the US occupation of Iraq had caused its oil output to fall below pre-invasion levels, resulting in a tighter world oil market and higher prices. Iran benefited greatly from the higher oil prices, as did another potential opponent of US global hegemony, Russia's president, Vladimir Putin, who in mid-2007 proclaimed his nation would reactivate its old Soviet-era naval base at Tartus, Syria, again send units of its Black Sea Fleet into the Mediterranean, and extend Russian long-range bomber patrols to America's Arctic borders and over the Pacific. But it was two other distinct events that catapulted Iran into the leadership of Muslim opposition to western influence.

First, in 2005, ordinary Iranians flocked to the polls and surprised everyone by electing Mahmoud Ahmadinejad as the new president of Iran. This was a stunning blow to Iran's conservative political establishment. Ahmadinejad's main rival, the wealthy, urbane veteran moderate politician Ali Akbar Rafsanjani, who had served as Iran's president from 1989 to 1997, had been expected to win handily.

Ahmadinejad, the son of a village blacksmith, had earned renown for courage and operational skill as a commander of Iran's Revolutionary Guards Corps commando units during the Iran-Iraq War. As mayor of

Tehran, he gained acclaim for his humble lifestyle, modesty and humility, and refusal to leave his very modest home for more opulent quarters. In a nation riddled with corruption, the pious Ahmadinejad stood out for remaining poor while in office. The Ahmadinejad house was open to anyone who wanted to come in and tell the mayor his problems. In short order, Ahmadinejad acquired the reputation of a champion of the poor. Many Iranians found there was something almost saintly about him, a view North Americans and Israelis certainly did not share.

The new president set about trying to implement domestic reforms in Iran and challenging its many foes abroad with a zeal and panache that were only exceeded by his lack of tact and self-restraint. Iran's centrist political establishment, led by Rafsanjani, had been trying for years to soften the strictures of the Islamic revolution, produce more economic growth through freer commerce, and improve Iran's frayed relations with the West. In the eyes of Iran's increasingly unhappy political establishment, the new firebrand president was a dangerous, populist loose cannon who was challenging their perks, promising the poor benefits he could not realistically deliver, and bringing down ever more trouble on Iran's head. At times, it seemed as if President Ahmadinejad was actually daring the West to do its worst against Iran.

Iran, for all its many faults, remains one of the Mideast's more democratic nations. North Americans are routinely told that Iran is "a medieval theocracy that advocates terrorism." In fact, even a quick look at that nation's turbulent political life will show that there is more open speech and criticism of government allowed in Iran than in many other US–supported Mideast nations, with the notable exceptions of Lebanon and Israel.

Iran is a hybrid state: a theocracy grafted onto a lively, if often chaotic, parliamentary democracy. Atop Iran's pyramid of government sits the Supreme Leader, usually a grand ayatollah from the nation's "Vatican" in Qum, appointed by a Council of Experts composed of senior religious figures. The Supreme Leader more or less fills the role of president in western democracies as head of state and commander in chief of the armed forces. Beneath him is the Council of Guardians, a sort of Supreme Court that can veto actions undertaken by parliament and remove other government officials. The Majlis, or parliament, is popularly elected and conducts much of the nation's day-to-day business. In Iran's March 2008 parliamentary elections hundreds of reformist candidates were barred from the race by conservatives in the Council of Guardians.

Checks and balances are the essence of Iran's Islamic government, just as they were for another post-royalist nation, the infant United States, though the comparison mostly ends there. Determined to avoid any future threat of autocracy or dictatorship, Iran's system of multi-level, overlapping, decentralized government has resulted in a very confused, complex system in which power has become overly diffused and decision-making diluted and uncertain.

At any given time in Iran, it is extremely difficult to tell who is in charge. Iranians' notorious love of argument, debate, and intrigue often twists even the simplest issues into Gordian knots. One school of thought holds that the presidency of Iran is largely a figurehead position, with real power held by the Supreme Leader. Another sees the president as the principal decision-maker and parliament as an active legislator and decision-maker.

Whatever the case, furious political debate always rages in Iran, with fevered accusations of corruption, treason, malfeasance, and nepotism common fare. Iran's feisty press amplifies the loud political debate and often goes after government corruption and mistakes. When media criticism grows too sharp, the government often shuts down its media critics in spite of laws guaranteeing freedom of the press. Politicians who become too irksome or boisterous are barred from office by the Council of Guardians. Goon squads from various religious organizations routinely try to intimidate other critics. Competing security organizations are constantly on the hunt for foreign spies and saboteurs. A climate of national paranoia and repression often prevails, fostered in no small part by ongoing western and Saudi attempts to overthrow Iran's government and stir up rebellion.

As a result, Iran has to be considered a half-democratic, half-repressive theocracy. It remains one of the few Muslim nations between Morocco and Pakistan whose president and parliament are directly elected by its people, and where often acerbic criticism of public figures is tolerated to a degree. Iran's Arab neighbors can only look on its rough-and-tumble semi-democracy with some measure of envy. In the Arab world, political leaders are never elected through honest votes, and criticism of high government officials or the leader brings swift retribution. In "democratic"

Turkey, America's role model for a good Muslim state, citizens can be jailed for criticizing the army or the nation's secular deity, Ataturk. Insulting Turkishness is a serious crime.

While nominally advocating free speech and open political expression, Iran remains a repressive regime where people are jailed, sometimes tortured, and too often executed. Women are constantly harassed by the police and religious vigilantes over their dress and deportment. Publications are routinely closed down for criticizing the government or advocating what is deemed un-Islamic behavior. There are reports of stonings in some rural areas. Most outsiders, including Muslims, find this side of Iran ugly, medieval, and embarrassing. By contrast, Saudi Arabia's routine public beheading of assorted malefactors goes largely unremarked in the West.

Both Iran and Saudi Arabia still practice traditional Islamic justice from the seventh and eighth centuries. Punishment conforms with the custom of eye for an eye; families often get to set the punishment for people who have killed or injured one of their own; Islamic judges, or "cadis," make swift, irrevocable decisions; thieves have their hands cut off; adulterers are supposed to be stoned (though this rarely occurs except in remote tribal areas); rapists, murderers, drug dealers, and child molesters face execution. Islamic law sees swift, draconian punishment as a far more effective social deterrent than long imprisonment. There is a general feeling under Sharia law, that locking up a man in a cage for years is inhumane.

Westerners recoil in horror at the application of Islamic law. But it must be noted that in Muslim nations or regions where Sharia is enforced, there is very little crime. You can leave your wallet in public in Saudi Arabia, and no one will steal it. Even in Egypt, where Sharia is not the law but remains blended into custom, one can walk through the poorest parts of Cairo without fear of robbery or molestation. Sharia law appears brutal and medieval, but Muslim nations do not keep armies of their citizens in prison, as does the United States, whose current number of convicts has reached a staggering 2.3 million.

In another irony, the nation closest to Iran in enforcement of religious observance and taboos happens to be one of the country's most bitter enemies, Saudi Arabia. Not only did the Saudi royal family largely fund the war against Iran, its agents waged a long, undercover struggle in Afghanistan, as well as in South and Central Asia, against spreading Iranian influence. The Muslim religious schools—madrassas—that have aroused such alarm in the West as hotbeds of terrorism were in large part funded by the Saudis to combat Iran's Shia agents of influence and traveling mullahs, an effort quietly supported by the United States.

Ever since the end of the Iran-Iraq War in 1988, the US and its allies have kept intensifying efforts to overthrow the Islamic Republic through subversion and punishing economic sanctions. This economic warfare has seriously retarded the growth of Iran's oil and gas industries and curtailed its exports. While rarely spoken of in western media, except when a European or Asian oil firm tries to do business in Iran and is hit by threats of US sanctions, Washington's imposition of harsh trade, military, and financial sanctions against Iran is viewed in Tehran as tantamount to open warfare and has seriously damaged Iran's economy.

This confrontation intensified with the advent of President Mahmoud Ahmadinejad. His vociferous and open defiance of American influence, and his frequent condemnation of Israel and Zionism, sparked outrage and fury in the United States and discomfort in Europe. The diminutive Iranian leader was crying aloud what other Muslim leaders only dared whisper. Many in the Muslim world thrilled to his fiery oratory, his refusal to give in to western threats, and his apparent determination to press ahead with Iran's nuclear enrichment program. Western critics called him a dangerous madman.

The second event that catapulted Iran into the unlikely role of the Muslim world's newest champion was the accidental little war that erupted in Lebanon in July 2006 (see Chapter 14). Israel's ferocious retaliation for a minor, routine border skirmish destroyed much of Lebanon's infrastructure and killed over 1,100 Lebanese civilians, bringing worldwide condemnation down on Israel's head. Israel's ground forces charged into southern Lebanon and in a month of heavy fighting were soundly beaten by Hezbollah's lightly armed fighters. It was a humiliating, mortifying disaster for Israelis, who prided themselves on always thrashing Arabs and inflicting ten casualties for every one they suffered. Israel's leadership was exposed as dazzlingly inept and amateur, and its vaunted military as something of a paper tiger, at least until the next war when revenge was all but certain.

Iran was Hezbollah's mentor and, with Syria, main supplier of arms and money. Iranian advisers had taught Hezbollah fighters close infantry tactics learned in the Iran-Iraq War and supplied the Lebanese militia with effective antitank weapons that shattered Israel's supposedly invulnerable Merkava heavy tanks. The entire Muslim world rejoiced at Hezbollah's David versus Goliath victory against the hitherto invincible Israelis, giving a good part of the credit to Iran, which lost no time in accepting the kudos.

Hezbollah's surprising victory not only humiliated Israel, it also deeply embarrassed the Arab states whose feeble armies and air forces had been so often routed or used for target practice by Israel's mighty armed forces. When the 2006 Lebanon border war erupted, Saudi Arabia, Jordan, and Egypt, the three pillars of the American Raj, even blamed and condemned Hezbollah, and sided with Israel. Or at least they did until euphoria across the Muslim world at Hezbollah's victory forced the rulers of these three US clients to cease their criticism and reluctantly show at least verbal support for Hezbollah.

This lesson in hypocrisy was not lost on the Muslim masses, who took it as yet another example of how the corrupt despots who ruled many of them had led them to nothing but defeat and humiliation. Zafar Bangash, a sharp-eyed observer of the Muslim world, later commented, and rightly so, that "over the past four decades, not one Muslim army had successfully defended its country's borders or the honor of its people." The sole function of the armies of Muslim states like Egypt, Pakistan, and Saudi Arabia was to suppress their own people, charged Bangash. These Muslim armies were not only centers of reaction but also the principal tool of western domination. No Muslim regular military forces had come to the aid of the Afghans, Bosnians, Chechens, Kashmiris, Palestinians, or Lebanese. Any successful resistance by the Muslim world had been done by irregular nationalist or Islamic organizations like Hezbollah, Hamas, and the Taliban—free-enterprise jihadi fighters.

Palestine and other afflicted Muslim lands would never be liberated, in the view of Islamists and Iran, until a Hezbollah-style revolution produced dedicated, incorruptible, well-trained fighters who could stand up to and defeat the Israelis and western powers. Hezbollah, and to a lesser degree Iraq's resistance forces and the Taliban, were showing the Muslim world the way to victory. Hezbollah's big brother, Iran, was suddenly the Muslim world's new champion, and, of course, the new public enemy number one for the United States.

One of the principal motivations for the US invasion of Iraq in 2003 was the potential threat to Israel posed by Baghdad's efforts prior to 1990 to develop nuclear weapons capability. Even though Israel had destroyed Iraq's sole nuclear reactor in 1981, and Saddam had eliminated what remained of Iraq's nuclear infrastructure after the 2001 war, partisans of Israel, led by Vice President Cheney, still considered Iraq a danger in spite of it being at least a decade or more away from developing a nuclear weapon, and lacking any means of delivering a warhead over anything farther than a few hundred miles. Israel and its American supporters were determined to eradicate any residual danger to the Jewish state. Cheney was even quoted as saying that the principal reason for invading Iraq was "for the security of Israel."

Washington was also concerned about a potential Iraqi nuclear weapon for another reason; not, as both Bush administrations falsely claimed, because a nuclear-armed Iraq might pose a threat to North America or Europe, but because it could limit the exercise of US power in the Mideast. Then secretary of state Colin Powell revealed this fact in an unguarded moment when he observed during an interview that any potential Iraqi nuclear capability "would limit our influence in the region." Translated into plain English, Powell was saying that the American Raj's hitherto unchallenged ability to overthrow regimes or wage war in the Fertile Crescent might be thwarted by Iraq's possession of a few defensive nuclear weapons. The United States' ability to attack North Korea had been blocked in the very same manner by Pyongyang's development of a limited but still strategically effective nuclear capability.

Precisely the same reasoning applied to Iran, but with even more force and urgency. Israel and its more sophisticated partisans knew that while the nuclear threat from Iraq had been exaggerated, Iran might one day challenge its Mideast nuclear monopoly and pose a very real danger to the Jewish state. There was, of course, nothing new about Iran's nuclear ambitions. In the late 1970s, shortly before the Islamic revolution, Iran's royalist government, as noted earlier, had been negotiating with Jerusalem to barter oil for Israeli nuclear warheads and the Jericho-1 ballistic missiles to carry them. During the same period, the US supplied Iran with basic nuclear technology.

In the early 1990s, Lieutenant General Jared Nasser, the director general of Pakistan's intelligence service, ISI, revealed to me that Iran had offered to pay Pakistan's entire defense budget for ten years in exchange for its nuclear weapons technology. Pakistan's government refused, though a decade later it would become involved in a covert international nuclear black-market operation led by Dr. Abdul Kadeer Khan.

Iran continued its dogged pursuit of nuclear capability. In 1975, it began construction, with German and Soviet/Russian assistance, of a large civilian power reactor at Bushehr on the Gulf, which remains unfinished to this day. During the late 1980s and 1990s, Iran initiated secret work on nuclear enrichment programs at a number of dispersed facilities at Nantaz, Isfahan, Arak, and a dozen other sites. When these nuclear sites eventually became known, Iran claimed its secrecy was due to the fear of US and Israeli attack.

In spite of the puzzlingly slow pace of development of Iran's nuclear programs, which Tehran resolutely insisted were solely for civilian purposes, international concern grew that Iran was covertly developing nuclear weapons capability. In 2006, Israel leaked Mossad reports claiming Iran would have a nuclear weapon within two years. The CIA estimated that it would take Tehran ten years, and another five years or so to develop effective delivery systems. American neocons lost no time in whipping up hysteria over the "worldwide threat" posed by Iran's nuclear program. Iran's Mahmoud Ahmadinejad poured fuel onto the fire by loudly trumpeting claims that Iran had achieved an "historic breakthrough in enriching uranium." Though he was talking about nuclear fuel to generate electricity, Ahmadinejad's gasconading convinced many around the globe that Iran was indeed well on the way to developing nuclear weapons.

In fact, according to nuclear experts, Iran has only managed to enrich a small amount of uranium, using newly developed centrifuge technology acquired from Pakistan, to around 3 to 5 percent. This low level of enrichment is adequate to fuel a civilian electric-power reactor but not for nuclear weapons, which require enrichment to over 85 percent. Ahmadinejad's claim that Iran would soon have a "cascade" of 30,000 or more gas centrifuges at Nantaz were dismissed by UN nuclear experts as gross exaggeration.

In 2004, a laptop computer was obtained by the CIA from "Iranian opposition forces" that allegedly came from a top-secret Iranian nuclear

laboratory. On it were designs for a ballistic missile nose cone and instruc-
tions on how to shape uranium into spherical cores needed to make a
nuclear warhead. Here, trumpeted the Bush administration, was the
smoking gun proving that Iran was developing nuclear weapons. But it
turned out the "Iranian opposition group" that provided the so-called
smoking gun was in fact the Mujahidin-i-Kalq, which, like Ahmad Chalabi's Iraqi opposition group, had close links with US intelligence and the
Pentagon, and received funding from Washington. The People's Mujahidin also had long-established links to the Mossad. Many Washington
intelligence professionals, burned by all the phony intelligence over Iraq,
believed the laptop and its contents had been cleverly concocted by the
Mossad, then passed to the Bush administration, which always was delighted to receive raw intelligence that appeared to validate its beliefs.

Whatever the case, Iran kept insisting its nuclear program was both
entirely within the bounds of the 1970 Nuclear Non-Proliferation Treaty
(NNPT), of which it was a signatory. Iran also claimed nuclear power was
absolutely necessary since its main resource, oil, was beginning to decline
at a time when the country's growing population of 70 million and its industry were increasing demand for energy.

The US, Britain, France, and Israel rejected out of hand Iran's insis-
tence that it had no plans to develop nuclear weapons. Just as the US and
Britain had done with Iraq in 2002–3, they demanded Tehran prove a
negative: that it had no nuclear weapons ambitions. This, of course, was
a logical impossibility.

The Bush administration launched a furious war of words against
Iran, supported by exactly the same kind of bogus information and junk
science from western-financed Iranian exile groups that proved so effective in whipping up war fever against Iraq. Vice President Dick Cheney
and his neocon allies issued a steady series of threats of war against Iran.
Israeli politicians and generals warned that their nation would attack Iran
with or without US help. In April 2008, Benjamin Ben-Eliezer, a right-
wing Israeli cabinet minister and former minister of defense, threatened:
if Iran attacks Israel, we will destroy it.

In December 2006, the UN Security Council, under heavy US pressure,
imposed limited sanctions on Iran as the first step in trying to shut down
its nuclear program. The European Union, Russia, and China reluctantly
went along with the sanctions in hopes that Iran would back down. Their

greatest fear was not Iran's nuclear program, but a US war against Iran that might destabilize the entire Mideast, provoke a firestorm across the Muslim world, and cause oil prices to skyrocket, thus endangering the international economy and global financial system.

Some important facts were obscured by all the hysteria and propaganda over Iran's nuclear program. First, the International Atomic Energy Agency (IAEA) made over 2,700 snap inspections in Iran and found no evidence of a weapons program. Traces of enriched uranium found in 2004 at Nantaz was determined to have come from a black-market centrifuge supplied by Pakistan. Second, Washington's claims that Iran had no need for nuclear power to generate energy were two-faced in the extreme. During the Ford administration, the Three Horsemen of the Neocon Apocalypse— Dick Cheney, Don Rumsfeld, and Paul Wolfowitz—negotiated to sell over 20 nuclear reactors to the Shah of Iran. Third, some western experts caution that because of contamination of Iran's uranium ore with heavy metals, it will not be able to enrich to more than 20 percent without extensive foreign technical support, which is unlikely to be forthcoming.

Most important, Iran has rigorously complied with the Non-Proliferation Treaty, putting its reactors under a regime of surprise, highly intrusive inspections. Under the treaty, Iran has every right to enrich uranium for civilian power use. Foreign powers are determined to deny Iran this basic treaty right, claiming that Iran might surge to develop highly enriched uranium.

The UN's chief nuclear inspector, Dr. Mohammed el-Baradai, and other UN inspectors and experts, have repeatedly stated they have found no evidence whatsoever of weapons programs in Iran. Under intense pressure from Washington, just as he was over Iraq, el-Baradai hedged by saying he cannot rule out that Iran has a covert weapons program, though 45 other nations are in exactly the same category. The US, which mounts 24/7 monitoring of Iran by satellite and drones, has yet to come up with any solid evidence to back up its incessant claims that Iran was violating the NNPT.

Amidst all the accusations against Iran, no one in the western world seemed to notice that the real violators of the international Non-Proliferation Treaty were the very same nations accusing Iran of violating the pact. A major provision of the original treaty calls on signatories to gradually eliminate all their nuclear weapons. Almost 40 years later, none of the original signers—the US, Britain, France, the Soviet Union, and

China—have complied. On the contrary, all five have steadily updated their nuclear arms. The Pentagon is currently studying a new generation of deep-penetrating tactical nuclear weapons, known in military circles as "Muslim busters." So the United States, a leading violator of the NNPT, unblushingly calls the Iranian kettle black. For the Muslim world, the entire issue of Iran's alleged nuclear weapons program is the latest and one of the most egregious example of America's widely criticized double standards.

Israel, which built its secret nuclear arsenal with French support and with technology and materials stolen by its agents from the United States, is estimated to have some 200 nuclear devices that can be delivered by a triad of medium-range ballistic missiles, sea-launched cruise missiles, and air-dropped nuclear weapons, as well as short-range tactical nuclear weapons and nuclear mines. Israel may also possess neutron weapons that produce intense radiation but small blast and thermal effects. Israel also has the Mideast's largest and most advanced chemical and biological warfare facilities.

The US has winked at Israel's nuclear and biological programs and even reportedly supplied the Jewish state with advanced nuclear and delivery-system technology. Israel's refusal to join the 118-nation Nuclear Non-Proliferation Treaty has been ignored by every American administration and, of course, Congress. Unlike North Korea's four or five estimated nuclear warheads, which are designed for defensive purposes to forestall a US nuclear or conventional attack by threatening to retaliate against South Korea, Okinawa, and Japan, Israel's large nuclear arsenal, which is believed to exceed those of Britain and France, appears designed for offensive war-fighting purposes, rather than self-defense against the Arabs or Iran, for which no more than two dozen warheads would likely suffice. One Israeli nuclear weapon dropped on the Aswan Dam, for example, would flood most of downstream Egypt. One theory holds that Israel developed such a large nuclear arsenal so as to be able to threaten the hostile Soviet Union as well as its unfriendly neighbors.

Calls by Arab states and Iran for creation of a nuclear-free zone in the Mideast have always been ignored by the US and Israel, though one might imagine that such a program, vigorously enforced by intensive inspections and coupled with Israel's effective anti-missile systems, would remove the threat to Israel of nuclear destruction. In fact, I have long proposed that the most effective inspections method would be to have inspectors from Israel and its neighbors permanently monitoring each other's nuclear facilities.

Muslim outrage and charges of hypocrisy intensified after the Bush administration initialed a strategic agreement with India in 2006 that legitimized India's nuclear weapons program. Until then, Washington had branded India, which refused to join the Nuclear Non-Proliferation Treaty, a "rogue" nuclear power and imposed trade sanctions on New Delhi. In an effort to build up India as a potential rival to China and enlist it in the war on terror, the Bush White House reversed long-standing US policy and blessed Delhi's extensive nuclear program of over 26 military reactors and about 100 nuclear warheads. The US agreed to resolve India's chronic shortages of nuclear fuel by supplying US fuel to its civilian reactors, allowing Delhi to devote its tight supplies of fuel to reactors making nuclear weapons. Certain advanced US nuclear technology would also be supplied to India.

India, in recent years, had become an important strategic ally of Israel in a sort of discreet anti-Muslim international. Israel quietly became India's second-largest arms supplier after Russia, and an important source of know-how and materials for India's nuclear weapons and missiles programs. The groundwork for the new US–India entente was laid in Washington by the Israel lobby, which gave the Indians, who had been in America's bad books for decades, entrée and political respectability.

The Muslim world and China were deeply dismayed by the new, proposed US–India–Israel entente, but most Americans remained unaware of this new alignment. They, and Congress, also ignored or remained blissfully unaware that their new ally, India, was rapidly developing intercontinental ballistic missiles (ICBMs) under cover of a civilian space program that could deliver nuclear warheads up to 7,000 miles away. India was also developing sea-launched, nuclear-armed ballistic missiles and powerful anti-ship missiles. Since it was unlikely that India would ever face a nuclear threat from Europe, Latin America, Japan, or Australia, what, one might ask, was the need for such long-range missiles when India's 4,000- to 5,000-kilometer-range Agni-III missiles were capable of covering India's main rivals, China and Pakistan, or most of Russia and the Mideast?

There was only one target worthy of India's long-range ICBMs—North America. But America's politicians, media, and big business were too giddy with the prospects of rich new commercial and arms markets in India to reflect on why India, where half its 1.1 billion people subsist in dire poverty, was spending billions of dollars deploying ICBMs and nuclear submarines. In the Indian Ocean, which Delhi calls its "mare nostrum," there was only one potential rival to India's fast-growing maritime power: the US Navy.

It did not take very long for Muslims everywhere to conclude that America's policy was nuclear arms for those who followed Washington's diktat, and no nukes for Muslims. Pakistan was an exception, since it had sneaked around US sanctions and was needed in the so-called war on terror.

American supporters of Israel were understandably panicked by ever more exaggerated, lurid claims by politicians and the media that Iran's nuclear program was threatening Israel with a second Holocaust.

The efficient Israel lobby went into high gear pressing Congress and the president to destroy Iran's nuclear infrastructure. US military experts estimated that at a bare minimum, "surgically removing" Iran's nuclear infrastructure in a "limited operation" would require massive and repeated air and missile strikes against at least 3,000 targets, including laboratories, factories, airfields and naval bases, communications nodes, ports, oil installations, military bases and government headquarters. In mid-2007, the White House ordered a major concentration of US strike forces against Iran, already virtually surrounded by US bases in the Gulf, Pakistan, and Central Asia, which has continued to this day.

As tension kept rising, Iran's president, Mahmoud Ahmadinejad delivered a fiery and deeply foolish speech in Tehran in which he claimed that the Jewish Holocaust had been greatly exaggerated and asked why Muslims should have had to pay for Europe's crimes against the Jews. Ahmadinejad quoted the late Imam Khomeini, who predicted that one day the Zionist state would be "swept from the pages of history" and replaced by a multi-religious, multi-ethnic state for Jews, Muslims, and Christians. Western sources, however, mistranslated Ahmadinejad's speech as calling for Israel's Jewish population to be "wiped from the map." This purposeful error, and invocations of the Holocaust, unsurprisingly brought Jewish passions to a boiling point, and intensified calls for war on Iran. The dwindling days of the Bush administration, and prospects of a possible Democratic victory in the 2008 elections, accelerated neocon efforts to promote war against Iran while Bush still held office. Meanwhile, the entire neocon community joined the campaign of Republican candidate John McCain, whose hard-line views on foreign policy, vows to keep US troops "as long as needed" in Iraq and singing, "bomb, bomb, bomb Iran" gave neocons an infusion of hope and newfound vigor.

The increasingly violent war of words between Iran and its western critics left unresolved the question of whether or not Iran was truly developing nuclear weapons. My judgment, based on Iran's previous history of seeking nuclear arms and its precarious geopolitical position, is that Tehran is indeed slowly working to develop a limited nuclear weapons capability, but primarily for defensive purposes. Iran's slowness in developing its nuclear program may well be due to furious debate within its chronically divided government whether or not to risk attack by the US and Israel in order to develop a handful of nuclear devices.

In the Muslim world's view, why should Iran not be entitled to nuclear weapons? Since 1900, Iran has been invaded by Britain, Russia, the Soviet Union, and Iraq. Iran has never launched a war of aggression in modern times. Muslims see Iran's support of militant Palestinian groups and Hezbollah as legitimate aid to those resisting foreign occupation, rather than terrorism, as Israel, the US and its allies claim. At present, Iran, a nation of 70 million with some of the world's leading oil and gas reserves, is surrounded by nuclear-armed powers: Israel, US forces in the Gulf, Russia, Pakistan, and India. Where is it written that among all these nations, only Iran must be denied the right to nuclear self-defense? Surely Iran has a far more logical need for nuclear weapons for self-defense than France or Britain, which are under the US nuclear umbrella.

Supporters of Israel claim Iran's development of nuclear weapons would pose a dire, unacceptable threat to its existence. Why the Iranian leadership would attack Israel with nuclear weapons and, in return, face certain total devastation by Israel's indestructible nuclear triad of land-, air-, and sea-based nuclear missiles, not to mention likely US nuclear retaliation, is never properly answered. Even the claim by some that a mad president could order an attack is spurious, since such a command would have to be approved by the Supreme Leader and the entire Council of Guardians who hold overall command of the armed forces.

The real danger of a few Iranian nuclear devices, as earlier noted, would come from Tehran's ability to create a nuclear umbrella that would limit the scope of US and/or Israeli military action against Iran and provide a bulwark for forces opposing US hegemony in the region. Contrary to US assertions, Iran would pose no strategic threat to North America, first because it has no nuclear warheads or intercontinental missiles capable of reaching North America; and second because, as noted above, even if Iran managed to develop a few crude ICBMs, or buy them from India, it would not risk nuclear eradication to lob a few missiles of highly doubtful accuracy at the United States.

Continental Europe and the Muslim world appear reluctantly prepared to accept a nuclear-armed Iran provided its strategic weapons serve only for self-defense against foreign attack or invasion. But having been humiliated by North Korea's development of nuclear weapons, Washington is determined to prevent Iran from following Pyongyang's lead. The prospect of Tehran's fiery mullahs armed with even a handful of nuclear weapons fills champions of the American Raj with dread.

President Bush's plan to install US antiballistic missiles and early warning radar stations in Poland and the Czech Republic to shoot down Iranian nuclear-armed missiles is another chimera: an unproven system to down missiles Iran does not possess, armed with warheads it does not yet have. In Washington's view, the system is designed to defend US bases in Europe against retaliatory attack from Tehran in the event of an American assault on Iran. The natives, remember, must not be allowed the Maxim gun.

Whether the US will be able to overthrow Iran's Islamic government and restore the tame royalist regime-in-waiting remains to be seen. Meanwhile, Iran's influence in the Muslim world continues to grow. However, the current fashionable thinking in the West of a Shia arc of influence seems overblown. It is difficult to imagine Shia Iran exercising decisive influence beyond its immediate neighbors along the Gulf, in Iraq, and in Shia parts of Lebanon.

Increasingly, some in the Sunni Muslim world are backing Iran, but from the quintessentially Mideastern premise that my enemy's enemy is my friend. There is no love lost for Iran or its clerical leadership. For many Sunnis, Iran remains an untrustworthy, semi-hostile apostate nation that always acts in its own narrow interests and ignores the broader interests and values of the Muslim world. Saudi Arabia, Egypt, and Jordan are actively working with the Bush administration to undermine Iranian influence in the Mideast.

The ghastly sectarian bloodbath in Iraq between the Shia majority and Sunni minority has certainly not burnished Iran's credentials in the Muslim world. Iraq's powerful Shia clergy is joined at the hip with Iran's religious establishment in Qum. The civil war in Iraq has rekindled both ancient animosities, and ingrained prejudices between Shia and Sunni. Some Sunni alarmists even claim Iran is seeking to revive the expansionist Safavid Empire (AD 1502–1736) in a rebirth of Persian imperialism. This is unlikely. Iran does exert strong influence among Shia is Iraq and Lebanon, but, for the time being, further expansion of its influence seems unlikely since Tehran is totally occupied with the rising threat of US and/or Israeli attack or internal subversion, and increasingly serious economic problems that are causing serious popular unrest. The flight of four million mostly Sunni refugees from Shia oppression in Iraq hardly recommends Iran to the mainstream Arab world as a liberator or savior. Many Sunnis, led by Osama bin Laden, condemn Iraq's Shia as stooges of the western powers and Israelis.

Turkey, Iran's historic enemy and rival, is watching Iran's growing influence in Iraq with mounting concern. In the view of many Turks, Iraq's oil, which once belonged to the Ottoman Empire, should be returned to their own nation, which has no oil, rather than be usurped by oil-rich Iran.

While the policies of Iran's Supreme Leader, Grand Ayatollah Ali Khamenei, have been cautious and generally pragmatic, there is a powerful hard-line faction in and out of government in Iran that is largely composed of war veterans of the Revolutionary Guards and Basij militia. This influential group, which includes President Ahmadinejad, a former Revolutionary Guards commander, sees the US as a paper tiger, and often appears to be actually encouraging an American attack.

In the view of these nationalist militants, nothing that US military forces could do to Iran—short of using nuclear weapons—could equal the destruction and pain caused by Iraq's eight-year invasion. Iran's soldiers and militia were hardened in this crucible and made insensible to losses and further suffering. Just as President George W. Bush boasted over Iraq, "bring 'em on," so Iran's hard-line veterans are similarly challenging the Americans. In their view, Iran could ride out a US air campaign, no matter how punishing. Any US ground invasion would founder in the immensity of Iran, and be met by ferocious resistance from its regular and irregular forces, led by veterans of the Iran-Iraq War. While poorly equipped and immobile, Iran's ground forces are large in number, highly motivated and would prove a formidable foe in a conventional war when defending the homeland.

"America will break its teeth on Iran, just as Germany did in Russia," a Revolutionary Guards officer told me. Iranian regular and Special Forces would then go on the offensive in Iraq, the Gulf sheikdoms, and against US bases in Afghanistan, Pakistan, and Central Asia. Iran might succeed in interrupting tanker routes through the Gulf, causing oil prices to rise to $140 per barrel or more. US forces in Iraq and Afghanistan would find themselves cut off, their supply lines interdicted, and their line of retreat blocked by hostile forces.

Americans who believe they could duplicate their easy victory against Iraq's armed rabble are mistaken. In 2003, Iraq was a small, demolished nation of only 25 million, at least half of whose citizens opposed the regime of Saddam Hussein. Iran, by contrast, is a large, cohesive nation with a profound sense of patriotism combined with the tradition of Shia martyrdom and self-sacrifice. The US may bomb Iran back to the nineteenth century, as it did Iraq, but it cannot occupy this large nation without a major land invasion. That, of course, seems impossible given that over half of all US maneuver brigades are hopelessly bogged down in Iraq and Afghanistan.

A full-scale war with Iran would produce a host of unpredictable dangers for the US and the entire Mideast. As a result, Iranian radicals are hoping for such a conflict that they believe would break once and for all the power of the American Raj. But given the US's recent history of attacking small nations such as Grenada, Panama, Libya, Somalia, or modest-sized ones like Iraq and Afghanistan, a US invasion of Iran seems unlikely, though a massive air campaign remains possible in the near future.

In spring 2007, I was invited to the Pentagon by Operation Checkmate, a highly classified US Air Force strategic planning group that reports directly to the powerful, four-star chiefs of staff, to brief them on Afghanistan, Pakistan, and the Mideast. In the course of the briefing I spoke with some of the planners who had engineered the 2001 and 2003 air campaigns against Iraq. I asked them point-blank if an attack on Iran was impending or planned. They strongly denied any attack was in the works. I took their denials with many grains of salt.

In March 2008, Admiral William Fallon, the respected chief of the US Central Command that covers the entire Mideast and South Asia, was forced to resign by the White House over his public opposition to a war against Iran. His ouster was the latest evidence of widespread and growing opposition to any new war in the Pentagon, CIA and State Department.

Iran's immediate neighbors, Saudi Arabia, Kuwait, and the Gulf emirates, who all have sizable Shia minorities, feel keenly the threat of Iranian militancy and the danger that any conflict with the US would quickly spill into their nations and interdict their oil exports. They are urging Washington to be cautious.

So Iran remains half in and half out of the Muslim world, both a possible defender against western domination and a potential threat as a new hegemon in its own right. Iranians' traditional arrogance and scorn for Arabs, Indians and Pakistanis, and its well-known feelings of racial and intellectual superiority over them, certainly do not advance Tehran's standing among Sunni Muslims, who have difficulty deciding whether the United States and Britain are a worse threat than resurgent Iran.

In the Mideast, Iran may be respected, but it is certainly not loved. Not a few Sunnis would like to see the western powers cut Iran down to size, just as happened to Saddam Hussein's threatening Iraq. After all, distrust the neighbor is an Arab maxim.

CHAPTER TWELVE
★ ★ ★

CHECHNYA:
GENOCIDE IN THE CAUCASUS

History may be the propaganda of the victors, but occasionally a small, forgotten people long submerged by a tide of imperial conquest manages to emerge for a few brief moments and make its voice heard. Such is the tragic story of the Chechens.

The Caucasian republic of Chechnya, or Islamic emirate of Ishkira, as its Islamists called it, was never part of the American Raj. It was, however, very much a part and involuntary member of the Russian-Soviet Imperial Raj, which used to be called until the 1990s "the last nineteenth-century colonial empire."

Its tragic story is being included in this study of America's influence over the Muslim world because the Chechens' heroic but hopeless struggle against Soviet/Russian rule and its savage repression enraged, pained, and shamed the entire Muslim world in much the same way two other heroic but hopeless struggles, the Warsaw Ghetto uprising of 1943 and the 1956 Hungarian uprising, aroused sympathy and deep anguish in the West.

Chechnya's tragedy, and the inaction of the Muslim world, turned many Muslims against their western-backed governments and generated intense anger against Russia and its erstwhile supporter, the United States. Many in the Muslim world believe to this day that Moscow, Washington, and London secretly colluded in the crushing of Chechen independence. After Iran, no more "Islamic republics" would be tolerated.

Of the four major issues that have inflamed passions across the Muslim world, Chechnya ranks with Palestine, Afghanistan, and Iraq, as a wellspring of sorrow and anger. By contrast, in the non-Muslim world, and particularly North America, the story of the Chechens' epic struggle for freedom from Russian rule is all but unknown, or dismissed as another example of Islamic terrorism.

Chechens are an ancient Indo-European people of the Caucasus Mountains, the great wall of snowcapped peaks that forms Russia's southern boundary from the Caspian to the Black Sea. Within this vast massif dwell over thirty major and at least one hundred minor different ethic and religious groups. During the sixteenth century, while under Ottoman rule, Chechens converted en masse from Christianity to Islam. Though Sunni Muslims, Chechens soon adopted the mystical Sufi creed of Islam from Central Asia based on secret brotherhoods, the adoration of saints, and the mystical ceremony of Zikr, in which initiates sought a vision of Allah, or union with him, through intense rituals of religiosity that resembled those of the Sufi Dervishes of Turkey.

In the eighteenth century, Russia's steady expansion into the regions around the Black and Caspian Seas eventually collided with the fierce, warlike Chechen and Dagestani mountain tribes of the Caucasus. Large-scale Chechen resistance to Russian imperial rule began in 1785, when Sheik Mansur rallied local tribesmen against the advancing Russians. After a six-year resistance, he was defeated and captured.

Thirty-one years later, a terrible storm broke upon the peoples of the Caucasus in the ruthless person of Russia's new imperial viceroy, Alexi Yermolov. This giant of a man set about crushing all resistance to Russian rule. Yermolov reserved special ferocity for those who most strongly resisted: Chechens, Dagestanis, and Cherkass (Circassians). He built a chain of forts across the region, one of which, Grozny, meaning "terrible" or "frightful," was to become Chechnya's capital.

In a boast that echoed down the ages and came to embody Russian colonial rule, Yermolov thundered, "I desire that the terror of my name should guard our frontiers more potently than chains or fortresses, that my word should be for the natives a law more inevitable than death." He held special hatred for Chechens, whom he branded "bandits," "assassins," and "treacherous." These epithets would come to form the prevailing Russian view of Chechens.

For the ensuing thirty years, Yermolov and his soldiers laid fire and sword on the Caucasus in a series of campaigns that were noteworthy for unusual savagery and brutality even during this era of rapacious European and American colonial expansion. The Chechens and their Muslim neighbors continued resisting the Russians; at the same time, large numbers fled to Turkey and the Levant. During the mid-1800s, Sheik Shamyl's revolt held the Russians at bay for thirty years. But after a quarter century of resistance, Shamyl and his Dagestani and Chechen mujahidin were finally surrounded and forced to surrender in 1859.

Other Muslim revolts kept breaking out against Russian rule. In the course of the Russian-Ottoman War in 1877, the entire Chechen people rose against the Russians. In the course of these rebellions, roughly 40 percent of the Chechen population, then estimated at about 220,000, were killed by Russian forces; 400,000 Cherkass were deported to the Ottoman Empire.

After Russia's Bolsheviks seized power, the Caucasus was allowed a grudging measure of autonomy by the new, weak Bolshevik regime. But once Stalin had consolidated his power, the Caucasus quickly felt the dictator's iron hand. Either a Georgian or Ossetian (a Christian Caucasus tribe of Turkic origins living in Georgia), Stalin hated Muslims and hated Georgia's historic foes, the Chechens.

In 1930, a second rebellion erupted after the Soviet NKVD (secret police) sought to impose collectivization on local farmers. It was quickly crushed. Six years later, Moscow detached part of Chechnya and created the new People's Republic of Ingushetia. There was no real difference between them, but Stalin was determined, following in the best British imperial tradition, to divide and rule these fractious, troublesome mountaineers. Dividing Chechnya, he reasoned with precise Caucasian logic, would further regionalize the mountaineers and accentuate petty differences between them. He would make of them an example they would not soon forget.

In July 1937, Stalin's NKVD execution units summarily shot 14,000 Chechens and Ingush, dumping bodies into a mass grave at Gori Yachevodskaya. While the entire world would hear of the massacre by the Nazis of an estimated 100,000 people, many of them Jews, at Babi Yar in Ukraine four years later, and the killing in 1940 of 22,000 Polish officers by the Soviets in the Katyn Forest, a crime blamed by Moscow on the Germans, this crime against the Muslims of the Caucasus remains unknown.

The supremely paranoid Stalin, believing false accusations that some Chechens had sided with the Germans during their brief, ten-week occupation of Chechnya and other regions of the Caucasus, decided in 1944 to deal with the Chechens in his trademark ruthless style. To quote one of Stalin's favorite maxims, "no man, no problem."

Stalin, well surnamed the Breaker of Nations, had the entire Chechen-Ingush population, some half-million people, rounded up in the winter by the NKVD and deported in unheated railroad cattle cars to Kazakhstan, 2,000 kilometers away, or even farther east into Siberia. The deportees were dumped into barren fields, in tiny hamlets, or in concentration camps in temperatures of –25 to –35C. Other Muslim peoples of the Caucasus and southern USSR—Kalmyks, Crimean Tatars, Karachai, Balkars—were also deported to the gulag in Stalin's mass ethnic cleansing, but none in such overwhelming numbers as the Chechens. Of the half-million Chechens and Ingush deported to Stalin's Siberian concentration camps or simply dumped in the middle of nowhere, at least half died. Death rates were similar for other deported Muslim peoples. Gas chambers and bullets were not needed; the lethal cold worked swiftly and cheaply.

Stalin's final solution to the "nationalities problem," as he called it, was directed by the ever-efficient Georgian, NKVD chief Lavrenti Beria, and eventually sent at least 2.5 million members of Muslim and non-Slav ethnic groups to the gulag, where one in three died of hunger and disease each year. This genocide went unnoticed in the West. Small wonder, since at the time the Soviet Union was the West's close ally in the Crusade for Freedom against National Socialist Germany. While Hitler's concentration camps are burned into our historical memory, those of Stalin, which preceded Hitler's industrial killing by a decade, are barely remembered outside Russia.

In the years following Stalin's death in 1953, the Soviet government finally freed survivors of his deportations from concentration camps or Siberian exile and allowed most to return to their ancestral homes. Another large group of deportees, Crimean Tatars, remained in exile until the years after 1967. Their homes had all been occupied by Slavic Russians; none received any compensation. Most of the Chechens who managed to survive Stalin's genocide eventually filtered back to Chechnya. Like two other groups of victims of genocide, Armenians and Jews, they retained a profound folk memory of their national suffering that bound them together and called out for vengeance.

Many Chechens, unable to find employment in their impoverished homeland, gravitated to the USSR's big cities. In Moscow, they came to dominate street markets and a more sinister métier, crime. Though small in number, thanks to their reckless courage, ferocity, and audacity, Chechens quickly became Russia's most feared gangsters. Everyone knew the Moscow warning "Watch out, or the Chechen will get you."

By the time the Soviet Union began to unravel in 1990, its Chechen population had risen to about one million, with 75 percent of them living in Chechnya proper and the remaining in Moscow and other Russian cities. In the late fall of that year, 1,000 prominent Chechens met in an historic conference that proclaimed their intent to seek national sovereignty, just as the leaders of fourteen other Soviet republics were doing.

Fruitless negotiations dragged on with Moscow during the tumultuous period when Russian Republic leader Boris Yeltsin was relentlessly stripping the federal chairman, Mikhail Gorbachev, of his powers and fatally undermining the structure of the Soviet Union.

The Chechens elected as their leader Dzhokar Dudayev, a respected former Red Air Force general who had commanded an air base for nuclear-armed bombers at Tartu, Estonia. The handsome, dashing Dudayev was a model Soviet officer; few of his military colleagues knew his family had been deported to Central Asia concentration camps by Stalin.

On November 1, 1991, President Dudayev proclaimed Chechnya's independence. Russia's feuding leadership, minus Yeltsin, who was hors de combat from drink, refused to accept Chechnya's declaration of independence, declared a state of emergency, and dispatched Interior Ministry troops to Chechnya. But lacking any plan for what to do next, Moscow soon withdrew its security forces.

Chechnya quickly became a sort of political no-man's-land, neither in nor out of the crumbling Soviet Empire. The ongoing power struggle in Moscow gave Chechens a brief respite. President Dudayev flew to Europe and the Mideast, urgently seeking diplomatic recognition of Chechen independence and aid for his tiny, impoverished republic of one million souls. Though he encountered considerable sympathy and verbal support, few nations were willing to anger Russia for the sake of a small Muslim nation in the Caucasus and refused his pleas for recognition.

In June 1992, the last Russian troops left Chechnya after selling most of their weapons to the Chechen government. However, in October, the Russian army invaded and occupied neighboring Ingushetia, even though it had chosen not to declare independence from the Russian Republic.

Chechen culture was based on xenophobic clans and Sufi religious brotherhoods. As is typical with most mountain peoples, the anarchic Chechens rejected central authority and often regarded even neighboring villages as hostile. During Chechnya's period of semi-freedom from Russia, its people squabbled furiously, intrigued against one another, and failed to produce a solidly established government. Worse, Chechnya became a haven for all kinds of illicit activities, prime among which were black marketeering and arms dealing. Chechen, Russian, Armenian, and Georgian gangsters had a field day.

Chechnya was believed to have earned nearly $1 billion by selling oil extracted from the north-south pipelines to the Caspian oil fields that made their nation so important to Moscow. Senior Russian officials and generals used Chechnya to illicitly sell Russian arms from military stores to all comers. Courageous Russian journalists who exposed such brazen corruption were beaten or murdered.

By early 1994, the Yeltsin government had begun a campaign to overthrow the new Chechen government, using its local pro-Moscow Chechens, Russian gangsters, small numbers of mercenaries, and agents of the security service the FSB (former KGB). All these limited, half-baked efforts failed. Meanwhile, a group of Russian hard-liners was gradually consolidating its power during the period when Yeltsin's drunken antics abroad were humiliating Russia. They sent a column of Russian tanks to seize Grozny in a coup de main. The attackers were ambushed and routed by Chechen fighters.

Moscow then geared up for a general war against the Chechens. Yeltsin's advisers suggested that a quick victory in Chechnya would boost his sagging fortunes just as President Bill Clinton's dispatch of troops to overthrow Haiti's elected but inept government had improved his political standing at home. On November 26, 1994, 40,000 Russian troops with armor, artillery, and powerful air support invaded Chechnya. Dudayev's frantic efforts to contact Yeltsin and head off the war were blocked. Moscow was determined to crush the Chechens and make an example of them to any other of Russia's independent-minded Muslims. There was also another reason: Moscow wanted revenge for its humiliating defeat by Muslims in Afghanistan.

Opposing the advancing Russian army were no more than a few thousand Chechen fighters armed with light weapons. They were commanded by another able Chechen veteran of the Red Army, Aslan Maskhadov. The

Chechen mujahidin put up a ferocious resistance in their villages and the capital, Grozny. It seemed impossible that Russia's armored juggernaut of T-72 tanks and BMP armored personnel carriers would not swiftly crush Chechen resistance. But in one of the most remarkable feats of modern military history, the Chechen irregulars fought the advancing Russians to a standstill, using highly effective small-infantry tactics and light RPG antitank weapons. Thirteen years later, lightly armed Hezbollah guerrilla fighters in southern Lebanon won an equally lopsided victory against invading Israeli heavy-armored columns.

Deeply frustrated by their inability to take Grozny, Russian commanders unleashed intensive bombardment of the capital with heavy artillery, rocket batteries, and saturation bombing that eventually razed much of the city. At least 30,000 civilians, Chechen and Russian, were killed in Grozny alone by Russian heavy artillery and bombs—and this was only the opening of the war. Russian forces—military, Interior Ministry, mercenaries, and FSB—launched a reign of terror across Chechnya, arresting suspects en masse, brutally torturing suspects, and executing anyone judged to be a mujahidin or sympathizer. In operations known as "zachistki," Russian troops would cordon off an entire village, arrest all males, loot houses, kill livestock, and rape women. This medieval brutality covered all of Chechnya and turned its civilian population into cowering fugitives. Thousands of Chechens were thrown into Russian concentration camps where they went through a filtration system consisting of torture, degradation, and intimidation. Some 100,000 Chechen refugees fled to Ingushetia.

The outside world received a steady stream of reports about the carnage in Chechnya but turned its back on the gruesome spectacle. The United States and Europe could have taken action to rein in Moscow's brutal behavior in Chechnya by ceasing their financial aid that sustained the bankrupt Moscow government. Human rights groups protested Russian atrocities against the Chechens, but their plaints were ignored by Moscow and by many western governments who did not want to anger the Kremlin. The European powers, who should have taken the lead in pressing Russia to halt its cruelties in Chechnya, evaded the issue for fear their growing trade with Russia and growing dependence on its deliveries of gas and oil would be negatively affected, or that Russia's Communists might return to power.

A fast-rising Chechen commander, Shamyl Basayev, desperate to halt the destruction of his nation, launched a bold foray into neighboring southern Russia, seizing Budyonnovsk, a provincial Cossack town of 60,000. Basayev and his 150 mujahidin shot up the town and seized some 2,000 Russian hostages. The enraged, humiliated Russians were forced to allow the Chechen raiders to escape. The Chechen leaders Aslan Maskhadov and Dzhokar Dudayev were furious at Basayev's unauthorized raid, but he insisted Russians had to feel some of the terror their troops were inflicting on Chechens.

As fighting raged across Chechnya and its fighters kept ambushing and destroying Russian columns in the mountains and forests of the south, limited help began to arrive from abroad. Money came from Islamic charities and wealthy individuals in the Gulf and Saudi Arabia.

Videotapes and recorded messages about the Chechens' struggle against impossible odds circulated widely throughout the Muslim world. Most Muslims had never previously heard of the Chechens, but their courage and intent to create a state based on Islamic principles of social welfare and justice aroused growing sympathy for their liberation struggle. Russia, and its predecessor, the Soviet Union, were still regarded by many Muslims as a ferocious enemy of Islam and leading oppressor of the Muslim people.

Small numbers of foreign mujahidin managed to make their way to isolated Chechnya, most through neighboring Georgia, which held no love for the Russians. Chief among the hundred or so foreign mujahidin was a young Saudi veteran of the Afghan jihad who fought under the nom de guerre Amir Khattab. His mother was of Caucasian Cherkass descent. These foreign fighters brought badly needed funds and inspired the Muslim world with their victories. They reminded Muslims that the Russians had slaughtered over two million Afghans, and were now doing the same to tiny Chechnya.

The presence of a small number of foreign Muslim fighters proved a boon to Moscow. The Kremlin directed all its media organs to unleash a powerful propaganda campaign painting the Chechen resistance as Islamic terrorists. Soon, there was no mention of Chechens in Russia's media or government statements without the appendage "Islamic terrorist." This campaign was highly effective, quickly spreading the notion in the United States and Europe that Chechens were terrorists with no legitimate political agenda. The Bush administration did the same thing in Iraq, convincing Americans that all its resistance groups were al-Qaida terrorists.

High-profile raids by Basayev and another daring Chechen commander, Salman Raduyev, who was later beaten to death in a Russian prison after his capture, provided the Russians with what appeared shocking examples of Chechen terrorism. Efforts by Chechens to tell their story to the world were pathetically ineffective and drowned out by Moscow's storm of invective.

In 1996, as the Chechens were fighting for their lives against Russian troops, US president Bill Clinton came to Moscow to show support for President Yeltsin, whose government had increasingly come under American financial influence. Much of Russia's war against the Chechens was secretly funded by cash from Washington laundered through a number of Russian businessmen with underworld connections. Clinton, in an April 21, 1996, speech in Moscow that horrified the Muslim world, seemed to compare Yeltsin's savage repression of Chechnya to America's own nation's civil war, and compared Yeltsin to US president Abraham Lincoln.

There was also another reason for Clinton's fulsome praise of Russia's savaging of Chechnya. The feeble Yeltsin government had given Washington carte blanche in the Mideast, and particularly US sanctions against Iraq. In exchange, Washington quietly backed and partly financed Russia's war in the Caucasus. At the same time, Yeltsin's Kremlin was selling the crown jewels of Soviet military technology to the US, reportedly including a top-secret, very powerful miniaturized nuclear reactor capable of tripling the capability of US intelligence satellites.

It is likely that the US National Security Agency or CIA provided Russia's FSB security service with advanced electronic-monitoring devices that could pinpoint the location of cell and satellite phones, and vector a missile to their location with great precision and deadly results.

On April 21, 1996, Chechnya's president, Dzhokar Dudayev, who had been evading Russian forces since the invasion, was talking on his satellite phone from a ravine near the village of Gekhi-Chu. He had just agreed to meet with Boris Yeltsin to try to end the war and had been lured into negotiating the details over his satellite phone. Dudayev had escaped a score of attempts by Russia's FSB to assassinate him. But this time, thanks to the new US–supplied tracking device, a Russian missile homed in on his telephone, killing the Chechen leader. This was a Parthian shaft from Moscow.

Dudayev's assassination provided Yeltsin and Moscow hard-liners with an ideal excuse to declare victory in a war that they were actually losing. Russian forces were stalemated by the Chechens and being bled dry. The brutal war was increasingly unpopular at home, and very expensive at a time when Yeltsin was fighting for reelection. So in May 2006, Moscow signed a cease-fire with the new Chechen government led by Aslan Maskhadov and Zelimkhan Yandarbiyev. Some fighting continued, but by August, a full peace deal, negotiated by the Russian paratroop general Alexander Lebed, came into force. Lebed, a very capable, much-admired leader and presidential candidate who favored full Chechen independence, was later killed in a suspicious helicopter crash in Siberia. Many Russians believe he was assassinated.

The Russians killed an estimated 100,000 Chechen civilians and fighters during the First Chechen War. At least 6,000 Russian soldiers died, and 17,000 were wounded. The tiny republic was devastated. Moscow acknowledged Chechnya's de facto independence, but did not accord it full de jure recognition. The western world did not even go this far, totally ignoring Chechen independence and spurning the country's desperate pleas for recognition and economic assistance. No nations challenged the air and economic embargo that Moscow maintained on isolated "independent" Chechnya.

Even so, Muslims were elated by Chechnya's resistance to Russia's brutal repression, and electrified by the second victory of Muslim mujahidin after Afghanistan. It appeared, at least to the jihadi movement, that their belief that ardent faith could overcome even the high-tech weapons and numerical advantage of European powers was indeed justified. They were soon to be disabused.

No Muslim powers recognized the Chechen republic, though Saudi Arabia and the Gulf emirates made token gestures. The only nation that did recognize the newly proclaimed Chechen Republic of Ishkeria was another former victim of Russian imperialism, tiny Estonia, where General Dudayev had been stationed. The world turned its back on Chechnya, thus assuring that its attempt to regain its freedom after more than three centuries of Russian rule was doomed.

The craven inaction of Muslim nations and their numerous talking-shop organizations was particularly shameful, a point not lost on its citizens, who railed against their governments for doing less than nothing to help the beleaguered Chechens. These were the same regimes that had stood by and watched the massacre and rape of Bosnia's Muslims and had done nothing to help Palestinians.

Russia's repression of Chechnya was condemned across the Muslim world but so, too, however unfairly, was the United States. Muslims began blaming America as well as Russia for the fate of the Chechens. The US government could have done a great deal to help Chechnya, as it would later do with newly independent Georgia and Armenia, but Washington was too absorbed with cultivating Yeltsin's client regime to care about human rights in the Caucasus, and the Chechens were Muslims. Once again, realpolitik won out.

There is, of course, the question of should the US have taken action to help the beleaguered Chechens? Is it Washington's responsibility to aid the oppressed around the globe? Of course not. The US cannot fulfill the role of world moral gendarme, but it has never hesitated to make certain humanitarian interventions when strategically or politically useful, such as in Somalia, Haiti, Bosnia, Indonesia and East Timor, Liberia, or Kosovo. The case of Chechnya was unique and demanded western action. Here was a tiny nation that had fought for its freedom for 300 years against the most savage repression, half of whose population had been sent to concentration camps, and that had as much right to independence as Ukraine, Georgia, Belarus, or Uzbekistan. Helping save the Chechens from Russian repression would have made America a hero in the Muslim world and gone far to repair earlier damage. If Jews merited their own independent state because of Hitler's Holocaust, then why not the Chechens, who had suffered even a higher proportion of deaths relative to their total population in Stalin's concentration camps?

During the three ensuing years after the First Chechen War ended in 1996, Russia's political landscape changed rapidly as the besotted, ailing Yeltsin became a near shut-in while his entourage vied for power and spoils. Hard-liners from the security organs and military relentlessly pushed aside democratic liberals and reformers, including those who advocated accepting Chechnya's independence. Such ideas were anathema to the hard men who bitterly mourned the demise of the Soviet Union.

I reported from fin de régime Moscow in 1988 and 1989, shortly before the USSR collapsed, that the KGB elite First Directorate had concluded the Communist Party was hopelessly rotten, corrupt, and incompetent, and could not be saved. The First Directorate was the KGB's premier arm, conducting all foreign intelligence and some domestic counterintelligence. Made up of the youthful cream of the Soviet "nomenklatura" elite, the First's men and women were highly educated and sophisticated, traveled abroad, spoke foreign languages, and had access to foreign media.

Equally important, they knew exactly what was going on inside the crumbling USSR and saw its implosion coming. So, as a number of senior KGB officers told me, the organization decided it would not sink with the party, but overthrow it and put its own members in key positions in government, security, and business. This process began in 1991 as KGB men moved into industry, the new FSB and SVR intelligence agencies, the Interior Ministry, media, banking oil and gas, and service industries. In the process of monopolizing the nation's assets, and crushing opposition, the new KGB elite frequently allied itself with shady businessmen and gangsters, both of whom had been running amok in the free-for-all of Russia's gold rush during the Yeltsin era.

The hard men who were quickly taking over the new Russia were determined to exact revenge on the Chechens, who were particularly hated in Russian security circles because of their historic defiance, and because they were Muslims. Hatred of Islam is a common prejudice among Russians. Russia's bitter historic struggle for hundreds of years against the Mongols and Tatars, many of whom later converted to Islam, left Russians infused by a deep folk-hatred for Muslims that became a companion for their traditional anti-Semitism. Russia's greatest poet, Pushkin, enshrined the sinister image in the national consciousness of the "creeping Chechen with his dagger." The Russian Orthodox Church, like its cousin in Serbia, actively whipped up medieval hatred of Muslims and urged liberation of Muslim lands.

The hard-liners, or "siloviki," steadily consolidated their power, discredited the moribund Yeltsin government, and cemented their alliance with the mafia-businessmen who were plundering Russia's industrial and resource assets. In August 1999, Yeltsin was forced to name the FSB's tough new director, Vladimir Putin, prime minister. Putin vowed to clean up the monstrous corruption that had engulfed Russia during the Yeltsin years and to exact revenge on the Chechens.

Beginning August 31, Moscow and other Russian provincial cities were hit by a wave of bombings. Planted in apartment buildings and a car, the bombs killed around 300 people, sowing fear and panic across Russia. The government lost no time accusing the Chechens, and specifically the Saudi jihadi Emir Khattab, of being behind the blasts. But at the height of the panic, a team of FSB men were caught red-handed by local police planting explosives in the basement of another apartment building. The FSB agents claimed they were merely running a security drill and the bags they were packing into the basement contained only sugar, not military explosives.

Russia's parliament, the Duma, opened an investigation. But the security services refused to comply with demands for information. Two members of the Duma's investigating committee were murdered and its lawyer was first beaten, then killed, in a suspicious car crash.

A Russian journalist, Yuri Felshtinsky, and a former FSB officer, Alexander Litvinenko, wrote a stunning, deeply disturbing book called *Blowing Up Russia*, in which they claimed to have uncovered evidence that the bombings had been staged by FSB and gangsters working for the intelligence agency. The book went on to describe in detail how hardliners had used gangsters and freelance ex-KGB men to murder opponents, and to undermine and eventually defeat Russia's democrats and moderate reformers. The Kremlin and FSB denied all the accusations, insisting it was waging war on terrorism. In 2006, Litvinenko was murdered in London by means of radioactive polonium-210. His killers were not caught.

Prime Minister Putin, who was barely known by Russians before the bombing scare, gained immediate popular attention and celebrity by blaming the Chechens and vowing to "kill the terrorists in their shithouses." Putin and his allies used the bombing crisis to enact new emergency regulations, silence what remained of the semi-free media, and crush what was left of the democracy movement. Russians gave Putin wholehearted support, transforming him overnight from a faceless intelligence officer into a national hero.

The Russian apartment bombing crisis bore an uncanny resemblance to another massive terrorist outrage that would occur two years later, the 9/11 attacks on New York and Washington. In both cases, the attacks were blamed on Islamic jihadis. The leaders of the attacked nations instantly were transformed from nobodies into vaunted war leaders who vowed to save their nations from Islamic terror. Both leaders used the attacks to fan nationalist hysteria that allowed them to launch wars, seriously curtail civil liberties, stifle opposition, and turn the media into a servant of state policy.

While there is a great deal of evidence pointing to government involvement in the Russian bombings, there is none to suggest that the destruction of the World Trade Center or part of the Pentagon was anything beyond what it appeared, an attack by Islamic extremists. But the coincidence is so uncanny, and the resemblance between the two events so close, that suspicions are natural and cannot be dismissed out of hand. A Scripps/*Washington Post* poll, as previously mentioned, showed that a surprising one-third of American respondents believed their own government was somehow involved in the 9/11 attacks. For both Moscow's antidemocratic hard-liners and Washington's antidemocratic neocons, the attacks were such a godsend that it strains credulity to imagine they were simply a bolt from the blue.

Putin's vow to wage war on the Chechen "terrorists" and his soaring popularity allowed the security organs to finally elbow aside the ailing Boris Yeltsin. After a bloodless palace coup, Putin was named acting president of Russia on December 31, 1999; three months later he was confirmed by the no-compliant Duma.

While these dramas had been going on in Russia, its security organs had been busy provoking unrest in Chechnya. There is strong suspicion to suggest that Chechen gangsters and local collaborators working for Moscow were behind many of the kidnappings, holdups, and beheadings there that shocked western opinion and reinforced the view that Chechens were indeed a bunch of bloodthirsty terrorists and criminals. Meanwhile, Chechen and Russian forces routinely engaged in border clashes and occasional raids.

Provocations and false flag operations have always been much beloved tactics of Russia's security forces, from the days of the czarist Okhrana to the contemporary FSB. Conjuring up crimes in Chechnya provided Moscow with a handy pretext to intervene, "to end terrorism and banditry," as the Kremlin proclaimed. The always feuding Chechens greatly aided Russia's campaign to discredit them by their usual fractious, often violent behavior and lack of national spirit or consensus in the face of a surging threat from Russia.

Once again, Chechen leaders pleaded with the outside world for help, and once again their pleas were spurned by the outside world, which, however sympathetic to the Chechens' plight, was not about to pick a fight with Russia over a tiny, obscure Caucasian people.

Moscow claimed a Chechen column led by Emir Khattab and Shamyl Basayev had raided an army base in neighboring Dagestan. This attack was a murky incident and may well have been a false flag operation. Some Russian sources even claimed that Basayev was a longtime KGB agent. In retaliation, Moscow unleashed a massive air campaign against Chechnya, bombing military bases, airports, cities, and towns.

On October 1, 1999, Russia launched its second, full-scale invasion of Chechnya, which Moscow trumpeted as a "counterterrorism operation." Grozny was again invested by Russian forces; its ruins were further demolished by Russian heavy artillery, bombing, and the use, for the first time, of deadly fuel air explosives that soldiers called mini–nuclear weapons. The Russian Air Force showered deadly cluster bombs on Chechen villages and fields.

This time, Russian ground forces were mostly made up of volunteers fighting for money known as "kontrakniki" rather than conscripts, as in the First Chechen War. Once again, the Chechens fought ferociously, inflicting heavy losses on the invading Russians. But the might of Russia's air and ground forces proved too much, even for the veteran Chechen mujahidin. After two years of relentless combat, the Chechens' depleted, outgunned units were slowly driven into the southern mountains or scattered into small groups.

As in the First Chechen War, Russian security forces brutalized the civilian population, resorting to widespread torture, savage reprisals, and concentration camps to break the spirit of the people and isolate them from the mujahidin. The World Health Organization estimated that 85 percent of Chechen civilians suffered from trauma and physical and emotional distress. Children were particularly afflicted by the savagery of the war.

The outside world saw and heard very little about this genocide in the Caucasus. Following a policy successfully developed during their occupation of Afghanistan, the Russians excluded nearly all journalists, diplomats, human rights observers, and aid workers from Chechnya. The few that managed to get in were kidnapped and often killed, supposedly by "Chechen terrorists," but, in reality, by pro-Moscow Chechen thugs. Russia simply shrugged off feeble protests by the European Union and even fainter rebukes from Washington.

While Russia was again laying waste to Chechnya, "brotherly" Muslim nations were once more averting their eyes. Some Muslim nations, notably Malaysia and Kuwait, even bought arms from Russia during this period. Not a single Muslim nation threatened a trade boycott of Russia's exports or a rupture of diplomatic relations. The slaughter in Chechnya was some-one else's problem.

Turkey, which had many citizens of Chechen descent as a result of Russian ethnic cleansing in the nineteenth century, could have provided invaluable aid to the Chechen cause. Though many of its citizens were anguished and enraged by the massacre of the Chechens, its military-dominated government, which was busy fighting Kurdish separatists, followed Washington's lead in dismissing the savaging of Chechnya as an internal Russian affair.

Once again, as in the case of Bosnia, while Muslim nations remained shamefully silent before the slaughter of their coreligionists, it was left to Jewish organizations to take the lead in denouncing the world's most recent example of genocide. In 2001, the Holocaust Memorial Museum in Washington, D.C., put Chechnya on its genocide watch list.

In April 2002, the Saudi jihadi Emir Khattab was assassinated. The FSB managed to get a Chechen collaborator to give him a message on paper impregnated by a fast-acting poison. Other Russian hit teams stalked all of the prominent Chechen leaders. In 2004, former Chechen president Zelimkhan Yandarbiyev was murdered in Qatar by Russian agents. There were no international protests over this brazen crime.

As Russian forces slowly ground down the Chechen resistance, they focused particular attention on eliminating moderate Chechen nationalists. As a result, by 2005, militant Islamist jihadis had assumed much more influence in the resistance. This, in turn, reinforced Russian claims that the Chechen nationalists were all Islamic terrorists who were closely linked to or under the direct orders of Osama bin Laden.

Moscow's campaign to portray the Chechens as members of al-Qaida proved an immediate success. The mere mention of the phrase "linked to al-Qaida" was guaranteed to produce a predictable Pavlovian response in Washington. The Bush administration swallowed Russia's false claims about the Chechen resistance, buying the line that they were anti-western

Islamic terrorists in the pay of Osama bin Laden.

The Russian journalist Anna Politkovskaya was one of the very few journalists who had managed to cover the Chechen conflict and report on the atrocities being committed there by both sides. Her book *The Dirty War* exposed Moscow's shocking brutality in Chechnya, its use of local criminals gangs, and the corruption and venality of Russian military and security officials, which even included selling the bodies of dead Russian soldiers back to their grieving families. Politkovskaya, a dour, courageous woman and fearless reporter, told me that she was without any doubt facing death for exposing Russian crimes. "I know I will die, but I must go on telling the world what is really happening in Chechnya," she said grimly. "I will go on until they kill me."

Deluged by death threats, Politkovskaya sought refuge for a time in Vienna, but returned to Moscow and continued reporting for her muckraking newspaper *Novaya Gazeta*. She wrote a series of articles exposing the criminality and brutishness of Moscow's latest Chechen puppet ruler, the warlord Ramazan Kadyrov. On November 7, 2006, Anna Politkovskaya finally met the fate she had long expected, but that she had refused to allow to silence her pen. A professional hit man shot her in the head in the entry of her apartment building, then vanished. The last courageous voice telling the world about the Chechen tragedy had been silenced.

The few senior members of the Bush administration who knew the facts about Chechnya still preferred to condemn the resistance as terrorists in order to secure Russia's help in fighting al-Qaida. In George Bush's worldview, shaped by the *Wall Street Journal* and Fox Television News, anything smacking of Islamic resistance was *ipso facto* terrorist. Any Muslims fighting for liberation or against injustice were without question terrorists. Case closed.

This foolish policy quite naturally reinforced the view that the United States had embarked on a worldwide crusade against Islam and was now its leading foe. While the Bush administration loudly condemned Saddam Hussein's Iraq, Iran, and North Korea for terrorism and human rights violations, it gave tacit support to Russia's crimes in the Caucasus and, later, to India's efforts to crush the Kashmir uprising. This double standard went unnoticed in North America but was clearly seen and deeply resented in many parts of the Muslim world.

Europe wanted no part of any group linked to al-Qaida, and gradually muted its criticism of Russia's repression and human rights violations. Given the growing importance of Russian natural gas to Europe, rebuking the Kremlin over Chechnya was deemed impolitic.

The Muslim world itself began shying away from giving even lip service to the Chechen cause, fearful the US would exact vengeance on any nation supporting terrorism. So, by 2005, the Chechens had become totally isolated and friendless. They were, in fact, condemned to death by the outside world.

In this same year, 2005, Russian forces finally succeeded in cornering and killing the then Chechen president, Aslan Maskhadov. His death tragically removed the most moderate and able Chechen leader, a man who could have forged an acceptable political settlement with Moscow. That, of course, was precisely what Moscow's hard-liners did not want to happen.

Driven to desperation as Russian forces ground Chechnya to a bloody pulp, small numbers of Chechen extremists staged high-profile atrocities in a last-ditch attempt to get Moscow to halt its assaults. In 2002, 39 Chechen male and female fighters seized 700 hostages in a Moscow theater, demanding a Russian pullout from Chechnya. Security forces pumped a toxic gas into the theater that killed all the Chechens and at least 129 hostages.

Two years later, Chechen gunmen seized a school in southern Russia in the town of Beslan, holding hundreds of terrified children hostage. Once again, the assailants called for Moscow to quit Chechnya. Russian security forces launched a bungled, and likely unnecessary, attack. In the end, over 300 civilians, 186 of them children, died. This horrible crime received intense worldwide publicity and totally turned international public against the Chechens. Shamyl Basayev, according to Russia's media and government, took personal responsibility for the outrage. The Beslan atrocity became the Chechens' badge of shame, utterly discrediting their cause and confirming them as mad-dog terrorists.

But serious doubts remain over Beslan. None of the attackers were previously known, nor were they identified with any Chechen resistance groups. What was left of Moscow's free press speculated that the attack had been yet another, and hugely successfully, false flag operation by Russian security organs using local Chechen gangsters and a faked message from Basayev. Russian reporters discovered that Moscow's security forces had opened fire first, detonating explosives and causing the heavy casualties.

If Beslan was a false flag operation, it worked brilliantly. If actually done by the real Chechen resistance, then Beslan was a demented act of extreme brutality by a people driven mad by the destruction of their own families and nation. In all the international outpouring of condemnation against the Chechens over Beslan, there was no mention of the tens of thousands of Chechen children killed in the two Russian invasions.

Given their total isolation, demonization, and tiny numbers, it was a near miracle the Chechens had managed to fight for so long. In July 2006, the last well-known Chechen leader, Shamyl Basayev, was killed in a Russian attack.

But nine years after Moscow's second invasion of Chechnya, small units of Chechen mujahidin are still resisting the Russian occupation. At the same time, Moscow is watching nervously as sparks of Islamic resistance flare among Russia's 22 million Muslims in other parts of the Caucasus Mountains and southern Russia.

Moscow has good reason for concern. The Muslim regions of southern Russia are the last remnant of its old, nineteenth-century colonial empire. While many Russians Muslims, notably in resource-rich Tatarstan and Bashkortistan, are content to remain within the Russian Republic, considerable unrest simmers among the Muslim Chechens, Ingushes, Cherkass, and Dagestanis of the Caucasus. Russia's leaders have long feared that Chechen resistance might ignite a wider revolt in turbulent southern Russia and calls for independence of this strategic region.

It was essential, in Moscow's view, to make a dramatic example of the rebellious Chechens. If these lions of the Caucasus could be crushed, no other malcontents would dare risk Moscow's wrath. The Kremlin claimed its ruthless campaign to crush Chechnya was actually saving lives by forestalling other revolts. In the end, Moscow got its revenge for Afghanistan. Yermolov would have been proud.

Estimates of casualties in the two Chechen wars vary considerably, from ludicrously low figures from official Russian sources to somewhat inflated numbers from the Chechen government. The most likely figure, using estimates by foreign aid organizations, is somewhere between 200,000 and 250,000 Chechens dead and at least the same number wounded.

On the eve of the first war, Chechnya's population was around 750,000. That means at least half the total population was either killed or wounded in the two Russian invasions. This toll clearly fits the UN's definition of genocide. In fact, the recent Chechen wars amounted to a second holocaust for this tiny people. First came Stalin's genocide, in which half of all Chechen were sent to concentration camps, and 50 percent died. Now, a second genocide occurred, in which half the population was killed or wounded and the country laid waste.

The children of the victims of genocide and Stalin's concentration camps came to be seen in Russia and the West as terrorists. By now, the Chechens have almost vanished from our collective consciousness. Another small, unimportant, irksome people whose Quixotic struggle for independence proved a minor irritant to smooth relations between the great powers.

Former members of the KGB and the military now filled 70 percent of all senior positions in Russia's federal government. Vladimir Putin and his hard men not only won their struggle to resume power, thanks to soaring oil prices, they also managed to double Russian's incomes, stabilize the country, and restore its battered pride.

We may already have forgotten the Chechens, but I believe that their lonely jihad against impossible odds, now nearly close to being snuffed out, will rekindle at a future date and flare anew in the Caucasus, serving as an ideological inspiration to new generations in the Muslim world, who will look back on the Chechens' struggle and fierce resistance as one of the most courageous acts in the history of Muslim peoples.

The crushing of organized Chechen resistance did not, however, cement Russian rule. Just as Moscow was announcing total success in Chechnya, unrest was growing in neighboring Dagestan and Ingushetia.

Somewhere in the heavily forested mountains of southern Chechnya, small bands of warriors are performing their mystical ceremony of "zikhr," and planning new attacks on their Russian occupiers. Chechens, as an old Caucasian saying goes, cannot ever be defeated. They can only be killed.

CHAPTER THIRTEEN
★ ★ ★

FINAL SOLUTION IN THE BALKANS

The ferocious conflicts that tore apart the Balkans from 1991 to 1999 marked the darkest, most shameful period in postwar European history. The atrocities and attempted genocide inflicted on almost a third of the Balkans' nine million Muslims enraged and horrified Muslims everywhere. Until the wars in Afghanistan and Iraq, the atrocities inflicted on the Muslims of Bosnia and Kosovo, and Europe's reluctance to prevent these crimes, became yet another burning cause for violent, anti-western movements in the Muslim world.

The Balkan Peninsula's Muslims, the human legacy of 500 years of Ottoman rule, were concentrated in two regions: first, in Yugoslavia's southern provinces of Kosovo and Macedonia, and its Sanjak of Novi Pazar; second, in neighboring Albania, whose population of about 3.6 million was 75 percent of Muslim origin, the remainder being split between Catholics in the north and Orthodox Christians in the south. Under Albania's postwar Stalinist dictator, Enver Hoxha, Islam and its culture had been all but eradicated.

By contrast, Islam had survived in Yugoslavia, though Muslims there were often treated as second-class citizens, or, in the case of the rebellious Albanian Muslims of Kosovo (known as Kosovars) much worse. Bulgaria also had a large Muslim population of one million, but a majority had been forced by the Communist regime in Sofia during the 1980s to change their names to Christian Slavic forms and cease the practice of Islam, thus making them nearly invisible. When Bulgaria was admitted to NATO, the alliance made no demand that Sofia restore the rights of its "hidden" Muslims.

Iraq was unfortunately not the only Frankenstein state created by the victorious British and French imperialists at the end of World War I. The Allies created a second geopolitical monster, Yugoslavia, by stitching together the mismatched body parts of a variety of deeply inimical Balkan ethnic and religious groups. Included in the borders of the new Kingdom of South Slavs were Serbs, Croats, Slovenes, Macedonians, Albanians, Bulgars, Gypsies, Hungarians, Jews, Vlachs, Turks, and Greeks. In many ways, Yugoslavia was a smaller mirror image of the defunct Austro-Hungarian empire, from which it had been created, filled with inimical, feuding groups who wished to either slaughter their neighbors or decamp from the ill-starred "federation."

During the First Balkan War of 1912, the kingdom of Serbia drove Ottoman forces out of the largely Albanian-populated region of Kosovo (Kosova in Albanian). For Serbs, Kosovo was a holy shrine, wrapped in potent nationalist and religious myths. There, in 1389, the medieval kingdom of Serbia was decisively defeated by the expanding Ottoman Empire. In ensuing centuries, Serbs and their Orthodox Church transmuted this epic defeat into a triumph of national sacrifice and Christian martyrdom. Kosovo became enshrined and mythologized as Serbia's Calvary, its Jerusalem, and the goal of passionate Serb irredentism.

Kosovo had been primarily populated by Albanians (Illyrians), a people of Germanic Indo-European origin, since the Iron Age. In the sixth and seventh centuries, invading Serb tribes conquered much of the Balkans, forcing its original Albanian inhabitants into the highlands of today's Albania and Macedonia, and Kosovo. But, according to Serb nationalist mythology, Kosovo had been Serb since the dawn of time and remained their nation's heartland, though "temporarily" inhabited by Albanians.

As soon as Serbs had driven Ottoman forces from Kosovo in 1912, they began ethnically cleansing its Albanian population. The Serb kingdom was landlocked: its most urgent strategic quest was securing Albania's deep-water Adriatic ports of Shkoder (Scutari), Durres (Durazzo), and Vlore (Valona). Landlocked Serbia's way to the Adriatic coast lay through Kosovo and Albania. It was during this first period of ethnic cleansing that an Albanian Catholic family named Bojaxhiu was driven from their home in Kosovo by Serbs. Their daughter, Agnes, would later become a nun, and go on to earn worldwide fame and beatification under the name Mother Teresa of Calcutta.

In the decade after the First and Second Balkan Wars of 1912 and 1913, an estimated 1.5 million Muslims were ethnically cleansed from the region. Most fled to Turkey. At the end of the brutal 1922 Greek-Turkish War, millions of Turks, other Muslims, and some 700,000 Greek civilians were uprooted and exchanged. During World War II, the chronic ethnic and religious animosities that had roiled Yugoslavia since its birth erupted into waves of murderous frenzies, as Serbs and Croats slaughtered one another, Jews and Muslims, committing some of the bloody era's most abominable cruelties.

Yugoslavia's wily, iron-fisted strongman Tito, a Croat, held the federation together from the end of World War II until his death in 1980 by skillfully playing off its tribal components. Once Tito was gone, the federation began to unravel as Serb nationalists sought to gain control of the decentralized government and bring the nation under their authority.

During the years 1986–89, Serb nationalists at the nationalist Serbian Academy of Science and Arts proclaimed Serbs victims of the gravest injustice at the hands of their Albanian and Croatian countrymen. Serb irredentists at the academy demanded an end to the autonomy of Kosovo, where Albanians represented the overwhelming majority. Serb nationalists claimed Albanians, backed by Serbia's old foe, Germany, were persecuting them, and clamored for revenge.

A Communist banker turned politician, Slobodan Milosevic, seized control of the surging Serb nationalist movement by vowing to "crush the Muslims of Kosovo" and create a Greater Serbia by unifying ethnic Serb regions of Yugoslavia. He urged his countrymen to "send the Turks (the Serbs' name for all Muslims) back to Asia Minor." Milosevic proved a master at conjuring up the ersatz romantic myths of Serb history, and rekindling historic hatred for Muslims among his Orthodox countrymen. Serbs, like Greeks, were raised on lurid tales of the centuries-long suffering of their innocent ancestors at the hands of the "savage Turks." Serbia's Orthodox Church, a bastion of nationalist irredentism and obscurantism, kept alive and inflamed hatred of Muslims as the direst enemies of Christianity and occupiers of Constantinople.

Milosevic rekindled and mixed these ancient religious toxins with the Serbs' violent nationalist passions, invoking five centuries' worth of alleged wrongs and portraying the Turks (read: Muslim Yugoslavs) as modern-day barbarians and subhumans bent on destroying Christian Yugoslavia and ravishing its women. "We are again threatened by Islam," he thundered.

Many urban, educated Serbs looked with derision at Milosevic's fulminations, but farmers and industrial workers flocked to his banner. News reports that Serbs were being driven from Kosovo by Albanian attacks inflamed public opinion and brought cries for a "new crusade" to "liberate Kosovo from the Turks." Yugoslavia's fast-declining economy and growing unemployment, and revived folk-hatred of all Muslims, added more members to the ranks of the neo-fascist nationalist movement.

Few in the West noted the new Serb demagogue or his ambitions. As one who followed the rise of Serb irridentism closely when few outside the Balkans were paying attention to this growing crisis, I warned in a number of articles that the nationalist-religious hatred preached by Milosevic risked unleashing a bloodbath that would tear apart Yugoslavia. For my pains, I was formally denounced by the Serbian Academy of Science and Arts as an "enemy of the Serb people."

Milosevic's attempt to tear down Tito's carefully balanced federal system and create Greater Serbia resulted in the violent disintegration of the federal republic and a series of bitter wars. In 1990, centuries of hatred between Orthodox Serbs and Catholic Croats erupted in a bloodbath as Serb forces massacred entire Croat villages and towns in a rampage of ethnic cleansing that shocked the world.

As bad as animosity was between Serbs and Croats, special Serb hatred was reserved for Bosnia's Muslims. Known as Bosniaks, they were descendants of Christian Serbs who had converted to Islam during the fifteenth century when the invading Ottomans were welcomed by many Slav Christians as liberators from fierce religious persecutions by fellow Christians. During the seventh century, Christians across the Mideast and North Africa had also converted en masse to Islam, which recognized and tolerated other faiths, for precisely the same reason.

In 1993, Milosevic and the Serb general staff determined to kill or expel most of Bosnia's Muslims and then annex the "liberated" regions to Greater Serbia. Serb forces besieged the Bosnian capital, Sarajevo, and Srebrenica, pounding civilians in both cities with heavy artillery. The regular army of Serbia went into action in Bosnia, while claiming it was only a volunteer force of Bosnian Serbs.

Gangs of Serb criminals and neo-Nazi paramilitary thugs acted as spearheads for ethnic terrorism against Muslims. Entire villages were burned, their inhabitants murdered. Thousands of Muslim Bosnian girls and women were gang-raped by Serbs in a carefully calibrated atrocity designed to demolish Muslim morale. Serbs knew that in Muslim society, raped women, tragically, became defiled, and outcasts. The gang rapes were also a powerful message of humiliation: the feeble Muslims could not even protect their own daughters and wives.

This was not the mere killing of civilians, looting or rape that is common in most conflicts. The war in Bosnia was distinguished by the particular racial-religious hatred and contempt felt by Serb ethnic cleansers for their Muslim victims, by the special sadism and humiliations inflicted on the victims, and by the evident elation and enjoyment of the men who were doing it.

We have seen this all before, of course. During World War II, teams of Nazi ss extermination troops and their eager East European allies inflicted particularly sadistic and humiliating punishments on Jews before massacring them. Gangs of Soviet NKVD killers behaved with equal ferocity in Ukraine, Poland, Chechnya, and the Baltic states. Pogroms became modern industrial-scale operations. The eruption of ideologically driven hatred and violent racism in 1990s Serbia eerily recalled Hitler's National Socialists. Many foreign observers, and certainly Jewish groups in America and Europe, believed they were witnessing the rebirth of Nazi thinking in Communist Serbia.

The leading contemporary authority on fascism and Nazism is Colombia University's Professor Robert Paxton. In his seminal book *The Anatomy of Fascism*, he precisely defines the over- and misused term "fascism," and carefully delineates the difference between genuine fascist and authoritarian regimes. His lapidary definition is worth careful attention. At the heart of fascist ideology, Paxton explains, are the following ideological themes: 1) a sense of overwhelming crisis beyond the reach of traditional solutions; 2) the belief that one's group is a victim, which thus justifies any action without legal or moral limits, against internal and external enemies; 3) the need for authority by "natural" leaders, whose instincts are superior and unfailing, and which fulfill the group's destiny; 4) the right of the chosen people to dominate others without restraint; 5) the need for constant struggle and warfare against internal and external enemies; and, 6) the belief that other groups are racially, intellectually, or morally inferior and need to be eliminated or expelled.

All of these elements featured prominently in the thinking of Serb extreme nationalists, who called for an end to their people's "historic victimhood," demanded expulsion of "subhuman" Albanians and other Muslims from Kosovo, and hailed dictator Milosevic as King Slobo, Serbia's long-awaited savior and liberator on a white horse. Those Serbs who refused to join the nationalist frenzy were denounced as traitors and agents of foreign powers. Serbs accused Germany and its "hireling" Croatia, and the United States, of plotting the ruin of their nation.

Paxton's catechism of fascism is not far off from the thinking of some of the more extreme American neoconservatives. In a truly disturbing observation that uncomfortably reminds us of America's own little gulag at Guantanamo, speaking of Hitler's new concentration camps, Professor Paxton also notes, "The new centers for industrialized mass killing were constructed outside the reach of the German normative state. Two (Auschwitz and Chelmno) were in territory annexed from Poland in 1939, and the other four (Treblinka, Sobibor, Majdanek and Belzee) were located in former Polish lands ..." In other words, outside the ambit of German law, just as Guantanamo is outside the reach of American and, apparently, international law.

The world sat by and watched as Bosnia's Muslims were being slaughtered, defiled, and driven to flight by Serb forces. No action was taken after Serb forces blew up mosques or burned entire villages and Sarajevo's priceless library. Demands by the European public to halt ethnic cleansing (a polite term for genocide) in Bosnia were ignored by governments that did not want to get involved. In some cases, foot-dragging by France and Britain led to accusations they were not unhappy to see Muslims being driven from Europe. The UN debated Bosnia, but avoided using the term "genocide," which would have been an immediate call to action.

France, the historic big brother of Serbia, thwarted attempts to end the war or impose an arms embargo on Serbia. Britain's Conservatives, who harbored deep anti-Muslim prejudices, secretly cheered on the Serbs and stalled attempts by the UN to end the conflict. The British feared old rival France would become the dominant new power and primary arms seller in the Balkans, and consequently sought to ingratiate itself with the region's apparent emerging power, Serbia. Greece, in an outpouring of Orthodox Christian solidarity, quietly aided Serbia throughout the whole war, delayed action to halt the conflict, and routinely violated international sanctions on Serbia.

In a remarkably unjust act, an international arms embargo was eventually imposed on Serbia and Bosnia, as if they bore equal responsibility for the war. Serbia already had a large army and very large caches of arms stored away by Tito and received a steady flow of weapons, munitions, military volunteers, and spare parts from old ally Russia.

Bosnia lacked even small arms and ammunition. There was no one to defend Muslim Bosniaks from rampaging Serb forces led by General Ratko Mladic and Bosnian Serb supremo Radovan Karadzic, or from murderous Serb paramilitary death squads, like the notorious Serb criminal Arkan's Tigers, the Scorpions, and proudly fascist White Eagles.

The world might have continued to ignore burning Bosnian villages and women keening over rows of dead bodies, had not western TV teams managed to capture grisly footage of heavy civilian casualties caused by the indiscriminate Serb bombardment of downtown Sarajevo. These anguishing news reports finally did stir anger and outrage across much of the civilized world, provoking demands for great-power intervention.

In spite of attempts by many Muslim regimes to block news reports from Bosnia, sufficient information leaked out to provoke horror and fury across the Muslim world. As Serb forces continued their massacres and atrocities, Muslim governments averted their eyes, issued feeble protests, and pretended the whole ugly business was not actually happening.

Muslim nations, with over 2.5 million soldiers under arms, could not manage to send a single fighting man to rescue Bosnia's suffering Muslims. Pleas from Bosnia for volunteer fighters from the Muslim world were blocked by Muslim governments and, at least initially, the United States and Europe. Turkey, with a highly capable, tough 600,000-man army, refused to intervene in any way, lest doing so somehow jeopardize its chance of joining Europe, inflame its own Islamists, or displease Washington. Considering Turkey was an important military power as well as the former ruler of Bosnia, Ankara's craven response marked a new low for Muslim nations.

The conflict in Bosnia was the very opposite of the modern, high-tech war with which we have become familiar. Muslims villagers were shot point-blank or had their throats cut. Muslim men were thrown into concentration camps and starved. Muslim women, and girls as young as twelve, were herded into small rape camps where Serbs took turns defiling them. It was all very up close, vicious, and personal.

As outrage flared across the Muslim world at Europe and their own do-nothing governments, the Saudis and Gulf emirates discreetly sent money to the Muslim government of Bosnia, but did nothing more beyond making these guilt donations. Iran became the only Muslim nation to take concrete action: it managed to send planeloads of small arms to Bosnia that were routed through Croatia. The CIA, which had by then grown alarmed by events in Bosnia, knew perfectly well about these arms flights but winked at them and allowed them through.

Small numbers of veteran mujahidin came from Afghanistan to help defend the Muslims of Bosnia from genocide. Their arrival was also finally sanctioned by the Clinton administration, which was reviewing America's neutrality in the Balkan conflict. But after 9/11 these same mujahidin would be branded "terrorists" and "part of the terrorist international." American Muslims who sent clothing, medicine, and cash to the beleaguered Bosnians would also later be branded "supporters of terrorism" by the Bush administration's Department of Justice and given long jail sentences.

For non-Balkan nations there was naturally deep reluctance to interfere in another nation's internal affairs, and equal reluctance to get involved in a confusing conflict in a region seen as only of minor importance. The ethnic war in Bosnia also rekindled old geopolitical rivalries in the Balkans that predated World War I between France, Germany, Austria, Greece, and Italy.

What ought the West or rest of the world have done in the face of these outrages? Europe should have swiftly taken the lead in forcing Serbia and its Bosnian-Serb allies to immediately cease attacks on civilians or face an oil embargo. Landlocked Serbia would have run out of fuel in days and been forced to relent. A trade and food embargo could also have been implemented. Europe's various military establishments were quite capable of punishing Serbia. A few Turkish or French divisions would have quickly ended the slaughter in Bosnia. It was intolerable and totally unacceptable for late-twentieth-century Europe to take no action in the face of the worst crimes against humanity on the continent since World War II, and an outbreak of rampant ethnic fascism. But Europe's nations were too busy squabbling to act.

None of this was America's business. The slaughter in Bosnia was entirely a European problem. But Europe was paralyzed. And so the slaughter went on.

In July 1995, Serb forces, under the command of General Ratko Mladic, besieging the Bosniak city of Srebrenica, began their final solution to the "Muslim problem" in that region. Srebrenica was an official UN–protected safe haven for Muslim refugees, many of whom were starving. Mladic's men swept aside a battalion of Dutch UN soldiers who were stationed there to protect Muslim civilians. The Dutch, in a notable act of cowardice, refused to fight. They allowed the Serbs to round up thousands of Muslims, who were falsely promised safe passage by General Mladic. In reality, 8,000 to 9,000 Muslim men were taken away by Serb soldiers and methodically murdered over days in the hills around Srebrenica. Before the battle, Bosnian-Serb leader Radovan Karadzic had issued his notorious Directive 7, in which he ordered Serb commanders Mladic and General Radislav Krstic to kill all male Muslims in the Srebrenica pocket.

Some of the Serb soldiers captured on video were seen laughing and smoking just before they shot their prisoners, or discussing ongoing executions. The idea behind the massacre was to erase a Muslim-populated region and eliminate Muslim men so they could not father any more children. Serb soldiers boasted that by raping Muslim women, they would repopulate Bosnia with Christian Serbs.

The Srebrenica massacre was the largest-scale atrocity committed by Serbs in Bosnia, and the worst war crime committed in Europe since World War II. The UN's International Criminal Tribunal in the Hague would later define this crime as an act of genocide. It was hardly unique, being fairly typical of many previous massacres in Bosnia, only on a far larger, more intensive and methodical scale. Outrage around the world was intense. Serbs and their supporters in America among anti-Muslim fundamentalist Christians and right-wingers rushed to defend the crime, claiming the Bosnians were Muslim terrorists even though the facts flatly contradicted them. Influential Serb communities across North America launched a powerful propaganda offensive to support this claim.

Canada's retired Major-General Lewis MacKenzie, who had been a UN commander in Sarajevo until he left under a cloud of accusations and controversy, became a self-appointed authority on Bosnia, lecturing, writing, and testifying before the US Congress against foreign intervention in the war. Bosnia was a civil war, he asserted, in which the West should not become involved. In a *Maclean's* magazine article, MacKenzie actually dismissed the genocidal Srebrenica massacre as an "overreaction" by Serbs. Articulate and persuasive, and hailed as a minor Canadian war hero, MacKenzie proved an effective apologist and propagandist for the Serb view until American reporters revealed his lecture tours and testimony to Congress has been covertly funded by Serb-American political advocacy groups. MacKenzie claimed he did not know who was paying him to travel and speak, leading to the inescapable conclusion he was either astoundingly naive or not telling the truth. Either way, MacKenzie was totally discredited as a voice on Bosnia, though he soldiers on to this day in advocating other anti-Muslim causes.

The massacre at Srebrenica finally spurred an international clamor to stop the war crimes and genocide in Bosnia. But effective action would likely never have materialized had it not been for the United States, which finally drew its sword and moved decisively to stop Serbia's ethnic terrorism. Jewish groups in America, who knew genocide when they saw it, took a leading role in demanding their government stop Serbia's Nazi-style atrocities in Bosnia. Other human rights groups took up the call and enlisted the support of the Clinton administration's secretary of state Madeleine Albright.

In one of its finer hours, the United States went into action in Bosnia, dragging its reluctant European allies with it. Washington secretly built up Croatia's armed forces and unleashed them, under US military supervision, against Serbia. In Operations Storm and Flash, the Croats routed Serb forces and, in the process, unfortunately expelled over 100,000 Serb civilians from the "liberated" Krajina region. US and NATO air forces launched an air blitz, paralyzing Serb military communications and threatening a wider bombing campaign.

In the end, the Serb nationalist-fascists had to face reality and give in. In November 1995, the Clinton administration convoked all the warring parties in former Yugoslavia to an air base in Dayton, Ohio, and grudgingly forced them into a peace deal that all detested but could not resist. The breakup of Yugoslavia was recognized and a shaky peace concluded. Regrettably, the fruits of ethnic cleansing were tacitly sanctified at Dayton, allowing Serbs and Croats to keep regions from which they had ruthlessly expelled their ethnic foes. Like most peace agreements, Dayton was unsatisfactory in many ways. But it ended the ghastly war and brought surcease to Bosnia's afflicted Muslims. It also saved Serb civilians from the revenge of the armed forces of Croatia and Bosnia, who had seized the initiative and were on the offensive when the cease-fire took effect.

The war in Bosnia created over one million internal refugees. Estimates of the death toll from 1992–95 vary from 200,000 to 250,000 originally advanced by UN sources, to some recent revisionist studies that claim the toll was around 100,000 dead. Serbia has refused to release casualty estimates. Nor is the much larger number of wounded and missing known, though it is possible they could be included in the higher estimates.

In any event, Muslims constituted 66 to 80 percent of the victims, with Serbs holding second place and Croats third. However, some Croat leaders claimed their total casualties alone amounted to 200,000. The death toll has become a highly politicized figure and may never be accurately known, particularly as Serb forces routinely sought to hide or destroy the bodies of their victims. At least 70,000, and perhaps as many as 160,000 Bosnian Muslims, were massacred by Serb forces or fell in battle. Had America not intervened, the butcher's bill would have been far higher.

The war left Bosnia's Muslims shattered, shell-shocked, and terrified. Many feared vengeance-seeking Serbs would return once US and NATO forces left. Serb war criminals Ratko Mladic and Radovan Karadzic still remained in hiding under the protection of the Belgrade government. As a final insult, a lawsuit by Bosnia charging Serbia with genocide was turned down by the International Court of Justice in the Hague because the Serb government refused to hand over evidence the court demanded. As a result, Serbia was only found guilty of failing to prevent genocide, not committing it.

Muslim extremists and radicals everywhere seized upon Bosnia's agonies as proof that only the jihadist movement could or would defend Muslims in peril, and the self-appointed defenders of Islam, like the Saudis, were fraudulent and thoroughly corrupt. They ignored the fact that it was the United States, not the mujahidin, who had saved the Bosnians. Never since the defeat in Palestine had the Muslim world been so deeply humiliated and filled with self-loathing.

These feelings only deepened when undaunted demagogue Slobodan Milosevic turned his anti-Muslim crusade on the rebellious Muslims and Catholics of Kosovo. Under Tito, the Albanian Kosovars had enjoyed a high degree of political, legal, educational, and cultural autonomy. In fact, Yugoslavia's Albanians were infinitely better off than those of Albania proper, who were, in effect, inmates in a giant Stalinist prison camp.

Milosevic stripped away Kosovo's autonomy, bringing it under direct Serb rule from Belgrade. Albanian universities were closed, legal and cultural institutions abolished, large numbers of students arrested, and most of the Albanian media gagged. In 1991, Kosovo Albanians held a vote in which 98 percent called for an independent state. The Albanian leader, Ibrahim Rugova, advocated passive resistance to the heavily armed Serb military and security forces that had imposed martial law on the restive province.

In 1996, Albanian guerrilla fighters, known as the Kosova Liberation Army, or KLA, began battling Serb security forces. Fighting intensified over the next three years as Serb regular and paramilitary forces inflicted a growing number of atrocities on Kosovars. The KLA, in turn, attacked Serb civilians and military forces, committing its own share of atrocities. Belgrade denounced the KLA as terrorists. Albanians hailed the guerrillas as freedom fighters.

In early 1999, Milosevic and his generals launched Operation Horseshoe, a campaign to drive Muslim and Catholic Kosovars to flight into neighboring Albania and Macedonia. Serb forces began ethnic cleansing on a mass scale, burning Albanian villages and killing many of their inhabitants. Once again the West and the Muslim world witnessed massacres of helpless civilians, arson, looting, and rape of Muslim women.

As in Bosnia, the Serbs attacked Muslim and Catholic Albanians with particular personalized ferocity and brutality. For Serbs, Albanians were even worse than Bosniaks: they were historic blood enemies who had sided with the Ottomans. Serbs called them Turk, ignoring the awkward historical fact that Serbs had, more often than not, cooperated with the Ottoman invaders after their initial defeats. Milosevic proclaimed the liberation of Kosovo from its Albanians, who constituted well over 90 percent of the population. Many of Kosovo's Serbs and Gypsies eagerly joined in the attacks against their Albanian neighbors, looting or occupying Albanian property.

Serbia's ethnic terrorism proved highly effective, but ultimately self-defeating. According to UN figures, some 800,000 Albanians—40 percent of all Kosovars—were uprooted and driven from their homes into panicked flight towards the borders of Albania and Macedonia. Long columns of refugees packed muddy roads or sought shelter in forests in the frigid winter weather. Unless action was undertaken swiftly, NATO and the UN warned, the refugees would begin dying in tens of thousands from exposure, disease, and hunger in the subzero weather.

Once again, the Muslim nations and Turkey, the former overlord of Kosovo, averted their eyes. The Turkish army would have soon put the Serb ethnic cleansers to flight, but no Muslim nation took action.

The United States finally forced a reluctant NATO to take action to end the unfolding humanitarian disaster in Kosovo. In March 1999, the western alliance, led by the US, launched an air campaign with 1,000 warplanes designed to punish Serbia into halting its second attempted genocide in a decade. Had the US not forcefully intervened, all or most of Kosovo's two million ethnic Albanians might have been driven from their homes, many to perish in the harsh winter weather. Albania, itself short on food and shelter, welcomed large numbers of the refugees; Orthodox-dominated Macedonia confined them to muddy tent camps.

The US–led air war and limited ground campaign were hardly a brilliant military victory, but, after killing some hundreds of Serb civilians, they forced Milosevic to surrender or face the total destruction of his nation's industry, communications, and military forces. Milosevic finally sued for peace and had to accept the NATO occupation of Kosovo and the de facto independence of its Albanians.

Nine years later, after endless and quite fruitless diplomatic wrangling, Kosovo—or Kosova, as the new state called itself—declared independence on February 27, 2008, and was quickly recognized by its protector, the United States, and the major European powers. Throngs of Kosovars filled the streets of the capital, Pristina, waving Albanian and American flags.

The United States had saved the Albanians of Kosovo, Muslim and Catholic alike. America had always been the traditional defender of Albania since President Woodrow Wilson prevented Serbia and Greece from gobbling up the little nation after World War I. Unfortunately, even tragically, the Muslim world never credited the United States with rescuing so many Muslims from attempted genocide. The Clinton administration should have been hailed from Morocco to Indonesia as a true defender of Islam.

Unfortunately, Washington failed to seize the opportunity offered by its rescue of the Balkans' oppressed Muslims to improve or even repair its tattered relations with the rest of the Muslim world. The Clinton administration did not recognize or understand the importance of its own humanitarian rescue mission, and turned its attention elsewhere. The second Palestinian intifada, which erupted in 2000, diverted the Muslim world's attention from the Balkans and generated renewed hostility against the US for its adamantine support of Israel. Over the eight ensuing years, the Bush administration utterly failed to remind the Muslim world of its defense of Balkan Muslims. The US invasions of Afghanistan and Iraq quickly erased positive memories of the gallant humanitarian action the United States had taken in the Balkans.

Among those few Muslims who did remember, there was often a cynical belief that the US had intervened in the Balkans in order to set up bases there from which to dominate the region. It was noted that the first temporary base set up by the US in Kosovo, Camp Bondsteel, remains active to this day, and reportedly houses a secret prison for captured Islamic militants. The Bush administration further reinforced this cynical but mostly mistaken view of America's motivation by forcing its new clients in Bosnia, Albania, and Kosovo to arrest and hand over small numbers of jihadists who had come to defend their coreligionists.

While the horrors inflicted on Bosnia's and Kosovo's Muslims by Europeans remains vivid in the mind of the Muslim world, what should have been America's shining, unforgettable moment of triumph in defense of Muslims quickly dissipated and, by now, is all but forgotten.

KASHMIR: THE FORGOTTEN JIHAD

For much of the Islamic world, the long, bitter dispute over Kashmir, the suffering of Kashmiri Muslims, and the anti-Indian jihad that has raged there since 1989 is the least emotive of the causes inflaming Muslim public opinion. It is also in a region well beyond the reach of the American Raj. So why, then, include it in this work? Because Kashmir represents probably the most dangerous current threat to world security: the ongoing risk of nuclear war between old enemies, India and Pakistan. Kashmir has poisoned relations between India and Pakistan for over half a century, led them into three full-scale wars, and continues to pose the danger of a nuclear exchange between them that could instantly kill an estimated 2 million people, injure 100 million, and contaminate the entire globe with radioactive dust.

An Arab foreign minister once told me, "Nearly all the world's worst problems are the fault of the British imperialists." An exaggeration, to be sure, but his comment has some validity. Two of the world's most dangerous and intractable conflicts, Palestine and Kashmir, were the result of Britain's colonial geopolitical constructions. The conflict over Kashmir, India's only state with a Muslim majority, dates back to the catastrophic partition of India by Great Britain in 1947. A year later, Britain's partition of Palestine would provoke another series of wars.

With 11.2 million inhabitants, mostly of Indo-European origin, though with a significant Tibetan-Mongol minority in Ladakh, Kashmir is larger in population than half the world's nations. Today, it is divided into three parts: the largest, with 8.5 million inhabitants, controlled by India; 2.5 million people in the Pakistani-controlled portion of Azad Kashmir; and a huge chunk of sparsely populated, frigid mountain territory annexed by China during the 1950s, known as Aksai Chin, which lies at a mean elevation of 5,000 meters.

Britain's hasty, poorly planned partition of India led to horrendous atrocities and massive population displacements as uprooted Muslims ran the gauntlet of hostile Hindus and Sikhs to reach the new state of Pakistan, and Hindus and Sikhs fled Punjab and East Bengal to India. An estimated one million people died in the communal carnage which neither the British nor even the venerated humanitarian Mahatma Gandhi were able to stop.

The princely mountain state of Kashmir was left to decide whether to join the new states of India or Pakistan, between which it lay. Kashmir's Muslim majority, 80 percent of the population, wanted to join Pakistan; its Hindus, Sikhs, and Buddhists sought union with India. The Hindu maharaja of Kashmir opted for India against the wishes of the state's Muslims. Violent riots ensued in which, Kashmiri nationalists claim, 200,000 Muslims were slaughtered—a figure that seems wildly exaggerated. Both Pakistan and India rushed troops into remote Kashmir. After indecisive fighting, in which India gained the upper hand, the newly founded UN imposed a cease-fire in 1949. India ended up controlling two-thirds of Kashmir, including the famed Vale of Kashmir, and Pakistan one-third.

The UN Security Council passed a resolution calling for a plebiscite to determine the future of Kashmir. Pakistan readily agreed, knowing any free vote would favor it. India, determined to hang on to strategic Kashmir, rejected the plebiscite, and set about integrating Kashmir into the Indian Union. Delhi has resolutely blocked any international intervention in the Kashmir dispute to this day.

Kashmir's Muslims repeatedly staged uprisings and protests against India's often harsh and corrupt rule—a rule, however, that was not much more brutal or corrupt than Pakistan's rule over its distant other half, East Pakistan (today Bangladesh). The Indian-run administration in Kashmir routinely rigged elections and ignored local demands for autonomy, or for opening links to neighboring Pakistan.

In 1989, a quite unexpected explosion of long-festering unrest occurred among Kashmiri Muslims that caught both India and Pakistan by complete surprise. A religious procession to a local shrine turned into protests, then a riot against Indian rule, and, soon, into a spontaneous armed insurrection. Delhi rushed army troops, paramilitary police infamous for cruelty, corruption, and looting, and battalions of regular police to counter the spreading rebellion. India repeated the extremely harsh tactics, such as torture, extrajudicial executions, hooded informers, and hostage-taking, it had successfully used a few years earlier to crush the Sikh independence movement in Punjab.

As fighting spread, small numbers of veteran mujahidin from the anti-Soviet struggle in Afghanistan began infiltrating across the cease-fire line, known as the Line of Control, which constitutes the internal border of divided Kashmir, and went into action against Indian security forces. In short order, Pakistan's powerful intelligence service, the ISI, organized important material support for the Kashmir Muslim mujahidin and their foreign jihadist supporters.

As I saw firsthand, the ISI open a score of training camps and supply depots in Azad (Pakistani) Kashmir and southern Afghanistan that supported the uprising in the Indian-controlled portion of the state. When the US invaded Afghanistan in 2001, it claimed that many of these ISI-run training camps in Afghanistan for the Kashmir jihad were al-Qaida terrorist training camps. It would have been too embarrassing to admit that what Washington called terrorist camps were actually being run by one of America's closest allies, Pakistan.

India immediately accused Pakistan of cross-border terrorism, and accused Islamabad of engineering the Kashmir insurrection. Some of the more than twenty Kashmiri insurgent groups were indeed run by the ISI, but others were not. Some sought total independence for Kashmir from both India and Pakistan, earning them deep hostility from both Delhi and Islamabad. Pakistan routinely jailed leaders of the moderate Jammu and Kashmir Liberation Front (JKLF) that advocated an independent Kashmiri state which happened to include much of Pakistan's strategic northern regions of Gilgit and Baltistan.

Fought among often densely populated civilian areas, the struggle in Kashmir quickly became marked by atrocities, brutality, war crimes, and routine violations of human rights. India's 400,000 regular troops in Kashmir maintained tight discipline, but its half million or so paramilitary soldiers and special police acted with brutality and indiscipline that far surpassed their already notorious reputation for such behavior in India.

Indian security forces found themselves attacked from all sides, and confronted by a sullen, hostile civilian population. Their ostensible Muslim allies betrayed planned security operations to the resistance. Women and children planted bombs. Muslims suspected of collaborating with Indian authorities were murdered. In short order, as is inevitable in all guerrilla wars and counterinsurgencies fought among civilians, India's soldiers and police turned increasingly brutal, vindictive, and demoralized. Torture and executions became the norm, entire village were burned down, Muslim girls and women gang-raped. Kashmiri Muslims retaliated by massacring Hindu and Sikh villagers. I have covered fourteen wars and conflicts. Kashmir was certainly one of the dirtiest, most cruel conflicts that I have ever witnessed.

The insurgency in Kashmir was in part fueled by many of the same type of ethno-religious hatreds seen in the Balkans. Hindu and Sikh Indians harbored the deepest animosity, even hatred, for Muslims, whom they had been taught were their faith's traditional archenemy. Muslims, in the view of Hindu nationalists and chauvinists, were unwanted interlopers and fifth columnists for Pakistan. Their presence in India was a daily reminder of past sufferings and the ultimate defeat and humiliation of Hindu India by the Muslim Mogul Empire. Many Hindus saw Muslims as violent, oversexed, meat-eating barbarians. For their part, many uneducated Muslims stereotyped Hindus as unclean, idolatrous, superstition-ridden inferiors who worship idols of monkeys and rats.

CHAPTER FOURTEEN
★ ★ ★

THE CURSE OF LEBANON

In the long-ago spring of 1975, after a trying, tedious stay in Egypt, I flew to Beirut, Lebanon, in search of some well-deserved diversion in the Arab world's famous seaside playground.

As I was being driven from the airport, the taxi driver told me he would have to take a long detour because of problems in one of the Palestinian refugee camps on the way to downtown Beirut. Lebanon was supposed to be the Switzerland of the Mideast. I accused him of trying to inflate the fare, an old trick of Beiruti taxi drivers. Just then, a stream of orange-red tracer bullets arced across the sky in front of us. Large explosions, likely mortar shells, came from our right. "OK. Take the detour," I yelled.

In downtown Beirut, we encountered more explosions and volleys of heavy machine-gun fire. The capital's streets, normally filled at dusk with strollers and hawkers, were dark and deserted. Stores and cafés were shuttered. With my uncanny, lifelong knack for being at the wrong place at the right time, I had managed to arrive in Beirut on the very first day of its bloody civil war that was to last another fifteen years.

In both the western and Muslim world, tiny Lebanon, a nation of just under four million people, was invariably regarded as the home of fun-loving, cosmopolitan Beirut and wily Levantine merchants. Lebanese were respected as businessmen and merchants, but widely unloved. In fact, Alexander the Great became so exasperated with their Phoenician fore-bearers during the sieges of the coastal ports of Tyre that he ordered large-scale massacre and crucifixion of the difficult Levantines.

For the Muslim world, Lebanon was a giant duty-free store where items denied in the more puritanical Muslim nations, like Scotch whiskey, pornography, nightclubs, girls in bikinis, and expensive courtesans, were readily available, for a high price, of course. Lebanon grew rich smuggling goods into Saudi Arabia and the Gulf, and from exporting its premium hashish, Bekaa Valley Gold, to Europe.

Lebanon was also the home of some 500,000 almost totally forgotten Palestinians, who had been expelled by Israeli forces from their ancestral homes in Galilee in 1948, and thereafter subsisted on western handouts in filthy slums called refugee camps. Few cared about them, either in Lebanon or the Muslim world. Like Palestinians elsewhere, they were a forgotten people—at least until 1970 when one of their radical groups, the Popular Front for the Liberation of Palestine (PFLP), blew up four western airliners in Jordan.

This shocking act etched the Palestinian cause onto the world's consciousness. The sharp irony was evident: without such violent acts, Palestinians would have remained an invisible people. I met the author of these attacks, the Marxist, Palestinian-Christian militant George Habash one evening in Tripoli, Libya. "The world didn't care about millions of Palestinian refugees," he told me. "We were against violence, but without it, the world would never have noticed our misery and suffering." Unfortunately, Habash was right. The notorious 1970 aircraft bombings put Palestinians on the world map and inaugurated the era of what westerners call terrorism.

On the surface, Lebanon seemed the happiest, least troubled land in the Mideast, an example, westerners used to say, of what other Muslim nations should be. But, like those other geopolitical time bombs created by western great powers, Yugoslavia, and Iraq, beautiful Lebanon was ticking away towards a devastating explosion.

In 1860, France's empire-building ruler, Napoleon III, sent troops to the region then called Mount Lebanon, to support local Christian Maronites, who had been fighting their traditional neighbors and foes, the Druze, a secretive Shia sect. France quickly established commercial and personal links with the Maronites that allowed the Christians to dominate Lebanon though it was still nominally ruled by the moribund Ottoman Empire.

After World War I, the former Ottoman province of Syria—which then comprised today's states of Syria, Lebanon, and parts of northern Israel and Jordan—fell to France as a spoil of World War I. In 1920, following the time-tested imperial practice of divide and rule, France detached the majority Maronite Christian region of Mount Lebanon and its littoral from Syria, declaring it the independent state, and new French protectorate, of Lebanon. France's Maronite allies were given control of government, the army, the security police, and much of the nation's fertile land. In addition, Syria lost in one blow its primary commercial port and opening to the outside world, Beirut. Around the same time, Britain was detaching Kuwait from Iraq for exactly the same reasons.

By 1975, Lebanon was seething with ethnic and political unrest. The nation's dirt-poor, marginalized Shia farmers in the south had surpassed the dominant Christian Maronites in numbers, and were demanding a voice in government. Mountain Druze clans and Sunnis were also chafing under Maronite rule. Lebanon's Palestinians were a constant source of friction and unrest.

The Palestine Liberation Organization (PLO) was based in Beirut. Its armed wing, Fatah, and, other Palestinian armed groups, controlled parts of southern Lebanon, which came to be known as Fatahland. Southern Lebanon's Shia farmers increasingly resented Fatah's intrusive, often arrogant presence, and its raids across Israel's northern border which inevitably provoked punishing retaliatory attacks.

Fighting between Maronites, Druze, Sunnis, Palestinians, and Armenians erupted in April 1975. The civil war transformed normally urbane Lebanese merchants into blood-crazed Rambos. One wealthy Maronite I knew well went from selling French sweaters and perfume in his Beirut boutiques to becoming a Christian militia leader. He invited me to come and see his extensive collection of Muslim ears, "all of which I have cut off personally," he beamed with pride. What madness, I wondered, could turn mild-mannered shopkeepers into sadistic killers?

Like all civil wars, Lebanon's conflict was cruel and vicious. Religion, land disputes, old vendettas, and long-pent-up hostilities added further ferocity to this tribal feud. The most important Maronite party was the Phalange, founded in the 1930s by Sheik Pierre Gemayel, who patterned his new party after Mussolini's black-shirted fascists. In spite of their fascist roots and far-right political platform, the Phalangists quickly received secret aid from Israel's Mossad, starting in the early 1970s. The Phalangists denied they were even Arabs. "We are Phoenicians," they claimed.

However, the Maronites proved better talkers than fighters. By 1976, they had been soundly beaten by a Druze-Sunni-Palestinian coalition and desperately called on Syria for help. The Syrian regime of Hafez Asad, which had close personal and business links with Lebanon's Maronite elite, and was a bitter enemy of Yasser Arafat's PLO, sent troops to rescue the beleaguered Christians, saving them from total defeat. Two years later, Israel staged a major foray into the southern half of Lebanon in an attempt to crush the armed Palestinian groups who had come to dominate the region.

Lebanon's civil war continued, marked by ever-worsening brutality and double-dealing. In 1982, Israel's then defense minister Ariel Sharon convinced Prime Minister Menachem Begin to authorize a "limited incursion" into southern Lebanon with the supposed objective of eliminating Palestinian guerrillas from the area north of Israel's border. What Sharon did not tell Begin was that he had far more ambitious plans in store, which, he believed, would solve the problems of Lebanon and the Palestinian Liberation Organization once and for all.

Sharon's plan was truly audacious and worthy of this dashing general and brilliant strategist. Israel would occupy most of Lebanon, drive out the Syrians, install a Phalangist Maronite puppet regime in Beirut under Bashir Gemayel, the son of the Phalangist Party's founder. Israel forces and the Phalangists would join to eradicate Yasser Arafat's PLO, ending any further Palestinian claims to lost lands in Israel. Finally, Israel would annex key water sources in southern Lebanon, thereby ending its chronic water shortages. If Syria tried to stop Israel, Sharon had drawn up operational plans to crush the Syrian Army, storm Damascus, and perhaps even annex parts of southern Syria to Israel.

Sharon's ambitious plan to turn Lebanon into an Israeli protectorate was finalized in 1981 and, reportedly, secretly approved by then US secretary of state Alexander Haig, a courtier-general of greatly inflated self-importance but limited intellect. President Ronald Reagan apparently knew nothing about the planned invasion. All that Sharon needed was a pretext to send his troops north.

This pretext came in June 1982, when a gunman from the Abu Nidal gang, which had nothing to do with the PLO and was, in fact, a bitter foe of Yasser Arafat, tried to assassinate Israel's ambassador to Britain. Sharon blamed the attack on the PLO and ordered the invasion of Lebanon. However, Israeli armored and mechanized divisions failed to halt their advance at the Litani River, as Sharon had promised, but raced north to Beirut, presenting Israel's furious Prime Minister Begin with a fait accompli.

Israeli forces laid siege to Beirut, a metropolis of some 1.8 million— almost half Lebanon's population—in a major effort to crush the PLO government and wipe out its fighters dug into the capital. However, Sharon, who was a master of fluid armored warfare, proved poor at siegecraft. One of Sharon's idols, US tank general George S. Patton, had been similarly stymied and held by for three months when he was unable to storm the World War I German forts west of Metz.

For eight weeks, Sharon employed massed batteries of US–supplied 155mm heavy guns and aerial bombing to slowly pulverize Beirut, which had already been damaged by the civil war. Israel shrugged off rising worldwide protests and continued its siege, heedless of civilian casualties within the city. Large parts of Beirut were pounded into rubble by Israel's heavy artillery. At the beginning of September, Israeli forces ringing Beirut, under the direct orders of Ariel Sharon, allowed Phalangist fighters to enter the city's squalid Palestinian refugee camps at Shatilla and Sabra. The Lebanese fascists went in armed with knives, crying for revenge for their leader, Bashir Gemayel, who had just been killed by a powerful bomb that was most likely planted by Syrian intelligence.

The Phalangists spent two days massacring Palestinian women, children, and old men. Senior Israeli officers observed the massacre from outside the camp; Israeli searchlights provided nighttime illumination so the Phalangists could continue their work. When it was over, around 2,200 Palestinian civilians had been slaughtered. Bodies had been cut open and left to rot, babies even ripped from mother's wombs.

Outrage over Shatilla and Sabra spread around the globe and was particularly intense across the Muslim world, where scenes of bloated, rotting bodies and wailing survivors, driven half-mad by horror, filled TV screens. Cries went up for jihad to save the Palestinians of Lebanon, but, as usual, no Arab or Muslim state responded.

President Reagan angrily demanded Israel cease its siege, which was poisoning America's relations with the Arab world. He also began planning to oust the dim Haig. Prime Minister Begin ordered Sharon to halt his siege and pull his troops back. Washington and Paris agreed to rush troops to Beirut. The two US and French battalions dispatched were billed as peacekeepers, but their hidden agenda was to interpose themselves in

Lebanon's civil war and defend the Maronite government.

In April 1983, a truck bomb was driven into the US embassy in Beirut, killing sixty-three people, including much of the CIA's senior Mideast staff gathered there for a regional meeting. A nebulous group, Islamic Jihad, claimed responsibility, but it was just as likely the attack was mounted by Syrian intelligence. Six months later, two huge truck bombs were driven into the US and French military compounds, killing 241 American and 58 French servicemen. Once again, the identity of the attackers remained uncertain, though the US and Israel would later blame Lebanon's nascent Hezbollah movement and one of its leading commanders, Imad Mugniyah, who, after a long career in the murky Levantine underground, was assassinated by a car bomb in Damascus on February 12, 2008. Syria quickly blamed Jordan's intelligence service for mounting the assassination of Mugniyah in league with Israel's Mossad and the CIA, a claim that was likely true.

The Americans and the French were enraged by what President Reagan called a "despicable act," unaware that their troops were not peacekeepers, as billed, but actually active participants in Lebanon's civil war. US and French forces attacked Syrian targets in Lebanon, including bombardment from the massive 16-inch guns of the battleship USS *New Jersey*, which proved most impressive but totally ineffective. However, the foreign military presence did have a positive effect in allowing the embattled PLO and its leaders to escape from the Israeli siege in Lebanon and transfer their operation to distant Tunisia.

Lebanon was soon forgotten in the West, but the Muslim world seethed with anger over Israel's invasion, siege of Beirut, and the ghastly atrocities at Shatilla and Sabra. The birth of many extremist jihadi groups dates to this period and can be directly linked to the carnage in Lebanon. In the Muslim view, tiny, defenseless Lebanon had been ravaged by Israel with secret American backing. General Alexander Haig's unauthorized green light to Ariel Sharon would come to haunt the United States nineteen years later.

Israel's invasion of Lebanon and the siege of Beirut killed an estimated 18,000 to 20,000 Lebanese and Palestinian civilians as well as thousands of Palestinian fighters and Syrian troops. Americans never paid attention to these casualty figures or to the continuing Lebanese morass.

By contrast, for the Muslim world, Lebanon remains to this day a subject that continues to incite anger against the United States, which is blamed, fairly or unfairly, for the 1982 Israeli invasion and subsequent atrocities. To Muslims, the mass murder and atrocities at Shatilla and Sabra have the same highly charged emotive effects as the massacres at Babi Yar and Musa Dagh have, respectively, for Jews and Armenians, though the numbers of victims in the Beirut camps were far lower than the other atrocities.

Over 400,000 horrified Israelis demonstrated, demanding a public inquiry into their nation's role in the massacres at Shatilla and Sabra. After an investigation many critics dismissed as a whitewash, an Israeli government commission found Defense Minister Ariel Sharon had "indirect personal responsibility" for the atrocities. Sharon was forced to resign. This mild sanction proved only a minor setback to his budding political career that would eventually take the general to the prime minister's office.

While the West soon forgot the carnage in Beirut, a young Saudi who'd observed the siege on TV, did not. In 2002, Osama bin Laden said in a taped interview that one of the primary goals of the planners of the 9/11 attacks was to exact revenge on New York for the 1982 destruction of Beirut. In his usual elliptical manner, bin Laden did not take credit for planning or initiating the 9/11 attacks himself, but left the impression he knew of them well in advance, and had given his blessings. Few in the US media ever made the connection between Beirut 1982 and New York City 2001. To do so would be anathema because such linkage would clearly define terrorism as a violent reaction to the West's own violent actions in the Mideast. The Muslims who attacked the United States, to repeat the neoconservative party line, had no legitimate political grievances; they were simply mad dogs and religion-crazed fanatics, end of story. Raising the specter of Beirut might start Americans and Britons wondering if their government's policies in the Mideast and greater Muslim world were the real reason so many violent groups were attacking the West.

France suffered its own bloody terrorist attacks emanating from Lebanon, but reacted in quite a different manner from the United States and Britain. Covert and overt French backing for Lebanon's traditional Maronite clients, and efforts by Paris to renew its previous political and economic influence in Lebanon and Syria, resulted in numerous intrigues and political machinations in the Levant by France's notoriously nasty, violence-prone intelligence service, Direction Général de la Securité

Extérieure (DGSE) (formerly Service de Documentation Extérieure et de
Contre-Espionnage (SDECE)). In the process, the French came to blows
with various Lebanese militant groups and clans. Some of them launched
violent counterattacks on France. Clan members of Lebanese militants
held prisoner by France also waged a bloody bombing campaign against
Paris shopping districts in an effort to get their relatives released from
detention.

During the mid-1980s, Paris was savaged by waves of terrorist bombings. The government of President François Mitterand wisely chose not to
militarize the conflict but to use the DGSE; France's internal security service, Direction de la surveillance du territoire (DST); the Gendarmerie Na-
tionale; and off-the-books thugs known as "barbouzes" (bearded ones) to
hunt down and eliminate the bombers who were terrorizing Paris. France
suffered for years before the terror campaign from Lebanon was finally
ended, but Mitterand refused all requests to launch more military missions
against Lebanon or Syria, curtail civil rights, or sharply increase already
substantial domestic surveillance of French citizens.

By contrast, President George Bush launched an exaggerated military
response to 9/11, which was a criminal, not military, act, by declaring an
apocalyptic global war on terror, invading Afghanistan and Iraq, and using
US armed forces to combat a threat better left to intelligence, security services, and police forces. France not only emerged successful from its clash
with violent Lebanese groups, equally important, it managed to do so
without antagonizing its own domestic Muslims or the greater Muslim
world. President Bush's overblown crusade to destroy a handful of irksome
jihadis using a military sledgehammer ended up turning the entire Muslim world against the United States and producing large numbers of new,
violent enemies where only a few had previously existed.

After the 9/11 attacks, President Jacques Chirac and the Ministry of
Foreign Affairs at the Quai d'Orsay advised Washington to follow France's
proven counterterrorist strategy, but the Bush administration, showing its
usual arrogance and hubris, brushed aside these sage recommendations as
a typically cowardly response from, in the words of one draft-dodging
neocon pundit, "cheese-eating surrender monkeys."

Shortly after Israel invaded Lebanon in 1982, I was accompanying an Israeli mechanized unit operating in southern Lebanon, a very dangerous combat zone infamous for ambushes and mines. The Israeli unit entered the southern Lebanese city of Nabatiyah, an important market center for the region's Shia farmers. The Shia had first warmly greeted the Israeli invaders, delighted to see gangs of swaggering Palestinian gunmen, who had long lorded over their region, put to flight. But the Israelis, imbued with their military superiority, and deeply contemptuous of all Arabs, treated the Shia with disdain and harshness.

At Nabatiyah's center, our unit encountered a very large, boisterous crowd of farmers and residents celebrating the important, emotionally charged Shia religious festival of Ashura, commemorating martyrdom and sacrifice. The Israeli convoy simply bulldozed its way through the crowd, firing over its head to disperse it. Some of the armed villagers fired back, provoking a nasty fracas that lasted for some hours. At the time, few gave any importance to this minor skirmish, but it marked the turning point in relations between Lebanon's Shia and the Israelis. Similar roughshod treatment of Shia by other Israeli military units, and shelling of their villages, quickly turned the Shia against the Israeli invaders.

The ongoing Israeli military occupation of southern Lebanon, eighteen years, had the completely unexpected consequence of transforming Lebanon's long-ignored, downtrodden Shia farmers into fierce warriors, the nation's most potent political movement, and Israel's bête noire.

During the 1970s, most of southern Lebanon's Shia clergy had been trained and had studied in madrassas in the Iranian Shia religious center at Qum. In the process, they became disciples of one of Iran's most important Shia theologian, Grand Ayatollah Ruhollah Khomeini, and imbued with his twin goals of driving western influence from the Muslim world and liberating Palestine. These Shia clerics returned home to southern Lebanon soon after Imam Khomeini's 1979 Islamic revolution in Iran and set about preaching the gospel of Islamic resistance, defense of Shia rights, and resistance to foreign influence.

Southern Lebanon was fertile ground for revolutionary agitation. Its mostly Shia inhabitants had grown from an isolated minority into over one-third of Lebanon's total population. The entrenched oligarchy of Maronite and Sunni warlords that ran Lebanon's politics and business, with occasional cooperation from Druze mountain warlords, excluded the

Shia and denied them any voice in the nation's political affairs or commerce.

The chronically corrupt government in Beirut was officially blessed as a democracy by the US and France. But, in reality, it was no more than a game of musical chairs between Maronite, Druze, and Sunni politicians, played to the tune of rigged votes, stuffed ballot boxes, routine bribes, and predetermined winners. Nearly all Lebanon's traditional politicians were on the regular payroll of Washington, Paris, or Damascus.

Southern Lebanon got almost nothing from the Beirut government. It had few schools or hospitals, only sporadic electricity, no pensions, and poor roads. It lacked proper water or sewer systems. No one in Beirut paid any attention to the remote south. But the Lebanese civil war began to change this equation. A new Shia political party was formed in southern Lebanon called Hezbollah, or party of God. Hezbollah vowed revenge on the Israeli-backed Maronite Phalangist militia for its many atrocities against Shia and Sunni Muslims during the civil war.

By the early 1980s, the Shia clergy and a small number of Iranian Revolutionary Guards seconded by Tehran to Lebanon, managed to field modest numbers of well-trained guerrillas to fight Israel's occupation. Unlike Palestinian guerrillas, who were invariably poorly trained, often lacking in martial spirit, and reluctant to die in combat, Shia guerrillas proved remarkably efficient fighters with a flagrant disregard for death that shocked even the battle-hardened Israelis.

While Hezbollah's influence was rapidly spreading, the Reagan administration's CIA chief, William Casey, convinced by Israel that the Shia movement had been responsible for bombing the US marine barracks in Beirut, decided to decapitate Hezbollah. The CIA used one of its well-known local proxies, the nation's shadowy, French-influenced military intelligence service known as the Deuxième Bureau, to mount a truck-bomb attack against the headquarters in southern Beirut of one of Hezbollah's leaders, Sheik Muhammed Fadlallah.

Deuxième's Bureau's agents detonated the large truck bomb next to Sheik Fadlallah's house. It missed the Hezbollah leader but killed 80 civilians and wounded 250. The sheik, who had a sense of humor not often seen among the dour Hezbollah, famously hung a banner across the ruined street, proclaiming, "Made in USA." Israel also launched three car- or truck-bomb attacks against Sheik Fadlallah. These also failed, but caused many civilian casualties.

British intelligence, MI6, also tried its hand at assassination. In 1996, MI6 mounted a plot, using local agents, to kill Libya's irksome leader, Muammar Khadaffi, using a car bomb. Khadaffi escaped but numerous Libyan civilians and bodyguards were killed. France also tried to assassinate Khadaffi during their confrontation over the Saharan state of Chad, which, at the time, was believed rich in uranium and oil. The late director of SDECE, Count Alexandre de Marenches, told me that his agents managed to secrete an altitude-activate bomb aboard the Libyan leader's private jet. When relations between Libya and France abruptly improved after their covert little war in Chad was amicably resolved, French agents were ordered to remove the bomb from Khadaffi's aircraft, a feat, Marenches told me, that "was ten times harder than getting it onto the plane."

Increasingly aggressive Hezbollah fighters battled Israel's occupation of southern Lebanon. For the first time, Hezbollah mujahidin staged suicide attacks—or "martyrdom operations"—as Hezbollah called them— against Israeli convoys and fixed positions. Hezbollah fighters proved highly proficient and deadly in small-unit infantry tactics, always a major weakness in professional Arab armies. Hezbollah's guerrillas were equipped with modern small arms and radios from Iran. Equally significant, Hezbollah showed that Israel's enormous superiority in high-tech weaponry could to some extent be neutralized in close infantry combat.

Israel's formidable air force, artillery, and even heavy armor lost their usual decisive battlefield effect when it came to fighting in built-up areas, villages, and southern Lebanon's rough, broken terrain. In addition, Hezbollah fighters developed the use of concealed roadside bombs to attack Israeli armor and supply units, a tactic that was later used to devastating effect against US forces in Iraq and NATO forces in Afghanistan. Israeli occupation forces came under constant attacks by Hezbollah fighters, who knew every meter of southern Lebanon and enjoyed the ardent support of its people. Israeli retaliation against Shia villages using heavy air and artillery attacks only generated more hatred for the occupiers.

Israel and its Lebanese allies responded by waging an increasingly dirty war in southern Lebanon against Hezbollah. Both sides used bombings, assassinations, kidnappings, and reprisals against civilians. Israeli intelligence agents, helicopter gunships, and commando assassinated many of Hezbollah's most important leaders, including, in 1992, killing the movement's head, Sheik Abbas Mousawi, his wife, and son. The Israelis continued thereafter to target Hezbollah's leadership in an attempt to wipe it out. During the 1996 war, Israeli warplanes dropped 23 tons of bombs alone on a single bunker in Beirut in which Hezbollah's current leader, Sheik Hassan Nasrallah, was mistakenly believed to be hiding. Israel also created a mercenary force in southern Lebanon composed of Maronites and renegade Muslims, grandly entitled the South Lebanese Army. The SLA was responsible for many atrocities against Shia villages and became infamous for brutality.

Israel set up a notorious prison camp in occupied southern Lebanon at Khayam for captured Hezbollah and Palestinians. Israeli psychologists and psychiatrists developed special techniques at Khayam to break the will of captured prisoners by physical and mental abuse, or outright torture. Degradation and humiliation of Arab prisoners was also extensively used. Photographs of such abuse were then used to blackmail prisoners into acting as agents for Israel's security services, Mossad and Shin Bet (Shabak). Israel ignored protests from various international human rights organizations over its mistreatment of prisoners, which, however cruel and in gross violation of the Geneva Conventions, was generally still less brutal than the often frightful abuse of inmates in Arab prisons. The SLA was disbanded when Israel withdrew from southern Lebanon and Khayam closed. But, curiously, Khayam's sinister spirit managed to live on and be reincarnated thirteen years later in Iraq.

Soon after the US occupied Iraq, it took over running one of Saddam's largest and most notorious prisons, Abu Ghraib. Israel shared with the US military the interrogation techniques it had developed at Khayam, and reportedly provided a cadre of specialists as advisers. The degradation and humiliation of Iraqis at Abu Ghraib Prison were not random acts of cruelty or beer-fueled hillbilly high jinks, as the Pentagon's spin machine claimed, but part of a softening-up process designed to break prisoner's wills and blackmail them into becoming informers. The Israelis had been doing it for decades, both in southern Lebanon and Israel proper. Blackmail had been one of the most successful ways Israel managed to recruit so many informers among Palestinian ranks. Hezbollah prisoners, however, were far harder to break.

During the second half of the 1980s, Israel began courting American evangelical Christian organizations, whose members increasingly came to Israel and the occupied West Bank on Holy Land tours. Israel allowed

Christian fundamentalists to set up a radio station in occupied southern Lebanon to broadcast messages of support and evangelical religious fervor to Maronite Christians.

This odd bedfellows relationship between Israelis and Christians from America's Midwest and Bible Belt, where anti-Semitism was endemic, flourished and quickly grew into a potent new movement known as Christian Zionism. These fundamentalist Protestants, in turn, became core supporters of George W. Bush and his conservative Republicans, further deepening the alliance and similar worldview between Israel's right-wing political parties and the White House.

So deep became the odd, three-way alliance between fundamentalist Christians, Israel's right-wing parties, and the White House that when Bush expressed his support for Israel's planned pullout from Gaza, a senior presidential aide was sent to assure one of the leading Christian fundamentalist groups that returning Gaza to Palestinian control would not derail the biblical prophecy that called for the re-creation of ancient Israel, and the ingathering of the world's Jews to the Holy Land. Once this ingathering was achieved, Christ would return to earth, the final battle of Armageddon would take place, and mankind would be destroyed in a fiery cataclysm, save, of course, for born-again Christians.

In response to Hezbollah's mounting military successes in the field, and its growing popularity in Lebanon, Israel's powerful information establishment launched a worldwide campaign to paint Hezbollah as a terrorist organization, citing its alleged involvement in the 1983 bombings of the US marine barracks and embassy in Beirut. Israel's supporters succeeded in putting the organization at the very top of America's enemies list—at least until Osama bin Laden came along. Israel's partisans warned of a deadly nexus of terrorism between Hezbollah, Iran, and Syria. In fact, while both Syria and Iran provided Hezbollah with cash and arms, they had much less influence over the movement's secretive, mercurial leaders than outsiders imagined. Hezbollah was hardly a puppet of Iran, as Israel claimed, any more than Israel was a puppet of the United States.

A similar campaign had worked extremely well against the Palestinians, who came to be seen by many Americans and Canadians, and their governments, as terrorists. In North America, Israel's partisans and media allies took up this theme and in short order convinced most people that Hezbollah was indeed a dangerous international terrorist organization that aimed to attack the United States and its allies. The 9/11 attacks on the US intensified Washington's hostility to Hezbollah in spite of the Lebanese movement's denunciation of the outrage and its offers to help find the perpetrators.

A pro-Israel former member of Canada's csis security organization played an important role in spreading false stories about Hezbollah's threat to North America. The US Congress, always responsive to Israel's needs, lost no time declaring Hezbollah a terrorist organization. The Bush administrations put Hezbollah at the top of its terrorist blacklist. Thus Hezbollah went from an obscure militia of Lebanese farmers to being America's newest enemy.

In the Arab and greater Muslim world, the view of Hezbollah was totally different. Hezbollah was hailed as a legitimate, heroic force of Lebanese patriots resisting Israeli military occupation, which the un had ruled was a violation of international law. But, at the same time, many Sunni Muslims felt uneasy supporting and lauding these fighters from the heretical Shia sect. Even so, after all the humiliations and defeats the Arabs had suffered in fighting Israel, Hezbollah's small victories in countless skirmishes and ambushes thrilled the Muslim world and, to some, seemed to offer a new, successful way of dealing with hitherto invincible Israeli and American military superiority. Increasing numbers of weapons and amounts of cash flowed to Hezbollah from its allies, Iran, and Syria.

By June 2000, Hezbollah's constant guerrilla attacks had grown so effective, and Israel's casualties so high, that popular outrage in the Jewish state finally forced the government of Prime Minister Ehud Barak to order Israeli troops to withdraw from Lebanon. For Israel, eighteen years of occupation of Lebanon had brought severe casualties, heavy financial cost, and had created a Hezbollah hornet's nest on the other side of its vulnerable northern border.

I saw the very same phenomenon occur when covering the war in Angola between South Africa and various Communist forces in the 1980s. The South Africans won almost every battle in the Angolan War, but steady personnel losses in the relentless bush war finally brought demands from voters at home for their soldiers to be withdrawn from what was clearly a war without end.

The same thing happened in Israel. Democracies (South Africa was then a democracy for its white and colored citizens, but not blacks) simply cannot bear the burden of an indefinite guerrilla war. Even in the former Soviet Union, popular outrage over the war in Afghanistan finally forced the Politburo to withdraw the Red Army. The United States is already suffering from this phenomenon over Iraq, and Canada and the United States in Afghanistan.

Israel's withdrawal from Lebanon brought acclaim for Hezbollah from across the Muslim world. For the first time, a Muslim military force had managed to best Israel's redoubtable armed forces. This triumph, and Hezbollah's ensuing victory in the 2006 war against Israel, underlined anew the apparent uselessness of traditional Muslim military forces, whose inability to defeat external enemies was only exceeded by their repression of the citizens they were supposed to be protecting.

Israel's 2006 defeat in southern Lebanon sent seismic tremors across the Muslim world, confirming to many of its peoples that the jihadi approach to resistance was indeed the proper path. Hezbollah's combination of ardent faith and willingness to take casualties, combined with modern weapons and effective military training, appeared to be the answer the Muslim world had so long been seeking. The largely Sunni jihadi movement had to grudgingly accept that the Shia "heretics" were on to a good thing.

But Hezbollah's most potent weapon was not its martial prowess but its impressive organizational capability. In fact, under its new leader, Sayyed Hassan Nasrallah, Hezbollah's civic undertakings became a model of Islamic social progress that was emulated by other like-minded movements, most notably the Islamic Salvation Front in North Africa, Hamas in the Palestinian Territories, and the grandfather of all Islamist movements, the Muslim Brotherhood in Egypt.

As noted earlier, most governments of Muslim nations have been too absorbed with preserving their own grip on power, and enriching themselves and their families, to pay attention to the needs of their rapidly growing populations. There was a severe deficiency across the Muslim world of schools, universities, clinics and hospitals, nurseries, and facilities to serve the elderly and waves of oncoming young. Government services were poor to nonexistent. Just obtaining a simple document, like a driver's permit or land deed, involved months of waiting in interminable lines, dealing with sullen bureaucrats, and, even more frequently, endless demands for bribes. Getting public facilities built or repaired, having garbage removed, or rabid dogs and rats controlled, is an often impossible task in many Muslim nations, particularly so in the Mideast and North Africa. In Pakistan, for example, assuring continued electric service to one's home requires large bribes of meter readers, who underreport consumption to the utility company in exchange for wads of cash.

Lebanon suffered from all these ills of governmental neglect, plus endemic corruption so brazen that it left even visiting Arabs aghast. Hezbollah, and other Islamist groups, moved into this civic void created by do-nothing governments. The Islamists opened schools where there had been none before. They set up hospitals, neighborhood clinics, child- and elder-care centers. Hezbollah created an old-age pension system and life-time support for the widows and families of its fallen fighters. Other Hezbollah cadres supervised proper waste disposal and crime prevention. All these may sound like normal government functions to westerners, but in the Muslim world, where government's only function was to soak its citizens for taxes or press-gang them into the army, Hezbollah's civic works and high efficiency were viewed by the recipients with admiration and gratitude.

Hezbollah's fierce determination to root out chronic corruption at all levels, and the unprecedented moral rectitude of its officials, earned the movement new adherents and growing political support. Unlike Lebanon's politicians, who were mostly on the pay of foreign powers, Hezbollah could not be bought. One of the reasons that Israel did so poorly in their 2006 war in southern Lebanon was the striking inability of its intelligence services to recruit agents from the Hezbollah movement.

Imitation being the highest form of praise, the Pentagon recently launched its own competitive version of Hezbollah's social welfare program, employing a Washington-based Iranian-exile physician to try to duplicate the Muslim movement's good social works in Afghanistan and Iraq. The Islamists referred to their social achievements as creating "Islamic space," a physical and mental place where Muslims would shelter, congregate, speak freely, and feel relatively safe from repressive government security forces.

By 1990, Hezbollah had become the de facto government of southern Lebanon and Beirut's southern neighborhoods. The party of God entered Lebanon's political system and won a sizable block of seats in parliament. Only the fact that Hezbollah was seen as a wholly Shia political movement prevented it from gaining more adherents in the rest of non-Shia Lebanon.

Israel may have withdrawn from the quagmire in southern Lebanon, but its right-wing leaders and public still longed for revenge against Hezbollah. The Israelis had long cultivated a mystique of military invincibility vis-à-vis the Arabs. So Israel's stunning defeat in Lebanon in 1990 was both deeply galling and deeply worrisome, since it suddenly revealed to their foes a vulnerability that had not before been apparent. This was also the Mideast, where defeats and wrongs called out for revenge, no matter how long it took. Israel's leaders determined to find a way to crush the dangerous Hezbollah movement once and for all.

When the Bush/Cheney team took office, they lost no time in making all of Israel's enemies America's principal foes. Israel accused Hezbollah of being behind the bombings of Jewish targets in Buenos Aires, Argentina, in 1992 and 1994. Hezbollah denied these accusations. The tangled case remains unresolved because of gross failures of Argentina's judicial system, unreliable witnesses, crass political interference, and, likely, bribery. But this atrocity, and the bombing of marine barracks in Beirut, are constantly cited by Washington as prima facie evidence of Hezbollah's role in international terrorism.

Both Hezbollah and Israel made it a practice to kidnap one another's soldiers or officials and civilians in the border region for use as bargaining chips in prisoner exchanges. In 1996, after a period of sharp border clashes, Israel thrust again into Lebanon in an attempt to uproot Hezbollah infrastructure and kill large numbers of its fighters. The operation was called Grapes of Wrath. Heavy shells, fired by Israel's US–supplied artillery, struck a number of UN posts, including one at Qana, in which large numbers of Lebanese civilians had taken shelter. At least 103 civilians were killed and 116 seriously wounded. Worldwide anger erupted over the so-called Qana massacre. Israel blamed a targeting error; UN observers claimed the targeting was deliberate; Hezbollah vowed revenge for what it called Israeli terrorism. In 2006, this forlorn village in southern Lebanon would again hit the world's front pages.

The blood feud between Israel and Hezbollah is best understood when seen against the backdrop of long-term strategic rivalry between Israel and Syria, Hezbollah's friend and provider. Both Israel and Syria were equally determined to expand their influence by making neighboring Jordan and Lebanon, both small, weak states with serious internal problems, into protectorates.

Syria still advances claims to Lebanon, parts of northern Jordan, and Israel on the basis that they were once part of the Ottoman-ruled province of Syria. Damascus has never accepted France and Britain's detachment of these territories. Syria's leader, the iron-fisted General Hafez Asad, was determined to exert control over Jordan and, even more so, Lebanon, and thus regain his nation's former coastline. Asad bankrolled, armed, and played off all the many Lebanese factions—Maronites, Druze, Sunni, Shia, Armenians, Palestinians—against one another, as well as opposing Israel and its western allies. The tough Asad sought to undermine Palestinian leader Yasser Arafat, intrigued against Jordan's King Hussein, and even launched an invasion of northern Jordan that was quickly stopped by Israeli military intervention. Syria's intelligence agents in Lebanon conducted assassinations, bombings, and kidnappings in a war fought largely in the shadows.

Israel's General Ariel Sharon and his right-wing Likud Party were equally determined to gain control of Lebanon and make it a protectorate under Lebanon's Phalangists. Israel covertly armed and financed the Phalangists, and assassinated their mutual foes. But, in the end, Israel failed to dominate Lebanon and had to endure the added indignity of seeing the 1989 Taif Agreement, which ended Lebanon's 15-year civil war by agreement among the members of the Arab League and warring Lebanese factions. Syrian troops were authorized by the League to occupy Lebanon and keep the peace.

Whereas Israel failed dismally in Lebanon, it wholly succeeded in asserting its influence over little Jordan. Ever since Jordan's first monarch, King Abdullah, had secretly colluded with Israel in 1948 to divide up the nascent Palestinian state, Jordan had been quietly aligned with the Israelis. As noted, in October 1973, King Hussein actually warned Israel's prime minister, Golda Meir, of the impending Arab surprise attack to regain territory lost in the 1967 war, even though Jordan was part of the coalition that was about to attack Israel.

Jordan has continued to maintain the appearance of Arab solidarity, but, in fact, it remains under the political, economic, and military coprotection of the United States and Israel. In a nation whose Palestinian citizens—over 60 percent of the total population—harbor no love for the long-running Hashemite dynasty, Israel's armed forces guarantee the survival of Jordan's royal government.

The 1989 Taif Agreement left Lebanon a de facto Syrian protectorate.

Many Christian, Sunni, and Druze Lebanese resented being lorded over by the Syrian Army and intelligence services, whose members were viewed as crude rustics by Beirut's sophisticated Levantines. The Syrians, by contrast, were delighted. Holding Lebanon brought them large amounts of profits from protection, smuggling, transport, and, perhaps most lucrative of all, control of the Bekaa Valley's lucrative hashish trade.

But the US and Israel, joined by France, were determined to break Syria's grip on Lebanon and put their own tame politicians back into power. Their chance came on February 14, 2005, when an extremely powerful bomb hidden on Beirut's seafront road near the St. George Hotel, where I always used to stay, blew up an armored limousine carrying Lebanon's (twice) former prime minister Rafik Hariri.

The portly Hariri was one of those larger-than-life characters, like arms dealer Adnan Kashoggi and Osama bin Laden's construction-tycoon father, Mohammed, who emerged from the Arab oil boom of the 1970s. Rafik Hariri, a Sunni Lebanese, made a fortune in construction in Saudi Arabia and was very close to its royal family. As is customary in Saudi Arabia, Hariri become a discreet business partner of a number of high-ranking princes. When Hariri returned to become prime minister of Lebanon, many called him the Saudi proconsul in Lebanon.

Hariri was a brilliant businessmen, worth well over $10 billion when he died, and a highly capable politician who managed to charm, arm-twist, or bribe Lebanon's feuding tribal politicians into cooperating. Rafik Hariri's greatest achievement was restoring war-battered Lebanon to reasonable financial health. He managed to stabilize Lebanon's credit, refinance outstanding loans, and embarked on a $12-billion campaign of massive reconstruction of demolished downtown Beirut.

Though posthumously portrayed by revisionists as an anti-Syrian hero, Hariri maintained good relations with all sides and was particularly close to Syria's ruling Asad family. He also maintained intimate relations with France's president, Jacques Chirac. French critics accused Chirac of receiving large financial gifts, stipends, and a luxurious Paris apartment on Quai Voltaire from Hariri.

Former Prime Minister Hariri's death remains a mystery to this day. The US, Israel, and anti-Syrian Lebanese immediately blamed Syria; the Bush administration engineered a United Nations investigation of Hariri's murder designed to bring down the Asad regime in Damascus. Syria's former intelligence chief in Lebanon, the widely feared General Ghazi Kanan, added to the wave of suspicion by shooting himself in Damascus, a death many believed was arranged to silence this key potential witness in the UN investigation.

Syria strongly denied any involvement in Hariri's murder and blamed Israeli agents for his assassination. But world opinion and the western media blamed the unloved, isolated government of Syria's president, Bashar Asad, and clamored for the culprits to be brought to justice. The US, France, Britain, and then the UN Security Council all demanded Syria withdraw its troops and intelligence agents from Lebanon.

The Bush administration seized on Hariri's killing to deliver an ultimatum to Syria: withdraw or face attacks by US forces in Iraq and, most likely, by Israel. Under enormous pressure, and without any ally save Iran, Damascus reluctantly complied and pulled all its soldiers and most of its agents out of Lebanon.

An anti-Syrian coalition of US–supported Sunni, Maronite, and Druze politicians was cobbled together and grandly titled the Cedar Revolution in the hope it would sweep away the remaining pro-Syrian president, Emil Lahoud, and his supporters in parliament. The Saudis helped finance the new anti-Syrian, anti-Hezbollah coalition. Washington demanded Hezbollah disarm; Hezbollah refused, using the lame excuse of Israel's continued occupation of a small chunk of Lebanese or Syrian territory known as the Shebaa Farms.

Hezbollah moved to support the pro-Syrian government and blocked attempts by the US and France to put the anti-Syrian factions in power. It did not take long for the political struggle in Beirut to be seen in Washington as a proxy war between, on one side, the US, France, Israel, and Saudi Arabia, and, on the other, Hezbollah, Lebanon's Syrian-backed president, and Syria.

The Saudis were particularly eager to see Hezbollah's wings clipped. The Saudi princes loathed and feared Hezbollah, and deeply feared that Iran was surrounding the kingdom with its proxies. Blasts by Iran and Hezbollah against "corrupt Arab oil monarchs" heightened Saudi fears.

Hariri's politically charged murder altered the Mideast power equation. On the surface, the Syrians looked the most likely culprits. Their hands were far from clean in Lebanon; deadly bombings had become a trademark of Syria's ruthless intelligence services. A number of anti-Syrian Lebanese politicians and journalists were blown up after Hariri's assassination, casting further suspicion on Damascus. Yet hardly anyone recalled pro-Syrian Lebanese who had been murdered in previous years. Or the startling case of Maronite warlord Elie Hobeika, then a leader of the Lebanese Forces Maronite movement. He was blown to bits in Beirut in 2002 by a car bomb just as he was preparing to leave to testify before a Belgian war crimes court that had indicted Ariel Sharon.

Hobeika, a former Phalangist leader, was widely accused of ordering and directing the massacres at Shatilla and Sabra. Hobeika announced he would testify to the Belgian war crimes court that the massacre had actually been carried out under Ariel Sharon's orders by Israeli mercenaries of the South Lebanese Army dressed in Phalangist uniforms. Hobeika's killers have never been caught. Many Lebanese believe they slipped in from an Israeli submarine or patrol boat. Asking the primary investigator's question "cui bono?" ("who benefits?"), Syria, curiously, comes up at the very bottom of the list. Hariri was on good terms with Damascus and had always been a loyal Syrian ally. The leading victim of Hariri's murder was, in fact, Syria, which suffered worldwide opprobrium, was literally run out of Lebanon, and saw the Asad regime accused of terrorism and murder.

Why would Syria risk such calamitous fallout by murdering a former Lebanese prime minister who was not at the time a decisive player in that nation's politics? An unauthorized plot by a rogue faction in Syrian intelligence was a possible explanation for the assassination. But the true beneficiaries of the crime appeared to be Syria's enemies: anti-Syrian Lebanese factions, Israel, the United States, and France.

Hariri had reportedly refused to implement Resolution 1559 that the United States rammed through the UN, calling on Hezbollah and other Lebanese militias to disarm. Hezbollah's military arm, according to Hariri, was alone preventing Israel from turning Lebanon into a protectorate. Lebanon's feeble little regular army was notoriously useless and timid. Hezbollah's fighters were Lebanon's real army.

Some Lebanese sources claimed Hariri and his business associates had diverted billions in reconstruction loans into their party or family coffers. A mafia-style hit over money could not be excluded as an explanation for Hariri's murder, even though the assassination bore the hallmarks of a professional intelligence job.

The kind of world outrage seen over Hariri's death had not, however, extended to a previous suspicious Mideast death, that of PLO leader Yasser

Arafat in November 2004. Many Arafat supporters still believe he was the victim of an untraceable poison. Arafat's removal opened the way for the American and Israeli–backed pliant Palestinian leader, Mahmoud Abbas, to take power. Arafat had refused to give in to US–Israeli plans that called for a fragmented Palestinian mini-state that accepted continued Israeli settlement.

Tensions boiled in Lebanon until June 2006, when, by his own remarkable public admission, Hezbollah leader Sheik Hassan Nasrallah made a serious mistake by ordering his men to seize some Israeli soldiers on Lebanon's southern border to use as bargaining chips for Hezbollah hostages and prisoners long held by the Israelis. What was supposed to have been a routine minor skirmish turned into a sharp fight, in which the Israelis suffered significant losses.

Just the week before, Nasrallah had taunted Israel's new, inexperienced prime minister, Ehud Olmert, calling him a "little man," and holding two fingers slightly apart in what everyone took as a very rude gesture questioning the Israeli leader's virility. Even more galling to the Israeli leader, Nasrallah sneered, "You are no Sharon," referring to the comatose former Israeli leader, a man much hated but also highly respected by the Arabs.

Olmert and his inept defense minister, labor union leader Amir Peretz, violently overreacted to what was a normal border clash by launching a full-scale war. Wars are fought to attain political objectives. Olmert and Peretz had none; their only goal was to kill as many Hezbollah fighters as possible, erase the affront of the border raid to their reputation, and punish Lebanon in hopes it would turn against Hezbollah. They foolishly listened to their equally inept chief of staff, air force general Dan Halutz, who promised to bomb Lebanon back to the Stone Age and crush Hezbollah from the air.

A vast Israeli air offensive was unleashed against all parts of Lebanon. Israeli navy units joined in. Hezbollah offices, residential areas, housing projects, power stations, water-treatment and pumping stations, gas stations, bridges, roads, Beirut airport, Shia villages in southern Lebanon, all came under intense air, naval, and artillery attack. Large oil storage tanks on Lebanon's coast were bombed by Israel, seriously polluting the Mediterranean with 15,000 tons of heavy fuel oil.

Israel's attacks killed just under 1,200 Lebanese and Palestinian civilians, wounded around 4,000, and caused at least four billion dollars' of damage—this on top of damage from the civil war and previous Israeli occupation that remained unrepaired. Thirty thousand private residences were destroyed or heavily damaged and 970,000 Lebanese made refugees. Shia villages of southern Lebanon that formed the backbone of the Shia movement were blasted by Israeli heavy artillery, using high-explosive and cluster munitions. Human rights groups estimated one million cluster bomblets were showered by Israel on Shia villages during the last seventy-two hours of the war; many remain unexploded to this day.

Hezbollah lost no time in showering northern Israel with an estimated 4,000 short- and medium-range artillery rockets that killed forty civilians and put hundreds of thousands of Israeli civilians to flight. Human rights groups would later accuse both sides of war crimes in their attacks on civilian targets.

The entire Muslim world was once again deeply angered by events in Lebanon. At first, there had been little support for Hezbollah's unprovoked attack. The feeling in many parts of the Muslim world was that the "crazy Shia" had kicked a hornet's nest and deserved to be badly stung. The Saudis, Jordan, and Egypt even condemned Hezbollah—at least until their people began cheering for the Lebanese movement.

As the ferocity and extent of Israel's retaliation against Lebanon became known, and television showed harrowing pictures of demolished apartment buildings and streams of panicked civilian refugees, public opinion across the world turned sharply against Israel. Except, as usual, in North America, where politicians and the media kept repeating the mantra "Israel has the right to defend itself" as if the small border skirmish had been a life-and-death struggle for national survival. The Bush administration and Britain's Tony Blair immediately backed Israel and launched efforts to thwart any international action to stop the carnage in Lebanon. The reason only became apparent after the war.

A year earlier, according to my military sources in Washington, the Bush White House and Israel had developed a plan to go after Iran by attacking its two principal allies, Hezbollah and Syria. Israel's armed forces would do the bulk of fighting in Lebanon. If a more general war developed with Syria, then US air and land forces would intervene. This covert, two-stage plan to strike at Iran was conceived by Vice President Dick Cheney's office and his neoconservative advisers with the same arrogance and wishful thinking demonstrated in US campaigns in Afghanistan and Iraq.

Had Prime Minister Sharon been in charge in Israel, he would never have been talked into this reckless scheme by Washington. But Israel's new leaders, Olmert and Peretz, were indeed tyros and political midgets, as Nasrallah had sneered. They charged into a war where more experienced and smarter politicians or military men would have feared to go.

The US–Israeli operation envisaged a quick defeat of Hezbollah, reoccupation of part of Lebanon by Israeli forces, and their movement from the Bekaa Valley towards Damascus. Joint air strikes on Syrian targets were also planned, according to my sources. Syria's isolated regime was expected to be overthrown by a military coup and replaced by pro-American generals. The fall of the Asad regime in Syria would help end Iraqi resistance to American occupation—or so it was believed in Washington and Jerusalem.

All that was needed was a pretext to launch the Bush administration's latest effort to redraw the Mideast's map. Sheik Hassan Nasrallah's reckless approval of the border raid on July 12, 2006, was the pretext Israel and the US had been awaiting. But everything went wrong for Israel and the Bush administration. Israel's heavy bombing of Lebanese civilian targets provoked worldwide criticism of Israel and its American and British sponsors. So, too, did Bush and Blair's crude efforts to block calls for a cease-fire. While piously urging peace to all concerned, Washington sent its relentlessly truth-challenged secretary of state, Condoleeza Rice, to keep the war going and ensure that the UN did not get involved until Hezbollah and Syria were defeated. But Hezbollah failed to cooperate in its own defeat. Its fighters in southern Lebanon proved startlingly effective in holding off the advance of Israeli armored units and inflicting serious casualties on the invaders. Israel's much-vaunted ground forces had grown slack and rusty from occupation duty in the Palestinian Territories and had lost their former combat edge.

Sheik Nasrallah's men fought from a warren of underground bunkers that proved largely immune to air attack, using caches of arms and munitions patiently stocked over years. Hezbollah's fighters proved they had mastered infantry tactics, and made decisive use of their knowledge of the broken landscape. Equally important, Hezbollah had acquired a supply of powerful, modern antitank missiles, likely from Syria and Iran, such as the European Milan and the Russian AT-5 Spandrel, and the deadly, laser-guided Kornet, whose tandem warheads penetrated the reactive armor on Israel's supposedly impenetrable Merkava tanks. To Israel's shock and dismay, the natives suddenly had the Maxim gun.

The Israeli armored advance into southern Lebanon ordered by Olmert was fought to a standstill by Hezbollah soldiers. Israel, which can mobilize almost 600,000 soldiers, 3,657 tanks, 5,400 heavy guns and over 10,400 armored personnel carriers was, in effect, defeated by a few thousand Hezbollah fighters with light infantry weapons. In a longer war, Israel would have certainly prevailed, but most Mideast wars are short affairs that quickly end when great powers force the combatants to stop. The 2006 Lebanon War was unusually long, spanning a full month, but apparently still not long enough for Israel to properly mobilize its forces and develop a military-political strategy that made sense. Had General Sharon been in charge, after a month of fighting, the Israelis would have conquered all Lebanon and Syria.

Understandably outraged Israelis and their media heaped curses and insults on the hapless Olmert and Peretz. Their poll figures dropped to 6 percent, even lower than those of Bush and Blair. Israel's right scourged Olmert and Peretz as pansies for not winning a lopsided war against a bunch of mere Arab terrorists. The left blasted them for launching a totally unnecessary war without any plan.

The Muslim world hailed Hezbollah for its fighting skill and faith. The watching jihadi movement took careful note that mighty Israel had been fought to a standstill by using a successful combination of western arms and modern infantry tactics, Vietnamese-style field fortifications and tunnels, high morale supplied by Hezbollah ideology, and religious faith.

Muslims and non-Muslims alike also took note of Hezbollah's remarkable efficiency in taking care of wounded and homeless Lebanese civilians after the July 2006 war and the speed with which its engineering and aid teams fanned out to clear wreckage and debris, restore electricity and water, and provide emergency shelter and food. Hezbollah's admirable performance won it praise around the globe and stood in striking contrast to the Bush administration's inept, plainly uncaring response to America's hurricane disaster in New Orleans. Some wags in New Orleans even called on Hezbollah to send emergency teams to their ruined city.

Hezbollah's unexpected victory wrecked the latest Bush/Cheney/Blair plan for attacking Syria and Iran, and derailed their attempt to impose a client Lebanese regime in Beirut. In fact, the July 2006 war was a huge fiasco for Washington and Britain, and a major defeat for their Mideast policies. Luckily for Bush, the tame US press never dug into his embarrassing strategic defeat. For most confused North Americans, the latest Lebanon war was another antiterrorist operation that had somehow gone wrong.

For the Muslim world, however, Lebanon marked a watershed. The entire Muslim world cheered Hezbollah and reveled in the defeat of Israel, the United States, and Britain. The hitherto invincible Israelis were shown to be human and, in this case, saddled with leaders almost as incompetent as their own. Hezbollah had shown the way to defeat western ground forces and diminish the previous devastating lethality of their air forces. Whether the Hezbollah model—which worked in a small geographical area among a homogenous, totally supportive population—could be duplicated elsewhere remained to be seen. But anti-western mujahidin in Afghanistan and Iraq certainly took notice and began studying Hezbollah's tactics.

Iran, as noted, suddenly became a new hero of the Muslim world and the de facto leader of forces opposing US domination. The "asymmetrical warfare" long feared by Pentagon thinkers had finally materialized. America's high-tech nuclear knights were now vulnerable to attacks by Shia farmers and Afghan or Somali goatherders, and their untold billions' worth of ultra-sophisticated weaponry and space-based communications networks held to ransom by small numbers of men armed with AK-47s, antitank missiles, and homemade bombs.

Woe be the day when jihadi forces discovered a weapon, like the US–made Stinger missile that helped defeat Soviet airpower in Afghanistan, capable of challenging the US Air Force's total mastery of the skies, the true source of America's world power. Or a means of jamming US satellite transmissions, without which America's armed forces would be blinded.

In the end, tiny, beautiful Lebanon had become an equal-opportunity curse for all concerned. The Lebanese suffered at least 150,000 dead and an equal number of wounded in their civil war and ensuing Israeli invasions, out of a population of under four million. Palestinian losses were proportionately heavy. Large parts of Lebanon were devastated.

Israel suffered serious casualties in Lebanon and incurred huge expenses with nothing to show but world condemnation and more Arab vows of revenge. In the 2006 war, Israel lost 114 soldiers and incurred more billions in costs. Syria lost the 1982 war against Israel and became isolated and faced regime change because of its occupation of Lebanon. France's covert involvement brought it a wave of terrorist attacks. By blundering into Lebanon, the US lost marines and CIA personnel, saw American citizens kidnapped, and generated increased hatred across the Muslim world for its clumsy efforts to turn this troublesome little nation into another member of the American Raj.

CHAPTER FIFTEEN
★ ★ ★

FIGHTING THE FIRES

The ultimate question facing us remains how to stop the accelerating confrontation and conflict between western powers and the Muslim world.
At the extremes, both sides in this looming conflict are filled with passionate self-righteousness and conviction that they are the innocent victims
of the other's nefarious intentions. The many governments involved are
on edge, fearing terrorist attacks or retaliation from their foes. Such is the
typical psychological state of nations about to go to war.

The solutions are perfectly clear; implementing them, however, will
be extremely difficult, but not impossible, provided the various parties are
patient and accept an incremental approach to East-West détente and an
end to state-sponsored hysteria.

ONE: The more than half-century conflict over Palestine is the primary,
though not the sole, generator of what we call terrorism and anti-western
hatred. As we have seen, the agony of the Palestinians has become the
agony of the entire Muslim world, and has poisoned relations between
Muslims, Jews, and Christians. For the Muslim world, Palestine has
become the icon of its own failings and the premier symbol of western
oppression.

So long as there is not a just solution to this half-century-old conflict,
the West and the Muslim world will remain at daggers drawn. As Osama
bin Laden repeatedly threatened, "There will be no peace for the United
States until there is peace in Palestine." Policy must not be driven by bin

Laden's bombastic threats, but his words in this case reflect the thinking of many Muslims around the globe.

At the same time, however, we in the West must not succumb to the idea that our lives and society are in existential peril from hostile Muslims. They are not. In fact, after seven years, western casualties in the so-called war on terror have been relatively modest compared to other conflicts, numbering, depending on the source of data, in the low thousands. Even these figures often include deaths in Iraq, Israel, and Lebanon whose internal conflicts would be going on with or without the war on terror. Since 9/11, not a single successful attack has been conducted against the United States. Meanwhile, some 43,000 Americans die in road accidents each year, a fact that generates surprisingly little public concern.

While US forces chase shadows through the mountains of Afghanistan and cities of Iraq, America has hardly any defenses and safeguards against imported toxic food, medicines, and raw materials that pose a far greater threat to the nation's well-being than Osama bin Laden. The Bush administration's glaring failure to properly regulate Wall Street's activities has brought on one of the worst financial crises since the Great Depression.

The reason cited by the 9/11 hijackers for attacking New York and Washington was not their hatred of "America's freedoms," as President Bush claimed, but the desire to punish the United States for its actions in Palestine and Saudi Arabia. This fact, however, was quickly obscured by the White House and media. Their motivation in no way lessens the criminality of the attacks, but it shows the depths of fury boiling in the minds of many Muslims. The 9/11 hijackers were so enraged at America's Mideast policies they were willing to go to their deaths, and kill scores of innocents, to demonstrate their opposition and wrath.

The intractable conflict over Palestine has, tragically, pitted the two primary victims of western racism, Jews and Muslims, against one another. Jews and Muslims have much more in common than either has with the Christian world. Those who think this idea surprising should reflect on the fact that for centuries Jews found refuge from Christian persecution in the Muslim world, where Jewish culture and learning flourished and were highly respected.

Once a peace settlement between Israelis and Palestinians is achieved, one that is seen by both sides as fair and ethical, Jews may, hopefully, begin regaining their former elevated status in Muslim nations. An Israel that has made peace with its neighbors should soon become an engine of economic and technological development for the entire Mideast, particularly so if in league with the forward-thinking Gulf emirates. Discreet contacts and business deals between the two are already well developed.

Israel boasts six world-class universities; the Arab world, none. Israel spends $112 per capita on scientific research; the Arab world less than $2 per capita. Israel has the world's highest per capita number of engineers, doctors, and readers of quality books. Average per capita income in Israel, which has no resources other than brains and generous aid from the US is over $26,000 as compared to $5,500 in the Arab world. Aside from such economic successes as Turkey, Dubai, Abu Dhabi, Qatar, and Malaysia, the record of Muslim development has been truly dismal.

It has long been an irony that Israel's struggle to annex small amounts of Arab land on the West Bank and monopolize Jerusalem has resulted in its near-total exclusion from doing business with most of the Muslim world's 1.5 billion people. Israel's agricultural, medical, and military technology, and thriving commerce, are ideally suited to serve Mideast, South Asian, and African markets. Today, there exists a small, discreet black market in the Mideast for much-admired Israeli technology and goods.

My extensive travels across the Muslim world for the past fifty years have shown over and over again that in spite of all the Arab-Israeli tensions and bloodletting, there remains a deep reservoir of respect for Jews and Israel across the Muslim world that today's destructive passions have not depleted. Many of Israel's Arab neighbors continue to wryly refer to Israelis as "the cousins."

Those who deem any lasting peace between Jews and Palestinians impossible, or unobtainable, should go to the beautiful French provinces of Alsace and Lorraine that border Germany for whose possession France and Germany waged three bloody wars from 1870–1945. The haunting, World War I battlefield of Verdun, where one million French and Germans were killed or wounded, is the most sinister and eloquent witness to the profound hatreds that drove the two sides. In 1984, President François Mitterand of France and Germany's Chancellor Helmut Kohl went to Verdun and stood before the Ossuary that holds the bone fragments of 130,000 unidentified French and German soldiers. In a remarkable, deeply moving gesture, these very conservative, formal men linked hands and solemnly vowed that France and Germany would never again fight, and henceforth be brother nations. Today, the long contested Franco-German border in Alsace and Lorraine is unguarded, and almost unmarked. The only way to know you have crossed the border over which so many millions fought and died is that, abruptly, you see advertising billboards in a different language.

This is certainly the greatest miracle I have seen in my six decades of life. No two national conflicts are alike, and one cannot in any way compare the one between Arabs and Israelis to those of Europe. But what was, and remains similar, is the depth of hatred, distrust, rancor, and desire for revenge in the European and Mideast conflicts. The political variables are totally dissimilar, but the human emotions involved remain the same.

Another such miracle as occurred along the Rhine can take place on the Jordan River. If French and German warrior peoples can forge a genuine, lasting peace of the brave, and a German general can lead France's annual July 14 military parade down the Champs Elysées, Muslims and Jews can achieve coexistence, and even their long-forgotten brotherhood as peoples of the Book.

The best chance for a lasting peace between Israel and the Palestinians clearly lies in a comprehensive plan originally presented to Israel in 2002 by the 22-member Arab League and the Organization of Islamic Conferences that represents most of the Muslim world. After the plan was initially rejected out of hand by Israel, the Arab League and Islamic Conferences re-presented it in 2007, and Israel agreed, without much enthusiasm, to study the historic proposal. It remains in limbo.

The Arab League plan calls for Israel to withdraw to its pre-1967 borders, the creation of an independent Palestinian state with its capital in East Jerusalem, and an unspecified "agreed solution" to the Palestine refugee problem. The plan's tacit understanding is that only a token number of Palestinian refugees would be permitted to return to what is now Israel. In exchange, all 22 members of the Arab League, and the Organization of the Islamic Conference, would recognize Israel in its 1967 borders and "normalize" diplomatic, commercial, and cultural relations with the Jewish state. Recognition of Israel's right to exist and normalized relations with the Muslim world has been Israel's oft-stated prime goal since 1948.

Many Arab leaders had backed the Arab League's peace offer because they saw creation of a viable Palestinian state as the best way to stabilize the Mideast and deprive extremist groups of their primary motivation.

Without a peace compact, they feared that Palestinians would grow more violent and Israel increasingly inclined to launch preemptive wars against its neighbors. These US–backed Arab moderates also rightly feared that their own people might overthrow them if nothing was done to end the suffering of Palestine.

But by the first half of 2008, steadily rising violence between Israel and Palestinians, and apparent rejection of the Arab League peace plan by Israel and the Bush administration left most Mideast nations believing the proposal was dead. The near civil war between the two leading Palestinian political movements, Fatah and Hamas, made any serious negotiations with Israel impossible, a point Israel's government never failed to underline.

A *New York Times* investigation revealed that soon after the free and fair election that brought Hamas to power in 2006, the US and Israel developed a plan to overthrow the new government by a combination of crushing trade and financial sanctions and isolation of Gaza. The CIA was tasked with arming and training Fatah security forces to mount a coup against Hamas. Such was President George Bush's response to the "democratic revolution" he was promoting in the Muslim world.

Meanwhile, Arab leaders came to fear that Israel's real intent was to keep stalling as settlements were expanded, to force Egypt to resume control and to police the Gaza Strip, and for Jordan to take over and police large Arab-population areas on the West Bank that Israel did not want to retain. The Golan Heights seemed destined to remain part of Israel.

There would be no real, viable Palestinian state, only a collection of little noncontiguous Arab reservations, isolated by large Jewish settlement blocks and Israeli-only roads. Jerusalem's announcement in March 2008 of new Jewish settlement activity only reinforced the prevailing pessimism. Israel's right-wingers adamantly refused to consider the return of even a token number of Palestinian refugees. Many Israeli peace activists lamented the failure of what they called "Israel's best-ever chance for peace." They were likely correct.

Land for peace has long been the obvious solution to the Arab-Jewish conflict, and one favored by 50 to 60 percent of Israel's voters, mostly on the center and left of the political spectrum. But ever since Ariel Sharon's right-wing Likud Party came to power and enlisted George W. Bush and Dick Cheney as its most prominent non-Israeli supporters, land for peace has been a dead issue. To the contrary, Israel's expansionist right and its American neoconservative adherents were determined at all costs to promote Greater Israel by sabotaging the Oslo Accords[1] and retaining at all costs the West Bank, Jerusalem's Old City, and Syria's Golan Heights. One of the neocons' primary objectives in engineering the 2003 US invasion of Iraq was to forestall the creation of a Palestinian state and crush one of its leading proponents, Iraq.

The catastrophic failure of Bush's Iraq adventure has led to the decline of neocon power in Washington and a modest revival of Israel's moderates, whose voice had virtually been silenced under the force of Palestinian suicide bombings and the wars in Iraq and then Lebanon. But the neocons remain embedded in Washington's power structure and flocked to the presidential campaign of Senator John McCain and his chief adviser on Israel, Senator Joseph Lieberman, known to wags in Washington as "the senator from Israel."

The Clinton administration's Mideast policy was shaped by a group of veteran Jewish Mideast experts and officials, such as Dennis Ross and Martin Indyk, who were closely aligned with Israel's center-left Labor Party. When Dick Cheney took office, he purged these so-called moderates and replaced them with hard-right ideologists. Paul Wolfowitz, Richard Perle, and Doug Feith at the Pentagon, John Bolton at the UN, and Elliott Abrams at the National Security Council. Their worldview and emotional loyalty lay with Israel's Likud Party. Hence their unofficial sobriquet, American Likud Party. Once in office, the American Likudniks quickly set about burying the Oslo Accords.

One of the most important elements of any peace initiative is for Washington to re-engage with Israel's moderates and support them against right-wing advocates of Greater Israel. Israel's human rights groups and moderates warn that the only way Israel can maintain control

---

1. Among other things, the Oslo Accords for the first time affirmed Palestinian support for Israel's right to exist. Israeli forces would withdraw from the Gaza Strip and the West Bank, and Palestinians would be granted limited self-government under a newly created Palestinian Authority.

of the West Bank's two million–plus Arabs is to deny them political rights and impose even harsher movement and residency restrictions. Israeli human rights advocates insist this would inevitably resemble South Africa's former apartheid system, or be even more restrictive. Israel must withdraw from most of the Occupied Territories if it wants to remain both Jewish and democratic, insists Israel's peace movement. The only alternative to apartheid, they warn, is ethnic cleansing.

For Israel, retaining the West Bank to provide strategic depth made military sense in the 1970s, but is no longer a valid concept at a time when the only potential threat to Israel comes from Iran's medium-range missiles, not the feeble, immobile, outdated armies or air forces of its Arab neighbors that have ceased to pose any kind of offensive threat to the Jewish state. From a military point of view, Israel can today live securely within its 1967 borders.

Nevertheless, to provide Israelis with an ironclad sense of security, part of a comprehensive peace plan should involve Israeli and possibly American, Canadian, and UN combat units and observation posts remaining in the Jordan Valley and on the Golan Heights for at least a decade, plus demilitarization of the entire border region, and agreement by Israel's Arab neighbors to keep their heavy-armored, mechanized and artillery units well away from its borders. Israel's absolute control of the airspace around its borders and its new constellation of satellites assures that the Jewish state can immediately spot and take action against any threatening concentration of enemy troops or intrusions from the neighboring Arab states. There will be no second big military surprise such as occurred when the Egyptians launched a surprise attack across the Suez Canal in 1973.

Evicting most of Israel's more than 400,000 settlers from the West Bank, expanded Jerusalem settlements, and Golan will be an excruciatingly difficult political undertaking for any Israeli government, as its fraught pullout from Gaza showed. But since a majority of such settlers moved into the Occupied Territories to secure low rents or subsidized mortgages, moving them out by means of generous financial inducements is certainly conceivable. Displacing religious fanatics will be a different story, and require a measure of force. But some 200,000 such extremists, many of them Americans, cannot be allowed to poison the Mideast, generate worldwide anti-Semitism, turn world public opinion against the United States and Israel, and thwart a lasting peace between Jews and Arabs.

Establishing a viable Palestinian state on the West Bank and Gaza is a solution that has by now been accepted by most parties to this endless conflict, including the United States. But what kind of state remains the key question. In the view of Israel's right, all large Jewish settlement blocs and water aquifers on the West Bank will remain part of Israel, even though the remaining settlement blocs will nearly bifurcate the new Palestinian state.

What Israel is offering Palestinians so far is a group of isolated, heavily policed enclaves, surrounded by Israel-controlled territory and high security walls, and chopped up by Israeli-only roads. Such a state would be little more than what the West Bank is today, a giant, self-administered outdoor penal colony, whose air, land and maritime links to the outside world would remain under permanent Israeli control.

Israel's right wing is determined to retain control of Syria's strategic Golan Heights with its important water sources and observation posts. Syria vows there will be no comprehensive peace deal with Israel until Golan is returned. Israeli artillery on Golan can reach downtown Damascus, just as Jordanian long-range guns could once reach the outskirts of Tel Aviv. However, in May 2008, Israel and Syria confirmed they had been holding unofficial peace talks in Ankara, Turkey.

Moderate Israelis understand it is to their nation's advantage to create a politically and economically stable Palestinian state. The Bantustans run by Palestinian yes-men envisaged by Israel's rightists and their neocon allies in Washington will simply turn into more breeding grounds for extremists and terrorists, and a constant source of anxiety and threat of violence to Israel. The last thing you want is to live next to a dangerous neighbor.

No viable Palestinian state is possible unless the majority of Israeli settlements and Israeli-only roads are removed. One way around this problem is an Israeli-Palestinian land swap that allows Israel to retain some of the major Jewish settlement blocs east of Jerusalem in exchange for ceding former Palestinian lands in Israeli Galilee. In mid-2007, Israel's new president, Shimon Peres, hinted at such a possible compromise. But subsequent events in Gaza quickly ended such musings. That was most unfortunate, since land swaps are the obvious way to an enduring peace.

It is highly doubtful that Palestinians will accept Israel's offer of returning an outlying, forlorn Jerusalem suburb for the capital of a mini-state. For Palestinians, and the entire Muslim world, restoration of Palestinian rights to East Jerusalem, also called the Old City, is a sine qua non of a peace settlement. Palestinians never tire of saying they are only being offered less than a quarter of what was their original Palestinian state. Take away Jerusalem, the Muslim world's third holiest city, and the Muslim-Jewish-Christian dispute will continue to fester.

Dividing Jerusalem's holy sites—notably the Jewish Wailing Wall and Al-Aksa Mosque—is perfectly achievable, provided extremists on both sides are prevented from wrecking such an agreement. Churches in Bethlehem are time-shared between various feuding Christian sects whose visits are kept carefully separated.

But extremists will, of course, try to sabotage any moves to peace, as in the past. One well-timed massacre can derail a peace process that has been years in the making. What other choice is there for both sides? Those who try to wreck a peace agreement need to be restrained, jailed, or exiled. Attacks by extremists intended to derail peace talks must be endured. Such attacks will be the price of peace. France, for example, went through a similarly painful process in the early 1960s when it was granting independence to its former colony of 160 years, Algeria.

Whatever the shape of the final Palestinian state, it will inevitably remain weak, dependent on outside aid and an economic and military protectorate of Israel. Whether it becomes a hostile hinterland or fruitful new market depends on how Israel and the US shapes its independence, and how successful a new Palestinian government is in curbing the violent impulses of Arab extremists who refuse to accept that a quarter of a pita is better than none. Success will also depend on the Palestinian government's perceived legitimacy and popularity. If it is seen as a tool of the US and Israel, like the unpopular regime of Mahmoud Abbas, then no genuine peace deal will work or be accepted by Palestinians.

The thorniest problem, of course, is restoring the rights of the 750,000 to 850,000 original Palestinian refugees, the 500,000 more evicted in 1967, their 5 million or more descendants, and the 50,000 or more Syrians ethnically cleansed after 1967 from the Golan Heights (Syria claims 250,000).

Israel absolutely refuses to take any sizable number of Arabs back, saying that doing so would "threaten the Jewish nature of Israel." There is indeed little doubt that moving millions of Palestinians back to Israel, many to their original homes that were bulldozed and the land long occupied by Jewish settlers, would be politically, economically, and legally impossible. Many Palestinians and other Arabs realize this, even though they and Iran keep insisting on a full right of return. The overwhelming view in the Muslim world, including Iran, is that Israel should be transformed into a secular, nonreligious democratic state for Jews, Muslims, and Christians alike, wherein no faith commands special rights or dominates. But few believe this will ever happen.

Israelis insist their crowded country has no room for Arab refugees. But if Israel could welcome and integrate one million Russian Jews, many of them actually non-Jews, or with only a drop of Jewish blood, as well as self-professed Ethiopian Jews, and large numbers of Asian guest workers, it surely could resettle a certain number of Palestinians. But how many?

A fair settlement that will be accepted by the Muslim world will require Israel to take back a sizable, though still token, number of Arab refugees. However, doing so means Israel also has to tacitly accept responsibility for the original expulsion of Palestinians, something it has long resisted doing and which violates Zionist ideology and the historical myth of "a land without people for a people without land."

We see the irony of Israel continuing to demand return or full compensation for Jewish property confiscated in Europe during the 1930s and 1940s, yet denying precisely the same right to Palestinians whose property was confiscated by the new Israeli state and given to Jewish settlers from Eastern Europe. One wonders why Palestinian groups have never brought lawsuits over this question before American, British, and European courts.

How many refugees could be resettled in Israel? Probably 100,000 to 200,000 over five years, selected by lottery from those Palestinian families who lost their homes in 1948 and 1967. Israel already has over one million Arab citizens. But such an addition would not greatly decrease Israel's security or upend its demographics, at least in the midterm, though it would produce subtle changes in Israel's domestic politics, with Arab parties and the left gaining a somewhat stronger voice.

Resettlement in Israel of these Arab refugees should be financed by the United States, Saudi Arabia and the Gulf emirates, the Arab League, and international Jewish organizations. The return of some Palestinians to their ancestral lands under Washington's sponsorship would send a powerful message to the entire Muslim world that America has again become a fair-minded protector of Muslims, just as it was in Bosnia and

Kosovo. This act would enormously improve America's image across Africa and Asia. A great deal of Muslim anger currently directed at Israel would be dissipated. Much of the Muslim world, and all Mideast regimes, are eager to put the Palestinian problem behind them and enter into productive relations with Israel.

Even Iran has repeatedly stated it would seek peace with Israel provided there was a just settlement of the refugee issue that most Palestinians accept. Iran has long maintained covert relations with Israel, waiting for the day when the plight of the Palestinians is resolved. The most effective way of alleviating Israel's growing security concerns about the possible development of Iranian nuclear capabilities is to resolve the Palestinian issue. Once settled, Iran would almost inevitably return to its former, pre-revolutionary military and economic alliance with Israel, and resume its role as Israel's primary oil supplier. Ending hostility with Iran is of many orders of magnitude more urgent than keeping West Bank settlements.

The rest of the Palestinian Diaspora must be encouraged to settle in the new Palestinian West Bank state created by the US and EU, or remain where they are, in their adopted homes across the Mideast. Unfortunately, a new Palestinian state on the West Bank and Gaza, seriously overcrowded and short of water, would not be economically viable without permanent infusions of foreign aid. In addition, creation of an independent Palestinian national state on the West Bank might cause Jordan, Syria, and Lebanon to try to force some or all of their resident Palestinian refugee population to move to the new state. Another humanitarian tragedy could be in the offing.

Once again, the wealthy western nations, the oil Arabs, and Japan would have to provide decent housing, schools, and services for a new Palestinian state and for marooned Palestinians left in Jordan, Syria, Lebanon, Iraq, Egypt, and the Gulf, and help them to develop commerce and industries. Such a Marshall Plan for Palestinians will take decades and be extremely expensive, but there is no alternative if the international community ever wants to resolve this festering problem. Perhaps the United States, which helped create Israel and displace its original inhabitants, and underpopulated Canada, might even find room for more homeless Palestinians.

At the same time, and equally important from a moral point of view, the Arab states must make whole the descendants of hundreds of thousands of Sephardic Jews who fled the Middle East during and after the creation of Israel. This means restoring lost property or adequate compensation at current market prices. Curiously, Israel's past governments have never made much of this issue, perhaps for fear that some or even many Sephardim might leave Israel and return to their old homes in Arab nations and Iran. It is time Israel's government address this important ethical issue and make fair compensation for Sephardic Jews a part of any general regional settlement.

It is also time for the Muslim nations, as part of a comprehensive peace settlement, to admit their guilt in encouraging their own ancient Jewish communities to flee and seizing their properties without compensation. Arabs and Jews badly need a South African–style truth commission to openly air all the wrongs that have transpired. Finally, the Muslim world would be extremely lucky to secure the return of at least some of its former Sephardic Jews, who were among its most productive and educated members.

Land, compensation, and resettlement will be the building blocks of peace. But there is another, often neglected, dimension: the psychological. If there is to be real peace, Palestinians have to be patiently relieved of their ingrained sense of humiliation, a primary driving force behind their fury and violence. The humiliations so long endured by Palestinians are also emblematic of the humiliations of the greater Muslim world.

Israel has relentlessly humiliated the Palestinians for the past fifty years. In 1969, Israeli prime minister Golda Meir famously exclaimed there was "no such people" as Palestinians. Prime Minister Menachem Begin called them "beasts walking on two legs." Israel's chief of staff, General Rafael Eitan, sneered that they were "cockroaches in a bottle." Everyday life for Palestinians in the Occupied Territories is a series of endless humiliations, some petty, some grand: interminable lines, body searches, identity papers, abuse at checkpoints, beatings, confiscations, house demolitions, arrests, reprisals. Any westerner, like myself, who has traveled with Palestinians across innumerable Israeli checkpoints quickly comes to share their boiling rage and frustration.

People will usually forgive you over time for killing their ancestors, relatives, or fellows, as the French and Germans have forgiven one another. But humiliation is rarely forgiven. This is precisely what the Nazis did to the proud Jewish people, packing them into cattle cars, stripping them naked, mocking their prayers, and branding them subhuman degenerates or simply "filthy rats." This targeted humiliation is what distinguished the

Nazis from the many other persecutors of Jews, and earned them the Jewish people's undying hatred. The Turks similarly humiliated another proud, ancient people, Armenians, who also have never forgotten. Serbs sought to inflict the same humiliations on Muslims.

An essential step in any lasting Arab-Israeli peace is to end these humiliations and, though it sounds naive to say so, begin treating one's foes with respect and dignity. This is no mere lefty-liberal panacea: in the Muslim world, dignity and respect are deemed cardinal virtues. Denying them, or failing to observe them, is a grave offense guaranteed to bring long-lasting hostility.

In a part of the world where symbolic gestures and proper manners are of paramount importance, and produce effects far beyond their actual import, both Israelis and Palestinians need to adopt public signs of respect and reconciliation that will provide way posts on the road to peace. When emotions are overwrought and supercharged, as they always are in the Mideast, and after so many decades of hatred and rounds of revenge and reprisals, even small gestures of humanity often can exert surprisingly potent effects.[2]

Israel's pro-peace center and left parties have wisely tried to do just that for years by holding out their hands to Palestinians and treating them with humanity. But they have been repeatedly thwarted by both extreme right-wing Jewish nationalists and bloody Palestinian terrorist incidents. The first step in any peace process is for Palestinians to permanently halt any and all attacks on Israeli civilians and stop launching provocative and utterly pointless rocket attacks at Jewish towns, and for Israel to halt its raids on Palestinian targets. A decision must be taken to break the cycle of violence and revenge.

Sadly, and ironically, the man who could have proved the most effective and powerful peacemaker with the Muslim world, former prime minister Ariel Sharon, is no longer available to make a beau geste like breaking bread with the leaders of Hamas, or personally returning a family of Palestinians to their lost homes. The lackluster politicians who followed him are hardly men for the job.

---

2.   Like opening roads and checkpoints, mixed school outings, visits by Israeli leaders to mosques and Arab leaders to synagogues.

The two Palestinian leaders who could have made similar dramatic gestures, Yasser Arafat and Sheik Ahmed Yassin, are gone, one removed by a mysterious malady, the second by an American-made Israeli Maverick missile fired by Israel. A third, Marwan Barghouti, often called the Palestinian Mandela, is in an Israeli prison, serving a life sentence on what Palestinians claim are trumped-up murder charges.

Only the United States has the power to push Israel into the final land-for-peace settlement that a majority of Israelis know must be made but whose politicians lack the courage and strength to deliver. Previous attempts by the US to forge a peace failed because Palestinians would not accept tiny, fragmented cantons, and Washington, for obvious domestic political reasons, would not put sufficient pressure on Israel to agree to a viable Palestinian state.

Such was the case with the last major push towards a settlement, the July 2000 summit at Camp David between President Bill Clinton, Israel's prime minister, Ehud Barak, and PLO leader, Yasser Arafat. The talks, which had seemed on the verge of success, broke down when Arafat refused to accept two truncated mini-states, with Israel still holding major settlement blocs, garrisoning the Jordan Valley, and controlling its links with the outside world. Clinton, with his domestic audience sharply in mind, quickly blamed the talks' failure on Arafat's "intransigence." The US media and Israel blasted Arafat for refusing to accept "the best deal Palestinians will ever get." Palestinians, by contrast, did not see it that way. For them, Camp David was a retread of the old Bantustan plan.

In April 2003, the United States, European Union, United Nations, and Russia all agreed on a road map to peace that called for an end to attacks on civilians, an end to Israeli settlement building, and swift moves to creating a viable Palestinian state. It was a good plan, but attacks on Israeli civilians continued and Israel kept assassinating Palestinian militants and building or expanding settlements on Arab land. Subsequent peace plans promoted by Washington turned out to be cynical political theater aimed at assuaging the guilt of US Arab allies. These efforts, championed by Condoleeza Rice, amounted to nothing and simply further angered Muslim opinion against the United States.

But this dolorous record does not mean the US must remain forever unable to forge a peace in a region of great strategic importance. By taking a forceful lead in pressing for peace, the US will be doing all parties involved—Israel, the Palestinians, and rest of the Middle East—an enormous service. All the influence of the European Community will be needed to press Palestinians into accepting an agreement with Israel that most will inevitably feel is unjust and unfair, but to which there is no reasonable alternative.

Unfortunately, there is no Israeli de Gaulle on the horizon endowed with his people's trust who can open the way to peace and quash fears about security. The only way the current crop of mediocre, unpopular Israeli politicians could ever accept a genuine peace deal with the Palestinians is to pretend they are doing so under irresistible American duress. They need to show voters that they fought valiantly against pressure from Washington, but, in the end, had to agree to terms in the face of threats of a cutoff of American political, economic, and all-important military support, such as President Dwight Eisenhower did in 1956 when he ordered Israel out of the Sinai desert. However, that was over a half century ago when American Jewish organizations were still in their infancy.

Israel's moderates will confront the same problem that Democrats in the US have been facing over Iraq. Many Israeli politicians would like to get out of the West Bank morass and make a real peace with their Arab neighbors, but advocating such an approach always brings accusations from the opposition of treason, "selling out our people," giving in to terrorism, and "abandoning our soldiers" and, of course, "abandoning the land God gave us." Democrats in the US faced similar accusations when they advocated pulling out of Iraq and were roasted as defeatists and traitors by flag-waving Republicans. As a result, the Democrats failed to end the Iraq War. Instead, they ran for cover for fear of being accused of that ultimate transgression, being unpatriotic.

Washington could follow Eisenhower's example of forcing Israel to do the right thing. Washington holds many levers to press Israel into peace: $3.6 billion to $5 billion of annual aid to Israel, supply of high-tech arms and vital spare parts, vetoing over seventy UN resolutions condemning Israel and ordering it to withdraw from the Occupied Territories, blocking international censure and sanctions, continued privileged access to American markets and technology, and granting of tax-deductible donations to pro-Likud "charities" and think tanks, like the American Enterprise Institute, Heritage Foundation, and Jewish Institute for National Security Affairs and a host of others, that promote Israel's interests in the

United States. The American Israel Public Affairs Committee, the chief lobbying group for Israel, could also have its tax-free status lifted and be asked to register as a foreign agent.

Pressuring Israel into a peace settlement, of course, risks deepening the siege mentality of its right-wing parties who, as in the current case of Iran's nuclear program, are loudly raising cries of a second Holocaust. But how else to push Israel into a necessary agreement it does not want to make? Particularly when they half believe that any peace deal will leave them worse off and even vulnerable. The old problem remains: Arab moderates will have to fight it out with their extremists and the same for Israel's pro-peace forces. Two civil struggles need be resolved before the peace process continues.

One key to peace is convincing Israel's influential supporters in the United States that tough diplomacy is the only way to end half a century of sterile conflict, bring peace and security to Israel and its neighbors, and end America's and Israel's war with the Muslim world.

The pro-Israel lobby in the United States has become as important as the White House and Congress in directing US Mideast policy. Its influential members badly need to stage a revolution of glasnost and perestroika to cast aside old thinking and look for new solutions. The longer the Arab-Israeli conflict burns, and the more the US suffers from the debacle in Iraq and rising global anti-Americanism, the more Jews in America and around the globe will be blamed. Anti-Semites are already having a field day. Frighteningly, I have even heard sources deep within the US intelligence community describe the neocon war-makers as "Israel's fifth column."

Unfortunately, as Uri Avnery—one of Israel's sharpest, most courageous thinkers—sardonically wrote, the US Congress, if ordered to do so by the Israel lobby, would repeal the Ten Commandments. Getting Israel's militant American supporters, who are often ready to fight to the last Israeli to retain the Occupied Territories, and the senators and congressmen who clap like trained seals when the American Israel Public Affairs Committee commands, to join in pressing Israel's right-wing politicians to sit down and make real peace will be a labor worthy of Samson. But the only other choice for Israel and the US is to face more decades of low-intensity conflict and the hatred of a Muslim world increasingly run by Islamist radicals. Israel must not be condemned to another half century of violence and hatred, nor to the threat of nuclear war with Iran.

There will be no resolution of the Israeli-Palestinian conflict until America's Jewish community decides it is time for real peace. This watershed cannot be reached until Jewish Americans start receiving accurate news about the Mideast instead of being force-fed a steady diet of alarmism from Israel's right-wingers and infusions of hysteria that purport to be news. A good place for them to start is by reading Israel's most balanced, level-headed newspaper, *Ha'aretz*, the UK *Independent*, and the always reliable, unbiased *Christian Science Monitor*.

It is also important to understand that North American Jewish opinion on Israel and the Mideast is far from monolithic. For example, surveys showed a majority of Jewish Americans, who predominantly vote liberal on all issues except Israel, were strongly opposed to the Iraq War.

A privately circulated 2007 internal survey of members by the moderate American Jewish Committee found interesting nuances in opinion. Sixty-nine percent said invading Iraq had been a serious mistake. Interestingly, while deeply concerned about Iran's nuclear ambitions, 69 percent also opposed a US attack on Iran. But 55 percent believed Israel and the Palestinians would never be able to resolve their differences. Even though negative over the prospects of talks between the Palestinian Authority and Israel, 46 percent favored establishment of a Palestinian state, while 43 percent opposed the idea. A majority opposed any concessions over Jerusalem. A disturbing 82 percent believed the Arabs' goal was the destruction of Israel.

As daunting as the challenge of convincing Israel's supporters to compromise on territorial issues, convincing Palestinians to forgo their rights to lost lands will be even more difficult. Israelis already have everything they want: the West Bank and Golan, major water resources, Jerusalem, open-ended US protection, and billions in US aid. Palestinians have nothing, and thus nothing to lose. At least half of Palestinians appear willing to make a land-for-peace deal with only a symbolic right of return to their lost homeland. Accepting a major injustice and living with it is one of the most difficult things to ask a human being. This is particularly so for Palestinians who have as deep an emotional attachment to their lost lands as Jews have to Israel. They also say, "next year in Jerusalem," as did Jews for so many centuries.

Convincing the rejectionists of Hamas, Islamic Jihad, and other militant groups to abjure armed resistance and accept a bitter peace agreement they and the entire Muslim world will view as profoundly unjust is, of course, another enormous challenge. Today, Palestinians lack leaders who can undertake this exceptionally difficult, dangerous mission. Palestinians need a supremely influential leader who can tell them, like the late Emperor Hirohito of Japan, that "today, you must endure the unendurable." The jailed Marwan Barghouti is probably the best man for this mission.

I once asked the late Palestinian militant leader George Habash how his people could ever hope to defeat nuclear-armed Israel and regain their lost lands. "We will fight for a thousand years, if necessary," he replied, "and drive Israel out just as our ancestors drove out the medieval Crusader states." His impossible dream went to the grave with him.

The massed heads of the Arab League and important Muslim nations must make the Arab rejectionists understand that their hopes Israel will somehow be defeated or driven out like the Crusader states, or pack up and leave after decades of harassment, are illusory. It will not be easy for militant Palestinian leaders to admit to their followers that all their past promises about "liberating Palestine" were so much hot air. Or face the fact that while Palestinians can vex or injure Israel, they will never be able to defeat or remove the Jewish state.

The best the Arabs can do is to marginalize their rejectionists or buy them off with plum jobs and stipends. It is worth noting that even the most militant members of the Provisional Irish Republican Army (IRA) eventually decided to give up their bloody but hopeless armed struggle and make peace with the British and Northern Irish moderates.

In spite of the adamant refusal of Hamas, Hezbollah, and other rejectionist groups to recognize Israel's right to existence, there is flexibility in their position. Both sides always adopt maximalist positions. Hamas has repeatedly demanded to know exactly what Israel the West is asking them to recognize: the Israel of pre-1967 borders; Greater Israel including the West Bank and Golan; or something in between. This is a good question. Since Hamas won a fair, democratic election to represent Palestinians, it also asks when Israel will recognize Hamas as the legitimate leader of the Palestinians. Israel says never, at least until Hamas drops its calls for the elimination of the Jewish state. Hamas's position is that while it totally rejects a state for Jews, it accepts a multireligious state with Jewish citizens.

Those Arab leaders advocating true peace with Israel will likely risk assassination and opprobrium. They will be branded traitors, just as Israel's peace movement, and Prime Minister Yitzhak Rabin, were by Israel's far right. The martyred Rabin paid with his life for his courageous advocacy of peace.

Arab extremists and militant Jewish settlers will stage bloody outrages to sabotage peace efforts. The path ahead is littered with mines, but there is no other road, other than the way to endless war. Unfortunately, the price of any real Arab-Israeli peace will be attacks by opponents of accord, but these must be patiently endured, the same way France gritted its teeth and rode out attacks by neo-fascists opposed to de Gaulle's plan to grant independence to Algeria. Eventually, such violence will ebb as movement for peace gathers momentum. The present miserable, bloody mess must not be bequeathed to the next generation of Jews and Arabs.

America's next president will hold in his hands the power to impose peace in Palestine. Whether he will have the will or fortitude to impose a peace that will bring the wrath of massed militant Christian and Jewish Zionists down on his head, and face down bitter opposition from Congress, remains to be seen. Presidents Clinton and Bush showed no inclination whatsoever to push Israel beyond its own negotiating limit. They were regarded as the most pro-Israel presidents in US history. The unfortunate fact remains, few presidents would be willing to face a domestic political firestorm for the sake of establishing a viable Mideast peace, no matter how much doing so benefits America's strategic interests.

Some Republican political strategists believe that a major factor in President George H.W. Bush's failure to be elected to a second term was the perception that he and his able secretary of state, James Baker, were "soft on Israel." Baker's attempt to halt US funding for illegal Jewish settlements marked him for good as an "enemy of Israel."

Palestinians, for their part, are going to have to overcome their endless, often childish squabbling and heal the breaches between Fatah and Hamas, which has allowed Israel's anti-peace rightists to insist they have no one with whom to negotiate. The current generation of Palestinian leaders will have to convince their followers that violence is entirely counterproductive, no easy task for a people who have seen negotiations produce nothing for three decades, and their living conditions steadily worsen.

In the end, only the United States has the ability and muscle to knock heads, twist arms, and use its immense wealth to impose peace on Arabs and Jews. Washington will have to begin supporting peace advocates in both camps, and isolating those thwarting a settlement. Israelis and Palestinians will inevitably become locked in internecine battles as they struggle to find the right path to a genuine peace.

The United States is far from a distant observer of the Mideast's problems. The American Raj holds supreme dominion over most of the region. Almost all the players involved in the Arab-Israeli conflict are patrons or clients of the United States. Israel has received over $110 billion in overt aid since its creation and depends on the US to retain its military superiority over all its combined neighbors. Egypt would quickly run out of wheat without US financial aid, and its armed forces would grind to a halt without US spare parts. Jordan's armed and intelligence forces are virtual offshoots of the US and British military. Its royal family is reported to have received $40 to $60 million per annum for decades in secret CIA stipends. Half of Lebanon's politicians are on Washington's payroll. Saudi Arabia's royal family relies on the US for defense, personal security, as a market for its oil, and repository for its billions in wealth. In the Mideast, the kingdom is known to one and all as Saudi America. The same applies to Kuwait and the Gulf emirates.

Palestinians belonging to Mahmoud Abbas's Fatah faction are virtual extensions of the US State Department. Fatah's finances, food, and diplomatic support come from Washington. The CIA and FBI train and arm its security forces. All of Fatah's communications are monitored by the US National Security Agency. Without the trickle of economic support provided Fatah by the US and EU, its Palestinians would starve.

Hamas and other rejectionist Palestinian factions are certainly not beholden to the US and its allies, but they depend on aid from America, Europe, and Saudi Arabia to feed their people, among whom unemployment runs between 60 and 70 percent. Hamas and its militant West Bank allies are sealed tightly into the Occupied Territories and have almost no egress to the outside world. The brief Palestinian breakout in January 2008 at Rafah from the walled-in Gaza Strip showed just how much Egypt was tacitly cooperating with Israel to keep Palestinians caged up in the Gaza penal colony.

With the exception of Syria, Hezbollah, and distant Iran, all the major players in the Israeli-Palestinian conflict, and all those who will form part of any peace process, are well and truly under the hand of the Raj.

Washington pulls almost all their strings. Israel is another exception. Though dependent on the US, it has succeeded in dominating Washington's conduct of Mideast policy. Nevertheless, it is still ironic and dismaying to watch the endless game of American shuttle diplomacy between Mideast capitals, as if a single government at the capitals visited by Condoleeza Rice had any real free choice or independence of action from the American Raj. It's all a game among client states, a squabble in an extended family. Yet even though everyone in the Mideast knows that Washington is the ultimate power, this dreary charade of political theater continues.

In yet another irony, exasperated US senators and congressmen keep demanding that America's allies "do more in the war against terror." But how can powerless puppets who have no real military or political power of their own do more? Their job is to take orders, say the right things, and hold on to power. When Iraq's US–installed prime minister, Nuri al-Maliki, dared voice some tepid support for Palestinian rights, he was roundly blasted by Congress and the US media, and told to shut up.

Critics of moves to genuine peace will claim that the status quo is preferable to forcing Israel back to narrow borders and possibly weakening its security. But with cash-strapped America bogged down in two wars in the Muslim world, as well as military operations in Somalia and western Africa, it is essential to begin reducing anti-American hostility as quickly as possible. Since the Israel-Palestine conflict is the primary generator of what the West calls terrorism, the quickest way to shut down this generator is to make peace in the Levant.

Even embarking on the initial stages of a real Arab-Israeli peace process will produce an immediate abatement of anti-western feelings across the Muslim world, and take the wind from the sails of extreme anti-American groups, like al-Qaida, who will be deprived of their most emotive, inflammatory issue. But America must be seen to be pressing for a genuine, fair peace rather than the previous bogus peace plans whose sole objective was to take pressure off the Saudis and Egyptians. More make-believe, mendacious peace summits or Condoleeza Rice's much-reviled peace shuttles designed to give the appearance of movement forward, while in reality reinforcing the status quo, will not be accepted by the Muslim world.

A permanent solution to the Israeli-Palestinian conflict will not eliminate all acts of terrorism, as other issues beyond Palestine also generate anti-western and inter-Muslim violence, and numerous extremist groups that have nothing to do with the Arab-Israeli conflict. As earlier stated, in the Muslim world, the primary motivation of the freelance violence we call terrorism is opposition to western-backed dictatorships. But Palestine is the key, and resolving this issue will likely reduce anti-western violence by a large measure and significantly reduce animosity towards the West.

An Israel that somehow manages to make peace with Palestinians will not find the absolute tranquillity it has so long sought. Acceptance by its neighbors, and an end to its regional isolation, means Israel will very likely be relentlessly drawn into the turbulent affairs of the Mideast and greater Muslim world, becoming a part of their intrigues, feuds, and shifting alliances. Israel will, in effect, become a superpower within the Muslim world and Mideast, as well as an important international state. Israel will never be able to escape the dangerous neighborhood in which it lives, but at least it can become one of the regular members, rather than an outcast and object of hatred and revenge. The Muslim world is an Ali Baba's cavern just waiting for the Israelis to explore.

TWO: Bring the festering wars in Iraq and Afghanistan to a speedy end. This is not the place for a lengthy discussion on how to extricate the US and its allies from these conflicts that have intensified its image as enemy of the Muslim world. But, like Palestine, the outline of a solution is simple and plain to see; its execution exceptionally difficult.

Iraq: the US has lost its war in Iraq in the sense that its plan to turn Iraq into another Arab protectorate like Saudi Arabia or Jordan appears to have failed. Washington had hoped to control Iraq's oil riches through a pliant, US–engineered Shia regime sustained by native troops backed by US airpower; in short, the traditional control model of the British Raj when it ruled Iraq. Holding on to Iraq will probably means a permanent US garrison and at least three to five military bases, as well as a huge, ongoing financial cost. Of the 2008 presidential candidates, only John McCain has stated an intent to keep troops in Iraq "for one hundred years, if necessary," he vowed, though he later backed away from this statement and called for most US troops to be withdrawn by 2013. The Democrats claimed to be determined to withdraw US forces from Iraq. But after two years in control of Congress, their record in achieving this goal has been a complete failure.

After five years of US occupation, Iraq remains racked by violence and instability. Oil production and power generation are lower than at the time of the US invasion in 2003. Four million Iraqis are refugees, two million of them externally, the rest as internal refugees. At least 40,000 Iraqi political prisoners are held in US-run prisons. No one knows how many Iraqis have died since 2003: estimates run into the hundreds of thousands.

After waves of bloody ethnic cleansing, Iraq has, for all intents, broken up into three nations run by Shia, Sunnis, and Kurds. Keeping 160,000 US troops and some 100,000 US-funded mercenaries in Iraq has strained the US Treasury and military forces. Estimates of the cost of replacing military equipment worn out by operations in Iraq are $60 billion. Some academic experts estimate the total cost of the Iraq War will reach two or even three trillion dollars when all costs are properly accounted for. Remember, the Bush administration's original cost estimate for the total war was forty to sixty billion dollars. The US invasion of Iraq has also played an important role in causing the price of oil to sharply rise to over $130 per barrel. Half of the US Army's combat battalions are bogged down in Iraq. If ever there were a Pyrrhic victory, it is Iraq. One more such victory, and the US will be undone. But if the neocons have their way, that next victory will be against Iran.

The US must thus face reality, no matter how painful or humiliating, and beat a retreat from Iraq. There is nothing wrong or dishonorable about retreat: it is a primary military maneuver. All great powers make strategic and tactical mistakes. All good generals leave an escape route open behind their forces.

The best way to end the chaos in Iraq, prevent it from spreading to its neighbors, and avoid the very real threat of intervention by powerful neighbors Iran and Turkey, is for the twenty-two members of the Arab League, in close cooperation with the United States, to send sizable military forces to stabilize Iraq and allow US forces a face-saving means of retreat.

There is no other standing multinational force capable of maintaining a modicum of order in Iraq. Arabic-speaking soldiers who understand local customs are essential for this mission. However, the divided Arab League may prove no better than the US at dealing with Iraq's feuding political factions, but at least it will be an Arab organization and take heat off the United States. It will give Iraqis time and protection to try to resolve their internal problems in a face-saving manner without tearing their nation apart and destabilizing the entire Mideast. The most important role the Arab League will play is to assure Iraq's borders and block its neighbors from trying to annex oil-rich parts of Iraq.

It is also worth recalling that the Arab League played a successful role in ending Lebanon's bloody 1975–90 civil war. Lebanon's conflict was even more complex than Iraq's, and just as bitter. One day, the Arab League will have to begin assuring the Mideast's stability and even its human rights. Intervention in Iraq could be a highly productive operation with long-term regional benefits. That is, provided the League's fractious members do not themselves begin tribal fighting over the bleeding carcass of Iraq.

Like Palestine, there will be no good solutions to Iraq, only bad ones and worse. Bad will still be better than none. The United States' presence in Iraq has become a major part of the problem there, not the solution. Compromise between Iraq's warring factions will be impossible so long as American power and money continue playing off factions against each other.

One thing is clear: the longer the Iraq War—what Saddam rightly named the Mother of All Battles—flares on, the more Iraq will become an incubator of terrorism and anti-American groups, and a proving ground for a new generation of jihadis, as the US National Intelligence Estimate rightly warned. The United States should not waste a moment in getting out of this ten-to-twelve-billion-dollar-a-month debacle that has run down its armed forces to the breaking point, earned America a sea of hatred, and is being largely financed by loans from China, of all places.

How many more trillions of dollars and lives will be wasted before the US finally admits defeat in Iraq and pulls its troops out?

Even with a peacekeeping force from the Arab League, there will still be intense violence and perhaps even chaos in Iraq after the US withdraws. But violence will after time abate as Iraqis are finally faced with the need to once again coexist, however painfully, as they did before the US invasion. Given time and freedom from outside pressures Iraqis will eventually develop a modus vivendi.

But the question remains, how to minimize Iran's fast-growing influence in Iraq, the eastern portion of which Tehran now dominates?

The other choice is to hand over a third of Iraq to Iran, a third to

Turkey, and forget about the Sunni center, a process that would throw the entire Mideast into convulsions and produce highly dangerous and largely unpredictable consequences. Many of the Mideast's unnatural borders, and, in fact, those of the Muslim world, were drawn by Imperial Britain and France. Any change to them threatens to destabilize this geopolitical house of cards. Denationalizing Iraq would, in effect, return it to its previous semi-autonomous state under the later Ottoman Empire. But, once again, three weak mini-states would be a constant lure for hungry neighbors. The only regional nation that would welcome such a development is Israel, whose right wing has long sought to break up Syria, Lebanon, Jordan, and Iraq. In this sense, President Bush's 2003 invasion handed Israel a geopolitical triumph. But how it develops in the long term remains to be seen.

Afghanistan: There are two ways out of the morass in Afghanistan. Either a stalemated war ending in ignominious retreat, as the British suffered in their infamous retreat from Kabul, and as the Americans did from Vietnam, or a negotiated settlement. As in Iraq, the longer the war in Afghanistan wears on, the more it will also serve as a vast training base and magnet for jihadists. Each new Afghan village bombed by the US Air Force produces ten new volunteers for the anti-western resistance.

The US and its NATO allies still claim they are fighting terrorism in Afghanistan. Most Americans and Canadians believe this, and support pursuing the war. Europeans are far more cynical: polls show a solid majority oppose NATO's operations in Afghanistan as an unnecessary, colonial war. In reality, what the US and its dragooned NATO allies have done, as we have seen, is get themselves stuck in an unwinnable war against much of the Pashtun tribal people—Afghanistan's largest ethnic group. If 160,000 Soviet troops could not defeat the Pashtun, 60,000 far less ruthless NATO forces are unlikely to succeed. The longer Canada, other NATO members, and, most lately, France, remain at war in Afghanistan, the more they will become targets for revenge attacks by extremists from the Muslim world. Their presence in Afghanistan degrades rather than enhances their security.

The answer to the Afghan morass is to stop demonizing and bombing the Pashtun Taliban, and bring them into the center of the nation's political process. It is time for the western powers to admit that the Taliban had little or nothing to do with the 9/11 attacks and is not a terrorist organization. The most constructive role the western powers could play is to get the many Afghan factions to meet in national assembly, or "loya jirga," and come up with a legitimate government that represents the interests of the nation's Pashtun majority as well as its Tajiks, Uzbeks, Hazara, and Turkmen.

Historically, Afghanistan has rarely had a real central government in the western sense. So let the unruly Afghans revert to their traditional, much-loved semi-anarchy—and then forget about them. The key to returning Afghanistan to its former obscurity and unimportance is to get all foreign influences out of that battered nation, which has been at constant war for nearly thirty years. That means agreement among the US, NATO, Russia, India, and its neighbors, Pakistan, Uzbekistan, Tajikistan, Turkmenistan, and Iran to stop meddling in Afghanistan and allow it to resume its former role as a buffer zone between the great powers. Whether its neighbors can avoid such temptation remains to be seen. History shows it is surprisingly easy to enter Afghanistan yet exceptionally difficult to withdraw.

In America, Afghanistan is still mistakenly seen as an antiterrorist war. Many Americans will object to pulling their troops out of Afghanistan that have been hunting for Osama bin Laden and his al-Qaida confederates. But after a fruitless seven-year manhunt, it is likely that bin Laden and what remains of his original handful of ardent supporters, if still alive, are hiding in Pakistan, not Afghanistan.

Invading Pakistan's autonomous tribal areas, as US defense secretary Robert Gates proposed in 2007, is a daft idea that would only widen and intensify an already unwinnable war in which US and NATO forces are already seriously under strength and overextended. It would also fit right into Osama bin Laden's strategy of drawing the US into yet another debilitating, hugely expensive war in the Muslim world, this time with Pakistan, a large nation with tough armed forces of 619,000 men.

Better to pull western forces out of Afghanistan and offer the Afghans large rewards to find bin Laden and company, which they might actually do once the onus of cooperating with foreign occupiers is removed. As for claims that a western pullout will allow jihadis to reopen training bases, they already have them aplenty in Afghanistan and now Iraq. According to the authoritative Senlis Council, by the end of 2006, the Taliban and its allies effectively controlled half of Afghanistan.

Besides, modern, urbanized jihadis operate over the Internet and can be trained in bomb-making and revolution in an apartment. They don't need Afghanistan as a base. The 9/11 attackers came from Hamburg, Germany, and may also have operated from Madrid, Spain. Holding on to turbulent, unstable Afghanistan for the sake of a future pipeline running from Uzbekistan to Karachi is simply not worth the financial and human cost of this war. Once western forces quit Afghanistan, it will quickly be forgotten, as was Vietnam in the 1970s. Future generations will ask, "What on earth were we doing there, chasing Pashtun tribesmen across the Hindu Kush?" A good question that should be asked today.

This proposal does not mean abandoning Afghanistan, as the US did after the Soviet withdrawal in 1989. Once Afghans manage to produce a legitimate government acceptable to all major ethnic groups, as was achieved, for example, in post-apartheid South Africa, then the US, Canada, the other western powers, China, and Japan should implement a major development to rebuild the shattered nation, train its cadres, and expand education, public services, and good government. Given the fractious nature of the Afghans, achieving even some of these goals will be difficult, but they are certainly better than the current policy of trying to bomb Afghanistan into submission to a puppet government imposed by Washington that has no authority beyond Kabul's city limits.

While the West will continue to exert strong influence over North Africa, sub-Saharan Africa, and the Mideast, Afghanistan and Central Asia are bridges too far. As Frederick the Great famously observed, "He who defends everything, defends nothing."

THREE: The Muslim world must be disabused of the mistaken, highly dangerous idea that the West, and particularly the United States, is set on destroying Islam. This canard, which has gained very wide currency, is being fanned by both Islamophobes in the West and anti-western fanatics in the Muslim world. For example, fundamentalist televangelist Reverend Rod Parsley, who Senator John McCain once called his spiritual guide, denounces Islam as a "false religion," and urges Christians to wage war against the false religion and destroy it. Parsley is one of America's most influential evangelical preachers, with a 12,000-member congregation, a 5,200-seat church, and a weekly television show. However extreme many Muslim preachers may sound, few if any call for the destruction of Christianity like Parsley and his twin demagogue, Reverend John Hagee of Global Evangelism television. Hagee, a major supporter of McCain, speaks twice daily on 75 radio stations and 125 television stations in the US and Canada, and has an e-mail list of two million supporters who are treated to his regular barrages of anti-Muslim invective and irrationality.

Hagee is the leading Christian Zionist who opposes a Palestinian state and supports Greater Israel and literal biblical prophecy. According to Hagee and other born-again evangelists, historic Israel must be created so the Messiah can then return and destroy the earth in Armageddon. All non–born again people, including Israelis, will be consumed in flames, warns Hagee and his followers.

When Parsley's and Hagee's views became widely known to the public, including Hagee's claim in 1900 that Adolf Hitler was an agent of Christ, McCain quickly backed away from these two demagogues, though he still sought their follower's support. The White House has got to cease projecting an image of hostility towards Muslims. Whenever Muslims hear President Bush fulminate against terrorism, what they really hear is the word "Muslim." Bush and Cheney are primarily responsible for projecting the image of a hostile, Islamophobic America to the Muslim world. Hopefully, their successors will be more circumspect and attuned to America's image abroad, and less eager to pander to religious fundamentalists at home. Fortunately, much of Muslim anger is focused on George Bush and Dick Cheney rather than on America. Unfortunately, Republican leader John McCain appears set on outdoing even Bush and Cheney in his overt hostility to the Muslim world.

The US must avoid classifying every act of resistance by Muslims to wrongs and injustice as terrorism. There are terrorists, to be sure, like al-Qaida and its offshoots, but there are still legitimate freedom fighters, like the Chechens of the Caucasus, and legitimate resisters against very real oppression, like Egypt's Muslim Brotherhood and democrats, and the Islamic Movement of Uzbekistan. The United States risks becoming a bulwark of reaction, the defender of an unjust status quo, like the old, ossified Austro-Hungarian Empire. America has to remember its revolutionary roots, and be seen as a friend and ally in struggles against injustice, oppression, and poverty around the world, though not always so successfully at home. The America that I grew up in certainly was.

Washington desperately needs some new official faces to speak to the

Muslim world and tell it that America is not an enemy of its people or religion. Former secretary of state Colin Powell would have been ideal for this role, but he is, alas, permanently discredited by his disgraceful UN performance just before the Iraq War. Senator Barack Obama, who is of partial Muslim descent, though he denies it, is another, but he is already very close to the pro-Israel lobby and, in an attempt to appear tough to American voters, foolishly declared he would attack Pakistan, provoking outrage and dismay across the Muslim world.

Still, of all the current crop of American politicians, the golden-tongued, convincingly sincere Barack Obama, who opposed the illegal Iraq War from the start, is the premier candidate to speak to the Muslim world and begin improving East-West relations. Not because he is a mulatto, nor half-Muslim by blood, but because he commands a unique degree of respect and trust abroad. Many non-Americans see in Obama the qualities of honesty, basic decency, and humanitarianism that are so painfully absent in Bush and his fellow Republicans. Barack Obama is the first senior American political leader who commands respect and admiration abroad in a very long time. Many Americans share these feelings.

Ending the appearance of hostility towards Islam requires adopting a number of important steps. Conduct of foreign policy must be removed from the Pentagon and returned to the State Department. Bush's militarized foreign policy has turned the world against the United States. It is the duty of the US Federal Communications Commission (FCC) to remove from the air rabid televangelists and talk-radio hosts preaching hatred of Islam and calling for mankind's destruction. They are money-grubbing pornographers of rank superstition, racism, and religious bigotry of the worst kind. Many sound like neo-Nazis. Their ravings, which many Muslims around the globe believe is America's authentic voice, do not constitute simple free speech. Tens of millions of Americans take their word as gospel.

The hatred and calumny preached by these grotesque charlatans and mountebanks violates US communications regulations. As Justice Felix Frankfurter said, such broadcast hatred is tantamount to crying fire in a crowded theater. If hate-spewing televangelists were to replace the word "Muslim" with "Jews," they would face dismissal, crushing lawsuits, and even arrest. New York broadcaster Don Imus was fired after a joking racial slur against a women's sports team, yet promoters of Islamophobia, like John Hagee, Pat Robertson, Franklin Graham, and Rod Parsley, continue their vicious public hate campaigns, reminding us that Islamophobia is today's only permissible public prejudice.

In a further irony, the neocons who have been promoting the big lie of so-called Islamofascism are themselves very close, as Professor Paxton showed, in Chapter 13, to traditional fascist ideas, and many of their fundamentalist evangelical allies near the same extreme.

Americans ought to understand the highly negative influence extremist evangelical Christian organizations exert on their political leadership, domestic, and foreign policies. These well-organized cultists often resemble Islamist cultists harkening back to Osama bin Laden and his fellow Salafists who want mankind to be ruled by Islamic law and a Muslim caliph. Their doppelgängers on America's Christian far right, known as Rapturists or Dominionists, want not only theocracy but advocate the total destruction of those who do not accept their religious teachings.

The beliefs of these extremist religious cults were popularized by the Left Behind series of best-selling books by Tim LaHaye and Jerry B. Jenkins, and *The Late Planet Earth* by Hal Lindsay. Farragoes of science fiction and doomsday cultism, these books have sold millions of copies in America's heartland. The Midwest and Bible Belt have always been populated by bizarre cults and religious oddities, but they rarely have played a major role in shaping foreign policy. As core supporters of the Bush administration, these millions of often heavily armed doomsday cultists have become a growing danger to their own nation, and the rest of the world. Politicians of the hard right, like Senators John McCain and Joseph Lieberman, have latched on to these Christian extremists who urge war against the Arabs and Iran.

Recent Gallup polls show 33 to 47 percent of American respondents describe themselves as either born-again Christians or the slightly broader Christian Evangelists. They are the fastest-growing religious sector in America. Seventy-nine percent of those identifying themselves as being on the Christian Right voted for George Bush in 2000. One survey quoted by PublicEye.org found that 40 percent of the total vote for Bush in 2000 came from Christian Evangelicals, making them the largest voting bloc in the Republican Party.

Evangelical Christians are not monolithic. Many groups and churches are moderate in their social and political views. Black evangelicals have little in common with white denominations and follow their own agenda. But the Republican Party has become so dominated by southerners and midwesterners and the born-again Christian Right that militant evangel-icalism has by now almost become the Republicans' official faith.

During the two Bush administrations, the organized Christian Right and its ally, various pro-Israel lobby groups, have become one of Washington's most powerful and influential forces. The Internal Revenue Service's failure to take action against patently political action organizations masquerading behind a cloak of Protestant, Catholic, or Jewish religious charity has violated the constitutional ban on religion in politics.

The question is, what can be done to curb the political meddling of these political-religious organizations? Free speech must not be abridged in any way, but tax-deductible lobbying and hate mongering can be. The IRS has reportedly begun investigating the charitable status of evangelical organizations active in politics, but no action is likely to be taken as long as Republicans control the White House.

Nevertheless, further tax investigations are overdue for politicized evangelicals and their spokespersons. Television stations should be pressed by the public not to sell airtime to religious fraudsters and hatemongers. Advertisers should be wary of sponsoring stations or networks that sell airtime to Christian TV networks that act as mouthpieces for the evangelical far right, and from which millions of poorly informed Americans get religious propaganda disguised as news. It is time to end the role of extreme evangelical churches as an unofficial arm of the Republican Party.

By the same token, it is incumbent upon the leadership of Muslim nations to take effective action, which some have so far not done, to end the preaching of violent, inflammatory religious doctrines towards the West. Muslim nations, like Turkey, Egypt, Jordan, and Saudi Arabia, completely control their tame religious establishments. In Turkey, for example, every Friday sermon delivered across the nation is written and distributed to mullahs by the state's ministry of religious affairs, and most clergymen are government appointed.

In its schizophrenic identity as both close ally and fierce critic of the United States, Saudi Arabia bears heavy responsibility for encouraging the preaching of anti-western sentiment. The Saudis, with American backing, sent large numbers of Wahabist-Salafist missionaries into the Gulf, Pakistan, and Afghanistan in the 1980s and 1990s to preach religious doctrines aimed at countering Iranian Shia influence. These Wahabi-Salafists converted large numbers of people to their rigid retro-beliefs and extreme hatred of Shia and, later, westerners. They were particularly effective among the Pashtun tribes of southern Afghanistan and Pakistan's Northwest Frontier that would soon come to form the core of the Taliban. Washington encouraged the spread of Salafism in South Asia until 9/11.

It is thus of prime importance to compel Saudi Arabia to cease exporting extremist religion. Saudi Arabia must also drop its unacceptable ban on churches and synagogues. Muslim nations have been shamefully silent on this issue. Constraints on non-Islamic faiths in other Muslim nations must cease if the Muslim world is to demand decent treatment by the West. This is an important issue the UN should address.

Iran, the other major sponsor of anti-western Islamic militancy, will not cease its efforts to export Shia revolution until the western powers cease their siege of Iran and attempts to overthrow its Islamic regime. For Iran, exporting anti-western animosity, however reprehensible, has become a weapon of self-defense.

In the West, the idea of shutting down madrassas has become common wisdom. But doing so will not work. These endowed Islamic religious schools are, in many cases, the only educational institutions in poor Muslim nations like Pakistan and Bangladesh. Most are supported by Saudi and Gulf charities. Without them, most children in these nations would be totally illiterate. Shutting down madrassas is no more likely than Muslim nations compelling the United States to shut down southern Baptist seminaries. These madrassas will mostly cease teaching anti-western lessons when the causes that incite such anger cease.

Finally, western powers and South Korea should discourage their aggressive evangelical missionary groups that are moving into the Muslim nations of the Mideast, Africa, and South Asia. Many are proselytizing under the false flag of being secular international-aid organizations. They are seen everywhere as western agents and invariably stir up violent opposition.

But we must not lose sight of two vital facts. First, as previously stated, in the Muslim world, and notably Pakistan, Egypt, Saudi Arabia, Jordan, and Algeria, religious-linked violent political activism is not primarily about global jihad, or attacking the West, but about domestic politics. That is, opposition to dictatorial, self-serving, self-enriching regimes that are doing the bidding of western powers. Second, much of the Muslim world's religious extremism is fueled by the burning issues of Palestine, Chechnya, Iraq, and Afghanistan, which we have previously examined. Removing them will shut off much of the oxygen that feeds today's fires in Islam. But there will remain a hard core of Muslim religious fanatics, concentrated in Pakistan and North Africa, who must be sternly dealt with by the governments of these nations. Though marginal and small in number, these groups remain a significant danger.

Finally, the US government would be wise to cease what Muslims see as its attempts to destroy one of the pillars of their faith by shutting down Islamic charities worldwide. Most of these charities were, and remain, perfectly legitimate organizations dedicated to aiding Muslims in need or peril. "Zakat," the regular giving of a share of one's income to the poor and oppressed, is a basic tenet of Islam that is mandatory for every Muslim. After 9/11, the Bush administration moved to shut down or cow into inaction North American and international Islamic charities. Serious criminal charges of "supporting terrorism" were brought against the charities' directors and donors. Many pled guilty to trumped-up charges when threatened with the death penalty after 9/11.

The US government lumped nearly all Islamic charitable efforts, from sending food and clothing to the terrorized Bosnians, arms and humanitarian aid for the Chechens, funds for Hamas social projects in the West Bank, as aiding terrorism. Donors went onto FBI suspect lists. Muslim-Americans who had sent funds and aid to Bosnia, Palestine, Kashmir, and Chechnya were put on trial for "aiding terrorism," and sentenced to long terms in prison. Not surprisingly, donations quickly dried up.

Closure of these Islamic charities choked off legitimate humanitarian aid across the Muslim world, leaving refugees and the poor without food, medicine, or shelter, and creating further bitterness against the West. A minor amount of funds for anti-western groups may have been interdicted, but most funding of jihadi groups was transmitted through the ancient "halawa" system of unofficial bankers that were untraceable, or delivered by hand. In any event, the jihadi movement runs on a shoestring. The total cost of the 9/11 attacks, for example, which inflicted over a hundred billion dollars' worth of damage, was estimated at $400,000.

Shutting down Islamic charities angered the whole Muslim world and was grossly unfair. For example, the leading source of terrorism in Britain was the Irish Republican Army. Its primary source of funds was New York and Boston. Fundraising for the IRA, with its powerful Irish-American urban backing, was never seriously halted by the US government. Had the

US Justice Department acted against the IRA in the same sweeping and highly unjust way it did against Muslim welfare groups, it would have shut down all Catholic charities as potential "supporters of terrorism" and put those Americans who had contributed to them onto a terrorism watch list and no-fly lists. Blatantly unfair to be sure, but this is what was done to Islamic charities and their contributors.

Ending the harassment and intimidation of Muslim charities, their directors and donors must be replaced by a more intelligent, targeted method of ensuring that these organizations are not being used to fund violence, particularly directed against Americans. It is also time to take a hard look at those right-wing Zionist charities that have been funding illegal Jewish settlement in the West Bank, and those Christian and Jewish charities that have blatantly become involved in Mideast politics.

FOUR: Stop sustaining authoritarian regimes across the Muslim world. One of the things that arouses the deepest anger abroad against America is Washington's persistent hypocrisy in preaching democracy to the Third World while supporting some of its ugliest dictatorships.

The US has rarely created authoritarian regimes in the Muslim world where none before existed. Instead, the expanding American Raj inherited some from Britain, like Jordan and the Gulf emirates. But, most often, the US bent existing nondemocratic power structure in the Third World to its will by either moving its own dictators into power, as in Egypt, Iraq, Pakistan, and Indonesia, or buying the loyalty of existing dictatorial regimes by large amounts of economic aid, arms, protection, and secret payments to their leaders. Sometimes, as in the case of Egypt under Anwar Sadat, and Afghanistan under Hamid Karzai, the newly installed leader was already a longtime CIA asset. In all cases, Washington developed an easy rapport and effective working relationship with such nondemocratic regimes. When confronted with genuine democratic governments, as in Algeria and the Palestinian territories, Washington quickly reacted by encouraging the overthrow of both elected governments.

By relentlessly supporting dictatorships, the United States, Britain, and France have become identified in the minds of many Muslims with their region's worst ills: often savage repression, violation of basic human and political rights, torture, censorship and denial of free speech, religious persecution, militarism, and endemic corruption. These evils existed in the Mideast long before the US was born, but the authoritarian regimes that today rule much of the Muslim world have perfected them. In fact, the only accomplishment of many of these police-state regimes is in the area of repression: public control, surveillance, intimidation, and crushing any and all genuine opposition. These authoritarian regimes' prime objective is not social advancement but keeping power at all costs.

Most westerners fail to understand that the generals, kings, and corrupt politicians of the Muslim world long backed by Washington, London, and Paris have, over the course of time, steadily eliminated almost all moderate political elements and intellectuals in their nations who might conceivably mount any significant opposition to the ruling regime. Criticism of the government was declared "treason," "Islamic terrorism," or "aiding the Zionists." Spies of the secret police were everywhere. Opposition to the powers that be often incurred punishment of entire extended families as well as the usual arrest and torture.

Across the Muslim world, what should have been the political center, the "political moderates" so long sought by westerners, was hollowed out or eradicated. Those who opposed the regime were either thrown in jail, driven into exile, bought off, or forced into terrified silence. This drove opponents, including Islamists, deep underground, leaving them the only remaining political opposition. Mosques became the sole place where opponents of the government could assemble and speak, though even there with trepidation because of ubiquitous government informers.

As Islamists increasingly became the dominant voice of opposition because of their organization, numbers, and faith, the Muslim world's dictatorships were quick to claim that they offered the only alternative to anti-western Islamic theocracy. Whenever the West made occasional feeble demands for political liberalization, dictatorial regimes would immediately cry, "It's either us or the terrorists." The western powers were easily sold this notion of *après nous le deluge*, and kept supporting nondemocratic regimes as the supposed lesser of two evils. After hectoring Egypt for its lack of democracy and flagrant repression, US secretary of state Condoleeza Rice watched in embarrassed silence, and to great scorn across the Mideast, as her chief client, Egypt's dictator, Husni Mubarak, ordered the arrest and torture of Ayman Nur, a young, would-be democratic politician who had the audacity to run against him in one of the nation's rigged elections.

The US, Britain, and France appeared to accept the elimination of the political center in the Muslim world and did almost nothing to support the real Muslim moderates it so loudly claimed to want to support. The faux moderates the western powers ended up supporting were those that readily obeyed orders from Washington, London, and Paris. The western media also adopted the term "moderate" to describe the West's pliant allies in the Muslim world. President Husni Mubarak of Egypt and King Abdullah of Jordan were moderates, in Washington's lexicon, though there was hardly anything moderate about these two absolute rulers, one a former general, the other a hereditary monarch.

Washington's noteworthy failure to support true moderate reformist Muslims within the Raj's huge footprint ensures that when revolutions inevitably sweep much of the Muslim world, those who eventually seize power will be violently anti-American extremists. One morning Americans will awaken to find there has been a coup in Saudi Arabia, its new leader, "Colonel Aziz," waving his fist and crying, as did Iranians after their revolution, "Death to America."

Since what we term "Islamic terrorism" is first and foremost violent opposition to the Muslim world's western-imposed regimes, it is obvious that one of America's and the West's most important steps in ending confrontation with the Muslim world is to begin supporting the democracy we preach. That means inculcating the philosophy and practice of genuine democracy into the Muslim world, funding and supporting the development of strong democratic institutions and non-governmental organizations, helping nurture a free press that is not subsidized by the CIA, and gradually helping remove authoritarian regimes and replacing them with popularly elected governments.

It is clearly urgent and essential for the western powers to open discourse with the Muslim world's democrats, real moderates, and Islamists, who are seeking to create modern, representative, effective governments. This invisible center of the Muslim political world has been silenced or drowned out by extremists and their own repressive regimes, and boycotted or ignored by the western powers. Yet in this centrist group lies the Muslim world's potential renaissance and fruitful accommodation with the West.

The most effective—and urgent—place for the United States and its allies to begin the process of building genuine democracy is in Egypt, the heartland of the Arab world. Egypt's dictator, President Mubarak, has ruled since 1981 with US support. But advancing age is bringing him near to the end of his long dictatorship. Mubarak's efforts to move his son Gamal into power have not yet succeeded, leaving the succession issue open and uncertain. Mubarak's departure from power offers an ideal time for the western powers, which supply half of Egypt's food, to demand that this ancient nation hold free and fair elections for the parliamentary government in the same manner as did Pakistan in early 2008. Free elections will inevitably bring the moderate Muslim Brotherhood to power. Moderate Muslims, as in Turkey's Justice and Development Party (AKP), are precisely what the West needs to assure order and stability. The alternative is either more dictatorship or a radical Islamist government.

Third World nations are not condemned to despotism, though it often appears to be the case. Dictatorship is sometimes a more efficient, even less risky form of government, particularly for poor, uneducated nations, than a rough-and-tumble democracy. But while one dictator may be honest and dedicated to his nation's best interests, like Kenya's Jomo Kenyatta, Egypt's Abdel Nasser, Cuba's Fidel Castro, or Yugoslavia's Marshall Tito, their successors almost inevitably are men of inferior qualities and lower morals, if not outright thugs or tyrants. Dictatorship is effective in the short term, but dangerous in the long run.

The West has an enormous amount to teach the Muslim world about democratic government, and the Muslim world has a huge pent-up desire for honest, democratic government. In the only free elections held in the Arab world, those in Algeria and Palestine, Muslims showed their passionate desire to vote. The United States, Britain, and France have to resolve to accept the results of such free elections and not reverse democratic votes through a military coup, as in Algeria, or punishing sanctions and subversion, as happened after Hamas won its resounding victory in Palestine.

A useful model for bringing democracy to the Muslim world is the way the United States used money, training, and election experts to help undermine Communist regimes in Ukraine and Georgia, and replace them with more or less democratic governments, that is, from the bottom up rather than the top down. Western non-government organizations, or NGOs, and forward-thinking individuals, like George Soros, spent tens of millions to educate Ukrainians and Georgians on electoral democracy, campaigning, building party membership, and spreading party policy.

Democratic institutions were designed and staffs prepared. Ukrainians and Georgians were taught how to generate political excitement and enthusiasm. Equally important, their western mentors tried to inculcate them with the basic democratic requirement of compromise and political accommodation.

The Orange revolution in Ukraine and the revolution of the Roses in Georgia succeeded brilliantly in ousting the decrepit Communist order. But the last western lesson—compromise—sadly failed to take root. Both Ukrainian and Georgian democrats were soon at one another's throats as old authoritarian impulses, political rivalries, jealousies, and fights to divide up the spoils of power undid the benefits of democracy. But if not quite Swiss-style democracy in Ukraine and Georgia, at least the former dictatorships were gone and most citizens realized that however imperfect their new political system, it was far, far better than the discredited older authoritarian order.

So, it will be a long, arduous struggle to bring democratic values and practices to Muslim nations where they have rarely been known or appreciated. But the majority of the Muslim world is now under 30 and, unlike their hidebound fathers, open to new thinking and positive influences from the West. The ideas and practices of democracy and free expression now course through the world's new nervous system, the Internet. We in the West just do not hear Muslim voices clamoring for democracy, free elections, and honest, clean government.

By contrast, an example of what not to do was Washington's tepid support for Turkey's democratic AK Islamist "light" party in the face of brazen threats of a coup by the reactionary Turkish Army and its supporters among Turkey's reactionary secular elite. Washington should have gone all out to show strong support for the moderate AK Justice and Development Party, Turkey's most successful, popular government since the 1930s, which brought improved human rights, fiscal stability, more rights for Kurds, and advanced freedom of speech. AK is precisely the kind of truly moderate (not just obedient) Islamic political party the West should be dealing with, one that emphasizes social justice and good government without imposing its religious doctrines on others.

Another even worse example of Washington's double standard was its efforts to keep one of its favorite military dictators, Pervez Musharraf, in power in Pakistan. While lecturing the world about the benefits of democracy and freedom, the Bush administration approved Musharraf's criminal purge of Pakistan's senior judiciary and the jailing and physical abuse of over sixty senior justices. Washington tried to engineer a still-born deal between Musharraf and the late Benazir Bhutto that would have perpetuated his dictatorship while using her as ersatz democratic window dressing. The US, Britain, and Canada, who claimed to be waging war in Afghanistan to promote democracy, sought long and hard to avoid recognizing Pakistan's newly elected democratic coalition government in a last-ditch effort to protect Musharraf. All told, it was one of the Raj's most shameful and perhaps most revealing days.

While encouraging the growth of democratic parties, it will also be necessary for the West to take more muscular action to ease out some of the Muslim world's autocratic heads of state. Since most Muslim regimes rely on the armed forces and secret police for their continued power, the best way to begin changing them—true regime change—not the phony version preached by the neocons with their hidden agenda—is to cultivate the democratic, reformist elements that are found even in the most conservative armies and security forces. The most progressive, forward-looking officers are usually in air forces, and thus offer fertile ground for democratic revolutions.

An excellent example of such a process occurred in the remote Saharan state of Mauritania. Its US- and Israeli-backed dictator, the widely hated despot Maaoya Taya, a key ally in the so-called war on terror, was overthrown in 2005 by a military coup. The new junta promised the usual democratic elections in two years. To just about everyone's astonishment, the junta, composed of young, reformist Islamist officers, kept its word and held absolute free and fair elections in 2007 that produced a fully functioning democratic government that has been a model for the troubled Sahel region and the rest of Africa.

The idea that the West must continue to assure its control over the Muslim world's oil and gas, and strategic real estate, by means of dictatorial puppet regimes—in effect, glorified overseers for foreign-owned plantations—is obsolete. It belongs on the ash heap of history with the Belgian Congo, the British Indian Raj, and French West Africa.

Democratic Muslim governments will have as great a need to sell their energy resources as autocratic ones. The US and its allies will inevitably end up competing in price with China, Japan, India, and Europe for oil and gas. Whether despots or democrats rule the Muslim world will not alter this fact. Paying higher energy prices would in any event be beneficial, curbing the wasteful use of fuel, lowering greenhouse gases, and providing the Muslim world with more funds for social and economic development at a time when current resources cannot handle an onrushing wave of young people.

Price competition and higher world energy costs are inevitable. Keeping generals and kings in power in the Muslim world may keep the West's cost of oil down by a few dollars a barrel, but in the end it will prove counterproductive since the western powers will continue to be afflicted by violence emanating from the Muslim world.

The cost of protecting western satraps and fighting off anti-western jihadis will far exceed the savings realized by controlling the monarchs who control oil. The US has spent over $700 billion to date in an effort to retain political control of Iraq's oil alone. That would buy enough oil on the open market to keep America in energy for a long time. The additional $300 billion or so spent on the war on terror has absolutely nothing positive to show except a few dead or caged jihadis. The faux war on terror and Iraq have produced a gargantuan expenditure that is second only to what America spent on World War ıı. The difference is, of course, is that World War ıı lasted only four years and America won.

The most effective way for the West to assure its continued access to the Muslim world's energy resources is to cultivate the growth of democratic, popular governments. Their natural affinity will be with the democratic West. In the end, the Muslim world must sell oil to live. Many arid Muslim nations must rely on imports of food from the West for up to 50 percent of their caloric needs. Without energy exports, there will be no hard currency to buy food imports. India and China will import increasing amounts of energy and other resources from Muslim nations, but they cannot fully replace the massive buying made by the profligate western nations.

The current mantra about America needing "energy independence" is an expensive chimera that has led to mass production of mainly corn-based ethanol that has caused a huge upsurge in food prices for Americans and the rest of the world. This, in turn, has sparked dangerous global inflation and is destabilizing many nations, including close US allies, like Egypt and the Gulf emirates that rely on subsidized wheat or foreign guest workers.

The loudest advocates of independence from Arab oil happen to be the very same neoconservatives who have been promoting conflict between the United States and the Muslim world. Exchanging food for oil is the perfect example of ideal terms of trade and the basic common sense of Adam Smith's free trade economics in which nations trade what they are most efficient at producing. The sole beneficiaries of the wrongheaded campaign to lower imports of oil from the Muslim world have been America's politically influential sugar and corn farmers.

The Muslim world must also be allowed to experiment with new types of government. Western-style parliamentary democracy may be fine for some nations, but others, such as the Arabian states or Afghanistan, may be more comfortable with the traditional Islamic form of democracy: clan and tribal councils, reporting to a national council, or "majlis," deciding on issues by lengthy dialectics and eventual consensus guided by a council of elders and Islamic law. Why the US accepts Islamic law in Saudi Arabia but finds it unacceptable in Iraq or Afghanistan remains unclear.

In the end, however, it will be up to the people of Muslim nations to begin changing their own political order. This beneficial process cannot begin until the United States acts firmly and decisively to prevent its client generals and monarchs from using their ferocious security organs and soldiers to crush political reformers and thwart the advent of democracy. Armies of Muslim nations must be kept out of politics and in their barracks. Most need to be reduced in size by at least one-half.

The United States has not always been seen as the reactionary defender of the status quo, nor as inevitable heir to the British Empire. As we have seen, as recently as 1960, America was still hailed as the world's champion of liberty, human rights and democracy and, particularly in the Muslim world, as a liberator from colonialism. The United States can regain this honorable reputation by slowly but surely unwinding the undemocratic Muslim regimes it has so long encouraged and defended, and, instead, champion the cause of political, social and educational reform across the Muslim world. Call this process soft interventionism.

In the course of this "green revolution," noisy, sometimes ugly Islamist groups may gain power, but that is the inevitably cost of democracy. The essence of the right of free speech is having to grit your teeth and listen to words that you hate from people you despise. It is also a truism that most extreme groups soon tone down their radicalism once confronted by the burdens and constraints of power.

FIVE: It is essential to Lower America's profile in the Muslim world. The British used to say about American troops based in their island, "They are overpaid, oversexed, and over here."

No one likes foreign troops, or to be reminded that their nations are vassals of a great imperial empire. Today, the United States has over 700 military bases scattered across the globe, from huge complexes in Germany, Japan, and South Korea to tiny outposts and radar stations in remote regions. During the Bush administration, US military forces have been quietly but steadily moving into the Horn of Africa, with a new base complex at Djibouti, and into North and sub-Saharan West Africa, both regions where new deposits of oil are believed to exist in quantity.

To lower tensions with the Muslim world, the United States should reduce its military profile from Morocco to Central Asia. US bases in the North Pacific, by contrast, should be retained because of the vital role they play in maintaining regional stability between China, Japan, the Koreas, and Taiwan.

One of the primary causes of anti-Americanism in Saudi Arabia, and another key motivation of the jihadis who attacked New York and Washington, was the presence and size of US military bases in the Saudi kingdom. Most Saudis saw the US bases as tantamount to military occupation of their nation. As earlier noted, the US wisely curtailed activities of its Saudi bases and moved many aircraft and ground units to Qatar, Bahrain, and Oman. But the feeling remains in Saudi Arabia and the Gulf that these were and still remain US occupation forces, ready, like the old imperial garrisons of the British Raj, to intervene to prop up local rulers and put down native uprisings. The spread of US operating bases to Pakistan and Central Asia has ignited more anti–US hostility in these regions and provoked similar feelings of occupation.

During the days of British rule, the symbols of occupation were the Royal Navy and red-coated troops with field artillery. Today, the modern symbols of US global power are its heavily guarded air bases, with their F-16s, A-10 Warthogs, helicopter gunships, and ability to quickly summon the modern version of the Royal Navy's Dreadnaughts, US B-1 and B-52 heavy bombers.

United States military bases in the Muslim world today serve three principal purposes: enforcing US regional dominance; keeping client regimes in power; and protecting oil. They are also stepping stones in the worldwide network of US bases that allow air, ground, and naval units to be swiftly moved around the globe and, when necessary, concentrated. But once the US and Britain substantially reduce their tensions with the Muslim world and begin encouraging the spread of democracy—whether western-style or traditional Islamic—the reason for having so many bases diminishes. The western powers could still maintain naval patrols in the Gulf and Arabian Sea to safeguard tankers and commerce, but removing land bases is essential if relations with the Muslim world are to be normalized. In any event, US military forces have become globally diluted and weakened by imperial overreach. They need to be trimmed back so that fewer bases can perform more effective roles.

Instead of lowering its military profile in the Muslim world, however, the Pentagon, as part of the Bush administration's imperial policies, has been steadily shifting its center of gravity in Europe from Germany eastward to new bases in Romania and Bulgaria. These bases now serve as key waypoints on America's new version of Britain's maritime Imperial Lifeline that once linked the far-flung parts of the empire, extending from Portsmouth through Suez and Aden to Calcutta, Colombo and Singapore. America's modern version of the Imperial Lifeline, the "air bridge," begins in North America and extends from Germany to Romania and Bulgaria's Black Sea coast, and then on to US air and naval bases in Egypt, Turkey, Saudi Arabia, the Gulf, Diego Garcia—an atoll in the middle of the Indian Ocean—and South Asia.

But current extensions of the American Raj's air bridge, and construction or improvement of four to six major US bases in Iraq, and others in Pakistan and Central Asia, strongly suggest the US intends a long stay in the heart of the Muslim world, a decision which, if true, suggests more, rather than less, future tensions. Deciding whether to stay and expand its presence in the Muslim world, and dealing with the emergence of Russia, China, and India as great powers and rivals will be the primary strategic concerns facing the next two US administrations and the western powers.

A just settlement in Palestine that offers tangible benefits and security to both sides, winding down of the wars in Afghanistan and Iraq, lowering of anti-Islamic rhetoric in the western nations, promoting democratic governments that improve rather than exploit or repress the Muslim world, and reducing America's exaggerated military profile in the Mideast and South Asia will cut off the fuel that inflames Muslims against the West.

Take away these primary issues, and the Muslim world will have little reason for hostility beyond the normal doses of envy, xenophobia, and foolishness common to all peoples. Even so, removing all these irritants is admittedly a huge, complex endeavor that could take a decade, but however difficult and daunting, this strategy is clearly the answer to eliminating the current rising tensions and dangerous animosity between the Muslim world and the West. There are simply not enough B-52s to bomb all the recalcitrant Muslims back into the nineteenth-century colonial era.

Making these sweeping changes, of course, will mean transforming American, British, and French policy towards the Muslim world from one of dominance, "dirigisme," and economic exploitation to cooperation with and tolerance of different political systems. For Canada, it will mean changing the perception in many Muslim nations that once-friendly Canada under the Harper government has become a dedicated foe and comrade in arms of the Bush administration.

Under the former Chirac government, France made important progress in this direction in its dealings with West Africa by recalling its Foreign Legion units and presidential advisers who used to exert the diktat of Paris on its former colonies, and cutting back substantially on overt and secret payments to their governments. France rightly concluded the cost of neocolonial domination, of running a latter-day African Raj, far outweighed the benefits derived from this arrangement and should be replaced by normal state-to-state relations enhanced by residual French economic, technological, and cultural influence, and carefully targeted aid programs.

However, France's new neoconservative-oriented president, Nicholas Sarkozy, has revived France's overseas ambitions by promoting his grand scheme of creating a Mediterranean Union which will essentially be a Franco-German protectorate over North Africa's oil and gas, while the US and Britain retain primacy in the central Mideast, Gulf, and Caspian Basin. In short, his plans call for a new western condominium over most of the Muslim world's energy riches. In April 2008, Sarkozy announced the dispatch of 1,000 more French troops to Afghanistan, a move widely interpreted in France as a rather embarrassing effort to play up to President George Bush. French voters have not reacted with much élan to the plans of the man many call the French George Bush. Britain, by contrast, remains ambivalent, torn between its traditional loyalty—some would call it subservience—to the US and domestic opposition to foreign adventures.

For their part, Muslim nations must curb fanatical, violence-preaching anti-western Islamist sects that have no part in the modern world. Blaming the West or Israel for the many failings and woes of the Muslim world is outdated and jejune. Muslims need to embark on a pitiless evaluation of their society's manifest political, economic, intellectual, technological, and cultural failings. Muslims have to be shamed into realizing that their dismal level of human and economic development ranks second last to that of black Africa and that they, an ancient and noble civilization, cannot go on in the twenty-first century being ruled by men with tanks or crowns.

Above all, the fact that a majority of the Muslim world's population is now below 25 years of age means its nations are facing an onrushing tsunami of young people for whom food, water, power, housing, education, and medical care are already often in critically short supply. Dealing with this demographic inundation will impose enormous strain on most Muslim nations and rock their social and political foundations. The dictatorships, inept military regimes, and medieval monarchies that have kept the Muslim world so backwards cannot even resolve today's problems; they will be wholly unable to address tomorrow's onrushing crises. This demographic storm could make today's concerns about Islamic fundamentalism look minor by comparison.

Neither Islamic jihadism—nor western antiterrorism campaigns—are going to address these impending dangers. To begin dealing with them, the Muslim world and the western nations have to end their growing confrontation and learn to coexist, as Europe's once-bellicose powers did, with the maturity, common sense, and intelligence befitting civilized peoples. It is time for mankind to begin ridding itself of its two worst scourges, religious fanaticism and nationalist passions. This, not empire building, should be our goal in the new century.

BIBLIOGRAPHY
★ ★ ★

Algar, Hamid. *The Roots of Islamic Revolution*. Toronto: Open Press, 1983.

Allon, Yigal. *Shield of David: The Story of Israel's Armed Forces*. London: Weidenfeld & Nicolson, 1970.

Anonymous. *Imperial Hubris*. Washington, DC: Brassey's International Defense Publishers. 2004.

Armstrong, Karen. *Holy War*. London: Papermac Macmillan, 1991.

Aruri, Naseer Hasan (ed.). *Palestinian Refugees*. Pluto, 2001.

Asad, Muhammed. *The Road to Mecca*. New York: Simon & Schuster, 1954.

Ashrawi, Hanan. *This Side of Peace*. New York: Simon & Schuster, 1995.

Avineri, Sholmo. *The Making of Modern Zionism: The Intellectual Origins of the Jewish State*. New York: Basic Books, 1981.

Avnery, Uri. www.Avnerynews.co.il; www.gushshalom.org.

Beilin, Yossi. *His Brother's Keeper*. New York: Schocken Books, 2000.

Benvenisti, Meron. *Conflicts and Contradictions*. New York: Random House, 1987.

Benvenisti, Keron, and Thomas L. Friedman. *Intimate Enemies: Jews and Arabs in a Shared Land*. University of California, 1995.

Black, Ian and Benny Morris. *Israel's Secret Wars: A History of Israel's Intelligence Services*. New York: Grove Press, 1992.

Borovik, Artyom. *The Hidden War*. London: Faber & Faber, 1990.

Brand, Laurie. *The Palestinians in the Arab World*. New York: Columbia University Press, 1988.

Brynen, Rex. *Israel and Palestine*. New York: Strauss and Young, 1952.

Brzezinski, Zbigniew. *Game Plan*. Boston: Atlantic Monthly Press, 1986.

——. *The Grand Chessboard*. New York: Basic Books, 1997.

Bulloch, John. *No Friends But the Mountains*. New York: Penguin Books, 1993.

Burgat, Francois, and William Dowell. *The Islamic Movement in North Africa*. Austin: University of Texas, 1993.

Buruma, Ian, and Avishai Margalit. *Occidentalism*. New York: Penguin, 2004.

Cockburn, Andres, and Leslie. *Dangerous Liaison*. New York: Harper Collins Publishers, 1991.

Cockburn, Andrew, and Patrick Cockburn. *Out of Ashes*. New York: Harper Collins, 1999.

Cohen, Avner. *Israel and the Bomb*. New York: Columbia University Press, 1998.

Cohen, Mitchell. *Zion & State: Nation, Class and the Shaping of Modern Israel*. New York: Columbia University Press, 1992.

Cooley, John K. *Unholy Wars*. London: Pluto Press, 1999.

Corera, Gordon. *Shopping for Bombs*. London: Oxford University Press, 2006.

Curtiss, Richard H. *The Lion's Last Roar: Suez, 1956*. New York: Harper & Row, 1978.

Dan, Uri. *To the Promised Land: The Birth of Israel*. New York: Doubleday, 1988.

Dayan, Moshe. *Diary of the Sinai Campaign*. New York: Da Capo Press, 1991.

de la Billière, General Sir Peter. *Storm Command*. London: Harper Collins, 1999.

Eban, Abba. *My Country: The Story of Modern Israel*. New York: Random House, 1972.

Edelheit, Abraham, and Hershel Edelheit. *History of Zionism: A Handbook and Dictionary*. Denver: Westview Press, 1999.

Eland, Ivan. *The Empire Has No Clothes*. Oakland: Independent Institute, 2004.

Ennes Jr., James M. *Assault on Liberty: The True Story of the Israeli Attack on an American Intelligence Ship*. New York: Random House, 1979.

Farsoun, Samih K., and Christina Zacharia. *Palestine and the Palestinians*. Denver: Westview Press, 1998.

Farwell, Byron. *Armies of the Raj*. London: Norton, 1989.

Findley, Paul. *They Dared Speak Out*. Westport: Lawrence Hill, 1985.

Finkelstein, Norman. *Image and Reality of the Israel*. New York: Verso Books, 1995.

Fisk, Robert. *Pity the Nation*, London: André Deutsch, 1990.

——. *The Great War for Civilisation*, London: Harper Collins, 2005.

Flapan, Simha. *The Birth of Israel*. New York: Pantheon, 1987.

——. *Zionism and the Palestinians*. New York: Barnes and Nobles Books, 1979.

Friedman, Robert I. *Zealots for Zion, Inside Israel's West Bank Settlement Movement*. New York: Random House, 1992.

Fromkin, David. *A Peace to End All Peace*. New York: Avon, 1989.

Gall, Carlotta, and Thoma De Waal. *Chechnya*. New York: New York University Press, 1998.

Gammer, Moshe. *Muslim Resistance to the Tsar*. London: Frank Cass, 1994.

Gause, F. Gregory. *Oil Monarchies*. New York: Council on Foreign Relations, 1994.

Gerolymatos, Andre. *The Balkan Wars*. Toronto: Stoddart, 2001.

Gilbert, Martin. *Israel, a History*. London: Doubleday, 1988.

——. *The Arab Israeli Conflict*. New York: Weiderfeld & Nicolson Ltd., 1993.

Gilmour, David. *Dispossessed, London*. London: Sidgwick & Jackson, 1980.

Glubb, John Bagot. *Peace in the Holy Land*. London: Hodder and Stoughton, 1971.

Goldberg, David J. *To the Promised Land*. London: Penguin, 1997.

Hawawi, Sami. *Bitter Harvest*. New World Press, 1967.

Hall, Richard. *The Balkan Wars*. London: Routledge, 2000.

Harkabi, Yehoshafat. *Israel's Fateful Hour*. New York: Harper and Row, 1988.

——.*The Arab Israeli Conflict on the Threshold of Negotiations*. Princeton: Princeton University Press, 1992.

Heikal, Mohamd.. *The Road to Ramadan*. New York: Balantine, 1975.

——. *Autumn of Fury*. London: Andre Deutsch, 1983.

——. *Illusions of Triumph*. London: Fontana, 1993.

Hersh, Seymour. *The Samson Option*. London: Faber & Faber, 1991.

Herzog, Chaim. *The War of Atonement*. New York: Stackpole Books, 1998.

International Institute of Strategic Studies. *The Military Balance*. London: 2000–2008.

Johnson, Chalmers. *Blowback*. New York: Metropolitan Books, Henry Holt, 2000.

Horne, Alistair. *A Savage War of Peace*. London: Pan Books, 2002.

Kally, Elisha, and Gideon Fishelson. *Water and Peace*. Westport, CT: Praeger, 1993.

Kapur, Ashok. *Pakistan's Nuclear Development*. Beckenham: Croom Helm, 1987.

Kapuscinsky, Ryszard. *Shah of Shahs*. London: Pan, 1986.

Katz, Shmuel. *Lone Wolf*. Barricade Books, 1996.

Khalidi, Rashid. *Under Siege*. New York: Columbia University Press, 1997.

Kimche, Jon. *There Could Have Been Peace*. New York: Dial Press, 1973.

Kimche, Jon, and D. Kimche. *A Clash of Destinies*. New York: Praeger, 1960.

Klieman, Aaron S. *Israel's Global Reach*. McLean, VA: Pergamon Brassey's International Defense Publishers, 1985.

Koestler A. *Promise and Fulfilment Palestine 1917–1949*. New York: MacMillan Co, 1949.

Kurzman, Dan. *Soldier of Peace*. New York: Harper Collins, 1998.

LaGuardia, Anton. *War Without End*. New York: Thomas Dunne Books, 2003.

Langer, Felicia. *With My Own Eyes*. Ithaca Press, 1975.

Laquer, W., and B. Rubin. *The Israel Arab Reader*. London: Penguin, 1995.

Laqueur, Walter. *A History of Zionism*. New York: Fine Communications, 1997.

Litvinenko, Alexander and Yuri Felshtinsky. *Blowing Up Russia*. London: Gibson Square, 2007.

Makiya, Kanan. *Republic of Fear*. London: Hutchinson, 1989.

Margolis, Eric. *War at the Top of the World*. 3d ed. Toronto: Key Porter Books, 2007.

McCoy, Alfred. *The Politics of Heroin*. Chicago: Lawrence Hill, 1991.

Meyer, Karl. *The Dust of Empire*. New York: Century Foundation, 2003.

Morris, Benny. *Righteous Victims*. New York: Alfred A. Knopf, 2000.

——. *The Birth of the Palestinian Refugee Problem, 1947–1949*. Cambridge: Cambridge University Press, 1987.

Nasiri, Omar. *Inside Jihad*. New York: Basic Books, 2006.

Nazzal, Nafez. *The Palestinian Exodus from Galilee 1948*. Beirut: Institute for Palestine Studies, 1978.

O'Balance, Edgar. *Afghan Wars*. London: Brassey's. 1993.

Odom, William. *The Collapse of the Soviet Military*. New Haven: Yale University Press, 1998.

Oren, Michael. *Six Days of War*. New York: Oxford University Press, 2002.

Ostrovsky, Victor, and Clair Hoy. *By Way of Deception*. New York: Harper Collins, 1990.

Oz, Amos. *Israel, Palestine and Peace*. New York: Harcourt, Brace and Company, 1994.

Ozal, Turgut. *Turkey in Europe*. London: K. Rustam, 1991.

Parsi, Trita. *Treacherous Alliance*. New Haven: Yale University Press, 2007.

Pappe, Llan. *The Making of the Arab Israeli Conflict*. London: I B Tauris and Co. Ltd, 1992.

Pappe, Llan, (ed.). *Israel/Palestine Question*. London: Routledge, 1999.

Paxton, Robert. *The Anatomy of Fascism*. New York: Alfred A. Knopf, 2004.

Peretz, Don. *Palestinians, Refugees and the Middle East Peace Process*. 1993.

Pettifer, James. *The Turkish Labyrinth*. New York: Penguin, 1997.

Politkovskaya, Anna. *A Dirty War*. London: Harvill Press, 1991.

Pollack, Kenneth M. *The Threatening Storm*. New York: Random House, 2002.

Porch, Douglas. *The French Secret Services*. New York: Farrar, 1995.

Quandt, William B. (ed.). *The Middle East*. Washington, DC: Brookings Institution, 1988.

Rabinovich, Itamar. *The Brink of Peace*. Princeton: Princeton University Press, 1999.

———. *Waging Peace*. Farrar Strauss and Giroux, 1999.

Reeve, Simon. *The New Jackals*. London: Andre Deutsch, 1999.

Ritter, Scott & William Rivers Pitt. *War on Iraq*. London: Profile Books, 2002.

Rosen, Nir. *In the Belly of the Green Bird*. New York: Free Press, 2006.

Roy, Olivier. *The Failure of Political Islam*. Cambridge: Harvard University Press, 1994.

Rubin, Barry. *The American Experience and Iran*. London: Penguin, 1981.

———. *Revolution until Victory*. Cambridge: Harvard University Press, 1997.

Rubinstein, Danny. *The People of Nowhere*. 1991.

Safran, Nadev. *From War to War*. New York: Pegasus Books, 1968.

Said, Edward. *Covering Islam*. New York: Pantheon, 1981.

———. *The Politics of Dispossession*. London: Chatto & Windus, 1994.

———. *The End of the Peace Process*. New York: Knopf, 2001.

Sayliyeh, Emile. *The PLO after the Lebanon War*. Boulder, CO: Westview, 1986.

Schiff, Ze'ev, and E. Ya'ari. *Intifada*. New York: Simon and Schuster, 1989.

Schiff, Ze'ev. *October Earthquake*. Tel Aviv: Tel Aviv University, 1974.

Seale, Patrick. *Asad*. Los Angeles: University of California Press, 1988.

———. *Abu Nidal*. New York: Random House, 1992.

Shahak, Israel. *Jewish Hsitory, Jewish Religion*. London: Pluto Press, 1994.

Sharon, Ariel (with David Chanoff). *Warrior*. London: Macdonald, 1989.

Shavit, Jacob. *Jabotinsky and the Revisionist Movement*. London: Frank Cass and Co, 1988.

Sherman, Martin. *The Politics of Water in the Middle East*. New York: St. Martin's Press, 1998.

Shindler, Colin. *Israel, Likud and the Zionist Dream*. London: I B Tauris and Co. Ltd, 1995.

Singh, Patwant. *The World According to Washington*. New Delhi: Rupa, 2004.

Sreedhar. *The Iraq Iran War*. New Delhi: ABC Publishing, 1985.

Steil, Benn, and Robert Litan. *Financial Statecraft*. New Haven: Yale University Press, 2006.

Stephens, Robert. *Nasser*. New York: Penguin Books, 1971.

Sumaida, Hussein. *Circle of Fear*. Toronto: Stoddart, 1991.

Telhami, Shibley. *Power and Leadership in International Bargaining*. New York: Columbia University Press, 1992.

——. *The Stakes*. Denver: Westview Press, 2002.

Thomas, Gordon. *Gideon's Spies*. New York: St. Martin's Press, 1999.

Timerman, Jacobo. *The Longest War*. New York: Knopf, 1982.

Timmerman, Kenneth R. *The Death Lobby*. London: Fourth Estate, 1992.

Tivnan, Edward. *The Lobby*. New York: Simon and Schuster, 1987.

Vatikiotis, P.J. *The History of Modern Egypt*. London: Weidenfeld & Nicolson, 1991.

Wirsing, Robert. *India, Pakistan and the Kashmir Dispute*. New York: St. Martin's Press, 1998.

Ziad, Abu-Amr. *Islamic Fundamentalism in the West Bank and Gaza*. Bloomington: Indiana University Press, 1994.

INDEX

★ ★ ★